SUPERVISION
A Guide to Practice

FOURTH EDITION

SUPERVISION
A Guide to Practice

FOURTH EDITION

Jon Wiles
University of South Florida

Joseph Bondi
University of South Florida

Merrill,
an imprint of Prentice Hall
Englewood Cliffs, New Jersey   Columbus, Ohio

Library of Congress Cataloging-in-Publication Data

Wiles, Jon.

Supervision : a guide to practice/Jon Wiles, Joseph Bondi.—4th ed.

p. cm.

Includes bibliographical references and index.

ISBN 0-02-427641-3 (hardcover)

1. School supervision. I. Bondi, Joseph. II. Title.

LB2806.4.W55 1996

371.2—dc20   95-6543

                                                                                            CIP

Editor: Debra A. Stollenwerk
Production Editor: Linda Hillis Bayma
Copy Editor: Colleen Brosnan
Text Designer: Ed Horcharik
Cover Designer: Brian Deep
Production Buyer: Pamela D. Bennett
Electronic Text Management: Marilyn Wilson Phelps, Matthew Williams, Karen L. Bretz, Tracey
    Ward

This book was set in ITC Garamond by Prentice Hall and was printed and bound by Quebecor
Printing/Book Press. The cover was printed by Quebecor Printing/Book Press.

 © 1996 by Prentice-Hall, Inc.
A Simon & Schuster Company
Englewood Cliffs, New Jersey 07632

Printed in the United States of America

10 9 8 7 6 5 4 3 2 1

ISBN: 0-02-427641-3

Prentice-Hall International (UK) Limited, *London*
Prentice-Hall of Australia Pty. Limited, *Sydney*
Prentice-Hall of Canada, Inc., *Toronto*
Prentice-Hall Hispanoamericana, S. A., *Mexico*
Prentice-Hall of India Private Limited, *New Delhi*
Prentice-Hall of Japan, Inc., *Tokyo*
Simon & Schuster Asia Pte. Ltd., *Singapore*
Editora Prentice-Hall do Brasil, Ltda., *Rio de Janeiro*

This book is dedicated
to Kimball Wiles,
a pioneer in supervision.

PREFACE

The role of supervision has changed significantly during the past decade as the role of teaching has changed. Our society has become increasingly complex, and teachers, in turn, have had their responsibilities expanded to meet the needs of students. As their role broadens, so also does the professional dimension of the job. Throughout the nation, legislatures and school districts have endorsed this new degree of responsibility by supporting school-based management and decision making.

Supervisors, working in schools with teachers and administrators, find themselves struggling for role definition. We see professional knowledge as the most promising asset for this very important function of instructional improvement. Professionalism can be defined as distinctive information in an area important to human development. For this reason, research is now a new and dominating part of this text.

We believe it is imperative for a supervisor to know more than those they are leading, and educational research on teaching since 1970 provides a solid foundation for such knowledge. Chapters 2, 6, and 7 introduce this body of knowledge, which should guide instructional improvement in the coming decade.

As in the previous edition, our text identifies critical skills as the defining feature of the role of supervision. Although titles and relationships will vary from job to job, the knowledge and skills needed for supervisory leadership remain constant. We see supervision in the mid-1990s as a coordinating function that ties together all activities concerned with the improvement of instruction. Critical to such a role is knowledge about teaching and learning, human development, curriculum development, human relations, uses of technology, staff development, administration, and evaluation. This text is organized around these major skill areas.

At the conclusion of each chapter are certain guiding structures that will assist you in analyzing the chapter material. Each chapter has a section, "Implications for Supervision," with questions relevant to the local district needs of the student. In the first eleven chapters, at least two case studies are presented for reader discussion with other class members. Selected learning activities are included in most chapters to encourage additional exploration of the topics beyond the classroom. Finally, further reading is recommended to expand your knowledge.

A list of "helping organizations" that are becoming increasingly important in the job demands of the 1990s is provided in the appendix. Name and subject indexes are provided for quick reference.

We hope that this text will enable you to bridge the rapidly changing face of education and give you a solid guide to supervisory leadership in the challenging years ahead.

We would like to thank the following reviewers for their helpful comments: Gillian E. Cook, University of Texas at San Antonio; John C. Daresh, University of Northern Colorado; Lucille M. Freeman, University of Nebraska-Kearney; Gene Gallegos, California State University, Bakersfield; Edna Jean Harper, Deputy Superintendent, Dayton (OH) Public Schools; Albert J. Pautler, Jr., SUNY University at Buffalo; India J. Podsen, Georgia State University; Walter E. Sistrunk, Mississippi State University, and Louis Wildman, California State University, Bakersfield.

BRIEF CONTENTS

CONTENTS

CHAPTER 3
Professional Knowledge About Teaching and Learning   57

CHAPTER 5
Designing and Developing Curriculum   143

CHAPTER 6
Improving Classroom Teaching   173

CHAPTER 9
Providing Effective Staff Development   249

CHAPTER 10
Administrative Functions 281

CHAPTER 11
Organizing for Evaluation 303

CHAPTER 12
New Directions for Supervision   337

CHAPTER 1 ≋

DEFINING EDUCATIONAL
SUPERVISION

SCENARIO: A DAY'S WORK

As was their custom, the supervisory team for the district sat down for coffee and doughnuts at 7:30 A.M. Today's agenda was a full one for the team in this school district of 15,000 students. The day would last well into the early evening.

Among the continuing tasks for Sally Jackson, the elementary supervisor, were computer contracts, the bilingual program review, counseling a teacher for retirement, the home schooling curriculum, and the new single parenting program being developed. These continuing concerns were sprinkled throughout a day that also included three formal meetings, standard office operations, and a commitment to be in two schools for special events. She knew she could count on a number of "drop-in" events to round out a fairly typical day as a school supervisor.

Sally was anxious to speak to her colleague, Ted, about the computer question because he had held responsibility for a review at the secondary level the year before. Computers were getting to be such a major expense item that they were actually redefining instruction in the schools. Making million-dollar decisions about such computer systems without clear direction made Sally very nervous.

Ted was helpful in painting the big picture that Sally so badly needed. There were, he told her, only a few big companies vying for the secondary contract last year and all of them painted rosy pictures of achievement possibilities. He had experienced difficulty with the technical vocabulary (file servers, main terminals, sysop, bundle swaps, ethernet equipment, and so on) and had finally resorted to contacting other districts to solicit information about their experiences with the various systems. Each district had its concerns, but all had reported that the systems were more expensive than they had anticipated and none had made the achievement gains they anticipated. The systems seemed to be more effective with certain groups of students and in certain subject areas. All of the districts warned that introduction of these sophisticated systems would alter the way instruction was conceptualized and that regular instructional programs would be affected. Then Ted asked whether she had been reading about a new microwave technology that transmits like a cellular telephone.

Sally next turned her attention to the review of bilingual programs in the district. Even though she worked in a medium-sized school district, many districts large and small were having to address this need without adequate preparation. Some 330 languages were spoken in the United States with Spanish being the most common second language. She had been given the responsibility to redesign the curriculum for limited English proficiency students following last year's discovery of rather stagnant achievement in these programs.

All educators had been informed that such students must be served. In Lau versus Nichols (1974), the U.S. Supreme Court ruled that students not receiving services to meet their linguistic needs suffered educationally. The district had responded with the goal "of providing limited English proficient students with appropriate, comprehensible instruction in English and in the academic content areas of math, science, social studies, and computer literacy, which will enable them to function successfully in the academic mainstream." How best to accomplish this aspiration still needed to be determined.

Sally knew that most of her students came to the district after experiencing an ESOL-only Headstart program in the community. However, a recent synthesis of research in the *TESOL Quarterly* had clearly stated that "a child who fails to reach competency in the first language and prematurely tried to learn a second language would be cognitively retarded in both languages."[1] Most of her district's non-English-speaking students were below the fiftieth percentile, and it was projected that they would not rise above that level in the elementary years. Something had to be done!

Sally's thoughts next turned to Bob Turner's imminent retirement at the end of the year. Bob was one of the most experienced teachers at the elementary level and, as was often the case, was completing service just when he was most needed. Sally recalled reading that many public school teachers who entered service in the 1960s were now eligible for retirement, as many as 50 percent in some districts would choose retirement by the year 2000, and the teacher training institutions weren't preparing enough replacements. Where would school districts like hers find qualified teachers who could operate in this increasingly complex learning environment?

Sally was quite certain Bob would rely on her to advise him on the most beneficial time to retire in order to maximize his benefits. She wrote herself a note to visit Personnel this morning to review state retirement formula as well as to check on any district incentives. Perhaps she should put together a newsletter since so many others were in the same situation.

Sally got some coffee and moved over to ask Mary about the state requirements for home schoolers. What had started out as something of a minor movement by politically and religiously disaffected parents was becoming a bit of a snowball.

Already, 15,000 students in the state were taking instruction at home, and many districts were unable or unwilling to monitor the studies and the qualifications of the parent-teachers.

Mary knew the legislation well since her office was generally the contact point for parents who wanted to instruct their children at home. She related that it was the legal responsibility of the public school district to screen the qualifications of the home teacher, to review the curriculum plan for the student, and to evaluate or review the evidence of student progress. Mary was quick to add that this was close to impossible since the legislature had not provided any resources for this task and that, further, the state department of education simply didn't have the resources to check on the districts.

Sally knew this condition only too well. How many other things was she responsible for without the authority or resources to do the job? But something about home schooling bothered her a lot. She could understand parents being fearful for the safety of their child, or concerned that some educational environments were not conducive to achievement, or even committed to making learning a semi-religious experience. What bothered her was the possibility that these young people were not being instructed at all or that perfectly able students were not benefiting from what she considered a high-quality program of education in the district. High school dropouts, she remembered, included about one third who were bright underachievers. Perhaps she should pull a few names and do some home visits to get more information.

The last item on today's "do" list was to coordinate development of the new single-parent program in the district. Now here was a condition screaming for attention. According to the National Center for Health Statistics, in 1990, over a million babies were born to single women; a 75 percent increase over 1980. What had always been a problem condition was becoming epidemic. In 1950, about 4 percent of all children were born to unwed mothers, and now the rate ranged between 20 and 60 percent for various ethnic groups.

The school problem relating to this statistic is that the loss of a second adult income in a child-bearing family means almost instant poverty and disadvantage for the child. The typical single-parent family headed by a female earns less than one half what the two-parent family earns. Related data shows the single parent moving more often and working outside of the home (nearly 70 percent).

Sally knew a little about the research on such children and found it scary. Children from such homes have been documented to have more social and personality problems, lower self-esteem, lower achievement motivation, lower tolerance for delay of gratification, poorer conscience development, less adequate peer relations, more anxiety, more rebelliousness, more aggressiveness, more depression, and a greater chance of drug dependence. In school, children from single-parent homes earned 50 percent more D's and F's and 50 percent fewer A's and B's than children from two-parent families. The mean grade point average for single-parent children, in one study, was 1.95 compared to an average of 2.37 for children of two-parent families. Promising among the more recent studies was the notion that a strong social support system can help overcome these pervasive statistics.

In a nutshell, thought Sally, family income stands out as the most crucial of the intervening variables that affect school success, and this variable is tied directly to the single-parent family trend. How could our new program help these parents overcome such a depressing projection? This task would be important and certainly require a lot of input from others.

Well, thought Sally, it's time to go. Finishing the last of her coffee, she stood to begin another typical day in the life of a school supervisor.

It's quite clear from this scenario of a typical day in the life of a school supervisor that the tasks are many and quite diverse. Sprinkled among the many perplexing tasks outlined in the scenario are numerous mundane and more predictable events that occur in the routine of school life in the district or school office. In short, the tasks of supervision are diverse and many. Supervisors must know a lot of things, and they must be able to activate that knowledge base through purposeful behavior on a daily basis.

Supervision occurs at many levels in education, and supervisors hold a variety of titles. In some school districts, the role of the supervisor is largely undefined, making the selection of daily tasks by the responsible individual even more important. Despite its lack of focus, supervision remains indispensable for the improvement of instructional programs in schools. *We see supervision in schools as a general leadership function that coordinates and manages those educational activities concerned with learning.*

A HISTORICAL PERSPECTIVE OF THE ROLE

To fully understand the nature of the supervisory role in schools, it is useful to trace the evolution of supervision in American education. You will note that this role has changed dramatically over the years and continues to change as this book is written. The definition of supervision is rooted in educational philosophy and the accompanying definition of the role of schooling.

In the early days of this nation, schools were formed to supplement the teachings of the family and church. Teachers were hired by local communities and buildings were erected for the purpose of educating. When too many children were present, requiring the services of multiple teachers, a "principal teacher" was employed to oversee the various functions. Eventually, a "superintendent" of schools would be hired to manage multiple-schools operations. When that person could no longer oversee the schools that were often spread over a wide geographic area, an assistant was hired. These assistants to the superintendent were the earliest supervisors. Since these persons assisted in oversight activities, their role was largely one of inspection.

Characterized by telling, directing, and judging, these supervisory visits to schools were often directly related to hiring and firing of teachers. A sample list of rules for teachers posted in 1872 suggests the kind of expectations that early supervisors might have been asked to reinforce:

1. Teachers each day will fill lamps, clean chimneys, and trim wicks.
2. Each teacher will bring a bucket of water and a scuttle of coal for the day's session.

3. Make your pens carefully; you may whittle nibs to the individual taste of pupils.
4. Men teachers may take one evening each week for courting purposes, or two evenings if they go to church regularly.
5. After ten hours in school, the teachers should spend the remaining time reading the Bible or other good books.
6. Women teachers who marry or engage in unseemingly conduct will be dismissed.
7. Every teacher should lay aside from each day a goodly sum of his earnings for his benefit during his declining years so that he will not become a burden on society.
8. Any teacher who smokes, uses liquor in any form, frequents pool or public halls, or gets shaved in a barber shop will give good reason to suspect his worth, intentions, integrity, and honesty.
9. The teacher who performs his labors fruitfully and without fault for five years will be given an increase of twenty-five cents per week in his pay providing the Board of Education approves.

The Civil War era was a true watershed in American life and in the spread of supervisory activity. As Trow has pointed out, the Civil War (War Between the States) "was a great watershed of American history, separating agrarian society with small farmers from an urbanized, industrial society."[2] From this point on, schools were larger, the population more diverse, and by the mid-1880s, even the mission of the American school was in question.[3] From a role as sort of a surrogate circuit rider, representing the superintendent at distant places, the supervisor of the late nineteenth century was involved in classrooms with teachers. As school districts grew in size, the role of supervisor often became bureaucratic. The American industrial revolution at the turn of the century encouraged education to model on the efficiency of business (as would be repeated in the 1980s), and the "inspector" became more of an efficiency expert. Callahan describes the tenor of this era:

> The procedure for bringing about a more businesslike organization and operation of schools was fairly well standardized . . . it consisted of making unfavorable comparisons between schools and business enterprise, of applying business-like criteria (e.g., economy and efficiency), and of suggesting that business and industrial practices be adopted by educators.[4]

In this area, supervision became tied to goals and objectives, and there were attempts to specify program dimensions and outcomes. Ideas like hierarchical control, division of labor, technical specialization, and reliance on rules and regulations influenced the practice of school supervision.

As America changed in the early decades of this century, so did public education change. Among the more important events influencing these changes in schools were the rise of conflicting philosophies of education (traditional, child-centered, social engineering), the birth of American psychology and its early orientation to testing, and a rising expectation for education following a world war and a prolonged depression. Where supervisors of the turn of the century focused on efficiency and results, supervisors of the 1930s held a wider perspective of their roles. Among the various factors expanding the role of the school supervisor were the dramatic growth of public education, an increase in the awareness of human development, and a new understanding of how education could be integral in the preparation for democratic citizenship.

In the period 1890 to 1920, the population of high school students in America increased from about 200,000 to over five million students. This twenty-five fold increase included large numbers of immigrant youths who were ill-prepared to enter society as participating citizens. In this period, the standard public school curriculum added subjects such as English, social studies, vocational education, and physical education as schools sought to accommodate diversity. Naturally, the development of new curriculum and new instructional techniques stretched the role of the instructional supervisor.

It was during this same era that a humanistic philosophy became firmly embedded in America. The writings of Europeans such as Pestalozzi, Rousseau, and Froebel were disseminated and studied by American educators. Those who responded to the idea that children, not subjects, were the focus of learning became known as "Progressives," and by the late 1920s, these educators were a major force in the form of the Progressive Education Association.

Finally, the First World War caught America by surprise, and few young persons were prepared for the encounter. In addition to having nearly one half of the recruits failing the physical exam, it was also discovered that these youths had a minimal understanding of democratic principles.[5] Preparing citizens to understand and participate in government required a broader definition of education at the public school level.

In addition, during the 1930s, industry and business theory in America was focusing on the worker as the key to greater productivity in the workplace. It took more, or so the theorists said, to be productive than simple efficiency. Worker productivity was often the result of how they were treated.[6] These thoughts influenced supervisors as they learned of these theories. Group dynamics, democratic leadership, and human relations became the "buzzwords."

During the 1940s, as Americans engaged in and then recovered from another World War, schools became more technically proficient. The military discovered during this conflict that training (determining in advance what is to occur) was more efficient than education and perfected learning techniques that led to a skill such as flying an airplane or driving a tank. These lessons of early "prescriptive learning" were soon applied in school settings. The interface of educators with early programmed instruction was comparable to today's interfacing with the new technologies of learning.

In the 1950s, public education was captured by the American response to the launch of the Russian satellite Sputnik I. Seemingly overnight, a primitive and agrarian nation had become a space leader, and Americans rushed to redesign their schools in order to "catch up." Under funding from the National Science Foundation, mathematics and science curricula were retooled in record time. Soon thereafter, the other subjects were redesigned in an era known as the "alphabet curriculums" including such curricula as MACOS (social studies), BSCS (biology), PSSC (physics), FLES (foreign language) and others. Quite naturally, supervisors were drawn into the development and implementation of these curriculum efforts.

During the mid-1960s and early 1970s, federal funding encouraged basic research in teaching and learning, and soon an emerging body of knowledge was available to supervisors. Quite early, supervisors began practicing what was known as "clinical supervision," in which the supervisor and the teacher sat down and analyzed teaching within the framework of pedagogy and the various research findings to support such practices.[7] As research continued to unfold in the mid-1970s, early prescriptions for teacher effectiveness began to emerge.

Events of the late 1970s and early 1980s soon overcame this professional thrust in supervision. In particular, an eight-year inflationary period halved school resource bases, causing many districts to retrench under the guise of "returning to the basics." Teacher unionism[8] grew dramatically in response to this pressure, and supervisors were soon assuming a "management role" as increased testing, evaluation, and reductions in force (RIF) became the fare-of-the-day in schools. During this period, too, the onslaught of technology and law brought many new titles to persons working in a supervisory role: supervisor of special programs, supervisor of special subjects, supervisor of technical applications.

The major influence in the 1990s, in defining supervision in public schools, has been a decentralization of management under a number of labels such as decentralized decision making, site management, school-based management, and teacher empowerment. Beginning with the 1986 Carnegie Task Force on Teaching, followed by the National Governor's Association Report (1987) and the National Education Association Recommendations of 1988, this progression of endorsements for teacher control of schools represents a new political reality in American education.[9] For supervisors, decentralization has meant a renewed search for their place in the hierarchy of instructional improvement.

What can be seen from this cursory review of 200 years is that the role of supervision has always been with us in American education, but the title and the tasks of supervision have changed as America has changed (see Figure 1.1). Supervisors have always been part-teacher, part-administrator, and continue to be so today. The exact blend of role and tasks depends on a host of variables including the supervisory setting and the degree to which supervisors are free to set their own job descriptions.

DEFINITIONS OF SUPERVISION

The definitions of supervision act to define the scope of responsibility of the role. Just as that role has changed over time according to events in the environment, the

Figure 1.1 The Evolution of Supervisory Roles

1840–1900	Inspection and enforcement
1900–1920	Scientific supervision
1920–1930	Bureaucratic supervision
1930–1945	Cooperative supervision
1945–1955	Technical supervision
1955–1965	Supervision as curriculum implementation
1965–1975	Clinical supervision
1975–1985	Supervision as management
1985–1995	Supervision as cooperative leadership

definition of supervision has evolved. At least six major conceptions of supervision are found in the modern literature:

1. Supervision as an act of administration
2. Supervision as an act of curriculum work
3. Supervision as an instructional function
4. Supervision as an act of human relations
5. Supervision as management
6. Supervision as a generic leadership role

Historically, supervision has been linked closely to administration. The first supervisors were, quite frankly, extensions of principals and superintendents. Some administrative definitions[10] focus on the accountability of administration for instructional outcomes. Another administrative type of definition of supervision, such as that of Glatthorn,[11] might focus on helping teachers develop plans. Harris and Bessent offer the following administrative perspective:

> Supervision is what school personnel do with adults and things for the purpose of maintaining and changing the operation of the school in order to directly influence the attainment of major instructional goals of the school.[12]

Another frequent definition found in supervision literature sees the supervisor as a curriculum worker. Cogan, as an example, gives the following definition of general supervision work:

> General supervision, therefore, denotes activities like the writing and revision of curriculums, the preparation of units and materials of instruction, the development of processes and instruments for reporting to parents, and such broad concerns as evaluation of the total educational program.[13]

Writing with the same orientation, Curtin observes:

> Curriculum practices can exist without supervision, although one would scarcely wish to vouch for their vitality. However, it is so blatantly obvious that supervision is utterly dependent on concern for curriculum that one need hardly bring up the matter at all. There is, if the newer concept of supervision is accepted. Of course, supervisors can "do" things that are not related to curriculum and instruction, just as they have in the past. They can gather statistics and information to no avail; they can observe teachers for no good reason; they can confer with teachers about irrelevancies; and they can conduct staff meetings that are unrelated to the imperatives of teaching. Enough of this exists today to make one uneasy. The only comfort that one can draw is that these activities are not supervisory at all. They are called "supervisory," and this tends to give the whole concept of supervision a bad name. Supervision must find meaning in curriculum. If it does not, it has no meaning.[14]

A third definition of supervision focuses squarely on instruction. An early example of this definition of supervision was provided by the Association for Supervision and Curriculum Development (ASCD), the major professional organization for school supervisors:

> Since the titles "supervisor" and "curriculum director" are often used interchangeably as to function, the terms might be used to indicate a person who, either through working with supervisors, principals, or others at the central office level, contributes to the improvement of teaching and/or the implementation or development of curriculum.[15]

The definition of supervision in terms of instruction continues today in the works of Marks, Stoops, and King-Stoops:

> Supervision is "action and experimentation aimed at improving instruction and the instructional program.[16]

A fourth definition of supervision found in the literature sees the supervisor in terms of human relations, working with all persons in the educational environment. The earliest proponent of this definition was Kimball Wiles:

> They [the supervisors] are the expediters. They help establish communication. They help people hear each other. They serve as liaison to get people into contact with others who have similar problems or with resource people who can help. They stimulate staff members to look at the extent to which ideas and resources are being shared, and the degree to which persons are encouraged and supported as they try new things. They make it easier to carry out the agreements that emerge from evaluation sessions. They listen to individuals discuss their problems and recommend other resources that may help in the search for solutions. They bring to individual teachers, whose confidence they possess, appropriate suggestions and materials. They sense, as far as they are able, the feelings that teachers have about the system and its policies, and they recommend that the administration examine irritations among staff members.[17]

A definition provided by Sergiovanni and Starratt follows this same theme:

> Traditionally, supervision is considered the province of those responsible for instructional improvement. While we hold this view, we add to this instructional emphasis responsibility for all school goals which are achieved through or dependent upon the human organization of the school.[18]

Finally, a draft from the 1982 ASCD Yearbook on supervision continues the human relations theme:

> By "supervisor" we mean not only those who have the word in the title, but also principals, superintendents, department heads—all those whose responsibilities include helping other staff members improve their performance.[19]

Supervision has also been defined as a form of management. Illustrating this position is a definition by Alfonso, Firth, and Neville:

> Supervision is found in all complex organizations. This is so because organizations are determined to maintain themselves and are sometimes concerned about their improvement or refinement. The connection between supervision and organizations is clear and direct. Organizational resources must be applied to the analysis of efficiency and effectiveness. . . . These descriptions of supervision within organizational production systems have implications of significant consequence to the educator engaged in instructional supervision. The school is a production system.[20]

The sixth definition of educational supervision is as a leadership function. According to Mosher and Purpel:

> We consider the tasks of supervision to be teaching teachers how to teach, and the professional leadership in reformulating public education—more specifically, its curriculum, its teaching, and its forms.[21]

It is our observation that all six definitions of educational supervision are valid and meaningful in the context from which they are drawn. If schools in the 1960s were frantically updating curriculum, then supervision had a strong curriculum orientation. Likewise, supervision in the 1970s and 1980s was primarily managerial. Definitions are obviously influenced by social and economic conditions during the times in which they were formulated.

DIMENSIONS OF SUPERVISION

The role of the supervisor has many dimensions or facets, and for this reason, supervision often overlaps with administrative, curricular, and instructional functions. Because supervision is a general leadership role and a coordinating role among all school activities concerned with learning, such overlap is natural and should be perceived as an asset in a school setting.

Supervision leadership involves thinking, planning, organizing, and evaluating processes. The thinking and planning phases of improving instruction are most like policy formation and administration. Organizing instructional programs is most like those functions of curriculum where a translation of ideas into programs occurs. The evaluation functions of supervisors are usually directed toward the instructional activities of the educational institution. Each of these three dimensions—administration, curriculum, and instruction—is treated as follows in terms of typical supervision tasks to be accomplished.

Administration

Among the many administrative supervision tasks usually encountered are:

1. *Setting and prioritizing goals*—Helping others in the school district focus on ends for schooling and establishing priorities among the many possible programs available to schools.

2. *Establishing standards and developing policies*—Translating goals into standardized levels of expectation, complete with rules and regulations to enforce such performances.

3. *Providing long-range planning*—Designing expectations in terms of actions and activities to be accomplished over time.

4. *Designing organizational structures*—Establishing structural connections between persons and groups within school districts.

5. *Identifying and securing resources*—Locating applicable resources and seeing that they are available to various organizational structures.

6. *Selecting personnel and staffing*—Identifying personnel needed to implement programs and assignments to organizational structures.

7. *Providing adequate facilities*—Matching available facilities with program needs; developing new facilities where needed.

8. *Securing necessary funding*—Raising the monies needed to adequately finance programs.

9. *Organizing for instruction*—Assigning staff and other instructional and support personnel to organizational structures.

10. *Promoting school–community relations*—Establishing and maintaining contact with those who support educational programs.

Curriculum

Curriculum-oriented supervision tasks are:

1. *Determining instructional objectives*—Translating goals into specific objectives for instruction.

2. *Surveying needs and conducting research*—Assessing present conditions to determine how school programs can effectively meet learner needs.

3. *Developing program and planning changes*—Organizing the instructional content and reviewing existing programs for greater relevance.

4. *Relating programs to various special services*—Tying together the many instructional components both within the school and in the community.

5. *Selecting materials and allocating resources*—Analyzing available instructional materials and assigning them to appropriate programs.

6. *Orienting and renewing instructional staff*—Introducing the school program to new teachers and assisting regular staff in improving their skills.

7. *Suggesting modification in facilities*—Designing a plan to restructure facilities to fit the instructional program and, where appropriate, suggesting the need for new facilities.

8. *Estimating expenditure needs for instruction*—Cost-estimating program development and making recommendations for the application of existing and anticipated funding.

9. *Preparing for instructional programs*—Forming various instructional units and teams; providing in-service opportunities for instructional development.

10. *Developing and disseminating descriptions of school programs*—Writing accurate descriptions of school programs and informing the public of successful activities.

Instruction

Some supervision tasks that are instructional in nature are:

1. *Developing instructional plans*—Working with teachers to outline and implement instructional programs.

2. *Evaluating programs*—Conducting testing and other types of evaluation to determine if instructional programs are meeting standards.

3. *Initiating new programs*—Demonstrating new techniques and otherwise establishing the groundwork for new programs.

4. *Redesigning instructional organization*—Reviewing existing instructional organization for effectiveness and, where appropriate, making alterations.

5. *Delivering instructional resources*—Ensuring that teachers have necessary instructional materials and anticipating future material needs.

6. *Advising and assisting teachers*—Being available to teachers in a consulting, helping role.

7. *Evaluating facilities and overseeing modifications*—Assessing educational facilities for instructional appropriateness and making on-site visits to ensure that modifications are as designed.

8. *Dispersing and applying funds*—Following the flow of monies to ensure their application to intended programs.

9. *Conducting and coordinating in-service programs*—Guiding in-service programs so that they are applied to instructional needs.

10. *Reacting to community needs and inquiries*—Receiving community feedback about school programs and sending information to parents of schoolchildren where appropriate.

While all of these tasks are supervisory in nature, they do intersect with administrative, curricular, and instructional domains. The unique role of supervisors is to bridge or coordinate these other areas as they conceptualize, plan, organize, and evaluate instructional programs. Like an engineer overseeing a construction project, the supervisor follows and directs the work flow in instructional improvement efforts (see Table 1.1).

SUPERVISION IN PRACTICE

The role of the supervisor in a practice environment, as can be seen from the scenario at the beginning of this chapter, is often self-determined. Beyond being responsible for instructional improvement and any tasks directly assigned to the supervisor, the job consists of patterns of activity that give purpose to the role. One survey of 1,000 supervisors by the Association for Supervision and Curriculum Development revealed:

> The data gathered by the survey substantiated the thesis that there was great confusion and little agreement when it comes to defining the distinct roles of supervisors and curriculum developers.[22]

Table 1.1

Administrative Tasks	Curricular Tasks	Instructional Tasks
1. Set and prioritize goals	Determine instructional objectives	Develop instructional plans
2. Establish standards and policies	Survey needs and conduct research	Evaluate programs according to standards
3. Provide long-range planning	Develop programs and plan changes	Initiate new programs
4. Design organizational structures	Relate programs to special services	Redesign instructional organization where needed
5. Identify and secure resources	Select materials and allocate resources	Deliver instructional resources
6. Select personnel and staff	Orient and renew instructional staff	Advise and assist teachers
7. Provide adequate facilities	Suggest modifications in facilities	Oversee modifications in facilities
8. Secure necessary funding	Estimate expenditure needs for instruction	Disperse and apply funds
9. Organize for instruction	Prepare instructional programs	Coordinate in-service activities
10. Promote school–community relations	Disseminate descriptions of school programs	React to community inquiries about school programs

◄─────────── THE SUPERVISION FLOW OF ACTIVITY ───────────►

Note: Supervisory activity overlaps and coordinates administrative, curricular, and instructional concerns and tasks.

Obviously, some of this disparity and lack of focus comes from the diversity of school districts in the United States—small and large, rural and urban, homogeneous and heterogeneous in student composition. There is also the issue of purpose as described by Mosher and Purpel:

> The difficulty in defining supervision in relation to education also stems, in large part, from unsolved theoretical problems about teaching. Quite simply, we lack sufficient understanding of the process of teaching. Our theories of learning are inadequate. . . . When we achieve more understanding of what and how to teach, and with what special effects on children, we will be much less vague about the supervision of the processes.[23]

As a form of prescription for what the practice of teaching "should" be, the same ASCD study proposed an active leadership role:

> The instructional supervisor should be more in the role of decision maker with authority than in an advisory one; should be more of a subject specialist in the supervised area than a generalist; should be more capable of planning and conducting research than merely an interpreter of research; should be more involved with the improvement of instruction than in curriculum development; should work with the teaching staff more in a directive fashion with authority than in a permissive manner; should be less involved in staff evaluation than responsible for such evaluation; and should exercise more budgetary or fiscal management control responsibility than no control over budget.[24]

The professional association of instructional supervisors is calling, then, for an active and directional leader who takes charge of the many areas related to teaching and learning. This active role, called the "dynamic supervisor" by Harris, is in contrast to a "tractive," or maintenance, role for the supervisor[25] (see Figure 1.2).

In a more recent study by Pajak[26] ($N = 1075$) aimed at identifying and verifying dimensions of proficiency associated with effective supervisory practice, 12 important dimensions of practice were noted. With three sample knowledge bases identified, they were, in order of importance:

Tractive Supervision	**Dynamic Supervision**
Enforcing statutory requirements	Planning new staff development
Assessing course outlines	Applying research findings
Reviewing enrollment patterns	Initiating pilot curriculum projects
Editing curriculum guides	Evaluating new technology
Enforcing legal requirements	Rewriting philosophy statements
Regulating visitors	Demonstrating new techniques

Figure 1.2 Tractive versus Dynamic Supervision

Communication
Knowledge of conflict resolution strategies
Knowledge of relationships within groups
Knowledge of relationships among groups

Staff Development
Commitment to ongoing professional growth
Orientation to providing assistance and support
Belief that teachers should participate in decisions about their growth

Instructional Program
Knowledge of instructional materials and resources
Knowledge of research on effective instruction
Knowledge of instructional methods and strategies

Planning and Change
Openness to new ideas, information, and criticism
Commitment to continuous improvement
Willingness to change

Motivating and Organizing
Belief in building a collective vision
Commitment to developing leadership in others
Commitment to democratic principles

Observation and Conferencing
Recognition of the need for a variety of supervisory approaches
Valuing collegial relationships with teachers
Commitment to the development of individual teaching styles

Curriculum
Knowledge of philosophical, sociological, and historical foundations
Knowledge of child and adult development
Knowledge of curriculum development processes

Problem Solving and Decision Making
Nonmanipulative
Regard problems as opportunities for improvement
Commitment to making decisions based on what is best for students

Service to Teachers
Commitment to working with teachers as colleagues
Protective of instructional time
Willingness to exert influence on behalf of others

Personal Development

Knowledge of self-image and its influence

Knowledge of one's own philosophy of schooling

Possessing a broad range of experiences

Community Relations

Desire to know and communicate with parents

Willingness to communicate with the community about goals

Sensitive to the cultural and socioeconomic context of the school

Research and Program Evaluation

Knowledge of a variety of evaluation strategies

Knowledge of test construction

Knowledge of data collection techniques

SELECTION OF SUPERVISORS

The supervision literature also prescribes a basic training and experience criteria for persons becoming supervisors. Among the most important college courses recommended, in rank order, are:

1. Supervision of Instruction
2. Group Processes and Human Relations
3. Curriculum Theory and Development
4. Educational Measurement and Evaluation
5. Educational Psychology
6. Organization and Administration of Schools
7. Educational Research
8. Philosophy of Education
9. Media and Technology
10. Sociology of Education
11. History of Education
12. Anthropology of Education

Selection criteria for supervisors, based on their training and experience, were recommended by the study participants:

I. Experience
   A. Minimum of two years of classroom teaching experience
   B. Minimum of one year of leadership experience (such as department chairperson, principal, internship, laboratory school researcher)

II. Preparation
   A. Certification as a teacher (assumes competence in the science of teaching and conditions of learning)
   B. Completion or equivalent of an educational specialist degree leading to certification as an instructional leader with courses and experience in:
      1. Supervision, including:
         a. Knowledge regarding the principles and nature of supervision, trends, and issues in supervision and models of staff development
         b. Ability to apply communication and group development skills
         c. Ability to evaluate staff personnel and to design improvement programs
      2. Curriculum, including:
         a. Knowledge regarding curriculum programs and processes of curriculum development
         b. Ability to evaluate curricular programs and plan appropriate strategies for their improvement
         c. Understanding of curriculum theory and design of various curricular models
      3. Instruction, including:
         a. Knowledge regarding principles and concepts, trends, issues, and models of instructional strategies
         b. Ability to design, develop, implement, and evaluate various instructional systems
         c. Understanding of instructional theory, utilization of media, and analysis of instructional factors
      4. Educational psychology, including:
         a. Ability to conduct appropriate research for determining teaching and learning problems
         b. Understanding of adult learning and the teaching/learning process
      5. Leadership, including:
         a. Processes and purposes of organizations
         b. Skills to organize and coordinate perceived resources for facilitating operations of, and changes in, curriculum and instruction
         c. Understanding of the function of supervision as provided by other educational leaders such as college professors, principals, and district curriculum leaders

LEADERSHIP BASED ON COMPETENCE

In the next few years, schools will be experiencing massive changes from both without and within. Supervisors, whom we have seen as historically defining their role by the status quo, will be forced to redefine that role based on new criteria. We believe that professional knowledge and technical skills will differentiate the new supervisors of the twenty-first century from those who cling to the past.

We envision the "new" supervisor as possessing extraordinary knowledge of the teaching–learning act, advances in technologically-assisted learning, and a host of other innovative and exciting databases. In short, we feel that supervisors should be "resident experts" or resources in many of the new areas affecting schools.

We also believe that supervisors will need to possess critical and distinctive human relations skills. As our society becomes more multicultural, as the family of old is replaced by new family forms, as the school attempts to gain the support of a community increasingly without children, as schools become more adept at public relations, these human skills will need to be carried out by highly competent leaders. The person who will fulfill such roles for the school or district will be the modern supervisor.

The following section lists eight generic skill areas that we feel form the nucleus of supervisory competence. These same skill areas are covered in entire chapters in this text.

Special Areas of Supervisory Competence

1. *Supervisors are developers of people.*   The best educational supervisors never forget that schools are learning environments designed to help children grow. The global task for all educators is to design the best possible learning experiences for those clients. Such a sensitivity to the growth of children requires a thorough knowledge of the development process as well as the special character of various groups of children in school.

All children in the United States spend better than a decade in schools enroute to becoming adult citizens. Those children come to school with varying degrees of readiness to learn, and they leave school with varying degrees of competence. The patterns of development among children are predictable and have been outlined in any number of models, hierarchies, and taxonomies. All students must master certain "developmental tasks" to grow up successfully.

There are differences as well as similarities among children in school that must be accommodated by school leaders. Children differ in the backgrounds and social experiences they have had prior to school. They differ in their natural capacities to learn in school. They differ in their values, as those values often reflect the values of their parents. Some children are stronger than others and more able to tolerate failure or success.

There are some children in schools who are so "different" that they wear the label "special." These students—those who are handicapped, gifted, or disturbed—are unable to adjust to a norm-based instructional program and require unique programming.

The danger for any educator, but particularly for someone with as much influence as a supervisor, is to become "prison dumb," or unable to remember what schools are all about. A special type of competence for supervisors, then, is never to forget why we operate schools and for whom the curriculum and the instructional program is planned.

2. *Supervisors are curriculum developers.*   It has been observed time and again that the "real" curriculum is what is experienced by students at the classroom level. While various district documents, textbooks, and guides tell us what should be taught, the actions of the teacher delivering the curriculum actually define the study program. Because they work directly with teachers on instructional problems, supervisors have the best opportunity to influence the development of curriculum.

Curriculum development can be conceptualized as a cycle that begins with the analysis of purpose for schooling. Clarifying philosophy and goals, pinpointing priorities, and extracting program concepts form this stage of development. The cycle continues with the design of the curriculum including developing standards and objectives and considering the approach to improvement. A third step in the curriculum development cycle is to implement or manage the proposed changes. Here, the direction of staff development and material upgrading is critical. Finally, the cycle concludes with an evaluation of the effort and the identification of further needs.

Supervisors, working with both administrators and teachers, also have a bird's-eye view of the curriculum development process. Because they work in classrooms with teachers to deliver the "real" curriculum, they are the primary quality control agents in most districts. The ability of supervisors to mold practices with general policy formation makes them the purveyors of critical information about curriculum improvement.

3. *Supervisors are instructional specialists.* Most supervisors are selected for their position because they are excellent teachers. The history of teaching in the United States suggests that good teachers become leaders, and rightly so. The primary task for anyone in a supervisory role is to improve learning opportunities for students.

Specifically, the instructional role of supervision has at least three dimensions: research, communication, and teaching. In the research role, the supervisor must understand the meaning of the many studies conducted in the area of teaching during the past 35 years. Recent studies of teacher and school effectiveness, learning styles, and the physiology of learners suggest many changes in the classroom. In this role, the supervisor is an analyst of instruction and a resource to relevant knowledge about the area of instruction.

Supervisors, as instructional specialists, are also communicators. As the supervisor moves among the rooms in a school building, he or she gains a unique perspective of the "whole" in the instructional program. Assisting with articulation (coordination) among grade levels or between levels of schooling, putting subject-area teachers in touch with one another across subject lines, or enriching the offerings of a single subject at a single grade level are among the supervisor's natural communications. Equally important is the ability of the supervisor to convey what is observed to those who plan school operations or to link teachers with larger resources available outside of the school site.

Finally, as instructional specialists, supervisors are teachers, most of whom were excellent in the classroom. Their expertise proves invaluable in helping novice teachers or in actually demonstrating new techniques to experienced teachers. Despite the sophistication of many school systems today, most real learning by classroom teachers still takes place by demonstration.

Helping classroom teachers by being knowledgeable, by sharing with and among teachers a host of new ideas, and by actually going into classrooms to demonstrate or model teaching are roles of the supervisor as the instructional specialist.

4. *Supervisors are human relations workers.* Most supervision work is informal and person to person, whether supervisors are working with individual teachers or in group settings. Supervisors also communicate with the teaching staff and the administrative staff. For these reasons and others, supervisors must be specialists in basic human relations.

The human relations skills called for in daily supervision are multiple. Supervisors must be sensitive to the needs of various client groups with whom they interact. They must employ diplomacy in their language usage, assuming that what they say will be heard and conveyed to others. Supervisors must be particularly good listeners, hearing not only what is said but also what is not said.

Supervision also includes a special capacity to motivate others. Often, the task of translating a policy or decision into behavior will fall to the supervisor because he or she is "on the line." Understanding what motivates people in a profession such as teaching is very important, and connecting such motivation to the tasks of the school as an organization requires skill.

Supervisors, too, must possess a special series of conferencing abilities as they work in small groups to improve education. Like the building administrator, the typical supervisor's day is usually a series of meetings in small groups to attack problems and provide solutions. Knowing how to manage such meetings effectively and how to actually accomplish tasks are primary human relations skills.

Finally, supervisors are regularly public relations specialists in schools. Although they may not always be dealing directly with media personnel or speaking for the school district to large groups, the troubleshooting nature of the job requires constant interface with important audiences who demand competence. Supervisors are always engaged in public relations activities as they go through the workday.

5. *Supervisors are staff developers.*   If the primary task for instructional supervisors is to improve learning opportunities for students, and if supervisors work most often in the classroom with teachers, then a major role is that of staff development or in-service specialist. Planning staff-development activities is the major method of improving instruction for the supervisor.

Because schools are human organizations, improving performance by teachers is more difficult than simply providing skill-development training. There is always an affective, or feeling, dimension to the area of staff development, and each supervisor must have a model of training ready as in-service experiences for teachers are planned. Most staff development, for instance, deals with the teacher as a person as a prerequisite to improving the teacher as an instructor.

Supervisors need the skill of being able to "see" teachers in planning staff development. There must be some way to profile the development of individual teachers so that growth can be continuous and directional. Some method must be used to make staff development respectable, overcoming a historic model of in-service to correct deficiencies in teachers.

Finally, supervisors must scout for talent when it comes to identifying and scheduling in-service assistance. Because much staff development in the past was irrelevant to the direct needs of classroom teachers, supervisors often find a basic skepticism among teachers about such assistance. Quality help must be found, and the delivery of that help must be linked to the improvement of classroom instruction. Making in-service work is a skill of the instructional supervisor.

6. *Supervisors are administrators.*   One of the most difficult tasks for the teacher-turned-supervisor is to accept an administration role in education. Historically, supervisors have been supervising teachers, but this role has changed during

the past 15 years. Heavy union activity and the resulting collective bargaining have pushed the field of supervision into a management posture. The supervisor who does not perceive his or her job as a subset of administration in the 1990s is apt to find tenure in the role short-lived.

As an administrator, the supervisor can expect to spend a major portion of the workday interacting with other administrators. This is not due to the location of problems as much as the location of solutions to instructional problems. The interrelatedness of a school "system" makes any decision a team decision. Although not yet a full-fledged member of the administrative team, the supervisor has become more administrative during the past five years.

As administrators, supervisors need basic administrative skills. They need to be able to manage assistants and secretaries. They should be able to manage information and establish effective recordkeeping in the instructional areas. They should become skilled at the use of administrative influence. To work effectively with other administrators, they must be able to think like an administrator.

There are many serious work issues that will define the meaning of the term "professional in supervision." Both women and men in supervision must be able to resolve a traditional male/female role dichotomy in working as an administrator. The supervisor-as-teacher may have difficulty in posing as an administrator. The degree of manipulation and politics may shock many new supervisors as they learn of the school–community relationship and power structures. In short, the supervisor as an administrator must possess an attitude as well as a set of skills.

7. *Supervisors are managers of change.* Twenty years ago, many supervisors conducted much of their business on an interpersonal basis, improving instruction by working directly with people. The size of today's school districts, plus the pressures of accountability, have diminished that interpersonal role. Supervisors are now often perceived as managers of meaningful change and are certainly held accountable for their actions.

Throughout the United States, state legislatures acted during the 1980s to legislate quality control in education. Testing programs, graduation requirements, and instructional competencies are only a few of the signs of the times. Most of this legislation enforces accountability that holds education programs up to public scrutiny in the area of performance. Because of this, educational supervisors are under some degree of pressure to get results. Instructional engineering has resulted in some school districts teaching to the test.

Even without the pressures of state law, a general "systems" mentality has taken hold in the area of instruction. Text series, worksheets, media, and computer programs are tied directly to performance, making the cycle of curriculum development also a cycle of accountability. Monitoring these results and making adjustments in the system are now a regular part of supervision. The management of budgets through the use of categorical funding (for certain uses only) has furthered this mechanical approach to instructional improvement.

Overall, this management function of supervision means that the instructional supervisor must be sharp with numbers, organized, and able to see all the pieces as an interacting whole.

8. *Supervisors are evaluators.*   The previously stated roles, collectively, place the supervisor in a constant evaluation position. Assessing teacher performance, program outcomes, texts and materials, consultant performance, and analysis of testing results—all are part of the evaluation role.

Supervisors are regularly expected to initiate general needs assessments and to conduct community surveys and follow-up studies of graduates. The organization of this information and the translation of this data into curriculum management plans or school improvement plans are expected roles for an instructional supervisor.

Finally, supervisors are expected to keep up with overall research in education and to translate these findings for other administrators and teachers. In some smaller districts, supervision is linked to evaluation directly in writing grants and in designing studies of student achievement.

These eight skill areas, then, form the foundation for supervisory competence in today's modern educational systems. Each of these skill areas will be treated in depth in Part Two of this book so that the reader can understand how these general competencies are applied on the job. Before addressing those areas, however, we need to gain a global perspective of the general leadership function in school supervision and how that leadership role operates at each level of schooling.

SUMMARY

Supervisors in schools have a very complex role that is often ill-defined. Historically, supervision has been defined as either an extension of administration or an overseer of teachers. Over the years, the role and tasks of supervision has been influenced by environmental factors that have caused supervisors to emphasize one area of operating over another. Definitions of supervision reflect these changing conditions and tasks.

As we enter the twenty-first century, the role of the supervisor will be defined by certain competencies that the individual brings to the job. We have identified eight such generic areas: developing people, curriculum development, instructional specialization, human relations, staff development, basic administration, management of change, and evaluation.

IMPLICATIONS FOR SUPERVISION

1. How are supervisors selected and evaluated in your school district?
2. What is the best way that a supervisor can become current in the knowledge of research on teaching?
3. What is the linkage between your school district and the nearest college or university where supervisors are trained? What should that relationship be?

∽ CASE STUDY 1 ∾

In the scenario found at the beginning of this chapter, Sally was confronted with a number of questions about her work role. Among those might be how to prioritize the many tasks ahead, how to decide if the day-to-day tasks are more important than the new ones confronting her on this day, what competence she possesses to address all of the tasks, and where she might find assistance in handling such a wide range of responsibilities.

Questions

1. How would you allocate the time in your workday if you were Sally? What is the basis of this allocation?

2. How many of these identified tasks are related in some way? What is the organizing principle for grouping these tasks?

3. Are any of the planned activities in Sally's day outside of her job responsibilities in your opinion? Why?

∽ CASE STUDY 2 ∾

Arriving on the job for the first time, Anne surveyed her new office. There was the standard issue furniture: chair, desk, filing cabinets, bookshelves, a waste can, and a coat hook. Her name appeared freshly painted on the door with the title, "Instructional Supervisor," beneath it. At last, she had finally arrived!

As Anne began to unpack some of the personal items that she had brought from home, her superior stuck her head in the door and greeted Anne, "Welcome to our crazy world at the district office."

Anne laughed. It felt good to be so informal. Turning serious for a moment, Anne asked her new boss where she thought Anne should begin.

"You know your job," replied the superior, "so just go to it."

As the woman disappeared down the hall, Anne sunk into her new chair and pondered, "Where do I start?"

Questions

1. How would Anne begin to define her position without any further direction?

2. How would variables such as the size of the district or Anne's training affect this defining process?

3. Should Anne seek additional counsel from other supervisors about her job and her responsibilities?

SUGGESTED LEARNING ACTIVITIES

1. Identify forces that may be changing the definition of supervision as you are taking this course.

2. In your own words, describe why supervision appears to be so loosely defined.

3. Construct a list of those things that make supervision a unique educational leadership role.

4. Study a school district familiar to you to assess how supervisors are deployed for leadership functions.

5. Identify a list of "tractive" tasks that a supervisor will face almost every day on the job.

BOOKS TO REVIEW

Ballentine, J. *The Sociology of Education: A Systematic Analysis.* Englewood Cliffs, NJ: Prentice Hall, 1989.

Glickman, C., ed. *Supervision in Transition.* Arlington, VA: Association for Supervision and Curriculum Development, 1992.

Owens, R. *Organizational Behavior in Schools,* 4th ed. Englewood Cliffs, NJ: Prentice Hall, 1993.

Sergiovanni, T., and Starratt, R. *Supervision: A Redefinition,* 5th ed. New York: McGraw-Hill, 1993.

Tanner, D., and Tanner, L. *The History of School Curriculum.* New York: Macmillan, 1990.

Wasley, P. *Teachers Who Lead: The Rhetoric of Reform and the Realities of Practice.* New York: Teachers College Press, 1992.

CHAPTER 2 ≈

THE FOUNDATIONS OF
SUPERVISORY LEADERSHIP

Leadership in schools is the product of many things including a clear vision, directional goals, and planning efforts; a constructed working organization; the selective application of resources, and, increasingly, the involvement of teachers and parents. All leadership reflects an approach or pattern of value priorities.

Several qualities are necessary to be an effective school leader: an understanding of the conditions of an organization, its tasks, and purposes, and the ability to interlock those tasks with the basic motivational needs of the persons who work and learn there. A leader makes basic assumptions about how the organization operates; when formalized, these assumptions become a theory of leading.

Administrative leadership theory, in its literature, has traditionally followed one of four major threads. The oldest viewpoint is one concerning the structure or bureaucracy of an organization. From this vantage point, the control and organization of schools can be seen as a major means of improving instruction. Supervisors can "organize" instructional improvement by structuring the way schools work and the relationships among the people who work there.

A second major approach to understanding leadership is the study of process, or the way organizations work. How are decisions made? What is the communication pattern? What is the relationship between line officers (superintendent, principals) and staff personnel (supervisors)? These processes can be altered to improve the way a school works and, therefore, to improve its instructional efficiency.

A third thread found in the literature of administration and supervision is a study of relationships—informal as well as formal. Here the supervisor may be concerned with one-on-one human relations, group work within organizations, or even climate control in the school environment. Such human interaction is a constant theme of supervision books because schools are so directly perceived as "human organizations."

Finally, a more recent theory is one dealing with the use of influence in organizations. Who, in schools, is really powerful and influential? How are decisions really made? This political area of organizational theory is discussed in a later chapter.

Collectively or individually, these approaches form the basis for an understanding of how schools or school districts work. The job of the supervisor is not only to understand these facets of the educational environment, but also to learn how to work within that organization to improve instruction. The deliberate mismatch of a supervisor's style with the organization and purpose of an educational institution has led to a majority of failures in supervision.

Once the supervisor knows the environment and understands how it works, he or she must then compare that purpose with his or her own conception of how a school should be structured so that it improves instructional experiences for learners. Viewing the process in the long run, as opposed to day-to-day, will help eliminate minor frustrations and improve job efficiency. The evolution of a clear theory, one that works, may take a considerable time.

ORIGINS OF LEADERSHIP THEORY

The evolution of leadership theory began thousands of years ago. The Egyptians, for example, demonstrated complex organizational skills in constructing pyramids in 5000 B.C. The Babylonians created the highly sophisticated Code of Hammurabi sometime between 2000–1700 B.C. Thousands of years ago, the Chinese had complex training programs for training leaders and scholars.

In the United States, the Industrial Revolution spurred the study of leadership behavior. By the early nineteenth century, the mechanization of industry led to classic problems of organization and role delineation among workers. By the first years of the twentieth century, ideas about leadership and administration were being catalogued and the first operational theories developed. We review these theories in order to provide the reader with four perspectives available to supervisors who work in schools.

Organizational Structures

The concern of leaders with organization structure evolved from the managerial complexities found in the mechanization of industry. Relationships among men and between men and machines were in transition because of increased industrial productivity and the need for greater efficiency of operation. Practice evolved to the theory stage at the close of the nineteenth century and found outlet in the writings of men such as Frederick Taylor, Max Weber, and Henri Fayol. These writers and others approached administration and management as a scientist might, using the scientific tools of research, measurement, and analysis.

Based on his extensive field experimentation, Frederick Taylor launched the serious study of organizational structure with his book, *Principles of Scientific Management* (1911), in which he advocated meticulous observation and study of the work process and reordering of organizations along functional lines.[1] Modern concepts such as specialization and standardization of work, use of mathematical models for production, the piece-rate system, and time standards for production were major contributions to the budding science of management. Other writers, such as Frank and Lillian Gilbreth[2] and Henry Gantt[3], filled in specific techniques of the scientific method by perfecting systems and record-keeping procedures for monitoring organizational productivity. Most of the work of this period focused squarely on the operation of the organization and ignored the human factors related to productivity.

Paralleling the scientific management movement around the turn of the century was an attempt by some practicing industrial managers to uncover general principles of organizations: to develop theory based on the structure of organizations. The best-known writer of this "universals" school of thought was Henri Fayol, French engineer, whose book, *General and Industrial Management,* was translated into English in 1929.[4] Fayol contended that management was general to all human endeavors and developed a set of principles applicable to all management activities. His fourteen principles included the concepts of division of labor, unity of command, subordination, remuneration, and esprit de corps.

Major concepts of the traditional monocratic, bureaucratic organization were

1. *Administrative efficiency*—The ultimate purpose of an organization is to establish conditions that will help it achieve its goals.
2. *Unity of purpose*—The effectiveness of any organization is enhanced when it has clearly defined goals and purpose.
3. *Standardization*—An organization is more effective when there exists a regular routine for all administrative operations.
4. *Stability*—The effectiveness of an organization is enhanced when policies and procedures are maintained until results are evaluated.
5. *Single executive*—Central coordination of activities provides for greater effectiveness in achieving the purposes of the organization.
6. *Unity of command*—The organization defines the role of each individual, and everyone knows to whom and for what they are responsible.
7. *Division of labor*—Labor and task division or specialization enhance productivity.
8. *Delegation of authority/responsibility*—Delegation of both responsibility and the authority to carry out tasks improves the effectiveness of the organization.
9. *Span of control*—Effectiveness is enhanced when each administrator is assigned only the number of persons that can be directly supervised.
10. *Security*—The organization is more effective when it provides for the security of its members.[5]

Early theorists thus recommended a pyramidal, hierarchal organizational structure that constrained power for decision making from superordinates downward to subordinates. The principles and practices that characterize this traditional structural pattern are known as "formal organization." The most thorough analysis of these elements of structural theory was developed by the German sociologist Max Weber, who fully defined the concept of a bureaucracy and adapted an administrative system to the needs of large and complex organizations.

In *The Theory of Social and Economic Organizations*,[6] Weber outlined the ideal bureaucratic structure in terms of components such as (1) fixed jurisdictional areas enforced by rules and regulations; (2) hierarchies of graded authority, assuring clear relationships between superordinates and subordinates; (3) authority derived from written documents and vested in offices, not men; (4) administration by fully trained and competent officials; and (5) the use of comprehensive planned policies to guide change. According to Weber, wide application of such characteristics produced the highest degree of efficiency and predictability in large, complex organizations.

The scientific management advocated by Taylor, the universal principles of Fayol, and the bureaucracy designed by Weber culminated in an administrative arrangement dominated by its concern for structure. The least complex formal organization was the line organization, so named because of the direct lines of authority between administrative officers. Line organizations have no staff, advisory, or auxiliary officers. A second type of formal organization has line relationships as well as staff members who are not links in the chain of authority. A third, more complex, type of formal organization might have both line and staff personnel, plus technical (functional) specialists, who service several layers of the hierarchy in an organization. This type is known as a "tall" organization, whereas one with few layers and wide spans of control is known as "flat." Figure 2.1 shows the various organizational styles.

During the early years of this century, most school districts in the United States were organized in a highly structured manner, according to the best available administrative theory. Today, most school districts employ a modified bureaucracy, which they find more flexible and responsive to a changing educational environment. Even in the large city systems, where bureaucracies are still entrenched, we see the emergence of technical specialists (such as computer programmers) who break down the monocratic structure with the influence of their expertise rather than their political savvy. Perhaps the greatest conflict for an individual administrator in a bureaucratic educational structure is the one between loyalty to administration and professional loyalty to issues and products.

Organizational Processes

A second focus in the study of organizations is the processes by which they function. Most contributions to this approach have come from the social and behavioral sciences. Collectively, the input from these fields make up organizational theory and its derivative, general systems theory.

A theory of leadership concerned with functional operation of an organization as an integrated whole evolved because of the inability of monocratic structures to change. In the 1920s, organizations underwent drastic changes because of the increasing scope and complexity of operations and advances in technology. The piecemeal evolution of major organizations in the face of such comprehensive

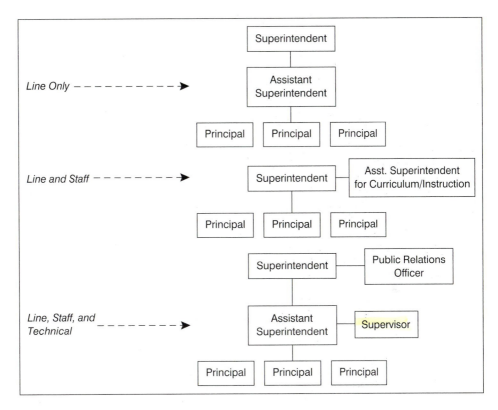

Figure 2.1 Formal Organizations

change resulted in dysfunctions and imbalance. During this period of change, organizations needed the capability of responding to their environment through self-regulation, self-adaptation, and self-renewal.

Organizations are social units purposefully constructed, and sometimes reconstructed, to meet goals. Those goals provide an identity to the organization and communication of the organization's mission to the environment. In times of substantial change, organizations that do not maintain goal-clarity, or fail to see themselves as a functioning whole, soon become obsolescent.

In this respect, the study of organizational processes emerged from need, because bureaucratic organization proved unable to monitor and accommodate major changes in the environment. In educational organizations, the highly structured bureaucracy had trouble dealing with a number of forces, including a changing mission with expanding boundaries, control of school resources by varying levels of government, and growing public access to educational decision making. Educational organizations responded by creating specialists and staff officers to perform the many peripheral roles associated with running the school. Supervisors are one such role.

Organizational processes encompass a cycle for dealing with change, the steps of which include analyzing, planning, implementing, and evaluating. Social science investigations have uncovered a staggering variety of specialized inquiry areas in analyzing the processes of organization. As Table 2.1 shows, each area of specialization includes many tasks.

Theorists of educational administration often selected various processes to explain the complexity of school operations. Griffith, for example, sees the specific function of administration as the development and regulation of a decision-making process.[7] According to Griffith, decision making follows identifiable steps:

1. Recognize, define, and limit the problem.
2. Analyze and evaluate the problem.
3. Establish standards by which the solution will be evaluated.
4. Collect data.
5. Formulate and select preferred solutions.
6. Put into effect the preferred solution.

Other theorists throughout the 1960s, 1970s, and 1980s have selected variables such as management techniques, fiscal analysis, and performance evaluation as handles for describing the processes of school administration.

By the early 1960s, the myriad variables represented by the various organizational processes found focus in general systems theory. Systems theory, a product of

Table 2.1 Sample Process Areas of an Organization

Area	Tasks
Planning	Forecasting
	Planning cycles
	Work flow analysis
	Fiscal projections
	Management techniques (management-by-objectives)
Decision making	Operations research
	Management information systems
	Cost benefit analysis
Project management	Task analysis
	Communications systems
	Long-range planning (program evaluation and review technique/critical path method)
Personnel administration	Job analysis
	Employee recruitment
	Testing/classification
Accountability and control	Fiscal projection
	Internal auditing
	Long-range budgeting (program planning budgeting system)

the physical sciences, provided the concept of interdependence in organizations and explained why changes in one part of an organization affected other parts or the whole of the organization. A system is simply a group of objects treated as a unit. With the adoption of systems theory in educational administration, all of the important processes of operating a school or school district could be seen holistically.

In modern organizational theory, the systems concept describes administration as the central force in organizations—a force that coordinates and relates activities. In this role, the administrator needs insight and skill in conceptualizing relationships. Robert Katz refers to conceptual skill as

> The ability to see the organization as a whole; it includes recognizing how . . . the various functions of the organization depend on one another, and how change in any one part affects all the others. Recognizing these relationships and perceiving the significant elements in any situation, the administrator should then be able to act in a way which advances the overall welfare of the organization.[8]

In school settings, a system might be defined as any set of components organized so that its goals can be accomplished. Thus, school programs are systems comprised of facilities, materials, funds, teachers, testing, and a host of other contributing variables for the purpose of educating children. The real value of a systems perspective for supervisors is as a means of identifying noncontributing conditions, or bottlenecks, in the flow of activity. Once identified, the system deficiencies can be targeted for redesign. Systems can also help the educator build models of preferred conditions for learning.[9]

Perhaps the high point in the study of organizational processes is the concept of Organization Development (O.D.), a planned and sustained effort to apply behavioral science for system improvement.[10] Organization Development consists of data gathering, organizational diagnosis, and action intervention. The fulfillment of the O.D. program is, in a real sense, changing the way a school works. The three elements of organizational process that appear important for meeting change are the roles people play, the goals of the organization, and operational procedures already in place. In effect, Organizational Development is a people-involving approach to systematic analysis. Through analysis, it is hoped, the members of the organization will become committed to the efficacy of the systems function.

The other key to the success of Organization Development methodology in improving institutional process is the commitment to deal with change over an extended period of time and to use some of the resources of the organization to maintain, rebuild, and expand its structure. O.D. technology approaches the goal of a self-renewing school.

Organizational Relationships

Although the study of organization structure and process has been a convenient way to look at supervision, another focus has been the relationship among people in organizations. Approached from a number of variables, such as communication, individual

needs, morale, motivation, and small group work, the study of organizational relationships has enriched the study of leadership and given clues to organizational function.

It was, in fact, a study of efficiency that ushered in the human relations era of
organizational analysis. During the 1920s, researchers at Western Electric's
Hawthorne Plant were attempting to determine the relationship between illumination and production. The chief investigator, F. J. Roethlisberger, was surprised to find
that production increased with every change in the experimental condition; whether
illumination was increased or decreased, productivity went up. A mysterious force,
later labeled the "Hawthorne Effect," was eventually determined to be a human attitudinal factor.

An early proponent of the human relationship approach to the study of leadership, Elton Mayo, proposed that an overemphasis of scientific method studies had
alienated workers and led to a form of psychological deterioration in organizations.
Mayo recommended more small-group interaction and face-to-face communication
to overcome these dehumanizing forces.[11] The early concern of Mayo and others for
attention to the psychosocial dimensions of an organization soon led to extensive
application of social science research to leadership theory.

One of the first major theories in this area was Kurt Lewin's "field theory." Lewin
held that causal relationships in organizations, or cause and effect, could be
explained in terms of (1) the psychological environment as it exists for groups or
individuals; (2) the needs, values, and desires of individuals in that environment; and
(3) the variables of life space, such as functions, behaviors, and flexibility. Lewin mentioned a "force field," in which certain driving or restraining forces competed to raise
or lower productivity. His basic formula, $B = F(PE)$ (behavior is a function of the person and the environment), introduced an entirely new element into the concept of
management.[12]

Later work in the social sciences focused more specifically on the nature of
humans and human behavior. An early contribution was the work of psychologist A.
H. Maslow, who proposed that human needs are arranged in hierarchical order.
According to Maslow, these needs had a prepotency effect, so that as one level of
needs was satisfied, the next level was activated. Maslow's model proposed five levels
of needs: (1) physiological needs; (2) security or safety needs; (3) social, belonging,
or membership needs; (4) esteem needs, including autonomy; and (5) self-actualization, or self-fulfillment needs. The value of Maslow's hierarchy for administration was
in providing an explanation of worker behavior and motivation.[13]

One piece of social science research built on Maslow's work was Frederick
Herzberg's "job enrichment" model.[14] Through extensive interviews with workers,
Herzberg determined that some job characteristics led to job satisfaction, whereas
others led to job dissatisfaction. Characteristics that led to job dissatisfaction were
called "hygiene factors" (salary, work conditions, job security), because they were
contextual and always in need of replenishment. Contrasted with hygiene factors
were "motivators" (recognition, responsibility, possibilities for growth), which satisfied the individual's need for self-actualization at work. Herzberg's work approached
prescription for administrators working in organizations with the so-called "human
factor." Maslow's and Herzberg's models appear in Figure 2.2.

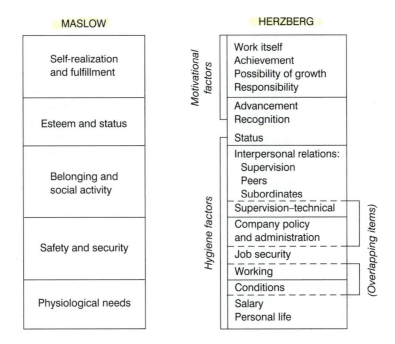

Figure 2.2 Maslow's Need-Priority Model Compared with Herzberg's Motivation-Hygiene Model
Source: Adapted from K. Davis, *Human Relations at Work.* New York: McGraw-Hill, 1967, p. 37.

By the 1950s, management theorists began to speak of the lack of congruence between the tasks of organizations and the needs of individuals. Argyris stated the condition in these three propositions:

1. There is a lack of congruence between the needs of healthy individuals and the demands of formal organizations.
2. The result of this disturbance is frustration, failure, short-term perspective, and conflict.
3. The nature of the formal principles causes the subordinate, at any given level, to experience competition, rivalry, insubordinate hostility, and a focus on the parts rather than the whole.[15]

Another theorist, Likert, called for management to modify the rigid communication patterns of many organizations and link formal and informal groups for greater productivity and effectiveness. Suggesting that people with membership in overlapping groups within an organization can play a critical role in promoting better communication, Likert developed his *linking pin theory* for modifying formal organizations.[16] Blau and Scott illuminated the role of informal groups:

The fact that an organization has been formally established does not mean that all activities and interactions of its members conform strictly to the official blueprint. In every organization there arise informal organizations . . . [which] develop their own practices, norms, and social relations.[17]

Finally, Douglas McGregor made the direct connection between leadership style, organization, and the individuals in the organization. McGregor suggested that underlying assumptions of the leader about human behavior were instrumental to both the design and operation of an organization. McGregor characterized two different styles of leadership, each of which would elicit different responses from individuals in the organization. One style, called "Theory X leadership," assumes a posture of distrust in viewing workers in the organization. The opposing style, "Theory Y leadership," believes in the capacity of workers to grow and contribute. This work of McGregor's provided new insights into how organizations might integrate individual needs with institutional tasks.[18] Figure 2.3 compares the characteristics of the two leadership styles.

Overall, the study of organizations from the perspective of relationships supplied practicing supervisors with many insights about their role in influencing human behavior. The study of relationships also opened a fourth approach to inquiry, the study of influence in the operation of an organization.

Theory X Assumptions	Theory Y Assumptions
People by Nature:	People by Nature:
1. Lack integrity	1. Have integrity
2. Are fundamentally lazy and desire to work as little as possible	2. Work hard toward objectives to which they are committed
3. Avoid responsibility	3. Assume responsibility within their commitments
4. Are not interested in achievement	4. Desire to achieve
5. Are incapable of directing their own behavior	5. Are capable of directing their own behavior
6. Are indifferent to organizational needs	6. Want their organization to succeed
7. Prefer to be directed by others	7. Are not passive and submissive
8. Avoid making decisions whenever possible	8. Will make decisions within their commitments
9. Are not very bright	9. Are not stupid

Figure 2.3 Organizational View of People
Source: From Douglas McGregor, "The Human Side of Enterprise," *Management Review,* November 1957, pp. 22–28, 88–92. Reprinted by permission of the publisher, American Management Association, Inc., New York.

Organizational Influence

A final avenue, and the most recently explored, evolved because the study of structure, process, and relationships failed to explain completely the operation of an organization. The study of influence in organizations has its origin in sociology and political science, and speaks in terms of power, authority, and persuasion. Emergence of this perspective has hastened since 1960 because of the issues of community pluralism, governance, and control brought about by shrinking resources and an increase in legal rulings on school issues and legal activity in our schools.

The study of influence includes at least four subareas: studies of change, leadership, decision making, and the role of politics. These subareas break down into more specialized studies, such as the influences of finance, media, technology, and other variables on an organization's operation.

The literature on change includes studies of types of change, models of change, strategies of changing, and barriers to change. One major distinction in the literature is the difference between planned change and evolutionary or natural change. Guba identifies three types of change: evolutionary (natural change), homeostatic (reactive change), and neomobilistic (planned change).[19] Bennis lists eight types of change: planned, indoctrination, coercive, technocratic, interactional, socialization, emulative, and natural.[20]

There are both adopted models and developed models of change. Stereotypic models include those of agriculture (change agent), medicine (action research), business (incentives), and the military (authority). Most models build on an original conception of five stages of change: awareness, interest, evaluation, trial, and adoption.[21] A more sophisticated version of the basic model focuses on the relationship between the change agent and the client system:

1. The development of a need for change
2. The establishment of a change relationship
3. The diagnosis of the client system's problem
4. The examination of goals and alternative routes of action
5. The transformation of intentions into action
6. The generalization and stabilization of change
7. The achievement of a terminal relationship[22]

Chin offers the most general conceptualization of strategies of change under the headings: rational-empirical, normative-reeducative, and power-coercive. The rational-empirical strategy is based on the assumption that people will follow their rational self-interests once these are revealed to them. The normative-reeducative strategy recognizes change as a sociocultural phenomenon that is reinforced by group values and attitudes. The power-coercive strategy, obviously, is based on the application of influence through position or some other irrefutable source.[23] Bennis identifies eight other traditional strategies of change: exposition and propagation, elite corps, human relations training, scholarly consultation, circulation of ideas to influentials, use of staff, developmental research, and action research.[24]

Finally, the literature on organizations points to a number of persistent barriers to change, including a lack of understanding of the change, human nature's tendency to favor the status quo, lack of skills for implementing change, poor leadership, and absence of precise goals for assessing the impact of change. Klein observes, however, that barriers to change are not all bad, because they

1. Protect the organization from random change which may be harmful;
2. Protect the system from takeover by vested interests; and
3. Ensure that unanticipated consequences of a change be spelled out and possibly avoided.[25]

Another area of study in the broad area of influence is leadership, that intangible driving force in planned change. Attempts to study and analyze leadership have evolved through three stages of inquiry: a study of leadership traits; an analysis of situation or environment affecting leadership; and a study of exchange or transactions between leaders and followers.

Although many traits have been considered unique to leaders (height, persistence, imagination), none has withstood objective analysis as an absolute predictor of leadership style or capacity. Stogdill suggested that leadership is linked to situations and identified six factors associated with leadership: achievement, responsibility, participation, capacity, status, and the situation. Stogdill stated, "A person does not become a leader by virtue of the possession of some combination of traits, but the pattern of personal characteristics of the leader must bear some relevant relationship to the characteristics, activities, and goals of the followers."[26]

Further research on leadership revealed another important factor in the formula of leadership: the follower. The follower is crucial in determining leadership because this person *perceives* the leader and the situation and reacts according to that perception. With this observation, leadership research emerged into the "exchange theory" stage, focusing on how leaders motivate groups to accept their influence and the processes underlying the prolonged exertion of that influence.

Other focuses of studying the area of leadership have included small-group management,[27] communications,[28] and perceptual psychology.[29] Collectively, these inquiries have led to the understanding that to be a leader, in the real sense of the word, a person must be perceived as a leader by the groups that make up an organization. The leader can have an impact on the perceptions of the organization's members by being aware of their needs and structuring the organization to meet their needs. Specific acts of leadership may include selectively applying roles and tasks to problems, encouraging desirable communication patterns, changing individual perceptions with information and experience, and tailoring rewards to motivational levels. Collectively, the leader's actions to influence the organization can be seen as the establishment of an environment to control transaction.[30]

A third area of study relating to influence has concentrated on decision making and policy formation. A pervasive element of administration is the need to coordinate activities; coordination is the bridge between planning and action. Policies facilitate coordination by providing a detailed conception of the method for accomplishing tasks and encouraging delegation of both authority and responsibility in organizations. The study of policy formation and implementation becomes particularly important in organizations such as schools that are open and subject to input from diverse sources.

Agger, Goldrich, and Swanson provide a six-step model of policy development that helps us understand this complex area. They refer to

1. Policy information
2. Policy deliberation
3. Organization of policy support
4. Authoritative consideration (support endorsement)
5. Policy promulgation
6. Policy effectuation[31]

Developing policy, or authoritative decisions for guiding other decisions, provides supervisors a way of governing and stabilizing organizations through times of change. Specialized areas in the study of policy include policy formation, access to decision making, influence of external bodies on policy formation, and conflict resolution. Interest in policy and decision making in schools is likely to continue and expand. As Campbell observes:

> The traditional belief is that education is a profession in which policy decisions are made by a representative board of lay persons and implemented by professionals. This ideology has been challenged on two grounds which, taken together, provide the rationale for new efforts in citizen involvement. The public has challenged (1) the effectiveness of schools and (2) the representativeness of the school policymakers.[32]

A final area of study of understanding the concept of influence has been the politics of education. Politics can be defined as the art or science of governing, but the concerns of inquiry have focused on the application of power to influence organizations. An early definition by Goldhammer and Shils held that "a person is said to have power to the extent that he influences the behavior of others in accordance with his own intentions."[33] Inquiry has delineated specialized study in areas such as power structures, passing bond issues, and budget control.

According to Nunnery and Kimbrough,

> The power structure of the community is the systematic, relative distribution of social power among citizens in determining the kind of community they want and the kind of institutional arrangement that will best serve them. The exercise of power by citizens is not equal; there is an unequal distribution of influence in the system.[34]

Hunter's study found a pyramidal type of informal power structure that included (1) the policymakers, (2) leaders who established policy positions, (3) those who implement policy, and (4) the professional educator and lay board. In other words, Hunter stated, "Those who held the formal power to make decisions tended not to appear in the policy-making group."[35]

Writing on this topic, Kimbrough observes,

> The entrenched power group is usually lodged deep in the socioeconomic fabric of the human group. Students who for the first time do empirical analyses of power in administration units in which an informal power group is predominant are awed by the extent to which its leaders are embedded in community affairs.[36]

In 1971, Nunnery and Kimbrough revealed the full extent of political activity in schools and their influence on the operation and administration of school districts:

> The school system is administered within a complex power structure. The typical board of education does not exercise final authority over educational policies. In reality it exercises power only to the extent that it can legitimize its decisions (make them acceptable) in the political system. It cannot enforce a policy that is unacceptable to the people it serves and retain power. Thus, schoolmen must continually seek public affirmation of operating policies.[37]

Inquiry into the function of organizations has been comprehensive and continuous in this century. Four main focuses—structures, processes, relationships, and influence—have served as organizers for this inquiry, as shown in Figure 2.4.

ROLES AND TASKS OF LEADERSHIP

Leadership in supervision is not a function of titles or appointed positions. Titles may legitimize formal authority, but they do not ensure leadership capacity. True leadership is a function of four complex variables: the character of the leader, the character of those being led, the character of the organization, and the character of the environment.

Leadership in educational organizations is a situational phenomenon. It is determined by the collective perceptions of individuals, is related to group norms, and is influenced by the frequency of interaction among members of the organization. Before leadership can be effective in an open organization such as a school, it must be acknowledged as a group activity.

To some extent, leadership is a product of the leader's vision. The way in which the leader conceives of the group's tasks, and the policies and practices to successfully achieve those ends, defines leadership. In the words of management specialist Douglas McGregor, "The theoretical assumptions management holds about controlling human resources determines the whole character of the enterprise."[38]

The way in which the leader sees the organization and its needs, when formalized, sets the foundation for a theory of leadership. Without such a theory, leader-

Figure 2.4 Study of Organizations 1900–1990

ship behaviors will be little more than a series of activities and projects that have little relationship to one another. Most often, conceptions of leadership are developed in terms of what the leader is to be and do, in terms of roles and tasks.

Leadership roles in supervision are multiple because of the numerous environments in which the supervisor operates and the supportive role of most supervisory positions. Here is a list of common leadership roles that can be applied to various situations:

Expert—Sometimes the consultant is the source of knowledge or skill in an area.

Instructor—The consultant may take the role of instructing about an area of knowledge.

Trainer—A trainer goes beyond instruction in that he or she helps people master "do it" behavioral skills in performing actions.

Retriever—The retriever brings what is needed to the client system.

Referrer—The referrer sends the client system to a source where it can find what it needs.

Linker—The linker provides a bridge to parties, or parts of a system, that need to be in contact.

Demonstrator—The demonstrator shows the client system how something is done but does not necessarily give instruction on how to do it.

Modeler—The modeler provides an example of how to do, or be, something by displaying that behavior.

Advocate—To best facilitate an intention, the consultant acts as an advocate for a goal, value, or strategy.

Confronter—A confronter points out a discrepancy to the client system.

Counselor—The role of the counselor generally includes listening, acting as a sounding board, and raising awareness of alternatives. It is a nondirective effort in helping the client think through issues.

Advisor—The advisor role differs from that of a counselor by being more directive about what the client might do and how to do it.

Observer—The observer comments on the things that exist and how things are being done.

Data Collector—The data collector gathers information about what exists and how things are being done.

Analyzer—The analyzer interprets the meaning of data found in the system.

Diagnoser—The diagnoser uses analyses, data, and observations in determining why things happen the way they do in the system.

Designer—The designer develops action strategies, training programs, and management models for use by the system.

Manager—The manager takes charge of the development process by ordering events to achieve accountability.

Evaluator—The evaluator serves to feed back information that will make the system more effective in its task.[39]

Like the roles of supervision, the tasks associated with successful practice are numerous. The tasks performed and the task pattern for any one supervisor will vary from organization to organization and work situation to work situation. However, some general tasks are found in most supervision leadership opportunities.

DEVELOPING AND OPERATING THEORY.   Leaders must be able to conceptualize tasks and communicate the approach to those tasks to others in the organization. The pattern of task identification and response forms the basis of an operating theory.

DEVELOPING ORGANIZATION AND A WORK ENVIRONMENT.   Supervision tasks are often nonpermanent responses to needs. In such cases, the way in which people, resources, and ideas are organized is left to the leader. An important task is to structure an organization and work environment that can respond to those needs.

SETTING STANDARDS.   Because supervision problems often involve diverse groups of individuals with different needs and perceptions, an important task for a curriculum leader is to set standards and other expectations that will affect the resolution of problems. Such standards may include work habits, communication procedures, time limitations, or a host of related planning areas.

USING AUTHORITY TO ESTABLISH AN ORGANIZATIONAL CLIMATE.   Persons assigned to leadership positions generally are able to structure organizations by suggesting changes and initiating policies. One of the most important tasks for a supervision leader is using such authority to establish a desirable work climate. Such a climate, discussed later in this chapter, is made up of the collective perceptions of persons affected by the structure of the organization.

ESTABLISHING EFFECTIVE INTERPERSONAL RELATIONS. Since leadership is a product of human exchanges or transactions within organizations, it is essential that interpersonal relationships contribute to the attainment of desired ends. The way in which a supervision leader interacts with others in the organization can assist in the establishment of a pattern of effective interpersonal relationships.

PLANNING AND INITIATING ACTION. The supervision leader is sometimes the only person with the authority to plan and initiate actions. Deciding when and how to initiate action is a strong leadership activity. Failure to lead planning or initiate action can undermine other leadership functions.

KEEPING COMMUNICATION CHANNELS OPEN AND FUNCTIONING. The supervision leader is often able to communicate with others in an organization when lateral and horizontal communication is limited for most members. The leader can use this unique position to bring together those persons who need to communicate with one another. The leader can also make changes in communication patterns, where necessary, to ensure that such communication channels are functioning.

LEADERSHIP STYLE

The study of leadership is a far-ranging inquiry characterized by sometimes conflicting expert opinion and a rich body of literature. There are some 130 different definitions of leadership in today's educational literature, a sample of which is provided for review:

> A leader is best when people barely know he exists. When our work is done, his aim is fulfilled, they will say, "We did this ourselves." Lao-Tsu, *The Way of Life*, 6th Century, B.C.
> Love is held by a chain of obligation . . . but fear is maintained by the dread of punishment which never fails . . . A wise prince must rely on what is in his power and not on what is in the power of others. Niccolo Machiavelli, *The Prince,* 1500 A.D.
> Leadership is the art of imposing one's will upon others in such a manner as to command their obedience, their respect and their loyal cooperation. *G-I Manual,* Staff College, United States Army, 1947.
> Leadership is the ability to get a man to do what you want him to do, when you want it done, in a way you want it done, because he wants to do it. Dwight Eisenhower, 1957.
> Leadership is the human factor which binds a group together and motivates it toward a goal. K. Davis, *Human Relations at Work,* 1962.
> Leadership is the process of influencing the activities of an individual or group in efforts toward goal achievement in a given situation. Hersey and Blanchard, *The Management of Organizational Behavior,* 1977.[40]

In addition, the literature on leadership often defines it by what it does or in how it is applied:

Leadership as the focus of group process—The leader is the nucleus of social movement. By control of social processes (structure, goals, ideology, atmosphere), the leader becomes the primary agent for group change.

Leadership as personality and its effects—The leader possesses the greatest number of desired traits. Using these, the leader exerts a degree of influence over those about him.

Leadership as the art of inducing compliance—The leader, through face-to-face control, causes the subordinate to behave in a desired manner.

Leadership as the exercise of influence—The leader establishes a relationship and uses this interpersonal influence to attain goals and enforce behavior beyond mechanical compliance.

Leadership as a power relationship—The leader is perceived as having the right to prescribe behavior patterns for others. Sources of power include referent power (liking), expert power, coercive power, and legitimate (authority) power.

Leadership as the initiation of structure—The leader originates and structures interaction as a part of a process to solve problems.

Leadership as goal achievement—The leader is perceived as controlling the means of satisfying needs as the group moves toward definite objectives.[41]

There have also been attempts in educational supervision literature to "prescribe" leadership under certain conditions. Wiles and Lovell attempt to state such "principles of leadership" in stating how leadership works in a school environment where there are multiple group needs:

1. Leadership is a group role . . . he is able to exert leadership only through effective participation in groups.
2. Leadership, other things being equal, depends upon the frequency of interaction between the leader and the led.
3. Status position does not necessarily give leadership.
4. Leadership in any organization is widespread and diffused . . . if a person hopes to exert leadership for everybody, he is doomed to frustration and failure.
5. The norms of the group determine the leader.
6. Leadership qualities and followership qualities are interchangeable.
7. People who give evidence of a desire to control are rejected for leadership roles.
8. The feeling that people hold about a person is a factor in whether they will use his behavior as leadership.
9. Leadership shifts from situation to situation.[42]

ANALYZING VARIABLES IN A SCHOOL CULTURE

As we have seen, leadership comes in many forms and is enacted through many roles. The supervisor, in working with the principal to improve instruction, will have to assess a number of factors in order to decide on an effective approach. Among the more obvious variables are the culture of the school itself, the clientele being served by the school, the personal leadership style and behaviors of the principal, the resources available for working, and any external forces operating to influence instructional improvement.

All schools have a culture, or way of working, that results from the interaction of the parts and the perceptions of members that drive such interaction. In assessing such a culture, the supervisor will note the communication patterns, reward systems, decision-making techniques, ways in which conflicts are resolved, and teacher, student, and administrative roles. Additionally, school records, significant or recognized events, and any sense of school history many reveal how persons see their school and why they act as they do.

The school clientele is an important variable for the supervisor to note. In the 1990s, schools vary widely in character including such things as wealth, racial, ethnic, or religious composition, general educational level of the parents, degree of parental participation in school decision making, and readiness for change.

Resources also vary among schools. In some districts, individual school buildings are allowed to supplement district allocations resulting in unequal resource bases. Active PTA's, business alliances, or influential parents suggest the presence of such a condition.

Working with the Principal

The personal leadership style and behavior of the principal may give clues to a successful way of working for the supervisor. In Figure 2.5, a simple conception of leadership styles is provided to indicate the variety of patterns you might encounter. In Figure 2.6, an analysis form is provided so that you may practice "typing" an administrator that you know.

The process of working with a principal will usually follow one of several patterns: (1) systematic, (2) permissive, (3) task oriented, or (4) mandated. In the case of systematic engagement (for example, systemwide requirements such as a new reading program), an accreditation, self-study, or some other comprehensive review will be addressed. Under these conditions, most principals view the supervisor as a resource to be used in meeting the requirement. The role of the supervisor is supported and directed by the principal.

In a more common pattern, the principal is simply permissive in allowing the supervisor to "practice" in the building. Here, norms and values will prove to be rather restrictive parameters on supervisor behaviors. For instance, calling a meeting after regular working hours (norm established, not contract established) may cause the principal to "redirect" the supervisor.

If the job of the supervisor is task oriented, such as evaluating new teachers using an established form, the supervisor can expect much greater autonomy. Any expansion of that role beyond the task, however, may interfere with, even threaten, the principal's way of operating.

Finally, if the supervisor's role is mandated, either officially by law or politically by the superintendent or board, the supervisor will pretty much have the "run of the place" in working to improve instruction. Using borrowed authority, the supervisor is elevated to being "in charge" of the mandated task.

1. "TELLS" Leadership
   a. Seeks unquestioning obedience
   b. Sometimes relies on fear, intimidation
   c. Gives orders
   d. Relies heavily on authority
   e. Sets all goals and standards
   f. Makes all decisions without consulting the group

2. "SELLS" Leadership
   a. Work assignments are allotted to workers
   b. Assignments are sometimes arbitrary
   c. Tries to persuade the group to accept assignments
   d. Seldom builds teamwork
   e. Does not motivate worker involvement
   f. Makes decisions without consulting the group

3. "CONSULTS" Leadership
   a. Does not rely on authority
   b. Develops considerable worker loyalty
   c. Does not hesitate to delegate
   d. Will usually explain why a task is to be performed in a certain way
   e. Takes time to inform his group what he thinks may be a solution

4. "JOINS" Leadership
   a. Builds teamwork by group involvement
   b. Accepts suggestions from the work group
   c. Treats each worker as an individual
   d. Helps workers achieve their potential
   e. Uses the decision of the group

5. "DELEGATES" Leadership
   a. Turns the decision-making process over to the group
   b. Accepts all group decisions that fit within accepted parameters
   c. Encourages subordinate participation in many activities
   d. Stimulates creative thinking in employees

Figure 2.5 Leadership Styles
Source: Michael C. Giammatteo, "Training Packing for a Model City Staff," Field Paper no. 15 (Portland, OR: Northwest Regional Educational Laboratory, 1975), p. 30.

To summarize, when instructional improvement is routine and systematic or the supervisor practices with "permission" of the principal, little autonomy will be present in the role. However, as the job is specific to a task or mandated by a higher authority, the supervisor gains autonomy and may move more freely within the school. Being aware of the school variables, the personality of the principal, and the type of work expected will help to make the supervisor much more effective at the school level.

Directions: Mark each item below with an L (like) or a U (unlike). Upon completion, attempt to determine how you might work with this individual to improve the instructional program of a school.

Items	**Examples**

1. Listening

   a. _____ Draws other people out
   b. _____ Gives no indication that he/she hears what is said
   c. _____ Hears content but not feeling
   d. _____ Blocks people out
   e. _____ Hears and interprets communications from sender's point of view
   f. _____ Hears words but does not comprehend them

2. Expressing Ideas to Others

   a. _____ Comes across clearly to individuals
   b. _____ Comes across clearly to both individuals and groups
   c. _____ Uses words well but doesn't convey ideas clearly
   d. _____ Is not easily understood
   e. _____ Conveys ideas but does so awkwardly
   f. _____ May not try sufficiently hard to get ideas across

3. Influences

   a. _____ By weight of ideas and logic
   b. _____ By force of personality
   c. _____ By being friendly
   d. _____ By scheming and manipulation
   e. _____ By involving others in the issue
   f. _____ By status and/or position

4. Decision Making

   a. _____ Focuses primarily on keeping people happy
   b. _____ Tries to get job done through getting people involved
   c. _____ Believes in making important decisions by himself/herself
   d. _____ Works for compromise between productivity and morale
   e. _____ Focuses primarily on getting job done
   f. _____ Follows leads of other people

Figure 2.6 Analyzing Principal Behaviors

Continued

5. Relationship with Others

   a. _____ Harmonizes and compromises differences in the group
   b. _____ Doesn't see need for supporting others
   c. _____ Keeps others involved
   d. _____ Insensitive to feelings of others
   e. _____ Tolerant of differences in others
   f. _____ Doesn't support things in which he/she doesn't believe
   g. _____ Puts others down with value judgment

6. Task Orientation

   a. _____ Works on task only if personally interested
   b. _____ Procrastinates in getting job done
   c. _____ Works on task only in spurts
   d. _____ Encourages involvement of others in work tasks
   e. _____ Works equally hard on important and unimportant tasks
   f. _____ Constantly presses to get job done

7. Handling of Conflict

   a. _____ Readily engages in conflict
   b. _____ Doesn't recognize any conflict
   c. _____ Tends to smooth or gloss over conflicts
   d. _____ Stirs up conflict for its own sake
   e. _____ Works through conflict openly
   f. _____ Goes out of way to avoid conflict

8. Willingness to Change

   a. _____ Defends ideas against all comers
   b. _____ Mulls ideas over thoroughly before committing to something new
   c. _____ Values change for change's sake
   d. _____ Quick to utilize new ideas
   e. _____ Will try new things only if his/her ideas
   f. _____ Usually thinks things through until it is too late to change

9. Problem Solving

   a. _____ Sets goals and keeps them in mind
   b. _____ Slows down groups by going off on tangents

Figure 2.6 *Continued*

NEW FORMS OF WORKING

Restructuring Schools

During the 1980s and into the early 1990s, a major change in public education was the increased involvement of teachers in governance. Flying under labels such as decentralized decision making (DDM), school-based management (SBM), teacher

c. _____ Considers all pertinent information
d. _____ Jumps to conclusions quickly
e. _____ Doesn't recognize existing problems
f. _____ Utilizes resources of others

10. Self-development

a. _____ Understands the reason for his/her task
b. _____ Is not self-critical
c. _____ Blames others for his/her own shortcomings
d. _____ Encourages comments on his/her own behavior
e. _____ Doesn't realize how others see him/her
f. _____ Is growing and developing in work effectiveness

11. Expressing Emotions to Others

a. _____ Clearly and frequently verbalizes his/her emotions
b. _____ Acknowledges emotions
c. _____ Has difficulty stating emotions clearly to others
d. _____ Uses emotional words but does not act/live out his/her feelings
e. _____ Uses only global words ("good," "comfortable," etc.) to describe emotions

Strategy for Working with This Leader

1.

2.

3.

4.

5.

Figure 2.6 *Continued*

empowerment, or "restructuring," the major thrust was to involve teachers more in the process of running the school. This development was very important to the supervisor since many of the new tasks assumed by teachers were historic supervision tasks. Also, this change meant that the supervisor's relationship with the school principal became more complex than in the past.

In many states, legislatures, with the prodding of state teacher unions, mandated that all districts develop a process to include teachers in policy formation and the operation of the school. The most common label given to the school site procedures was S.I.T. (School Improvement Teams). Under this arrangement, teacher representatives would meet regularly with administrators to set goals, review expenditures, procure resources, and even assess teaching performance. Although most teachers embraced this movement as long overdue, problems did arise (see Figure 2.7)

The actual procedure of working "collaboratively" is still being established as this book is written. Several widely disseminated labels have guided most action. One twenty-year-old idea that has been reviewed by many staffs is M.B.O. (management by objectives). Here, decentralization of a task occurs, and teachers are given responsibility at the school level for areas such as curriculum development, teacher evaluation, or community involvement. The role of the principal is to manage these efforts, and the supervisor serves as one of many resources available to the teaching staff (such as providing ideas for teacher evaluation).

Another very popular set of principles being considered is T.Q.M. (Total Quality Management). This concept is based on a list of some fourteen principles that have governed Japanese industrial development since World War Two, credited to W. Edward Deming, an American.

Deming believed that workers are assets who should be involved in improving the products they produce. Deming felt that building quality into products as they are being made is better than inspecting for quality after the job is done, as was the standard practice.

On Teacher Empowerment

Following are Seven Ironies of School Empowerment, as identified by Carl D. Glickman.

1. The more an empowered school improves, the more apparent it is that there's more to be improved.

2. The more an empowered school is recognized for its success, the more non-empowered schools criticize it.

3. The more an empowered school works collectively, the more individual differences and tensions among its staff members become obvious.

4. The more an empowered school becomes a model for success, the less the school becomes a practical model to be imitated by others.

5. The more an empowered school has to gain, the more it hesitates to act.

6. The more an empowered school has to gain, the more it has to lose.

7. The more an empowered school represents a democracy, the more it must justify its own existence to the most vocal proponents of democracy.

Figure 2.7 Shortcomings of Teacher Empowerment
Source: Carl D. Glickman, "Pushing School Reform to a New Edge. The Seven Ironies of School Empowerment," *Phi Delta Kappa,* September 1990, p. 113. Excerpted from "Teacher Empowerment—Sharing the Challenge: A Guide to Implementation and Success," by Gary Heller. The article appeared in the February 1993 Bulletin.

His move to "drive out fear" in the workplace and instill quality through consistency of purpose struck a responsive chord for the American teacher empowerment movement.[43]

Finally, our own Curriculum Management Planning (CMP) process has proven to be a useful application of the concept of teacher involvement. Working closely with strong teacher unions in cities such as St. Louis, Dallas, and Miami, the CMP allowed wide involvement in school and district redesign efforts. This technique is discussed more fully in Chapter 5.

GOALS FOR IMPROVING INSTRUCTION

Supervisors must select among many tasks those that will have the most impact on improving instruction. Among these are:

1. Developing a clear mission statement and gaining commitment for that statement from the administration, teachers, and community.

2. Working to get the involvement of all persons who contribute to improving instruction with particular emphasis on students.

3. Determining physical and resource needs and working to satisfy those needs.

4. Setting high expectations for teachers, students, and parents.

5. Clarifying the relationship between curriculum and instruction.

6. Establishing an information-gathering technique that will ensure that all major decisions are made with the best available information.

7. Establishing a curriculum system that rationalizes all K–12 teaching in terms of the relationship among the parts.

8. Promoting an openness to change that sees teaching and learning as evolutionary rather than static.

ISSUES FOR SUPERVISORS

Following are some particularly troublesome issues that may arise from the style of supervisory intervention in a school.

The School Mission

Americans have a wide range of opinions about the purpose of schools. Specific arguments may revolve around buzzwords such as "basics" or "cooperative learning," but the issues underlying these concerns are foundational. Schools in the United States initially adopted an educational pattern found in Europe in the seventeenth century: a system of education rationalized by the mastery of specific content. In the nineteenth century, a different concept of educating was imported from Europe—a child-centered program drawing its rationale from the needs of growing children. Both of these purposes of educating have been preserved in the modern American system.

An important philosophical question underlying the design of school curricula, however, is whether the intention of the program is to (1) "round out" the student so that all graduates possess common knowledge and attributes, or (2) whether the schooling experience should "accentuate the uniqueness" of the individual in an effort to gain the full potential of the student for society. The issue of the school's mission is best seen in the competition between goals of the school: learning competencies and graduation requirements on the one hand, and efforts to serve special students and find unique characteristics (gifted, talented, special education) on the other.

Although both goals are worthy, a school must be organized in different ways to accomplish these different ends. To encourage sameness and uniformity of graduates, the school has to employ high degrees of structure so that students experience nearly identical programs. To encourage uniqueness, flexibility has to be encouraged, so that each student has the freedom to develop to his or her capacity, whatever that is. Arguments over course materials, teaching methods, building designs, and so forth, spring from this key difference in the intention of the program.[44] Supervisors need to know which of these purposes seems more important to them, because they have an unusual degree of control over these variables.

The Scope of Responsibility

One issue that separates many supervisors is the perceived scope of their responsibility. Few job descriptions are meant to be comprehensive or restrictive in nature, and the residual dimensions of school leadership (the assumed duties) will provide supervisors with many choices beyond that which is identifiable as their direct responsibility. For example, is the supervisor responsible for helping a teacher who has a problem outside of school that is affecting school performance? Is the supervisor responsible for providing a quality school program for students who are beyond the benefit of the standard school curriculum?

In many cases, the nature of what constitutes the job of supervisor—even what is meant by the term itself—will be decided by the person who fills the position. Defining the scope of the job will, of course, reflect a larger definition of the purpose of schooling and the nature of leadership in education.

The Focus of Leadership

It is evident that supervisors can and will significantly influence how educational programs are organized and how they will operate. By the control of task focus, communications, resource allocation, and evaluation, the supervisor will set a tone for working. In channeling activities, the supervisor will focus more on either tractive (static) or dynamic (change-oriented) operations.

Within this choice of tractive or dynamic leadership style lies the supervisor's definition of professionalism in education. For some leaders, professionalism is the efficient application of administrative skills to operate an educational program. A model for this type of supervisor might be an engineer who keeps the machinery operating efficiently. A different conception of leadership and professionalism might be a supervisor who constantly improves schools, using as a model the architect who is always in the process of enacting a vision.

Public Involvement

A fourth issue that regularly separates school leaders is whether the public should be directly involved in school operations. Although reason would seem to prevail on a case-by-case basis, involvement or noninvolvement of citizens actually constitutes an entire operational strategy for some administrators.

Many districts conduct assessments of need to gain information for making decisions about school programs. Whether the public should be involved in gathering and analyzing such information and whether the public should be involved in the actual decision making resulting from that analysis is an administrative issue. One argument for public involvement is that the public sponsors the schools with its tax dollars and entrusts its children to their educational programs. By this argument, involvement in decision making is only natural, almost a right of every interested parent. On the other hand, many school administrators feel there is no clear consensus on many educational issues, and public involvement in decision making only polarizes the many public groups that support the schools. Those who take this position draw an analogy to representative government or refer to professional judgment to support their feeling that the school administrator has no real obligation or mandate to involve the public in the daily decision-making operation of the schools.

In truth, this issue revolves around the concept of trust and democratic principles. It is also true that the issue has never been satisfactorily resolved, so it remains both recurrent and pressing.

Use of Influence

One of the most difficult issues for new supervisors is the use of influence. Most new supervisors like to think of public school leadership as a democratic process where they, as professionals, oversee many competing forces in the formulation of ideas and policy. In reality, things are not always simple.

A school supervisor is a highly trained professional, more knowledgeable about the field of education than most. Such knowledge should mean that the supervisor has information and skills that the average teacher or citizen does not possess. The issue in the use of influence arises when the supervisor knows that teachers or the public are making a poor choice from among limited alternatives. At what point does the supervisor offer professional expertise that may not have been solicited? By the same token, when does the sharing of such knowledge become a form of manipulation? An honest supervisor will acknowledge that even methods of leadership (how a committee is formed) constitute a degree of manipulation.

Obviously, to lead a public institution such as a school, the supervisor needs a clear conception of democratic principles and their use. However, it makes a tremendous amount of difference whether the leader considers himself or herself a controller of events by virtue of position, or simply one more force or influence in a democratic arena.

Moral Integrity

A final issue, which some would call an imperative, is moral integrity in supervision. Unlike supervisors in other professions, school supervisors carry a special burden stemming from the value-laden nature of education and schooling. The public holds special expectations for schools, due to the special nature of the commodity that is the subject of educational influence. For this reason, supervisory behavior will be monitored constantly by a number of concerned groups.

Not only must the school supervisor be exemplary in his or her behavior but also must insist that others around them hold high standards for performance. If there is a breakdown in the quality of control of instruction, it is the responsibility of the supervisor of instruction. If materials are less than adequate, it is the responsibility of the supervisor of instruction. If there is a problem in a school under the supervision of a district leader called the supervisor, it is the responsibility of the supervisor and no one else. In short, the buck stops at the level of the supervisor, and the integrity of that person must be impeccable simply because of the very important nature of school work. Supervision is the critical link between the classroom teacher and the administration; it is the primary quality control agency in schools.

In Figure 2.8, you are encouraged to react to these issues on a personal level.

SUMMARY

Leadership by a school supervisor is the product of many behaviors including establishing a mission, setting goals, forming a working organization, applying limited resources, and involving teachers, parents, and the community in developing a program. Understanding the condition of the organization is the first step in becoming a leader.

Leadership theory looks at four key variables in organizations: structure, processes, organization, and influence. Using one or all of these, the supervisor defines roles and tasks of leadership. When addressed comprehensively, a leadership style emerges.

School supervisory leadership is unique in that it is often superimposed over the official (formal) leadership of the principal. Assessing the style of the principal, the type of tasks, and the condition of the school will enable the supervisor to experience greater success. Particularly sensitive in the 1990s is the inclusion of teachers in major instructional decision making and school governance through school improvement teams.

Choices, from all of these variables, lead to both redefined goals and issues in practice.

IMPLICATIONS FOR SUPERVISION

1. What are the steps by which a supervisor develops a theory of leading?
2. How can your school district be seen as a "system"? Can this be reduced to a drawing or schemata?
3. What is the message of Maslow or Herzberg in working with teachers?

Directions: Mark an X over that number which best describes your current feelings about each issue. (1 = strong feeling; 3 = no opinion.)

Schools should round out pupils and promote commonality				Schools should accentuate the uniqueness of pupils
1	2	3	2	1

Supervisors should stick to their appointed roles and duties				Supervisors should pursue whatever duties necessary to succeed
1	2	3	2	1

Supervisors should not allow extensive public involvement				Supervisors are obligated to involve the public extensively
1	2	3	2	1

Supervisors should not use their position to influence the public				Supervisors must use their position to influence the public
1	2	3	2	1

School supervisors are much like other supervisors in terms of moral integrity				School supervisors must possess an exceptional moral integrity in leading
1	2	3	2	1

Figure 2.8 Defining Supervisory Values

ᔥ CASE STUDY 1 ᔥ

After a lengthy search process, you have been offered a general supervision position in a mid-sized district. This district is financially affluent, and the salary is generous. During your interview, however, the board chairman drew you aside and told you something that you considered bothersome. His words were, "If you ever feel like making a big decision of an instructional nature, see me first."

Questions
1. Why do you suppose a would-be supervisor would find such a comment bothersome coming from the chairman of the board of education?
2. What action should you take prior to accepting or rejecting this position?

⇜ CASE STUDY 2 ⇝

A veteran teacher has been appointed "acting" supervisor for the year by the superintendent of schools. Almost immediately, the supervisor senses that the once warm and friendly relations with fellow teachers is changing. Since the teacher is only in an "acting" or temporary role, she is puzzled.

Questions

1. Can you explain what is happening to this newly appointed supervisor?
2. Given the new empowerment of teachers, what should be the role of this acting supervisor? Spell out the relationship in ten points or less.

SUGGESTED LEARNING ACTIVITIES

1. Develop a list of your own assumptions, principles, and observations about the leadership process. Can these statements be presented in the form of a theory of leadership?
2. Make a list of adjectives to characterize the desirable school supervisor.
3. Describe how the supervisor's leadership style either matches or fails to match the needs and purposes of an organization.

4. Interview a fellow student for ten minutes and try to determine what kind of leadership style they would have. What are the questions that were productive in this activity?

BOOKS TO REVIEW

Allen, D. *Schools for a New Century.* New York: Praeger, 1992.

Bacharach, S. *Education Reform: Making Sense of It All.* Boston: Allyn and Bacon, 1990.

Benfari, R. *Understanding Your Management Style.* Lexington, MA: Lexington Books, 1991.

Block, P. *The Empowered Manager: Positive Political Skills at Work.* San Francisco: Jossey-Bass, 1991.

Bolman, L. and Deal, T. *The Path to School Leadership.* Newbury Park, CA: Corwin Press, 1993.

Cambone, J. et al. *We're Not Programmed for This: An Exploration of the Variance Between the Ways Teachers Think and the Concept of Shared Decision-making in High Schools.* Cambridge, MA: Harvard University, 1992.

Clark, C. *Site-Based Management.* Arlington, VA: AASA, Educational Research Service, 1990.

Conley, D. *Managing Change in Restructuring Schools.* Eugene: Oregon School Study Council, 1993.

Deal, T. *The Principal's Role in Shaping School Culture.* Washington, DC: U.S. Office of Education, 1990.

Erlandson, D. et al. *The Management Profile.* College Station: Texas A&M University Principal Center, 1991.

Fernstermacher, G. *Where Are We Going? Who Will Lead Us There?* Washington, DC: AACTE, 1992.

Gorton, R., and Theirback, G. *School-Based Leadership: Challenges and Opportunities.* Dubuque, IA: Wm C Brown, 1991.

Guy, M. *Ethical Decision-Making in Everyday Work Situations.* New York: Quorum Books, 1991.

Hallinger, P. et al. *Restructuring Schools: Principals' Perceptions of Fundamental Educational Reform.* Cambridge, MA: Harvard University, 1992.

Hoyle, J., *Skills for Successful School Leaders.* Arlington, VA: AASA, 1990.

Jablonski, J. *Implementing Total Quality Management.* San Diego: Pfieffer, 1991.

Kowalski, T. *Case Studies in Educational Leadership.* New York: Longman, 1991.

Milstein, M. *Changing the Way We Prepare Educational Leaders: The Danforth Experience.* Newbury Park, CA: Corwin, 1993.

Murphy, Joseph, ed. *Restructuring Schooling: Learning from Ongoing Efforts.* Newbury Park, CA: Corwin, 1993.

Nanus, B. *Visionary Leadership: Creating a Compelling Sense of Direction for Your Organization.* San Francisco: Jossey-Bass, 1992.

Roseander, A. *The Deming Road to Quality and Productivity.* Milwaukee: Marcel Dekker, Inc., 1991.

Rost, J. *Leadership for the Twenty-First Century.* New York: Praeger, 1991.

Sarason, S. *The Predictable Failure of Educational Reform.* San Francisco: Jossey-Bass, 1990.

Sashkin, M., and Walberg, H., eds. *Educational Leadership and Culture.* San Francisco: McCutchan, 1993.

Sergiovanni, T. *The Moral Dilemma of Leadership.* San Francisco: Jossey-Bass, 1992.

PROFESSIONAL KNOWLEDGE ABOUT TEACHING AND LEARNING

The role of a school supervisor is often loosely defined but encompasses significant responsibilities. In the past, labor–management relationships and expanding school responsibilities clouded the role and authority of the school supervisor. More recently, school-based management and cooperative leadership styles have further brought into question the exact purpose of educational supervision. We believe that the true role for any supervisor is to improve the learning experiences for students and, to be effective in this role, the school supervisor must possess a new professional competence. What will make the supervisor powerful and influential in coming years will be his or her knowledge about teaching and learning.

EARLY STUDIES ON TEACHING

During the past twenty-five years, there has been a quiet revolution in the knowledge gained about classroom learning. Although much of what has been learned has created more questions than answers, the body of knowledge has grown dramatically. We would hasten to observe that what is available to school supervisors today is not of a prescriptive quality, but, nonetheless, teaching has become more scientific and predictive since 1970. We know much more than we are using, and supervisors who possess such knowledge are useful and productive in improving instructional opportunities. No modern supervisor can afford to be ignorant of this emerging knowledge base.

There have been studies of teaching for over a century in the United States, many with curious outcomes. In one classic study, high school students from thirty unconventional schools outperformed a comparable group of conventional school students during the college years. It is puzzling to teachers how students who learn math and science by gardening (organic education) can outperform comparable students who study a precollege curriculum in a classroom.[1]

Many of the earliest studies of teaching and learning contained methodological flaws: too few students, uncontrolled variables, bad data treatment, and numerous errors in study procedures. Early studies were also hampered by the sheer volume of data generated. In the Coleman study of disadvantaged learners (1964), over 600,000 students were studied to determine the effects of home on school. Unfortunately, such a study generated overwhelming data before computers were available to process the information.

We can, in fact, say that modern educational research on teaching and learning began when computers became widely available to researchers. This new era is generally believed to have begun with a review of previous research by Barak Rosenshine and Norma Furst in the late 1960s. Examining only those studies from the past that focused on teacher variables and student gains in cognitive achievement, Rosenshine and Furst identified eleven teaching behaviors that seemed significant in promoting positive student outcomes. The positivism of this review defined teacher research in the 1970s and 1980s and remains the basis of many teacher education programs and staff development designs even today.

The eleven variables considered to be significant included

1. Clarity and teacher organization
2. Variation in activities, materials, and media
3. Enthusiasm of the teacher
4. Task orientation and academic focus
5. Student opportunity to learn (understanding of the task)
6. Use of student ideas in class
7. Justified criticism during instruction (later praise as well)
8. Use of structuring comments
9. Questions (high and low) appropriate to cognitive level
10. Probing or encouraging questions that allow student elaboration
11. Challenging instructional materials[2]

The investigation of the eleven variables went forward with vigor under the influence of heavy federal funding for educational research in the early 1970s. Using what became known as process–product research (the teacher behavior being the process and the student learning outcome the product), researchers tried to correlate the various behaviors under controlled conditions. Two large studies, the Texas Teacher Evaluation Study (1973) and the California Beginning Teacher Evaluation

(1973–74) generated massive data. Other studies followed traditional federal programs such as Head Start and Follow Through.

The contribution of these early process–product and ethnographic (anthropological) studies was significant. For the first time, objective and measurable data was used to define effective teaching (having an effect) in terms of student performance. However, these early works were also frustrating. Researchers had hoped to come up with principles of learning. In the words of Stake and Denny:

> The researcher is concerned with the discovery and building of principles—lawful relationships with a high degree of generalizability over several instances or class of problems. . . . he seeks to understand the basic forces that interact whenever there is teaching and learning.[3]

Unfortunately, most of what was revealed by these early scientific studies was negative rather than positive. Writing in 1977, Brophy and Evertson concluded that single-shot studies were not going to do the job:

> The majority of significant relationships with learning gain (MAT test) were negative. In short, we found out more about what not to do than we did what to do . . . the upshot of all this is that teaching involves orchestration of a large number of different behaviors which the teacher must have mastered to at least a certain minimal level and can adapt to different situations, as opposed to application of a few basic teaching skills that are "all-important." The behaviors are many and complex rather than few and simple. There are no magical keys to successful teaching.[4]

This revelation was echoed in the research findings of Soar who studied teacher-initiated structuring behavior in low socioeconomic status students:

> These findings suggest that an intermediate amount of different kinds of teacher behavior are best for a particular goal and a particular group of pupils, but they don't begin to answer the question of the classroom teacher—how much a certain behavior is best for which goal for which pupil? What we have so far is an organizing principle (certain behaviors are functional for certain pupils with certain tasks) which can be used by the teacher and the researcher to begin thinking about effective teaching; we do not have specific answers for the teacher's question.[5]

A similar finding was logged in by McDonald in reviewing the California project data in 1975:

> Did we find any single teaching skill which correlated with learning in both reading and math at both grade levels? No such skills were found. Performances which correlated significantly with outcomes were different by subject matter and by grade level.[6]

Rather than seeing these early studies as failures, you should note the progress made over the traditional concept of "good" teaching—a subjective judgment based on intuitive criteria. The studies of the 1970s identified a number of distinctive teaching acts and found that some of them were effective under certain conditions. In addition, these early correlations were statistical in nature and replicable over similar studies.

The real value of the early process–product studies was that they showed teaching as a multidimensional act, with emphasis on some set of skills for some specified purpose. This theme was explored by McDonald in 1976 during a review of the BTES data:

> The practical object of research on teaching is to describe teaching effectiveness. This requires that we state a desired effect—a desired change in children—and the actions which produce it.[7]

Effectiveness Defined by Purpose

As researchers analyzed early returns from the assessments of Rosenshine and Furst's eleven variables, it became obvious that only one kind of teaching was being measured. Since the outcome desired in most early studies was defined as an achievement gain on a standardized achievement test (CTBS, MAT, ITBS), only teaching skills that contributed to such learning was identified as "effective." Further complicating these matters was the design of early studies which used predominantly young, under-achieving, poor minority youth as subjects. This choice of subjects was thought to produce the "purest" student capable of showing the most gain if the correct teaching skills were employed.

One of the byproducts of this focus in early research was a premature acceptance of the results by some governmental officials who sought a quick answer to a complex question. Early summaries of the data, for instance, provided a highly structured prescription that featured teacher talk, lots of seatwork, and drill formats (Figure 3.1). Seeing such clarity, states such as Florida and Tennessee rushed to legislate the formula (Figure 3.2).

Later analyses, often called "meta-analyses" in the literature, found additional patterns in the data if different criteria were used to assess effect. The idea of a teacher interacting with a student to gain input, or allowing the student to take charge of learning through personal application of information, revealed that all teacher effectiveness studies are value-laden. In other words, educational philosophy and educational learning theory would determine whether any teacher behaviors were contributing to learner success. As Rosenshine concluded in the mid-1980s,

> It would be a mistake to claim that the teaching procedures which have emerged from the research apply to all subjects, and all learners, and all time. Rather, there are procedures which are most applicable to the "well-structured" parts of any content area and are least applicable to the "ill-structured parts of the content area.[8]

We believe that the preceding is true and would stretch this distinction further by including attitudes and skills as possible outcomes in addition to the content that Rosenshine addresses. There are, of course, many choices in educational destination and a set of teaching behaviors most appropriate for each destination.

Ineffective and Effective Behaviors for Teaching the Classroom Lesson

Ineffective Behaviors	Effective Behaviors
1. *Communicating lesson objectives*	
Not describing the lesson's purpose or what students are expected to learn.	Stating goals or major objectives at the beginning of the lesson.
Not calling students' attention to main points, ideas, or concepts.	Telling students what they will be accountable for knowing or doing.
	Emphasizing major ideas as they are presented.
	Reviewing key points or objectives at the end of the lesson.
2. *Presenting information systematically*	
Presenting information out of sequence; skipping important points or backtracking.	Outlining the lesson sequence and sticking to it.
Inserting extraneous information, comments, or trivia into the lesson.	Sticking to the topic; holding back on complexities until the main idea is developed.
Moving from one topic to another without warning.	Summarizing previous points; clearly delineating major transitions between ideas or topics.
Presenting too much complex information at once or giving directions too quickly.	Breaking complex content into manageable portions or steps; giving step-by-step directions, checking for understanding before proceeding.
Not leaving sufficient time to cover each aspect of the lesson thoroughly.	Maintaining an efficient pace in early activities so that ample time remains for later ones.
3. *Avoiding vagueness*	
Presenting concepts without concrete examples.	Providing a variety of apt examples.
Using overly complex vocabulary.	Using words that students understand; defining new vocabulary terms.
Overusing negative phrases (e.g., not all insects, not many people, not very happy).	Being specific and direct (e.g., the beetles, one third of the people, enraged, discouraged).
Being ambiguous or indefinite: *maybe, perhaps, sort of correct, more or less right, you know, right most of the time, not always.*	Being specific, precise, referring to the concrete object, stating what is and is not correct and why.
4. *Checking for understanding*	
Assuming everyone understands, or simply asking, "Does everyone understand?" or "Does anyone have any questions?"; then proceeding without verification.	Asking questions or obtaining work samples to be sure students are ready to move on.
Moving to the next topic because time is limited or because no students ask questions.	Asking students to summarize main points to verify comprehension.
Not calling on slower students; relying on feedback from only a few volunteers.	Reteaching unclear parts.
	Systematically checking everyone's understanding.
5. *Providing for practice and feedback*	
Not assigning classwork or homework.	Being sure students have adequate practice so that critical objectives are mastered.
Giving assignments that cover only a portion of the learning.	Reviewing assignments to be sure that all of the lesson's skills and concepts are reinforced.
Not checking, reviewing, or discussing students' assigned work.	Checking work regularly, reexplaining needed concepts, reteaching when appropriate.

Figure 3.1 Early Summary of Teacher Effectiveness Research
Source: Edmund T. Emmer, Carolyn M. Evertson, B. Clements, et al., *Classroom Management for Secondary Teachers* (Englewood Cliffs, NJ: Prentice Hall, 1984), pp. 119–120.

Phase I Observation Instrument				
	Frequency	*Comments*	*Frequency*	
1. Begins instruction promptly/ maintains instruction				
2. Handles materials in an orderly manner		Punctuality Management transition Wait time avoidance Controlled interruptions		
3. Orients students to classwork		Lesson initiation Academic transition signals		
4. Conducts beginning/ ending review		Lesson-initiating review Topic summary within lesson Lesson-end review		
5. Maintains academic focus				Uses talk/activity unrelated to subject
6. Modulates speech				Uses loud/ grating/ high pitched/ monotone/low inaudible
7. Utilizes verbal-nonverbal behavior to show interest/ enthusiasm				Uses sarcasm/ frowns/ humdrum/ glares/shows disgust

Figure 3.2 Sample State Instrument Based on Preliminary Findings of Teacher Effectiveness Research
Source: Florida Beginning Teacher Program, 1985. Reprinted with permission.

Phase II Observation Instrument					
		Frequency	*Comments*	*Frequency*	
8. Treats concepts-definitions/examples/nonexamples					Gives definitions or examples only
9. Applies laws, rules, principles					
10. Uses linking words (thus, therefore, etc.)					
11. Emphasizes important points					
Phase III Observation Instrument					
		Frequency	*Comments*	*Frequency*	
	Single Factual				Uses multiple questions asked as one
12. Asks questions					Uses nonacademic/procedural questions
	Requires analysis/reasons				
13. Recognizes/amplifies/corrective feedback			Acknowledges a student response Extension of student response by probing (amplifying)		Ignores/harshly responds to student talk
			Discussion of student response by peer involvement		

Figure 3.2 *Continued*

14. Gives specific academic praise				Overuses general praise/ nonspecific
15. Provides for practice and checks for academic comprehension				Extends lecture/ changes topics/ no practice

Phase IV Observation Instrument				
	Frequency	*Comments*	*Frequency*	
16. Utilizes correct spelling/ grammar/mathe-matics/etc.				Makes academic errors—spelling/ grammar/ mathematics/etc.
17. Gives directions/ assigns/checks comprehension of homework/ assignment/ feedback				Gives inadequate directions/ no homework check/feedback
18. Circulates and assists students consistently				Remains at desk/ inappropriate circulation/ assistance
19. Stops misconduct and maintains instructional momentum		Reacting to an irrelevant stimulus		Delays/does not stop misconduct
				Stops misconduct/ loses momentum

Figure 3.2 *Continued*

PHILOSOPHIES AND LEARNING THEORIES

Various families of educational philosophy and learning theory coexist in American schools. This somewhat unique phenomenon exists because we have an open, decentralized, politicized education system in American in which no body mandates purpose. The traditional, bedrock philosophies of Perennialism and Idealism reflect a time when education was defined as "knowing" and the basic purpose of schooling was the transmission of knowledge. A sort of middle-of-the road philosophy, Realism, was a compromise as educators tried to extend this traditional mission to all youth in our nation. Finally, philosophies such as Experimentalism (Progressivism) and Existentialism reflect the growing trend of defining education in terms of social ends or individual development (see Figure 3.3). In a nutshell, American education has a full range of philosophies, and each would define the purpose of teaching differently.

Likewise, there are a number of families of learning theory in American schools. These can be grouped into three approaches: behavioral, developmental, and perceptual. The behavioral theory of learning is an external perspective of teaching and learning in which the teacher acts and the student reacts (stimulus–response). Such an approach is highly directive. The developmental learning theory is also external (locus of control with the teacher) but acknowledges that student development is an important factor in planning the teaching act. In this case, the teacher is interactive, to a point, and then guides the learning experience to a predetermined outcome. The perceptual theorist is distinctively different from the behaviorist and the developmentalist in that the student is seen as the critical factor in teaching and learning. The perceptual learning theorist holds that each student is unique and is the one who gives meaning to the teaching–learning act. Hence, this teacher is more of a "guide on the side" than a "sage on the stage."

If we compare the philosophies and learning theories in terms of their mission and beliefs, we can see an emerging continuum which, on the one hand, is quite controlling and directing (Perennialism, Idealism using behavioral learning theory) and, on the other hand, is quite nondirective and student oriented (Experimental, Existential, using perceptual approaches). Further, we can differentiate all teaching on the basis of how much structure or flexibility exists in the teaching–learning act. The directive teacher desires control and employs high structure to eliminate distortion in the teaching–learning act. The nondirective teacher is purposefully flexible in order to meet the unique and individual needs of the students.

McNeil and Wiles have identified three styles of teaching using this distinction: direct, indirect, and self-directed. Given this model (see Figure 3.4), it is possible to understand how research prescriptions might evolve. Using traditional criteria, a directing teacher who is conveying predetermined subject matter efficiently will find a highly structured prescription makes sense. This teacher is "on-task," fully involved in transmitting knowledge, closely guiding learning through structuring comments and questions, and reinforcing correctness by narrow and specific tests. Grades are used as a reinforcer, just as punitive discipline is used to focus student behavior.

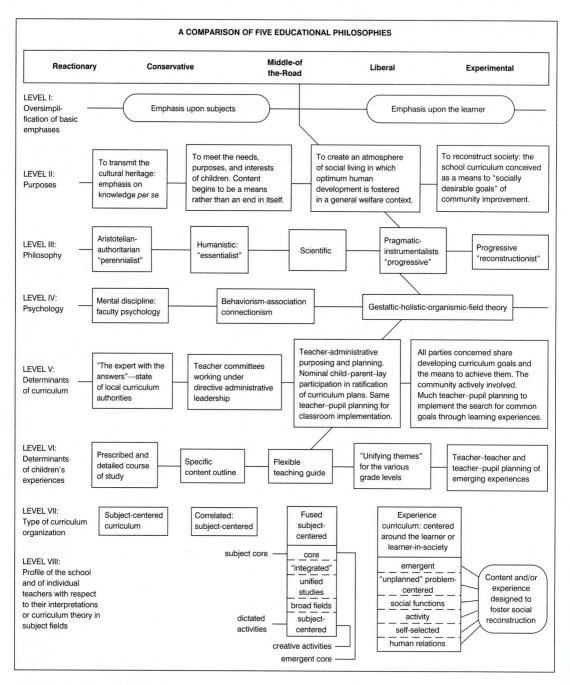

Figure 3.3 Philosophies of Education Compared
Source: Jon Wiles, *Promoting Change in Schools* (New York: Scholastic, Inc., 1993), p. 16. © 1993, Scholastic, Inc. Reprinted by permission of Scholastic, Inc.

Perennialist	Idealist	Realist	Experimentalist	Existentialist

Behaviorism	Developmental	Perceptual

Direct teaching	Indirect teaching	Self-directed teaching

High structure --- Flexibility
Teacher control ....Student control

Figure 3.4 Comparison of Philosophies, Learning Theories, and Teaching Styles

If, however, the teacher is to be more interactive (indirect), the above prescription is inappropriate. A teacher who fails to interact with the student will be unable to determine the developmental level of the student (and will, therefore, miss motivational opportunities by matching needs and task). This teacher will operate a little slower, meander through material using student questions and supplemental methods to "round up" learners, and then bring lessons to completion.

If the teacher is a Perceptualist, seeing the student as the key to "learning" rather than the teacher, he or she will make every effort to get the student involved. The Experimentalist will stress application and relevance, whereas the Existentialist will probably encourage the student by teaching learning skills and by providing intellectual "setups" or learning opportunities.

We can see, by this conceptualization of the teaching act, that effectiveness is determined by purpose and that the prescription for the pattern of skills used by the teacher is defined by what works to encourage the desired form of learning. Our review of teacher effectiveness research found that the meta-analyses of the 1980s and 1990s have revealed patterns other than direct teaching prescriptions. Supervisors must be aware of these developments in order to match curriculum and instruction in their schools and districts.

Most supervisors are elevated from the ranks of teaching and quickly find themselves operating as leaders in an environment of bewildering complexity. Armed with only their own teaching experience, they are often asked to prescribe behaviors for other teachers at levels and in subjects foreign to their experience. It isn't surprising that so many new supervisors seek refuge in rules, regulations, unimportant tasks, and the day-to-day routine. This reactive or "tractive" pattern isn't necessary, because general prescriptions for teachers can be formulated following a careful study of the teaching literature.

What do teachers need? Most classroom teachers, experienced or novice, need to have a way of organizing their own actions on a daily basis. What every teacher should seek is to be consistent and effective in promoting learning. They can't, and don't, expect the supervisor to know everything about pedagogy, but it is reassuring for a teacher to learn that their supervisor is current and insightful about the teaching act. The professional knowledge base of the supervisor is the basis for the establishment of a professional relationship with the teacher.

In the remainder of this chapter, we will attempt to summarize some of what is known about the context, the organization, and the act of teaching. All of the topics covered have been researched extensively, and these studies provide some interesting clues about why some teachers are more effective than others. Our first section looks at the context of schooling including social influences, school readiness, compensatory programs, parenting, and the classroom environment.

THE CONTEXT OF SCHOOLING

Social Influences

Schooling is a social experience and, all things being equal, the higher the social economic status of the student (SES), the greater his or her educational achievement.[9] In fact, the standard deviation of student achievement is, in most cases, dependent upon socioeconomic factors.[10] The effects of socioeconomic factors on schooling success has been studied heavily for over thirty years.[11]

The social components that detract from or contribute to a child's success in school include social status, language abilities, level of parent education, and parental involvement in a child's schooling. Improvement in any of these conditions will generally improve school performance. Even the size of the school attended affects attendance, with children from low SES generally benefitting from smaller schools.[12]

Special conditions in the society have a greater impact on the achievement of low-performing students. A cut in budget, for instance, has a greater impact on special programs. Reconstitution of the family through divorce or abandonment usually means greater family mobility and less parental attention.

Especially important today are two problems—cocaine and homelessness—that affect many young children. It is estimated that 23 million Americans (roughly 10 percent) have tried cocaine and that five to six million are addicted. A euphoric drug that reaches the brain pleasure center in five to seven seconds, cocaine is passed through the placenta to the fetus in pregnant women with each use.[13] About 11 percent of all babies in the United States are drug exposed; 70 percent of these have been cocaine exposed. Cocaine exposure causes disabling effects on organ development, resulting in visual, speech, and motor retardation and abnormal social and "attachment" development.[14]

Another example of a current social influence in schools is the new wave of homeless children in America. Estimated at between 300,000 and two million, homeless children present a special challenge to a society that counts on an educated population. Approximately 17 percent of these children do not attend school at all.[15] The homeless child is protected by the McKinny Act (1987), and the cost of ensuring educational opportunity for such children is about $25 million annually. However, a child who is attending school but has no home is more concerned with Maslow's lowest needs—shelter, nutrition, and safety—than with educational excellence.

In summary, it has been shown that "advantaged" children perform in a different way than do "disadvantaged" children in school settings. This accident of circumstances affects the ability of these children to learn in a school setting. Studies of intervention with parents[16] and facilitating school group experiences[17] show that schools can make a difference in the lives of such children.

Readiness

Closely related to social and economic background is the readiness of students to benefit from schooling. How students perceive their social environment accounts for such important schooling factors as feelings of self-worth, peer acceptance, motivation, and attribution of academic success. Without appropriate support and preparation, a student can enter school without the necessary skills and never catch up to their peers.

In the Havighurst study cited in the last section, 500 nine-year-olds were divided into four socioeconomic groupings and studied over time. The unstable families in the study had a disproportionate number of maladjusted children who had identifiable school problems. For example, the most disadvantaged group had 4.5 times as many absences and 4.9 times as many instances of tardiness as the least disadvantaged group. The former group had no higher than a C+ average in their studies.

The in-depth study of this group of disadvantaged students indicated three problem patterns: poor learning ability and aggressiveness toward others, withdrawn and shy, and a lack of motivation. These children also lacked achievement drive, models of success, parental and peer expectation, and intrinsic pleasure in learning. Recognizing the scope of the problem and the importance of early childhood learning, the federal government in the mid-1960s moved to intervene in the lives of low SES students or students lacking readiness to learn. These programs of compensation are discussed in the next section.

Any number of specific learning difficulties can prevent a child from having a successful start in school. Among the most common neurodevelopmental dysfunctions are:

1. *Attention*—Concentration disrupted by daydreaming and lack of school focus.
2. *Memory*—Inability to make specific mental placement of information.
3. *Language*—Manipulation of spoken and written words.
4. *Visual/spatial*—Interpretation of symbols and sound/sight relationships.
5. *Sequencing*—Ordering and arranging ideas, information, or events.
6. *Motor*—Difficulties in hand/eye coordination or body movements.

One of the responses in the early 1990s to this wide range of possible difficulties affecting readiness in students is the "Full Service School" which provides services such as health and nutritional support, basic medical services, family support, parent counseling, and even adult education. These schools attempt to help students by fill-ing in the gaps in their backgrounds that might be preventing their full participation in the learning experience.

Newer research concerning school readiness is providing interesting insights about the variables that contribute to success. In one study, it was documented that our dependence on verbal performances in the early years may be giving educators a false view of student capacity. Often, verbal calculations (recitation, reading out loud) reflect linguistic knowledge rather than true ability.[18] In a second series of studies of children, it was found that those who were started in school too early (so-called "sum-mer children") were retained more frequently, referred for psychological help more often, had overall poorer academic performance, and had less social acceptance. In one study in Montgomery County, Ohio, it was found that a higher suicide rate was found in those summer children who began schooling at a younger age.

Compensatory Programs

Compensatory programs (comp ed), programs that compensate, seek to remedy deficiencies in a disadvantaged student's background by providing specific curricula designed to make up for what is lacking. These programs have been heavily funded by the federal government since the passage of the Elementary and Secondary Edu-cation Act (ESEA) of 1965.

Perhaps the best-known compensatory program is "Head Start." This program for preschoolers, ages two to three, uses the criteria of family income and requires that 10 percent of the children have handicaps to select children who are likely to be disadvan-taged by school age. Heavily researched in the 1970s and 1980s, Head Start has been found to promote industry, initiative, dependability, social control, better reading and math skills, and a greater likelihood of promotion.[19] A 1985 followup of Head Starters found that those attending were more likely to graduate from high school and less likely to be placed in special education.[20] Some nutritional gains were found as well.[21]

Research findings concerning Head Start have been challenged, and some evi-dence exists that the gains of Head Starters evaporate with time. Nearly everyone believes that Head Start provides a "higher platform" for children starting school, and, recently, the Council on Economic Development recommended an investment of $5000 for each three- and four-year-old. In return, it was calculated, society would get a $7 return for each dollar invested in terms of fewer expenditures on remedial education, welfare, and criminal justice.[22]

Because educators noted a subsequent drop in achievement of Head Starters when the program ended, a second program, "Follow Through," was begun which is still found in schools. This program also found that fewer participants were held back a grade, dropped out, and were less likely to have special education designation than might have been anticipated without intervention.

A third compensatory program found in most public school systems is "Chapter One," a program providing extra educational services to low-income and low-achiev-ing students. At a cost of over $5 billion, Chapter One has now served over five mil-lion students in forty-five states.

Chapter One uses five basic designs including in-class, pull-out (the student leaves the class for instruction), add-on (the student attends an extra class), replacement (the student goes to a Chapter One class instead of the regular class), and school-wide (all students in the school receive the same treatment). To date, using reading gains as the indicator, the pull-out design works best (but also is most disruptive to the regular program). Ranging up to the sixth grade, Chapter One appears more effective with younger pupils.* The cost of individual programs has not been correlated with student achievement gains.[23] Extending the Chapter One program into grades seven and eight is forecast for the late 1990s.

Yet another type of compensating program deals with language. Programs of English as a Second Language (ESL) and English for Speakers of Other Languages (ESOL) are found throughout the United States. The basis of most programming is the U.S. Supreme Court ruling in Lau v. Nichols (1974) that affirmed the responsibility of schools to take action so that non-English-speaking students have equal access to educational opportunity.

Among the major findings to date are that young children have higher proficiency levels in languages prior to puberty,[24] that speaking, per se, does not cause language acquisition,[25] and that children who know one language well learn a second one better.[26] Of all programs studied, the "immersion" model that places children in the English-speaking room early scored worst in achievement, whereas extended instruction in a native language through grade 6 showed the most achievement gains. The worst-case scenario, quite common in public schools, is to place a non-English speaking-student over age twelve, with poor language skills in his or her native language, in a regular classroom.[27]

Language will be especially important in the future. According to demographers, by the year 2020, 46 percent of all people in the United States will be a "minority," and many will have a language other than English as a native tongue. The ratio will be higher, of course, among the school-age population.[28]

Parents and Guardians

From a contextual vantage point, what goes on at home before and during the early school years is very important to school success. In fact, some researchers believe that parents and the home have at least as much influence on student learning and behavior as do the teacher and the school.[29] If this is true, supervisors should help teachers learn how to gain parental support for learning.

Six types of at-home behavior have been suggested as important for student success at school:

1. *Task structure*—Children participating in activities at home.
2. *Authority structure*—Home responsibilities, participation, and decision-making.

---

*In 1996, Chapter One will become Title I. It will serve students according to their income level rather than their achievement level.

3. *Reward structure*—Parents recognize student growth and advancement.

4. *Grouping*—Parents influence peer relations.

5. *Standards*—Clear and realistic expectations for behavior.

6. *Time structure*—Parents insist on time management for schoolwork.[30]

Studies reveal a great deal about what kind of parent involvement helps students achieve in school. It comes as no surprise that children with higher socioeconomic status have parents who are more involved in school.[31] Parents from a higher socio-economic level, however, more often criticize the teacher and school.[32] Surprisingly, it is not the amount of parental participation at school (volunteer work) that influences student success,[33] but rather the goal setting and planning that a parent does with his or her child. Overall, research supports the notion that parent involvement is associated with academic achievement, better attendance, reduced dropouts, decreased delinquency, and fewer pregnancies while in school. Most importantly, parental support is crucial regardless of the economic, racial, or cultural background of the family.

One of the major problems in studying family support is the changing nature of the American family. As late as 1960, only 5 percent of all children in America were born out of wedlock. The average in the early 1990s is about 22 percent of all children born to single mothers, with the figure ranging upward to 60 percent for some ethnic groups. Many educators have been quick to note that the decline in achievement tests scores has occurred in the same period as the decline in the two-parent family.[34]

The number of single-parent families in the United States are increasing ten times faster than the number of two-parent families, and females head up nine out of ten of these newer single-parent homes.[35] It has been estimated that in the 1990s one-half of all American public school children will spend time in a single-parent home.[36]

For the 15 million children in single-parent homes, it makes little difference if the cause of the condition is divorce, separation, death of a parent, or a single mother's choice. There are, however, some startling statistics that accompany this status that directly affect schooling. For example, 60 percent of these single mothers will have more than one child; 50 to 90 percent of these families will fall below the poverty level earning less than half the income of a two-parent family; the single parent will be more likely to be employed outside the home; the parent will have less time to attend to the child's intellectual and emotional needs; the child's sense of security will be diminished; the child's chances of abuse and neglect are increased in such a household (2.7 million cases were reported in 1990).

In school, children of single parents were found to exhibit a number of personality differences including low self-esteem, low achievement motivation, poor peer relations, and high anxiety. These children also were more likely to be rebellious, act out, become juvenile delinquents, and use drugs and alcohol at school.[37] More troubling for supervisors are the findings of a National Association of Elementary School Principals study of 18,000 children from single-parent families. In this study, it was documented that such children are more likely to be low achievers, earning half the A's and B's of the children from two-parent families and with a solid 38 percent getting mostly D's and F's in school.

Researchers have found that parental separation tends to have more effect on boys than girls,[38] that death of a parent is less detrimental than separation, and that problems at school due to a divorce tend to decrease after the initial year.[39] Giftedness in children does not shield the child from such problems.[40]

There is hope that school intervention can help overcome these conditions caused by our changing society. Numerous studies have found that when communication is established with the parent about the role he or she can play, student school performance is improved. The seventeen-year study by Dr. James Comer of Yale University serves as a benchmark in documenting the positive effects of parent involvement. It is noteworthy, however, that the variable that is most critical appears to be family income.

Classrooms

It has been estimated that students spend about seven hours per day in schools, and many of these 1260 hours per year are in a classroom. It is vital, then, that supervisors understand the impact of this contextual variable on learning. The physical setting of a classroom affects the psychology, emotion, and physiology of learning, and it can cause both physical and mental dysfunction.

Physical space, seating patterns, light, color, noise, and temperature all combine to orient the child to the learning experience. One of the most interesting things about schools is how little space they allocate to each student. Most school classrooms are about 30 × 30 feet or 900 square feet. When divided by 30 students, each student has approximately a 6 × 5 foot space. After subtracting space taken up by desks, hat racks, learning centers, and so forth, each student's personal space shrinks to about 3 × 3 or 9 square feet. What is interesting about this allocation is that it is a "short duration" space like a phone booth. By contrast, prison cells and fallout shelters are spacious. Surely, being contained in such an area for long durations is counterproductive.

Seating patterns appear very important to different kinds of learning. Although some studies support straight rows and others support circles (tables), one study determined that people sitting at a 72 × 36-inch table had different communication patterns according to location. Those at right angles to each other communicated with each other twice as often as those seated side by side, and those side-by-side talked three times as often as those seated across the table from each other. No conversations were recorded by those at the far ends.[41]

Not only does distance affect communication,[42] but we have noted in numerous schools that the pattern of furniture is important. A cafeteria, for instance, with tables arranged in a herringbone pattern will feel less institutional than will one with tables arranged in rows.

Choice of seating affects learning as well. Problem children will choose to sit in only the back and sides of a classroom whereas nonproblem children will use the full space. Teachers, unconsciously, teach to the front and middle of the classroom[43] and to the side of their handedness (right-handed teachers look right; left-handed teachers, left). Younger children are found to be more "on-task" when the gender of seating is mixed. Older children are more on-task when there is a segregation of gender.[44]

The look of the room also draws a response from student learners. One researcher reports that students in rooms created purposefully ugly (as opposed to beautiful and average) worked faster and reported irritability and fatigue. Specifically, light, color, noise, and temperature can induce fitfulness or calmness in students.[45]

Light seems to have a most important impact on student learning. Light that is too bright or too dim can have a negative emotional response on learning.[46] Visual fatigue is accelerated when the amount of light alternates frequently from one level to another. Further, students exposed to ultraviolet light (UV) are found to have better attendance and better academic performance.[47] Sodium bulb lights seem to have the opposite effects on learning. It is prescribed that agitated and tense students should be placed in soft lit areas, whereas unresponsive students should be located in brightly lit areas.[48]

The color of a learning space seems significant in relation to learning. Color has been shown to have a physiological effect on the level of blood pressure, respiratory rate, task confusion, and reaction time. Bright warm colors produce activity, whereas cooler colors produce thought and contemplation.[49] For this reason, it is prescribed that elementary rooms be painted yellow, peach, or pink (activity colors) and secondary rooms be in shades of blue or green. Teachers can use bulletin boards to establish a "color set" for learning.

Noise definitely impacts learning in the classroom, with sounds above 70 dB producing accelerated heart rate, elevated blood pressure, and even higher cholesterol rates. Since the ear is a second route to the brain, noise affects thinking. One study documented a 19 percent increase in energy expended in a noisy classroom as contrasted with a quiet classroom.[50]

Finally, temperature and humidity affect learning. The ideal temperature for learning is probably between 68 to 74 degrees Fahrenheit, but younger children require cooler rooms because of their higher metabolism rate. Adults have been shown to operate efficiently at 80 degrees.[51] A temperature that is too high can produce stress, cause people to work more slowly, and increase the frequency of mistakes.[52]

The effect of humidity on learning and health is surprising. Humidity that is too low causes negative physical reactions. In one study, classrooms with humidity ranges from 22 to 26 percent had thirteen percent more illness than those at 27 to 33 percent humidity.[53]

ORGANIZING FOR LEARNING

In addition to the physical environment of a school, any number of organizational factors influence classroom instruction. Items such as discipline, failing or retention of a student, awarding marks for achievement, and using testing for placement are standard practice in most school districts. Yet, these factors are not often supported by professional study and may even be detrimental to learning. In this section, we look at four such areas.

Management and Discipline

The notion of a teacher managing a classroom or disciplining unruly students seems simple enough. Discipline can be defined as "methods used by teachers to bring about student conduct orderly enough for productive learning." However, a word-by-word breakdown of the preceding definition shows key action words such as "methods," "orderly," and "productive." A clear definition of learning must precede a definition of discipline.

Several large patterns emerge from studies on discipline. First, effective and ineffective teachers tend to respond to student misbehavior about the same way, but effective teachers are better at preventing disruption in the first place.[54] Another finding is that classroom climate, or how formal groups interact, is directly related to teacher behavior.[55] Another key difference between discipline programs and styles is how much the teacher chooses to involve the student in the process of control.

The many variables of discipline include commitment, teacher expectation, rules, classroom climate, principal involvement, community roles, and authority invoked. By far the most widely used discipline program is "assertive discipline" now used by over 400,000 teachers. A meta-analysis of all studies on this approach found "no significant difference" when compared to other or no program.[56] Few quality studies were available according to the researchers.

Finally, literature on discipline indicates certain techniques effective at certain ages. Preschoolers tend to react to physical controls. Lower elementary students respond to materialistic consequences. Upper elementary students are sensitive to social rules and norms. Early middle schoolers respond to peer pressure, whereas upper middle schoolers begin to use inner direction and individual responsibility for control. With high school students, freedom seems to be an effective variable in building a program.[57]

Retention

One of the most common practices in American education is grade retention. The underlying principle of "failing" or "flunking" a child, or of "holding a child back," seems to be that low achievement at grade level is more traumatic than being placed with younger age students. Studies show that about 5 to 7 percent of all public school students are retained annually,[58] and that some 16 percent of all students will be retained twice by the sixth grade.[59] The annual cost of retaining 2.4 million children has been estimated to be $10 billion.

The practice of retention dates from the 1840s when the Prussians adopted the first age-grade system. It continues today because parents, administrators, and teachers believe it works. Nearly 800 studies of retention have been conducted with few supporting the practice. Major reviews of these studies have found no evidence to support the practice of retention.[60]

Studies show that the students who are retained come from a certain background; the most common pattern is a disadvantaged student, a minority, or a male.

Students who are younger, have a perceived behavior problem, and live in the South are more likely to be retained.[61] Students tend to be retained at certain grade levels (traditional transition levels), and the practice has been reinforced in the past decade by competency testing laws. In one New York study, the best predictor of who might be retained was the school lunch program (children enrolled in the free lunch program were also from lower income homes).

The effects of retention have been widely documented, and suggest a highly undesirable byproduct. Dropouts are five times more likely to have repeated a grade, and students who are retained twice have virtually no chance of high school graduation.[62,63] A 1988 Texas study estimated that repeaters were 2.7 times more likely to quit than comparable students who were promoted to the next grade.[64]

Other negative byproducts of retention that have been documented include poor school adjustment, low self-esteem, low attendance, more behavioral problems, and less popularity.[65] Although advocates of retention believe that the social costs are minimal, one study found that students reported the prospect of repeating even more stressful than being caught stealing or "wetting in class." In that study, 88 percent of the students ranked retention as the third most stressful even after losing a parent and going blind.[66] One 1989 study found the majority of students believed that retention was "punishment for being bad in class."[67]

A major California study documented that the anticipated academic benefit from retention was nonexistent. Even when intervention programs are attempted, there is no significant difference after three years in any subject or skill area. In the words of the researcher, "When low-achieving students are retained, they remain low achievers—when promoted they continue to be low achievers."[68]

There remains a widespread belief that early intervention can make a difference, and programs to help retainees account for about 7 percent of school expenditures (including summer school programs). Short-run gains have been documented, but no long-term successes have been documented. Ironically, the best candidates for early intervention and retention are those who are academically able, making progress, but immature.[69]

Prescriptions for the many students in this category, as an alternative to retention, include compensatory reading, transition (nongraded or multi-age) classes, tutoring, extended day classes, double promotions, and spreading the nine-month work over an eleven-month (summer) year.

Testing and Evaluation of Students

Schools spend a great deal of time assessing students by testing and sorting them according to their graded performances. Students take competency exams in most states to demonstrate progress through a prescribed curriculum and take S.A.T.'s to get into college. In classrooms throughout the country, teachers prepare "report cards" at regular intervals. How accurate are these tests and assessment activities? What should the supervisor know? Research in this area is extensive and raises many questions about practice.

Most school tests are treated as "norm-referenced" in that they are used to compare and contrast student progress against that of other students. In recent years, for example, American students have been compared unfavorably to students from other nations. Listen to former President George Bush:

> The ringing school bell sounds an alarm, a warning to all of us who care about the state of American education . . . every day brings new evidence of a crisis.[70]

The former President was referring to the scores on an International Assessment of Educational Progress that showed American students lagging behind the scores of students in other industrial nations. While the newspapers played the story heavily, educators soon learned that the President hadn't done his homework.[71] The use of the tests was political!

On standardized tests, supervisors need to understand that test makers, such as the Educational Testing Service, constantly renew their tests and, in fact, have something of a "conflict of interest" in presenting a portrait of declining scores. Given the composition of the test takers and the sheer number of students taking these tests, compared to twenty years ago, our standardized scores show remarkable health.

Supervisors need also to view state competency tests with a wariness, for they, too, are often presented politically rather than educationally in their reporting. In one recent study of the Florida state competency exam, for example, it was found that no correlation existed between passing or failing the state test and later academic success in higher grades as measured by grade point average.[72]

Teacher-designed tests, too, have been found by research to be faulty in many ways. For example, it has been found that teachers use short-answer tests extensively, often omit directions and scoring criteria, sometimes use illegible tests, and have over 90 percent of all questions low–level.[73,74,75] In one study, it was found that the order in which the teacher read test papers determined the grade of students.[76] Another researcher estimated that about 84 percent of a student's grade is a measure of competence, and 16 percent is explained by the teacher's judging habits.[77]

If teachers use grades as a means of control, the reliability of testing and grading declines further. Factors such as social class, gender, handwriting, physical attractiveness of the student, verbal patterns, and even the name of the student have been shown to distort the grading process.[78] While all districts have grading policies, the teacher is the sole arbitrators in implementing that policy.

INSTRUCTIONAL VARIABLES

A large number of instructional variables related to student learning have been studied and represent the foundations of a prescription for teaching. Each of the variables are, of course, influenced by the purpose of the teaching act. Among some of the best evidenced areas are ability grouping, praise, questioning, memory and attention to learning, self-concept development, grouping, motivation and attribution, thinking skill development, gender bias, and learning styles.

Ability Grouping

The practice of grouping students by ability is widespread in American education and developed from a set of beliefs about the purpose of schooling. The assumption that the learner has fixed and measurable abilities that must be assessed and then matched with appropriate teaching suggests a mechanical model of education in which learning is "engineered." In contrast is a view of learning that sees students as growing, but at different rates and perhaps in different ways. Here, the task of schooling is to facilitate and document progress in learning. Elkind refers to these two assumptions as "psychometric" versus "developmental" philosophies of education, and the two are shown in comparison in Figure 3.5.[79] Most arguments for ability grouping are made from a psychometric perspective.

The origins of ability grouping (or tracking) in the United States is a system created in the Boston Public Schools in 1908 to "fit" education to the student. Over fifteen hundred studies have analyzed this practice since then. The vast majority advise against this practice.

If the operational hypothesis is that students in various ability groups learn more (academic gain) than would normally be expected in mixed ability groups, then there is almost no support for the practice. While various studies (Kulik, Nevi and Dar, Jaeger, Wolff, Hill, and Kerckhoff)[80,81,82,83,84] reveal greater gains among high ability students when ability grouped, such studies cannot attribute the gain to grouping alone. For instance, other studies attribute such "relative gains" to smaller classes,[85] different teacher expectations, use of different teaching strategies and communication patterns by the teacher, and even the removal of "high student" influence from the comparison classrooms. One major study of tracking by Robert Slavin documented that grouping

Developmental Philosophy	Psychometric Philosophy
Learner has developing mental ability	Learner has measurable abilities
Differences found in rate of growth	Differences reflect amount of ability
Task to match curricula to student rate of development	Task to match student with others of like ability
Learning a creative activity	Learning set by principles that are independent of content
Aim of education to facilitate learning	Aim of education to promote measured achievement . . . to maximize acquisition of knowledge and skills
Assessment by documenting work accomplished	Assessment by testing and comparing to like students

Figure 3.5 Contrasting Views of Development
Source: David Elkind, "Developmentally Appropriate Practice: Philosophical and Practical Implications," *Phi Delta Kappan,* October 1989, pp. 113–116.

the upper two thirds of the students together, as opposed to the more traditional "upper, middle, and lower thirds," can be done without a loss of achievement.[86]

Besides indicating that teacher behavior, not grouping per se, is a critical variable in higher achievement when students are grouped, there is also evidence of significant teacher bias. One study, for instance, found Asian and Hispanic students with comparable profiles grouped differently.[87] Studies of Hispanic children and their performance in public and private settings also raise serious questions about teacher expectation and treatment.[88]

What appears in study after study is that teachers make judgments about student ability on factors other than ability (appearance, clothes, ethnicity) and that once such judgments are made, students tend to remain in that ability group for the rest of their school careers.[89] Once grouped, students experience discrimination in grading patterns,[90] and there is some research to suggest that girls, the poor, and minorities are further discriminated against at the secondary level.[91]

Although numerous adverse byproducts of ability grouping, such as lowered self-concept and retardation of academic motivation, are regularly reported among low ability groups, it is interesting to note that research shows that not all high ability students benefit from the practice. There is a relationship in learning between self-cognition, behavior, and achievement, and some high students lose confidence under grouping conditions.[92] This phenomena is referred to in the literature as the "big fish, small pond" syndrome.

It should be noted that most students of ability grouping are concerned with "low" students, and the existence of high mixed populations available for study (for example, gifted mixed with low) are rare. Sample variables to contend with are sex, SES, school characteristics, student ability, self-concept, academic effort, teacher grading patterns, and the subject.

Teacher Expectation

Teachers regularly make inferences about future student behaviors, and teachers treat students differently based on these expectations. Such teacher behavior affects and influences student academic performance.

Studies on teacher expectation date from 1938, and the most widely known publication on the subject is Rosenthal and Jackson's classic *Pygmalion in the Classroom*.[93] In this study, researchers sought to influence teacher expectancies positively by providing them with test scores that were said to be predictive of learning growth spurts. In reality, the scores were no different between the experimental and control populations; the difference was in the mind of the teacher. In the lower grades, students whom teachers thought should spurt ahead did, creating a self-fulfilling prophecy. Although the methodology of this study has subsequently been questioned, the study did seem to demonstrate that a teacher's favorable expectation can be responsible for student academic gains.[94]

Some researchers have suggested that the difference in school success between advantaged and disadvantaged students may quite simply be rooted in their teachers' expectations for achievement. A study by Farkas, for instance, stated that "teacher judgments of student work habits, behavior in class, and appearance have a causal effect on the rewards teachers used and join with other factors to almost completely account for the grade differentials observed for gender, ethnicity, and poverty groups."[95]

It has been documented that once a teacher decides a student is of "low ability," they will wait less time for answers to questions, provide more answers for the student when questioning, reward incorrect answers by the low student, give more criticism of the student after the answer, provide less praise for the low student, and seat the low student further from the teacher.[96] It is interesting to note that research shows that teacher prediction of student performance is usually quite correct.[97] Further, students of all ages know that the teacher judges them and that treatment is differential according to expectations.

More recently, teacher expectation has been linked to teaching styles. It was found that "since teaching often reflects the teachers' personal thinking style, the teacher inadvertently rewards students whose style (learning style) corresponds to the teachers' teaching style . . . at the expense of those whose styles differ. Thus, the teacher labels as "slow" or "stupid" those students who learn well but in ways different from the teacher."[98]

Student behaviors in the classroom, particularly language patterns, influence teacher expectation. Nonstandard English, for example, has been shown to alter the way a teacher thinks of a student.[99] One British study found the impact of speech even greater than a writing sample or photograph.

Finally, and most disturbing, is the documentation that teacher expectation can even alter the measurable I.Q. of a student.[100] This finding evidenced the fact that teachers who reached "expectation induction" early altered their teaching behaviors accordingly and either increased or retarded student intellectual growth as measured by such testing.

Use of Praise

Behaviorists tell teachers that if a pleasant consequence follows a behavior (reinforcement), the behavior is more likely to occur in the future.[101] Many teachers believe that the use of praise or criticism (negative reinforcement) can alter student behavior. The research on praise supports this notion, but only under certain conditions. Researchers have determined that praise in classrooms is infrequent, often noncontingent, and global rather than specific. Further, in many classrooms, praise is determined more by the students' need for praise than by the quality of student conduct.

Researchers identified early that praise occurs infrequently; perhaps only once or twice a day for most pupils.[102] A 1974 study estimated the frequency at 6 percent of the time. These researchers also determined that "high expectation" students received more praise than "low expectation" students.[103]

Regardless of the frequency, response to praise varies with the student and, in particular, according to variables such as grouping, socioeconomic level, ability level, age, personality, gender, and learning style.[104] For some students, being praised may promote feelings of embarrassment or being manipulated,[105] whereas other students may see praise as the way in which the teacher establishes superiority or creates dependence.[106] In one study of second graders, praise actually lowered student confidence and reduced participation.[107] Another study showed praise lowering self-esteem. In general, the older the student, the more likely false praise is perceived as a putdown.[108]

It has been learned that students can actually elicit praise from the teacher, even at the preschool level, through training in certain behaviors. Teachers have been found to praise only the students who regularly smile and participate in class discussions.[109]

In short, the effect of praise or criticism is influenced by the students themselves. The key to understanding the effect of praising is how the person receiving the praise interprets that teacher behavior. Praise that is insincere or nondirective (see Figure 3.6) is ineffective. Also, it has been found that such general praise is often accompanied by negative affect in nonverbal expression. In a similar fashion, praise perceived by the student as "evaluative" is often rejected as counterproductive. By contrast, some higher ability students see teacher criticism as an indication that they are intelligent.[110]

Guidelines for effective use of praise are outlined in Figure 3.7. Effective praise should be specific to the task, sincerely expressed, delivered in private when possible, credible and relevant. Criticism should be delivered from close proximity, be spoken softly, and the use of eye contact or touch reinforce the meaning.

Questions

Questions asked in a classroom are often the intellectual link between the thoughts of teachers and students. As such, this teaching variable has been heavily researched since 1970. It is generally accepted that teachers ask many more questions than students; fifty thousand questions per year for the teacher versus ten questions per year for the average student. The nature of these questions tell more about the cognitive processes of the questioner than those of the listener.[111]

Studies of questions asked reveal that some 20 percent are procedural and another 60 percent are factual; the remainder may be higher level in nature.[112] Continuous procedural questions were found to promote listlessness among the listeners.[113] There is a correspondence between the cognitive level of the teacher question and the student response (see Figure 3.8).[114]

Three studies of the relationship between higher level questions and achievement have failed to establish a causal relationship.[115,116,117] This is probably due to the nature of the achievement assessed rather than to an absence of effectiveness in questioning. In general, direct questions (didactic) bring short and direct answers; open-ended questions employing more "wait time" on the part of the teacher elicit longer and more complex answers by the student.[118]

By far, the greatest number of teacher questions are didactic in nature. These short and direct questions can be used for the following reasons with effect:

1. To stimulate student participation.
2. To initiate a review of materials previously covered.

1. You're on the right track.
2. You're doing a super job.
3. You did a lot of work today.
4. Now you've figured it out.
5. Now you have the hang of it.
6. That's exactly right.
7. That's absolutely correct.
8. That's the way.
9. You're really going to town.
10. You are really something.
11. You're doing just fine.
12. Now you have it.
13. Nice going.
14. That's coming along nicely.
15. That's great.
16. You did it that time.
17. You really outdid yourself.
18. Right on.
19. Great work.
20. Fantastic.
21. Terrific.
22. Good for you.
23. Good work.
24. Excellent.
25. Super job.
26. Good job.
27. That is the best you've ever done.
28. Good going.
29. Way to wrap it up.
30. That's a neat idea.
31. That's really nice.
32. Wow, that's incredible!
33. Keep up the good work.
34. Good thinking.
35. Super!
36. How did you ever think of that?
37. That's awesome.
38. You make it look so easy.
39. I've never seen anyone do it better.
40. You're doing much better today.
41. Way to go.
42. That's superb.
43. You're getting better every day.
44. Wonderful.
45. I knew you could do it.
46. You're doing beautifully.
47. You're really working hard today.
48. That's the way to do it.
49. Keep on trying.
50. That's it.
51. Nothing can stop you now.
52. You've got it made.
53. You're very good at that.
54. You're learning fast.
55. You're really on top of things.
56. I'm very proud of you.
57. You certainly did well today.
58. You've just about gotten it.
59. That's really good.
60. I'm happy to see you working like that.
61. I'm proud of the way you worked today.
62. You can be proud of your-self.
63. Great effort today.
64. That's the right way to do it.
65. You're really learning a lot.
66. You're impressive.
67. That's better than ever.
68. That's quite an improve-ment.
69. You made my day.
70. You're really concentrating.
71. I've noticed the improve-ment in your work.
72. That's marvelous.
73. Beautiful.
74. Perfect.
75. That's not half bad.
76. That's just fine.
77. You've got your brain in gear today.
78. That's it.
79. You figured that out quickly.
80. You remembered.
81. You're really improving.
82. I think you've got it now.
83. Well, look at you go!
84. You've got that down pat.
85. That's perfection.
86. Tremendous.
87. Outstanding.
88. I couldn't have done it better myself.
89. That's what I call a fine job.
90. You did that very well.
91. You're getting better and better.
92. Congratulations.
93. That was first-class work.
94. You're unreal.
95. How did you think of that?
96. That's sensational.
97. That's the best ever.
98. Good remembering.
99. You haven't missed a thing.
100. You make teaching a plea-sure.
101. You make my job so much fun.
102. You got everything right.
103. You've mastered that.
104. You've been practicing.
105. That's very nice.
106. You sure fooled me.
107. Your behavior has really improved.
108. One more time and you'll have it.
109. You're doing much better.

Figure 3.6 109 Ways to Praise

Effective Praise	Ineffective Praise
1. Is delivered contingently	1. Is delivered randomly or unsystematically
2. Specifies the particulars of the accomplishment	2. Is restricted to global positive reactions
3. Shows spontaneity, variety, and other signs of credibility; suggests clear attention to the student's accomplishment	3. Shows a bland uniformity, which suggests a conditioned response made with minimal attention
4. Rewards attainment of specified performance criteria (which can include effort criteria, however)	4. Rewards mere participation, without consideration of performance processes or outcomes
5. Provides information to students about their competence or the value of their accomplishments	5. Provides no information at all or gives students information about their status
6. Orients students towards better appreciation of their own task-related behavior and thinking about problem solving	6. Orients students toward comparing themselves with others and thinking about competing
7. Uses students' own prior accomplishments as the context for describing present accomplishments	7. Uses the accomplishments of peers as the context for describing students' present accomplishments
8. Is given in recognition of noteworthy effort or success at difficult (for *this* student) tasks	8. Is given sans regard to the effort expended or the meaning of the accomplishment (for *this* student)
9. Attributes success to effort and ability, implying that similar successes can be expected in the future	9. Attributes success to ability alone or to external factors such as luck or easy task
10. Fosters endogenous attributions (students believe that they expend effort on the task because they enjoy the task and/or want to develop task-relevant skills	10. Fosters exogenous attributions (students believe that they expend effort on the task for external reasons—to please the teacher, win a competition or reward, etc.)
11. Focuses students' attention on their own task-relevant behavior	11. Focuses students' attention on the teacher as an external authority figure who is manipulative
12. Fosters appreciation of and desirable attributions about task-relevant behavior after the process is completed	12. Intrudes into the ongoing process, distracting attention from task-relevant behavior

Figure 3.7 Guidelines for Effective Praise
Source: From J. G. Nicholls, "Quality and Equality in Intellectual Development: The Role of Motivation in Education," in J. E. Brophy, "Teacher Praise: A Functional Analysis," *Review of Educational Research* 51, 1 (1981): 5–32. Copyright 1981 by the American Educational Research Association. Reprinted by permission of the publisher.

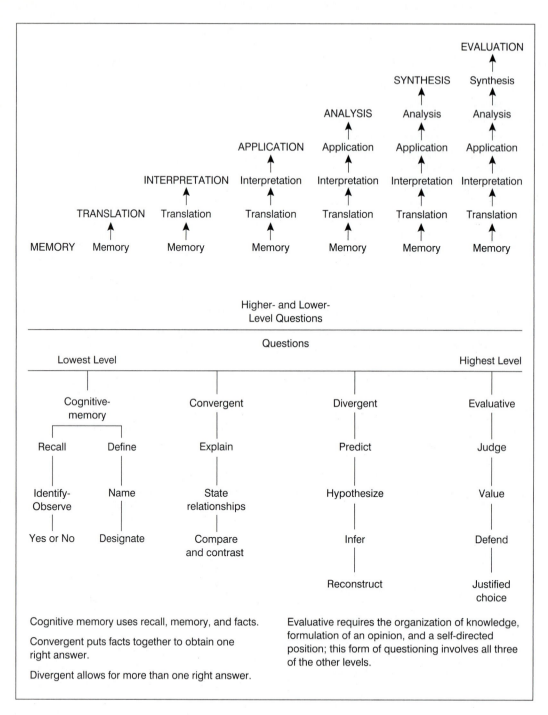

Figure 3.8 Higher- and Lower-Level Questions
Source: N. Sanders, *Classroom Questions: What Kind?* (New York: Harper and Row, 1966), p. 10.

3. To initiate discussion of a topic or issue.

4. To involve students in logical thinking.

5. To diagnose student knowledge and thinking ability.

6. To determine the extent to which objectives have been mastered.

7. To encourage student participation in class discussion.

Memory and Attention

Studies of students' memory and attention in the classroom have been on-going since the 1920s in the United States. Quite simply, memory can be defined as the ability to focus the mind,[119] and some students do this better than others. In general, the primary elements affecting retention of information seem to be prior knowledge and the instructional methods employed by the teacher.

The development of memory is thought to occur in the sixth or seventh postnatal month, at which time ideas or objects can first be associated with other items in the long-term memory. Memory is increased when the individual relates the item or information to his or her personal knowledge base. When students are unable to correlate subject matter or other school learnings with their knowledge or experience, inattentiveness arises.

There are two ways that researchers have attempted to learn about student attentiveness and mental activity. One, the behavioral approach, observes student engagement and speaks to teachers of concepts like academic learning time (ALT). In a major study of twenty-five second-grade classes and twenty-one fifth-grade classes, it was found that the time on task was associated with achievement.[120]

The second way, the cognitive approach, focuses on the mental processes used by the student to determine the degree of attentiveness. The perspective sees teachers increasing student attentiveness and learning by facilitating learning through questions, relating learning to previous student knowledge, and teaching thinking skills associated with school success. It has been shown that students who use certain cognitive strategies do, in fact, increase their attentiveness.[121]

Studies of learners reveal that some students don't grasp information easily and can't maintain academic attention. Overall, brighter students are more attentive and slower students more passive. It is believed that certain teacher behaviors trigger this latter condition in slower students.[122] It also has been found that girls tend to be more attentive than boys[123] and are less likely to become inattentive because they employ superior planning processes.[124] As academic difficulty increases in a classroom, attention decreases correspondingly; however, students who are verbally fluent tend to have better attention and memory regardless of difficulty.[125] Any positive academic feedback from the teacher will increase student attention to task.[126]

Prescriptions for increasing student attentiveness and memory of prescribed learning are plentiful. In Figure 3.9, Sousa identifies eight strategies to improve retention of learning.

1. Place new learning at the beginning of a learning sequence and a student review at the end. Use the in-between time for practice.

2. Find ways to link new learning to something that the student already knows and, therefore, has the most relevance.

3. Keep in mind the influence already in the student's memory will have on new learning. Find ways to have this old learning help and not interfere with new material.

4. Provide a variety of unique and clear verbal cues that students can use to tag the new learning accurately before storage.

5. Use simple diagrams, graphs, or pictures to help students with visual cues.

6. Space out the new material so the learner has time to rehearse it and attach meaning to it.

7. Remember that massed practice is for immediate learning, but that distributed practice in short, intense periods is what leads to retention.

8. Organize the new material so students can easily classify and link it with the appropriate network in long-term memory.

Figure 3.9 Eight Strategies to Improve Retention of Learning
Source: D. Sousa, "Helping Students Remember What You Teach," *Middle School Journal* 23 (1992): 21–23.

Attribution

In the search for qualities that determine school success, researchers have looked at variables such as the student, the teacher, the parent, the home and school environment, and the methodology of instruction. In the early 1970s, researchers began to identify a possible cause of low motivation in school[127]; students with low motivation rarely attributed success to themselves.[128] By contrast, successful students were more likely to attribute school success to internal and controllable factors such as effective study techniques.

Research has documented that low achievers often have "learned helplessness," and that this condition is most prevalent in girls and upper level students.[129] Such learners believe that effort is unrelated to outcomes and, therefore, futile. Training students to attribute outcomes to controllable causes and to interpret failure as a natural stage in learning has shown promise.[130,131] Specifically, such training involves appropriate praise, minimizing criticism, and giving effort feedback to students.

Thinking Skill Development

During the 1980s, researchers have investigated the manner in which thinking occurs in students. Four areas have evolved with which every supervisor should be familiar in order to lead teachers in planning instruction. Those areas include metacognition, semantic mapping, scaffolding, and scheme theory.

"Metacognition" refers to the student's awareness of his or her mental processes. Such awareness is critical to planning and setting goals, assessing content, and monitoring for understanding. Teachers can help students in metacognition development by modeling, "thinking out loud," rehearsing for coming tasks, employing anxiety reduction techniques, using directional questioning, and using games as analogies.[132]

Research has found that most students are not aware of their own thinking as they approach tasks,[133] and younger children, in particular, do not recognize major blocks to understanding in their own thinking.[134] It appears that all children, regardless of ability level, can benefit from such training. Metacognition training has been shown to aid in memory development.[135]

Another area under investigation is semantic mapping, a technique designed to help students tap into their prior knowledge base and expand that knowledge base through vocabulary development. In this thinking skill, students give their associations (concepts) for the topic to be studied. The procedure gives the students "anchor points" and bridges what is known to what is to be learned. As a generic thinking skill, it is effective in all subject areas and uses all of the elements of learning including reading, writing, speaking, and listening.

A third kind of thinking skill that has been researched and found effective with elementary and middle school students is scaffolding.[136] Originally an extension of a theory of "proximal development" which seeks the difference between actual and potential development of a student,[137] the term now refers to techniques that structure learning. Outlines and question stems are used to transfer thinking to form a "framework" or scaffold for further learning. This approach to learning requires constant teacher monitoring of student progress.

Finally, researchers have developed an understanding of how old information structures new learning under the label of "schema theory." According to schema theory, the organized, structured, and abstract bodies of information (schemata) that we all possess through personal experience "structures" new learning. Said another way, the way in which new information is perceived and interpreted is predetermined by existing understandings which may, or may not, be accurate. This research indicates that it is very important for teachers to learn what their students know prior to placing new knowledge (schema) on old knowledge (schemata).[138]

Collectively, these four new areas of inquiry suggest that supervisors must learn how learning occurs to be useful to classroom teachers in improving instruction. While the areas cited are new and lacking in longitudinal studies, they promise to provide supervisors with more relevant and useful knowledge in the years immediately ahead.

Self-Concept

The idea that the self-concept of a student (self-esteem) is a critical variable for school success has been around since the 1940s. Self-concept is thought to be related to attitudes toward school and teachers, basic responsibility for learning, motivation, participation, and personal and social adjustment to name a few items known to affect school success. The topic has been researched with mixed results.

It is generally recognized that personality factors contribute something beyond intellectual abilities in the performance of academic tasks. Students who feel secure and confident generally experience a positive schooling experience. These feelings of confidence and well-being are generally higher in boys than in girls,[139] are somewhat subject or content specific, and have been found to be valid predictors of academic success as measured by college attendance.[140] Grades, not surprisingly, are reinforcers for academic self-concept, and high self-concept is correlated with attribution.

Recent studies have indicated the role of self-concept in linking cognition and affect; how students feel about themselves has a direct relationship to classroom experience which, if successful, increases feelings of academic self-worth.[141]

Self-concept has been shown to be multifaceted, hierarchal, and somewhat differentiated with age.[142] There is a sharp but natural drop in the academic self-concept of students during puberty,[143] but it rises again in grades nine to twelve.

Gender Bias

The research on gender bias tells us that girls appear to be better students than boys, are better behaved, and receive better grades. They even score better on achievement tests than boys do in the elementary grades. However, with each year in school, the achievement of girls drops; by the time they take the Scholastic Aptitude Test in high school, the average girl will score fifty-seven points lower than will the average boy.[144] Why?

Research has looked at the possibility that girls are treated with an inclination or preference that somehow interferes with an impartial judgment due to sex classification. For instance, it has been shown that teachers direct more cognitive questions and statements to girls in reading classes but more to boys in math classes.[145] Such treatment may lead to feelings of lowered academic self-concept.[146,147]

Clearly, in the past, there has been extensive documentation that women and men are portrayed differently in books, magazines, and other media. In 1972, the National Council of Teachers of English concluded that an overwhelming number of books found in schools depicted women and girls in a demeaning fashion. Another study by Women on Words and Images entitled "Dick and Jane as Victims: Sex Stereotyping in Children's Books," looked at 2,760 books and found none that portrayed men and women as equals. Since children seem to read stories about same-sex characters, girls were seen as being programmed for inferiority.

Attitudes of administrators show great discrepancy between the attitudes of men and women concerning gender bias and content of school materials. Also, practices such as lining students up by their gender, grouping students competitively by gender, and greeting classes each day by gender ("hello, boys and girls") are prevalent in the 1990s.

Although the results of gender bias appear verifiable, causation has not been proved. Among current theories of why, for instance, girls decline in mathematics are

1. They mature early and boys catch up.
2. Male teachers dominate the subject in the upper grades and treat girls differently.

3. Girls evidence maturity in the middle grades by affiliation whereas boys evidence maturity by independence resulting in a more confident learner.

4. The hormone testosterone in males activates a part of the brain associated with mathematical logic. This latter biological theory seems supported by the fact that women who excel in math generally have elevated levels of testosterone.

Small Learning Groups

Teachers have a number of choices in grouping students, including whole-class instruction and subgrouping instruction. The latter category can be ability groups or mixed-ability groups. In addition, teachers can pair students in a number of patterns, and they can allow them to work independently. Some of the general purposes for grouping are shown in Figure 3.10. Research has looked at most of these combinations, and the findings are interesting.

Whole-group instruction through lecture has shown superior achievement under certain conditions. The "drill and practice" methodology of Mastery Learning

Purpose	Choice
1. To give students necessary information	
2. To demonstrate a skill or technique	Whole-group lecture
3. To practice listening and note taking	
1. To share ideas, knowledge, and experiences	
2. To make applications to real-life conditions	Whole-group discussion
3. To check student understandings	
4. To reveal student interests	
1. To conduct planning	
2. To share ideas or perceptions	Small-group work/projects
3. To carry out specific learning tasks	
4. To allow student leadership	
1. To allow students to work at their own pace	
2. To allow practice in managing time	Individual work
3. To allow students to pursue their own interests	
4. To employ a learning modality that fits students	

Figure 3.10 Grouping Students Purposefully

and "time on task" studies[148] reveal that when the teacher is introducing new materials, covering material in a sequence, or asking students to master material verbatim, whole-class instruction is effective.

If the objective of instruction is not so direct or requires cognitive or affective input from students, small-group instruction may be appropriate. Small-group arrangements seem to be of two varieties: giving and receiving help, and cooperative learning. Giving and receiving help (tutoring) is usually either cross-age or of a peer design.

Research has shown consistently that when grouping is of the cross-age tutorial pattern, both the tutor and the tutee benefit. When tutoring is done by peers, good things happen also. In one study of four hundred students at the University of Kansas (Classwide Peer Tutoring Program), students in peer formation scored significantly higher than those in regular whole class arrangements.[149] In another study of 118 pairs of students who were asked to discuss academic motivation problems, opinions became alike, indicating the potential for increases in academic attitude under peer arrangements.[150]

In cooperative learning designs, small groups of students work together, and their grade is based on common, or group, performance. Such cooperative groups can be same ability or mixed ability in design depending on the objective of the lesson. Cooperative learning has received more attention in the educational journals of the 1990s than any other form of classroom instruction.

Most studies and meta-analyses of cooperative learning have documented positive results in areas as diverse as standardized achievement test scores, improving race relations, improving attendance, and mainstreaming special education students.[151,152] Not all reviews have been positive, however, stating that cooperative learning is effective only under certain circumstances.

Among the positive findings have been higher achievement and increased retention of learning,[153] more on-task learning,[154,155] greater achievement motivation,[156] and higher self-esteem among students engaged in cooperative learning.[157] The largest number of supportive studies for achievement have been in the form of cooperative learning known as "Teams-Games-Tournament."[158]

Critics of the highly publicized research on cooperative learning are many, and their reservations are diverse. Stallings, for instance, states that the cause of achievement under the TGT pattern is more like rewards and incentives than the act of cooperating.[159] Some critics have noted that the measures of the success of cooperative learning have been low-level thinking skills.[160] Most studies have been conducted in grades seven through nine, and the greatest successes in cooperative behaviors have been recorded in rural rather than urban communities.[161]

Perhaps the most damning observations of cooperative learning research have come from Chambers who observes that "students low in prior achievement who work in successful teams can benefit academically, but students low in prior achievement who work in unsuccessful teams are at a disadvantage academically."[162] This concern is amplified by another researcher who states that "high achieving students tended to either dominate in the group or choose to work alone, and some poorer students manifested passive behaviors in the cooperative small group setting . . . low achieving students were relatively passive in cooperative learning small groups in comparison with their high achieving peers."[163] Noted researcher Thomas Good adds, "if teachers did not address this problem, passive students were content to allow other students to do the work."[164] Finally, Hooper concludes, "The benefits expressed by the less able students in heterogeneous groups are made at the expense of their more able counterparts."[165]

Learning Styles/Teaching Styles

Educators have possessed an interest in styles of teaching and learning for a long while. In the 1920s, for instance, Carl Jung identified different behavior types and found that there are two ways of perceiving the world: through sensation and intuition. He also hypothesized that people made decisions in two ways: logical and emotional. This early work has formed the framework for many of today's learning style inventories.[166,167,168]

The basic excitement over this research is the premise that if a teaching style and a learning style could be "matched," higher achievement would occur. Not only would such a match help to explain why some students "bond" with some teachers, but also why the many types of methodology (mastery learning, individualized instruction, cooperative learning, computer-assisted learning, and so on) are appropriate for only some students.

Research on teaching styles and learning styles has tended to follow specific systems. Some researchers feel an eclectic teaching style (many approaches) would best fit all students.[169] Another study found that adolescent learners and girls favored more direct teaching styles.[170] Still a third study using the Hanson and Silver instrument found that 60 percent of the average students favored a "sensing" or affective approach to learning whereas 60 percent of the bright and gifted students preferred an "intuitive" teaching style.

Research on teaching and learning styles continues today, but without the objectivity necessary to document causal relationships through controlled research.

A summary of the research areas presented is offered as a twenty-point suggestion for supervisors of instruction in Figure 3.11.

Having reviewed some of the more heavily researched areas influencing the effectiveness of the classroom teacher, you may well conclude that a modern supervisor is a student of learning. Possessing knowledge about the various studies on teaching enables the supervisor to improve learning experiences for students. Clearly, because of the vast amount of material, some important ideas are sometimes hidden in the volumes of data:

1. A teacher's effectiveness is defined by the purpose of the curriculum.
2. Many patterns of effectiveness exist in teaching.
3. Seeing the pattern of need and prescribing a pattern of teaching based on reasonable evidence is the supervisory task.

Context	1. Lower the school entry age and stress life skills and language at an early age.
	2. Develop a K-8 compensatory education package to reinforce early gains throughout the formative years.
	3. Conduct instruction in the student's first language until that language is mastered, no matter how long such language is required.
	4. Increase efforts to involve and train parents, especially single parents, in the education of their children.
Environment	5. Place fewer students in each classroom, or make classrooms larger, for the purpose of increasing personal space and instructional flexibility.
	6. Ensure that no classroom or learning space has sodium vapor or blinking lights.
	7. Code room color to learning task when possible.
Organization	8. Invest staff development in classroom management (offense) rather than discipline techniques (defense). Make discipline programs age-appropriate.
	9. Do not retain children (grade failure) except in the case of bright but immature kindergarten pupils.
	10. Put achievement test schools and teacher grades in perspective; they should be seen as general indicators subject to gross distortions.
Instruction	11. If ability grouping is used, combine middle and upper students and be aware of the danger of high placement for some students.
	12. Continue to make teachers aware of teacher bias in "expectation" and grouping.
	13. Accelerate exploration of matching teaching styles with learning styles.
	14. Tailor the use of praise in school to patterns appropriate for the groups being taught.
	15. Understand that questioning is the link between teacher thoughts and student thoughts and that questions structure the level of thinking in a classroom.
Staff Development Areas	16. Accelerate study of attribution theory as a means of increasing academic motivation in all students.
	17. Help students gain control of learning by teaching thinking skills and modeling ways of approaching learning.
	18. Review self-concept programs for both appropriateness and results.
	19. Recognize that gender bias is a two-way street. Follow carefully the medical research on gender performance that is currently unfolding.
	20. Note the limitations on small-group and cooperative learning programs and the increasing criticism of social dynamics in some cooperative learning programs.

Figure 3.11 Twenty Suggestions from Research for Instructional Improvement

For example, Figure 3.12 shows one conception of five educational goals and the strategies of teaching that seem appropriate to meet those goals. Each of these goals would call for a different set of teaching behaviors. Teachers who employ, for example, mastery strategies when they were really teaching for understanding (concept attainment) would probably be unsuccessful. The supervisor, noting the disharmony between the teacher's intentions and the student's learning performance, would prescribe a new pattern of behaviors. The circumstances under which the behaviors would be employed (what kind of children, what subject, and so on) would be further determined by research. To the degree that the supervisor knows what the teacher should do to be effective and is correct in the new prescription for the teacher, the supervisor will be an invaluable resource to that teacher. If, however, the supervisor doesn't see the pattern or is incorrect in the prescription, the teacher will have little respect for what the supervisor is trying to accomplish. Said quite simply, if the supervisor knows the research, the odds are greater for gaining respect from the teacher being assisted.

SUMMARY

Research on teaching and learning represents the best possible professional link between supervisors and teachers. To the degree that supervisors are aware of what is known about teaching and learning and can use this knowledge to provide prescriptions to teachers with needs, a professional relationship will be established. If supervisors are ignorant of this knowledge base, their role in improving instruction is severely limited to their own experience.

Most of what we know about teaching and learning has been learned in the past twenty-five years. Aided by computers, researchers have been able to isolate key teaching acts and measure their impact on students under controlled conditions. In the 1990s, research has led to the understanding that the effectiveness of a teacher is determined by both the mission of the curriculum and the patterns of strategies the teacher employs. The supervisor must understand that a set of skills for direct instruction (mastery learning, didactic questioning) will be effective for some outcomes (knowledge tested by achievement tests) but may be quite ineffective for other kinds of intended outcomes such as building affect or teaching thinking skills.

Knowledge of the research increases the odds that the supervisor can make a successful prescription for the teacher in need. By seeing the patterns and assessing the evidence for various prescriptions, the supervisor can be dedicated to improving instruction for students.

IMPLICATIONS FOR SUPERVISION

1. What is a minimum baseline of research data that should be monitored by any school district?
2. In the areas of teacher effectiveness research presented in this chapter, which bodies of knowledge might be combined to form an approach to instruction? How might crossing three areas such as praise, self-concept, and attribution contribute to such an approach?
3. Try to envision a perfect world in which each child's needs are met by a tailored instructional plan based on sound research. What steps would lead us to that state of practice?

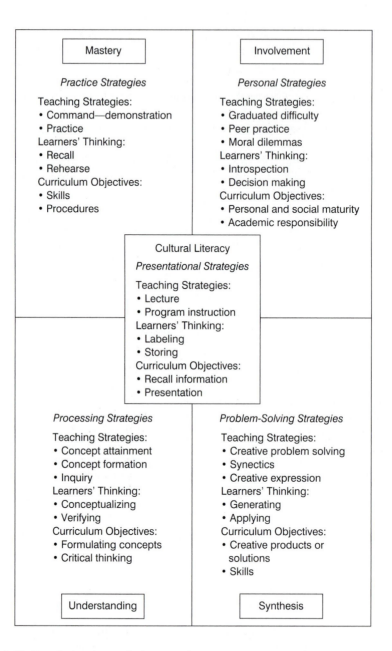

Figure 3.12 Five Conceptions of Educational Purpose
Source: Richard Strong, Harvey F. Silver, and Robert Hanson, "Integrating Teaching Strategies and Thinking Styles with the Elements of Effective Instruction," *Educational Leadership* 42 (May 1985): 9–15.

⊱ CASE STUDY 1 ⊰

A new eighth-grade teacher has requested assistance from the supervisor because she is having difficulty motivating some boys in her general science classes. "These students," she states, "just don't believe in themselves." The teacher continues to describe a small group of boys who are unsuccessful in school and who have learned to expect failure. The teacher has tried giving easier tests, heaping praise on their efforts, using rewards to encourage success, as well as any number of interesting lessons to motivate them. Nothing works for this teacher, and the attitude of these boys is spreading to the other students.

Questions

1. As a supervisor, what questions would you ask the teacher in order to establish the purpose and pattern of instruction in this room?

2. What sort of approach is suggested by the research cited on attribution, self-concept, praise, and questioning?
3. Can you tailor a prescription for this teacher that should lead to an improved condition in the classroom?
4. In what area of research do you need to increase your knowledge base in order to be more helpful to this teacher?

⊱ CASE STUDY 2 ⊰

In reviewing the socioeconomic data of the families of students in the district, the supervisor discovers a large (48 percent) number of children from poor backgrounds. The vast majority of these students are living in single-parent families. Data presented in this chapter suggests that these students will not fare well in school.

Questions

1. What does research reveal about the academic prospects of such students?

2. What appears to the actual cause of this condition?
3. Are there exceptions to this otherwise grim projection?
4. Can you develop an intervention program that would remove many of the aggravating conditions in this situation?

SUGGESTED LEARNING ACTIVITIES

1. Using the research cited in this chapter, try to develop a teacher evaluation form you could defend in a court of law. Are there any general criteria good under all circumstances?
2. Develop a general prescription for a teacher using the direct, indirect, and self-directing style of teaching. What are the differences in these prescriptions?

3. Identify the most important research findings presented in this chapter. What areas should receive funding for further inquiry in the 1990s?
4. Attempt to create a hierarchy of skills needed by a classroom teacher. How would this structure help define staff development in a school district?

ADDITIONAL READING

Airasian, P., and Madaus, G. "Linking Testing and Instruction: Policy Issues," *Journal of Educational Measurement* 20 (1983): 103–118.

Allan, S. "Ability Grouping Research Reviews: What Do They Say About Grouping the Gifted?" *Educational Leadership* 48 (March 1991): 60–65.

American Association of University Women. "Shortchanging Girls, Shortchanging America." Initiative for Educational Equity, 1992 ERIC ED 339 674.

Anderson, R. C. "The Notion of Schemata and the Educational Enterprise," in *Schooling and the Acquisition of Knowledge* (Hillsdale, NJ: Lawrence Erlbaum and Associates, 1977).

Aronson, E. et al. *The Jigsaw Classroom* (Beverly Hills: Sage, 1978).

Ascher, C. "Grade Retention: Making the Decision," Office of Educational Research and Improvement, Washington, DC, 1988.

Babey, E. "The Classrooms: Physical Environments That Enhance Teaching and Learning." Paper at the American Association of Higher Education, Washington, DC, 1991.

Bacoats, G. "The Relationship of the Florida State Student Assessment Test and the Grade Performance of Students in a Medium Sized School District in Florida." Ph.D. diss., University of South Florida, 1993.

Baenan, N. "Perspective After Five Years—Has Grade Retention Passed or Failed?" Austin Independent School District, Austin, Texas, 1988.

Balow, I. "Retention in Grade: A Failed Procedure," California Education Research Cooperative, Riverside, California, 1990.

Bardos, A. "Gender Differences on Planning, Attention, Simultaneous and Successive Cognitive Planning Tasks," *Journal of School Psychology* 3 (1992): 297–299.

Baron, E. *Discipline Strategies for Teachers.* Bloomington, IN: Phi Delta Kappa Foundation, 1992.

Birely, M., and Hoelin, L. "Teaching Implications of Learning Styles," *Academic Therapy,* March 1987, pp. 437–442.

Blase, J., and Kirby, P. "The Power of Praise: A Strategy for Effective Principals," *NASSP Bulletin* 76 (1992): 69–77.

Bosma, M., and Jackson, S. *Coping and Self-Confidence in Adolescence.* Berlin, Germany: Springer-Verlag, 1990.

Brophy, J. "Teacher Praise: A Functional Analysis," *Review of Educational Research* 51, 2 (1981): 5–32.

Brophy, J. "Educating Teachers about Managing Classrooms and Students," *Teaching and Teacher Education* 4 (1988): 1–16.

Brown, G., and Wragg, T. *How Questions Can Stimulate Children's Learning.* New York: Routledge, 1993.

Bull, R. "The Effects of Attractiveness of Writer and Penmanship on Essay Graders," *Journal of Occupational Psychology* 52 (1979): 53–59.

Carlson, W. "Questions in the Classroom: A Sociolinguistic Perspective," *Review of Educational Research* 61 (1991): 157–178.

Carter, E. "Decreasing the Incidence of First Grade Retention Through Diagnostic–Prescriptive Intervention," 1990, ERIC 327341.

Carter, R. "How Invalid Are Marks Assigned by Teachers?" *Journal of Educational Psychology* 43 (1952): 218–228.

Chambers, A., and Abrami, B. "The Relationship Between Student Team Learning Outcomes and Achievement: Causal, Attributes, and Affect," *Journal of Educational Psychology* 83 (1991): 145.

Chipman, S. et al. "Content Effects on Word Problem Performance: A Possible Source of Test Bias?" *American Educational Research Journal* 28, 4 (1991): 897–915.

Cole, M. "The Zones of Proximal Development: Where Culture and Cognition Create Each Other," in *Culture, Communication, and Cognition,* ed. J. Wertsch. New York: Cambridge University Press, 1985.

Collier, V. "How Long?: A Synthesis of Research on Academic Achievement in Second Language." *TESOL Quarterly* 23 (September 1988): 509–530.

Combs, A., ed. *Perceiving, Behaving, Becoming.* ASCD Yearbook, 1965.

Cotton, K. "Schoolwide and Classroom Discipline," *School Improvement Research Series,* V, pp. 1–12.

Crawford, J. *Bilingual Education: History, Politics, Theory, Practice.* Newark, NJ: Crane Publishing Company, 1991.

Crone, P., and Tashakkori, M. "Variance in Student Achievement in Effective and Ineffective Schools: Inconsistencies Across SES Categories." Paper, American Educational Research Association, 1992.

D'Angelo, D. "Chapter One: A Catalyst for Improving Parent-Involvement," *Phi Delta Kappan,* January 1991, pp. 350–354.

Daines, D. *Teacher Oral Questions and Subsequent Verbal Behaviors of Teachers and Students.* Provo, UT: Brigham Young University, 1982.

Daniels, J. "Empowering Homeless Children Through School Counseling." *Elementary School Guidance and Counseling* 27 (December 1992): 105–111.

Darling, S. "Parents and Children Learning Together," *Principal,* November 1992, 10–13

Davidson, C. *Studies of Various Vigo County School Corporation Groups—What a Difference a Day Makes.* Rosemont, NJ: Programs for Educators, Inc., 1986.

Davidson, N. "Life Without Father: America's Greatest Social Catastrophe," *Policy Review* 51 (1990): 40–44.

DeAndrea, D., and Morioka, J. M. "Building Strategies to Meet the Developmental Needs of Homeless Children." Ann Arbor: University of Michigan Press (ERIC/CAPS), 1992.

Dickinson, D. "An Examination of Programs That Involve Parents in Efforts to Support Children's Acquisition of Literacy." W. T. Grant Foundation, Worcester, MA, 1988.

Digby, A. *Cooperative Learning: A Guide to Research.* New York: Garland Publishing, 1991.

Dunkin, M., and Biddle, B. *The Study of Teaching.* New York: Holt, Rinehart & Winston, 1974.

Dunn, R., and Dunn, K. *Teaching Students Through Their Individual Learning Styles.* Reston, VA: Reston Publishing Company, 1978.

Dweck, C. "The Role of Expectations and Attributions in the Alleviation of Learned Helplessness," *Journal of Personality and Social Psychology* 31 (1975): 674–685.

Dweck, C. "Motivational Processes Affecting Learning," *American Psychologist* 41 (1986): 1040–1048.

Elkind, D. "Developmentally Appropriate Practice: Philosophy and Practical Implications." *Phi Delta Kappan* (October 1989): 113–116.

Emmer, E., and Ausikker, A. "School and Classroom Discipline Programs: How Well Do They Work?" in *Student Discipline Strategies: Research and Practice,* ed. D. Moles. Albany: State University Press, 1990.

Epstein, J. "Longitudinal Effects of Family-School Interaction on Student Outcomes" in *Research in the Sociology of Education,* ed. A. Kerchhoff. Greenwich, CT: Kingsman.

Evertson, C. et al. "Improving Classroom Management: A School Based Program for the Beginning of the Year," *Journal of Educational Research* 64 (1989): 82–90.

Fagan, T., and Held, C. "Chapter One Program Improvement," *Phi Delta Kappan* 72 (1991): 582–584.

Farkas, G. et al. "Cultural Resources and School Success: Gender, Ethnicity, and Poverty Groups Within an Urban School District," *American Sociological Review* 55 (1990): 127–142.

Fielder, E. et al. "In Search of Reality: Unraveling the Myths About Tracking, Ability Groups and the Gifted," *Roeper Review,* September 1993.

Fisher, C. W. "Teaching and Learning in the Elementary School: A Summary of the Beginning Teacher Evaluation Study." Report VII-1, BTES Technical Report, 1978.

Flavell, J. "Metacognition and Cognitive Monitoring," *American Psychologist* 34 (1979): 906–911.

Forrest, D., and Waller, T. "What Do Children Know About Their Reading and Study Skills?" Paper, American Educational Research Association, Boston, 1980.

Fredericks, A. "Single Parent Families: Tips for Educators, *Reading Teacher,* April 1991, pp. 604–608.

Gall, M. "The Use of Questions in Teaching," *Review of Educational Research* 40 (1970): 707–720.

Gallicchio, B. "Motivating Average Students in Groups," *Educational Digest,* May 1993, pp. 49–52.

Garner, R. *Metacognition and Reading Comprehension.* Norwood: NJ: Ablex Publishing, 1987.

Gehshan, S. "College Admission Tests: Opportunity or Roadblocks," *AAUW,* June 1988, pp. 1–6.

Gerlach, J., and Hart, B. "Gender Equity in the Classrooms: An Inventory," *Phi Delta Kappan* 54 (1992).

Glass, K. "Sonic Environment," *CEFP Journal,* July–August 1985, pp. 8–11.

Good, T. "Two Decades of Research on Teacher Expectation: Findings and Further Directions," *Journal of Teacher Education* 38 (1987): 32–48.

Good, T. "Using Work Groups in Mathematics Instruction," *Educational Leadership* 47, 4 (1990): 4.

Gordon, T. *Teacher Effectiveness Training.* New York: Wyden Press, 1974.

Graham, S., and Folkes, V. *Attribution Theory: Applications to Achievement, Mental Health, and Interpersonal Conflict.* Hillsdale, NJ: Lawrence Erlbaum and Associates, 1990.

Greenwood, G. "Research and Practice in Parent Involvement: Implications for Teacher Involvement," *The Elementary School Journal* 91, 3 (January 1993): 279–286.

Gurkey, T., and Gates, S. "Synthesis of Research on Mastery Learning," *Educational Leadership* 43 (1986): 3–8.

Hales, L., and Tokar, E. "The Effects of Quality if Preceding Responses on the Graders Assigned to Subsequent Responses to an Essay Examination," *Journal of Educational Measurement* 12 (1975): 115–117.

Hallihan, M. "The Effects of Ability Grouping in Secondary Schools," *Review of Educational Research* 60 (1990): 501–504.

Hamachek, D. *The Self in Growth, Teaching, and Learning.* Englewood Cliffs, NJ: Prentice Hall, 1965.

Hart, T. "Involving Parents in the Education of Their Children," *OSSC Bulletin* 3, November 1984.

Hathaway, W. "A Study into the Effects of Light on Children of Elementary School Age—A Case of Daylight Robbery." Alberta Department of Education, 1992, ERIC 343686.

Havighurst, Robert. *Growing Up in River City.* New York: J. Wiley and Sons, 1962.

Henak, R. "Addressing Learning Styles," *The Technology Teacher,* November 1992, p. 25.

Henerey, S. "Sex and Locus of Control as Determinants of Children's Response to Peer Versus Adult Praise," *Journal of Educational Psychology* 67 (1979): 604–612.

Hetherington, E. "Cognitive Performance, School Behavior and Achievement of Children From One-Parent Households." National Institute of Education, 1981.

Hill, C. "Cooperative Learning and Ability Grouping: An Issue of Choice," *Gifted Child Quarterly* 36, 1 (1992): 11–16.

Hooper, G. "The Effects of Interaction During Computer-Based Mathematics Instruction," *Journal of Educational Research* 85, 3 (1992): 180.

Howze, K. and Howze, W. "Children of Cocaine: Treatment and Child Care." Paper, National Association for the Education of Young Children, Annual Conference, 1989.

Hubbell, R. *A Review of Head Start Research Since 1970.* Washington, DC: U.S. Department of Health and Human Services, 1985.

Hughes, J. "What's in a Grade?" Paper, Speech Communication Association, Washington DC, November 1983.

Imai, M. "Properties of Attention During Reading Lessons," *Journal of Educational Psychology* 84 (June 1992): 160–172.

Inhelder, B., and Piaget, J. *The Early Growth of Logic in the Child.* London: Routledge & Kegan, 1964.

Irwin, C. *Research Methodologies Used in Women's Gender—Equity Studies.* Detroit: Wayne State, 1992.

Jaeger, R. "Weak Measurement Serving Presumptive Policy," *Phi Delta Kappan,* October 1992, pp. 118–128.

Jordon, N. "Differential Calculations Abilities in Young Children From Middle and Low Income Families." *Developmental Psychology* 28, 4 (1992): 644–653.

Karweit, N. *Repeating a Grade: Time to Grow or Denial of Opportunity.* Baltimore: John Hopkins University, May 1991.

Kelly, K., and Jordon, L. "The Effects of Academic Achievement on Self-Concept: A Reproduction Study," *Journal of Educational Psychology* 84 (1992): 345–355.

Kerckhoff, A. "Effects of Ability Grouping in British Secondary Schools," *American Sociological Review* 51 (December 1986): 842–858.

Knirk, F. "Facility Requirements," *Educational Technology,* September 1992, pp. 26–32.

Kohn, A. "Group Grade Grubbing Versus Cooperative Learning," *Educational Leadership* 48 (1992): 83–88.

Kulik, J., and Kulik, C. "Meta-Analysis: Findings on Grouping Programs," *Gifted Child Quarterly* 36, 2 (Spring 1992): 73–76.

Kwallek, N., and Lewis, C. "Effects of Environmental Color on Males and Females," *Applied Ergonomics,* 1990, pp. 257–278.

Laharderne, H. "Attitudinal and Intellectual Correlates of Attention," *Journal of Educational Psychology* 59, 5 (1968): 321–323.

Lahti, J. In *Handbook of Research on Teaching,* 3rd ed., ed. M. Wittrock. New York: Macmillan, 1986, p. 704.

Larsen-Freeman, K. "Second Language Acquisition Research: Staking Out the Territory." *TESOL Quarterly* 25, 2 (1991): 215–260.

Licht, B. et al. "Children's Achievement-Related Beliefs: Effects of Academic Area, Sex, and Achievement," *Journal of Educational Research* 82, 5 (May/June 1989): 253–260.

Lynsynchuk, L. "Reciprocal Teaching Improves Standardized Reading Comprehension," *Elementary School Journal* 90 (1990): 469–484.

MacDonald, C. *Ballpoint Pens and Braided Hair: An Analysis of Reasoning Skills and the Curriculum.* Pretoria, South Africa: Human Sciences Research Council, 1990.

Marsh, H. "Failure of High Ability High Schools to Deliver Academic Benefits Commensurate with Their Students' Ability Levels," *American Educational Research Journal* 28 (Summer 1991): 445–480.

Marsh, M. "Age and Sex Effects in Multiple Dimensions of Self Concept: Preadolescence to Early Adulthood," *Journal of Education* 81 (1989): 417–430.

Marsh, M. "Content Specificity of Relations Between Academic Achievement and Academic Self-Concept," *Journal of Educational Psychology* 84, 4 (1992): 3–51.

Mativa, N. "Socio-economic Status, Aptitude, and Gender Difference in CAI Gains in Arithmetic." *Journal of Educational Research* 63, 1 (1987): 11–12.

McCarthy, B. "Using the 4MAT System to Bring Learning Styles to Schools," *Educational Leadership* 48, 2 (1990): 31–37.

McCormack, S. "Assertive Discipline: What Do We Really Know?" San Diego County Schools, 1987.

Meichenbaum, D., and Asarnow, J. "Cognitive Behavior Modification and Metacognition," in *Cognitive Behavior Interventions,* ed. P. Kendall (New York: Academic Press, 1979), pp. 137–211.

Mendler, A. "Discipline with Dignity in the Classroom," *Education Digest,* January 1993, pp. 27–29.

Merret, F., and Wheldall, K. Teacher Use of Praise and Reprimands to Boys and Girls," *Educational Review* 44 (1992): 73–79.

Meyer, P. et al. "The Informational Value of Evaluative Behavior: Influences of Praise and Blame on Perception of Ability," *Journal of Educational Psychology* 71 (1979): 259–268.

Milne, A. et al. "Single Parents, Working Mothers, and the Educational Achievement of School Children," *Sociology of Education* 59, 3 (1986): 14–139.

Moely, B. et al. "How Do Teachers Teach Memory Skills?" *Educational Psychologist* 21 (1986): 55–71.

Morine-Dershimer, G. "Pupil Perception of Teacher Praise," *Elementary School Journal* 82, 5 (1982): 421–434.

Mulryan, C. "Student Passivity During Cooperative Small Groups in Mathematics, *Journal of Educational Psychology* 85 (1992): 261–273.

Mystrand, M., and Gamoran, A. "Student Engagement: When Recitation Becomes Conversation," National Center on the Effectiveness of Secondary Schools, Madison, WI, Report, February 1990.

National Education Association. "Academic Tracking." Executive Committee, June 1990, pp. 1–31.

Neill, S. *Classroom Nonverbal Behavior.* New York: Routledge, 1991.

Newby, T. "Strategies of First Year Teachers," *Journal of Educational Psychology* 83 (1991): 195–200.

Newman, F., and Thompson, J. *Effects of Cooperative Learning on Achievement in Secondary Schools: A Summary of Research.* Madison: University of Wisconsin–Madison, 1987.

Noely, B. "The Teacher's Role in Facilitating Memory and Study Strategy in Elementary School Classrooms," *Child Development* 63, 3 (June 1992): 653–672.

Oakes, J. *Keeping Track: How Schools Structure Inequality.* New Haven: Yale University Press, 1985.

Oakes, J. "Grouping Students for Instruction," in *Encyclopedia of Educational Research,* 6th ed., ed. M. Aiken, 2 (1992): 562–567.

Oelbrich, J., and Hare, E. "The Effects of Single-Parenthood on School Achievement in a Gifted Population," *Gifted Child Quarterly* 33, 3 (1989): 115–117.

Okebukola, P. "The Influence of Preferred Learning Styles on Cooperative Learning in Science," *Science Education* 70 (1986): 509–576.

Parsons, J. et al. "Sex Differences in Attribution and Learned Helplessness," *Sex Roles* 8, 4 (1982): 421–432.

Peterson, P. et al., "Student Attitudes and Their Reports of Cognitive Processes During Direct Instruction," *Journal of Educational Psychology* 74 (1982): 535–546.

Pflaum, S. *The Development of Language on Literacy of Young Children.* Columbus, OH: Merrill, 1986.

Poulson, M. "Children at Risk Due to Prenatal Substance Exposure." Paper, Los Angeles Unified School District, December 1989.

Redfield, D. "A Meta-Analysis of Experimental Research on Teacher Questioning Behavior," *Review of Educational Research* 51, 2 (1981): 237–245.

Risenmy, M., and Ebel, D. "Retention and Transfer of Children's Self-Directed Critical Thinking Skills," *The Journal of Educational Research* 85, 1 (1991): 14–25.

Rodenbush, S. "Magnitude of Teacher Expectancy on Pupil I.Q. as a Foundation of the Credibility of Teacher Induction," *Journal of Educational Psychology* 76 (1984): 85–97.

Rosenberg, M. *Conceiving of Self.* New York: Basic Books, 1979.

Rosenshine, B., and Guenther, J. "Using Scaffolding for Teaching Higher Level Cognitive Strategies," in *Teaching for Thinking,* ed. H. Walberg. Reston VA: NAASP, 1992, pp. 35–48.

Rosenshine, B., and Stevens, R. "Teaching Functions," in *Handbook of Research on Teaching,* 3rd ed., ed. M. Wittrock. New York: Macmillan, 1986, pp. 376–390.

Rosenthal, R., and Jacobson, L. *Pygmalion in the Classroom.* New York: Holt, Rinehart & Winston, 1968.

Ryan, S. A., ed. *Report of the Longitudinal Evaluations of Preschool Programs,* Zigler and Butterfield. Washington, DC: Department of Health, Education, and Welfare, 1975.

Sadker, M. et al. "Gender and Educational Equity," in *Multicultural Education: Issues and Perspectives,* 2nd ed., ed. J. Banks. Boston: Allyn & Bacon, 1993.

Salmon-Cox, L. "Teachers and Standardized Tests: What's Really Happening?" *Phi Delta Kappan* 62, 9 (1982).

Sanders, M., and McCormick, E. *Human Factors in Engineering and Design.* New York: McGraw-Hill, 1987.

Sanders, N. *Classroom Questions: What Kind?* New York: Harper & Row, 1966.

Schunk, D. "Socialization and the Development of Self-Regulated Learning: The Role of Attributions," American Educational Research Association, Boston, 1990.

Sharan, A. "Cooperative Learning in Small Groups—Recent Methods and Effects on Achievement, Attitudes, and Ethnic Relations," *Review of Educational Research* 16 (1980): 241–271.

Shepard, L., and Smith, M. "Synthesis of Research on Grade Retention," *Educational Leadership,* May 1990.

Shiang, C. *The Effectiveness of Questioning on the Thinking Process.* San Francisco: American Educational Research Association, 1989, ERIC ED 013704.

Shoho, A. "A Historical Comparison of Parental Involvement of Three Generations of Japanese Americans in the Education of Their Children." AERA Paper, 1992.

Shreeve, W. "Single Parents and Student Achievement: A National Tragedy." HDA Research Report, 1985.

Slavin, R. "Cooperative Learning," *Review of Educational Research,* 1980, pp. 315–342.

Slavin, R. "Achievement Effects of Ability Grouping in Secondary Schools: A Best-Evidence Synthesis," *Review of Educational Research* 60 (1990): 471–499.

Slavin, R. "When and Why Does Cooperative Learning Increase Achievement: Theoretical and Empirical Perspectives," in *Interaction in Cooperative Groups,* ed. R. Hertz. New York: Cambridge University Press, 1992, pp. 145–173.

Slavin, R. "Synthesis of Research on Cooperative Learning, *Educational Leadership* 48 (1992): 71–82.

Smith, A. "The Impact of Head Start on Children, Families, and Communities." Final Report, U.S. Department of Health and Human Services, 1985.

Snyder, S., and Esposito, J. "Designing Schools That Work," *American School Board Journal,* 1993, pp. 49–51.

Southwest Educational Development Laboratory. "Follow Through: A Bridge To the Future," Austin, TX: 1992.

Sprinthall, N., and Sprinthall, K. *Educational Psychology: A Developmental Approach.* New York: McGraw-Hill, 1990.

Stallings, J. "Research on Early Childhood and Elementary Teaching Programs," *Handbook of Research on Teaching.* New York: Macmillan, 1986, pp. 746–750.

Sternberg, R. "Thinking Styles: Keys to Understanding Student Performance," *Phi Delta Kappan* 71 (1990): 366–371.

Sylvester, R. "What Brain Research Says About Paying Attention," *Educational Leadership* 50, 4 (December 1992): 71–75.

Tauber, R. "Criticisms and Deception: The Pitfalls of Praise," *NASSP Bulletin* 74, 528 (October 1990): 95–99.

Thomas, A. "Alternative to Retention: If Flunking Hasn't Worked, What Does?" Oregon School Study Council (Eugene, Oregon), 35, 6 (February 1992).

Titus, T. "Adolescent Learning Styles," *Journal of Research and Development in Education* 23, 3 (Spring 1990): 165–170.

Toch, T. "Giving Kids a Leg Up: How to Best Help Kids Succeed in School." *U.S. News and World Report,* October 22, 1990, p. 63.

Uphoff, J., and Gilmore, J. "Pupil Age at School Entrance—How Many Are Ready for Success?" *Young Children* (January 1986), pp. 24–29.

Valdiviesco, R. "Hispanics and Schools: A New Perspective," *Educational Horizons* 11 (1986): 190–196.

Van de Mars, H. "Effects of Specific Verbal Praise on Off Task Behavior of Second Grade Students in Physical Education," *Journal of Teaching Physical Education* 8 (1993): 162–169.

Vygotsky, L. *Mind in Society: The Development of Higher Psychological Processes.* Cambridge: Harvard University Press, 1978.

Walberg, H. "Long-Term Grouping for Better Learning," *Education Digest,* May 1994, pp. 4–6.

Webb, N. "Student Interaction and Learning in Small Groups: A Research Summary," in *Learning to Cooperate, Cooperating to Learning,* ed. R. Slavin. New York: Plenum, 1985.

Weikart, D. *Quality Preschool Programs: Long Term Social Investment.* New York: Ford Foundation, 1989.

Weiner, B. *An Attributional Theory of Motivation and Emotion.* New York: Springer-Verlag, 1986.

Weinstein, C. "The Physical Environment of the School: A Review of the Research," *Review of Educational Research* 49 (1979): 577–610.

Wheelock, A. *Alternatives to Tracking and Ability Grouping.* New York: American Association of School Administrators, 1994.

Whelen, C., and Teddlie, C. "Self-Fulfilling Prophecy and Attribution for Responsibility: Is There a Causal Link to Achievement?" March 1989, ERIC Ed 323211.

Williams, A. "Class, Race, and Gender in American Education," *AAUW,* November 1989, p. 5.

Wynne, E. "Persisting Groups: An Overlooked Force for Learning," *Phi Delta Kappan,* March 1994.

Yawkey, T. *The Self-Concept and the Young Child.* Provo, UT: Brigham Young University Press, 1990.

Books to Review

Aiken, M., ed. *The Encyclopedia of Educational Research,* 6th ed. New York: Macmillan, 1992.

Beach, D., and Reinhartz, J. *Supervision: Focus on Instruction.* New York: Harper and Row, 1989.

Gage, N. L. *The Scientific Basis of the Art of Teaching.* New York: Teachers College Press, 1978.

Wittrock, M.,ed. *Handbook of Research on Teaching.* New York: Macmillan, 1986.

CHAPTER 4

PROMOTING HUMAN DEVELOPMENT

Supervision, as a leadership specialty in professional education, is first about helping people grow and develop. Schools are human organizations; their ultimate product is an adjusted and knowledgeable young adult. The supervisor's job is to work with people to improve the educational process and to aid the growth and development of students. In working with teachers, supervisors must never forget that the improvement of teaching is a means, not an end. The goal of supervision is to contribute to a better learning experience that will help people develop.

Having made this observation, it follows that all supervisors must know how children and adults grow and develop. They must possess some conception or model of normal development, and they must fully understand patterns of deviation in growth and development. Finally, supervisors must possess a skill that allows them to link clearly the development of students to the instructional programs and behaviors of teachers. Without such an understanding of development and the linking of instruction to development outcomes, the schooling experience is reduced to a mindless process based on the historical repetition of academic activity.

As we enter a new century, it is helpful to review the rich literature on human development. In this chapter, the supervisor can examine principles of human growth and development, look at human needs, and match those needs against the realities of our modern society. Of particular significance are the noble goals of *America 2000,* a plan that called for all children in America to be prepared to start school ready to learn, contrasted with the realities of poor childcare and continued family breakdown. At no other time in the history of our country have we needed stronger advocates for children. Those in supervisory leadership roles can, and should, be those advocates.

A good place to start for supervisors building a knowledge of human development is to examine some of the better known models of human growth.

MODELS OF HUMAN GROWTH

Many contributions have been made over the past seventy-five years to our understanding of how humans develop. Although statistical summaries have been available throughout the century, the patterns of growth are now much clearer thanks to the contribution of many models of development. These models are not certain prescriptions of how each person will develop, but they do provide us with a way of seeing the entire process of development. Some of these models focus on physical growth. The utility of these models for supervisors is that they provide the "big picture" of the unfolding process of student development, thereby organizing the many isolated pieces of information encountered in school environments.

Models of physical development are plentiful in the literature of education and psychology. For nearly ninety years, educators have measured and charted growth patterns of infants and children. It is possible to predict with considerable precision the normal course of motor development from birth to three years of age:

Birth	Exhibits reflect behavior
	Motor behavior highly variable
	Head sags when not supported
3 months	Holds head erect and steady
	Reaches for objects but misses
	Steps when held erect
6 months	Bears weight when in standing position
	No thumb apposition yet
	Can follow distant object with eyes
12 months	Can walk with support
	Can sit up alone, pull self upright
	Places objects on top of one another
24 months	Walks well
	Can kick large ball
	Can turn pages of book one at a time
36 months	Rides a tricycle
	Can button and unbutton
	Walks down steps with alternative footing[1]

Most models of physical development are constructed from statistical averages gleaned from studies of large numbers of children. Information from the studies is useful to the supervisor in planning physical education programs, developing facility specifications, analyzing art curricula, and many other everyday instructional tasks.

Another set of models available to supervisors traces the growth and development patterns in terms of social progression (see Figure 4.1). Probably the best-

Figure 4.1 Aiding Human Development

Examples of Developmental Tasks

Early Childhood
Developing motor control
Emerging self-awareness
Mapping out surroundings
Assigning meaning to events
Exploring relationships with others
Developing language and thought patterns

Middle Childhood
Structuring the physical world
Refining language and thought patterns
Establishing relationships with others
Understanding sex roles

Late Childhood
Mastering communication skills
Building meaningful peer relations
Thinking independently
Acceptance of self
Finding constructive expression outlets
Role projection

Preadolescence
Handling major body changes
Asserting independence from family
Establishing sex-role identity
Dealing with peer group relationships
Controlling emotions
Constructing a values foundation
Pursuing interest expression
Utilizing new reasoning capacities
Developing acceptable self-concept

Adolescence
Emancipation from parent dependency
Occupational projection selection
Completion of value structure
Acceptance of self

known of these models are the "developmental tasks," first suggested by sociologist Robert Havighurst.[2]

The developmental tasks focus on those skills that children must master to function in American society. These maturation measures occur both in and out of school. For teachers, knowledge of these needs and interests of students represent a source of motivation during instruction when these tasks are addressed.

Still another model of social development is provided by Abraham Maslow in his Hierarchy of Needs:

Self-realization and fulfillment
Esteem and status
Belonging and social activity
Safety and security
Physiological needs[3]

According to Maslow, human beings tend to their personal/social needs in a specified order of development. At the bottom level, and always satisfied first, are physiological needs (food, sleep). At the top level is the most sophisticated human need: finding meaning in life. According to Maslow, an individual cannot satisfy higher needs until lower needs have been met.

This single model is very important to an understanding of student behavior in school. Children who are hungry are poor students. Students who are insecure at home or in school are poor students. Students who need attention or friends are rarely good students. Even students who are overly concerned about being recognized (grade chasing) are not good students. A teacher who wants discipline in the classroom and students fully engaged in the learning process must help them address these lower-level needs that retard academic performance.

One of the most interesting models of emotional development to be contributed during the last thirty years is the Stages of Moral Development by Lawrence Kohlberg.[4] Kohlberg's concern with how children gain self-control resulted in a six-tier model:

Levels	Stages
1. Preconventional	1. The punishment and obedience orientation
	2. The instrumental–relativist orientation
2. Conventional	3. The interpersonal concordance orientation
	4. The "law and order" orientation
3. Postconventional	5. The social–contract legalistic orientation
	6. The universal ethical–principle orientation

In his model, Kohlberg believes little children behave because they fear punishment by larger authority figures. At some point around the middle school age, however, students must assume an internal code of behavior if they are to behave moralistically as adults. It is interesting to think about the discipline programs of schools and their contribution, if any, to this transition by the student. It is equally interesting to think about the consequences for society if students do not assume responsibility for their behavior as they grow up.

Finally, there are a number of models of intellectual growth available to supervisors, the best-known of which is Jean Piaget's Theory of Intellectual Development. According to this model, a human being's mind develops in four distinct stages, somewhat related to chronological age, and the pattern of development is a defined path that never varies:

Age 0–2	Sensorimotor stage	Trial and error learning based on organized motor activity
Age 2–7	Preoperational stage	Use of symbols to represent objects Development of language and use of dramatic play
Age 7–11	Concrete operations	Use of concepts, logical thinking
Age 11–15	Formal operations	Use of abstract as well as concrete thinking[5]

Piaget's model, although badly overextended by many educators, does provide a way of thinking about mental maturation. Questions, such as when a young person becomes capable of abstract thinking, have tremendous implications for academic programming in areas like math and science. Supervisors need to consider this development when determining the appropriateness of content and instructional methodology.

Models such as those outlined direct our understanding of the quantitative growth and development of students in school. It is helpful to know, for instance, that first-graders are about forty-six inches tall and weigh just under fifty pounds; sixth-graders, five feet tall and about ninety pounds. This data and these models tell us about normal development and what we can anticipate in working with children. They also should alert us to "qualitative" growth, leaps in functioning, intelligence, creative capacity and so on, that make individuals distinct and unique.

Supervisors can easily organize their thinking about school programs in terms of four general stages of development: early childhood (grades K–3), late childhood (grades 4–5), preadolescence (grades 6–8), and adolescence (grades 9–12). However, they must remember that there is a wide spectrum of differences in the normal range of development at any stage (see Figure 4.2). Supervisors must also tailor school programs to students' developmental characteristics (physical, social, emotional, and intellectual). An example of matching programs to developmental needs is illustrated in Figure 4.3.

THE GROWTH ENVIRONMENT

In addition to knowing about how growth occurs in students, it is also important to recognize the environment in which development occurs. No other single factor has so influenced the planning of school programs in the past two decades as the changing milieu of the American society.

It is not an overstatement to say that the social structure in America today is far different from that of the past two hundred years. Once a nurturing environment

6 feet 2 inches tall	or	4 feet 7 inches tall
Trips going up the stairs	or	An Olympic goal medal winner with a perfect 10.0 in parallel bar competition
An alcoholic or a drug addict	or	A Sunday school leader and Little Leaguer
Wears dental braces	or	Competes in Miss Teenage America
Looking forward to quitting school	or	Curious and enthusiastic about learning
Unable to read the comic page	or	Reads the *Wall Street Journal*
Has trouble with whole numbers	or	Solves geometry problems easily
A "regular" in juvenile court	or	An Eagle Scout
Already a mother of two	or	Still plays with dolls

Figure 4.2 Portrait of a Thirteen-Year-Old
Source: Reprinted with the permission of Simon & Schuster, Inc. from Merrill/Prentice Hall text, *The Essential Middle School,* 2nd ed., by Jon Wiles and Joseph Bondi, p. 34. Copyright © 1993 by Prentice-Hall, Inc.

characterized by strong institutions and a nuclear family structure, American society since the 1980s has splintered into a new set of arrangements. The statistics on the breakdown of the family and neglect of children are staggering. Consider the following statistics:

- Since 1987, one fourth of all preschool children in the United States are classified as poor.
- Each year, over 350,000 children are born to mothers who were addicted to cocaine or other drugs during pregnancy. Kindergarten costs for these students are about $40,000 each—an equal amount is needed for children with fetal alcohol syndrome.
- Women ages 15 to 34 who have a first child before their first marriage is approximately 25 percent for whites and 70 percent for blacks.
- Today, 15 million children are reared by single mothers, whose family income averages about $1000 below the poverty level. Since 1975, children have been poorer than any other age group in our society. The poverty rate for families headed by a single woman who are also high school dropouts is 90 percent.
- In 1994, 20 percent of America's preschool children had not been vaccinated against polio.
- The number of children with learning disabilities has increased by 40 percent between 1993 and 1995 to over two million children.
- One fourth of pregnant mothers in the United States receive no physical care from any source during the first trimester of pregnancy. About 20 percent of children with handicaps could have been born healthy if mothers had had one physical examination during the first trimester of pregnancy.

Characteristics of Emerging Adolescents	Implications for the Middle School
Physical Development	

Accelerated physical development begins in transescence, marked by increase in weight, height, heart size, lung capacity, and muscular strength. Boys and girls are growing at varying rates. Girls tend to be taller for the first two years and tend to be more physically advanced. Bone growth is faster than muscle development, and the uneven muscle/bone development results in lack of coordination and awkwardness. Bones may lack protection of covering muscles and supporting tendons.	Provide a health and science curriculum that emphasizes self-understanding about body changes. Guidance counselors and community resource persons (e.g., pediatricians) can help students understand what is happening to their bodies.
	Schedule adaptive physical education classes to build physical coordination. Equipment design should help students develop small and large muscles.
In pubescent girls, secondary sex characteristics continue to develop, with breasts enlarging and menstruation beginning.	Intense sports competition; avoid contact sports.
	Schedule sex education classes; health and hygiene seminars.
A wide range of individual differences among students begins to appear. Although the sequential order of development is relatively consistent in each sex, boys tend to lag a year or two behind girls. There are marked individual differences in physical development for boys and girls. The age of greatest variability in physiological development and physical size is about age 13.	Provide opportunities for interaction among students of different ages, but avoid situations where physical development can be compared (e.g., communal showers).
	Emphasize intramural programs rather than interscholastic athletics so that each student may participate regardless of physical development. Where interscholastic sports programs exist, number of games should be limited, with games played in afternoon rather than evening.
Glandular imbalances occur, resulting in acne, allergies, dental and eye defects—some health disturbances are real, and some are imaginary.	Provide regular physical examinations for all middle school students.
Boys and girls display changes in body contour—large nose, protruding ears, long arms—have posture problems, and are self-conscious about their bodies.	Health classes should emphasize exercises for good posture. Students should understand through self-analysis that growth is an individual process and occurs unevenly.
A girdle of fat often appears around the hips and thighs of boys in early puberty. Slight development of tissue under the skin around the nipples occurs briefly, causing anxiety in boys who fear they are developing "the wrong way."	Films and talks by doctors and counselors can help students understand the changes the body goes through during this period. A carefully planned program of sex education developed in collaboration with parents, medical doctors, and community agencies should be developed.

Continued

Figure 4.3 Development of Emerging Adolescents and Its Implications for the Middle School
Source: Jon Wiles and Joseph Bondi, *The Essential Middle School* (Tampa, FL: Wiles, Bondi & Associates, 1980), pp. 29–34.

Physical Development

Students are likely to be disturbed by body changes. Girls especially are likely to be disturbed by the physical changes that accompany sexual maturation.

Receding chins, cowlicks, dimples, and changes in voice result in possible embarrassment to boys.

Teacher and parental reassurance and understanding are necessary to help students understand that many body changes are temporary in nature.

Boys and girls tend to tire easily but won't admit it.

Advise parents to insist that students get proper rest; overexertion should be discouraged.

Fluctuations in basal metabolism may cause students to be extremely restless at times and listless at others.

Provide an opportunity for daily exercise and a place where students can be children by playing and being noisy for short periods.

Encourage activities such as special-interest classes and "hands on" exercises. Students should be allowed to move around physically in classes and avoid long periods of passive work.

Boys and girls show ravenous appetites and peculiar tastes; may overtax digestive system with large quantities of improper foods.

Provide snacks to satisfy between-meal hunger as well as nutritional guidance specific to this age group.

Social Development

Affiliation base broadens from family to peer group. Conflict sometimes results due to splitting of allegiance between peer group and family.

Teachers should work closely with the family to help adults realize that peer pressure is a normal part of the maturation process. Parents should be encouraged to continue to provide love and comfort even though they may feel rejected.

Teachers should be counselors. Homebase, teacher-adviser house plan arrangements should be encouraged.

Peers become sources for standards and models of behavior. Child's occasional rebellion does not diminish importance of parents for development of values. Emerging adolescents want to make their own choices, but authority still remains primarily with family.

Sponsor school activities that permit students to interact socially with many school personnel. Family studies can help ease parental conflicts. Parental involvement at school should be encouraged, but parents should not be too conspicuous by their presence.

Figure 4.3 *Continued*

Social Development	
	Encourage co-curriculum activities. For example, an active student government will help students develop guidelines for interpersonal relations and standards of behavior.
Society's mobility has broken ties to peer groups and created anxieties in emerging adolescents.	Promote "family" grouping of students and teachers to provide stability for new students. Interdisciplinary units can be structured to provide interaction among various groups of students. Clubs and special-interest classes should be an integral part of the school day.
Students are confused and frightened by new school settings.	Orientation programs and "buddy systems" can reduce the trauma of moving from an elementary school to a middle school. Family teams can encourage a sense of belonging.
Students show unusual or drastic behavior at times—aggressive, daring, boisterous, argumentative.	Schedule debates, plays, playdays, and other activities to allow students to "show off" in a productive way.
"Puppy love" years emerge, with a show of extreme devotion to a particular boy or girl. However, allegiance may be transferred to a new friend overnight.	Role-playing and guidance exercises can provide the opportunity to act out feelings. Provide opportunities for social interaction between the sexes—parties and games, but not dances in the early grades of the middle school.
Youths feel that the will of the group must prevail and sometimes can be almost cruel to those not in their group. They copy and display fads of extremes in clothes, speech, mannerisms, and handwriting; very susceptible to media advertising.	Set up an active student government so students can develop their own guidelines for dress and behavior. Adults should be encouraged not to react with outrage when extreme dress or mannerisms are displayed.
Boys and girls show strong concern for what is "right" and for social justice; also show concern for those less fortunate.	Foster plans that allow students to engage in service activities, for example, peer teaching, which allow students to help other students. Community projects (e.g., assisting in a senior citizens club or helping in a childcare center) can be planned by students and teachers.
They are influenced by adults—attempt to identify with adults other than their parents.	Flexible teaching patterns should prevail so students can interact with a variety of adults with whom they can identify.

Figure 4.3 *Continued*

Social Development

Despite a trend toward heterosexual interests, same-sex affiliation tends to dominate.	Plan large group activities rather than boy-girl events. Intramurals can be scheduled so students can interact with friends of the same or opposite sex.
Students desire direction and regulation but reserve the right to question or reject suggestions of adults.	Provide opportunities for students to accept more responsibility in setting standards for behavior. Students should be helped to establish realistic goals and be assisted in helping realize those goals.

Emotional Development

Erratic and inconsistent behavior is prevalent. Anxiety and fear contrast with reassuring bravado. Feelings tend to shift between superiority and inferiority. Coping with physical changes, striving for independence from family, becoming a person in his/her own right, and learning a new mode of intellectual functioning are all emotion-laden problems for emerging adolescents. Students have many fears, real and imagined. At no other time in development is he or she likely to encounter such a diverse number of problems simultaneously.	Encourage self-evaluation among students. Design activities that help students play out their emotions. Activity programs should provide opportunities for shy students to be drawn out and loud students to engage in calming activities. Counseling must operate as a part of, rather than an adjunct to, the learning program. Students should be helped to interpret superiority and inferiority feelings. Mature value systems should be encouraged by allowing students to examine options of behavior and to study consequences of various actions.
	Encourage students to assume leadership in group discussions and experience frequent success and recognition for personal efforts and achievements. A general atmosphere of friendliness, relaxation, concern, and group cohesiveness should guide the program.
Chemical and hormone imbalances often trigger emotions that are little understood by the transescent. Students sometimes regress to childlike behavior.	Adults in the middle school should not pressure students to explain their emotions (e.g., crying for no apparent reason). Occasional childlike behavior should not be ridiculed.
	Provide numerous possibilities for releasing emotional stress.
Too-rapid or too-slow physical development is often a source of irritation and concern. Development of secondary sex characteristics may create additional tensions about rate of development.	Provide appropriate sex education and encourage participation of parents and community agencies. Pediatricians, psychologists, and counselors should be called on to assist students in understanding developmental changes.

Figure 4.3 *Continued*

Emotional Development

This age group is easily offended and sensitive to criticism of personal shortcomings.	Sarcasm by adults should be avoided. Students should be helped to develop values when solving their problems.
Students tend to exaggerate simple occurrences and believe their problems are unique.	Use sociodrama to enable students to see themselves as others see them. Readings dealing with problems similar to their own can help them see that many problems are not unique.

Intellectual Development

Students display a wide range of skills and abilities unique to their developmental patterns.	Use a variety of approaches and materials in the teaching-learning process.
Students will range in development from the concrete-manipulatory stage to the ability to deal with abstract concepts. The transescent is intensely curious and growing in mental ability.	Treat students at their own intellectual levels, providing immediate rather than remote goals. All subjects should be individualized. Skill grouping should be flexible.
Middle school learners prefer active over passive learning activities and prefer interaction with peers during learning activities.	Encourage physical movement, with small group discussions, learning centers, and creative dramatics suggested as good activity projects. Provide a program of learning that is exciting and meaningful.
Students are usually very curious and exhibit a strong willingness to learn things they consider useful. They enjoy using skills to solve "real-life" problems.	Organize curricula around real-life concepts (e.g., conflict, competition, peer group influence). Provide activities in formal and informal situations to improve reasoning powers. Studies of the community and the environment are particularly relevant to the age group.
Students often display heightened egocentrism and will argue to convince others or to clarify their own thinking. Independent, critical thinking emerges.	Organized discussions of ideas and feelings in peer groups can facilitate self-understanding. Provide experiences for individuals to express themselves by writing and participating in dramatic productions.
Studies show that brain growth in transescents slows between the ages of 12 and 14.	Learners' cognitive skills should be refined; continued cognitive growth during ages 12 to 14 may not be expected.
	Provide opportunities for enjoyable studies in the arts. Encourage self-expression in all subjects.

Figure 4.3 *Continued*

- The "Norman Rockwell" family—a working father, a stay-at-home mother, and two children of school age—constitutes only 6 percent of U.S. households today.
- On any given night, between 50,000 and 200,000 children have no home. About 40 percent of shelter users are families with children.
- In 1994, there were over 2.2 million reports of child abuse or neglect, triple that of ten years ago.
- AIDS is the top killer of men 25 to 44 years of age and the fourth-leading killer of women in that age group.
- 85 percent of the nation's prisoners are high school dropouts.
- Blacks, who make up only 12 percent of the U.S. population, were nearly one half of those murdered in 1994.
- For 1994, 830,000 people were on welfare in New York City, a total larger than the population of all but ten American cities. New York City had a half million drug users in 1994.
- In 1994, more than 1.6 million youngsters—including a half million elementary children—were latchkey kids.
- Nine of every 1000 U.S. babies die before their first birthday—one of the highest infant-mortality rates in the industrialized world.
- About 60 percent of two-year-olds still haven't had shots against the most common childhood diseases.
- One in three victims of physical abuse is a child less than one year old.
- One fourth of U.S. babies live in families with incomes under the federal poverty level ($15,000 for a family of four in 1995).[6]

In light of these statistics, it is important to note that the first goal of education in the America 2000 Plan outlined by the President and fifty governors in 1991 was that "all children in America will start school ready to learn by the year 2000." Other goals included:

- All disadvantaged children and those with disabilities will have access to high-quality and developmentally appropriate preschool programs that help prepare children for school.
- Every parent in America will be a child's first teacher and devote time each day to helping his or her preschool child to learn; parents will have access to the training and support they need.
- Children will receive the nutrition and health care needs to arrive at school with healthy minds and bodies, and the number of low-birthweight babies will be significantly reduced.
- All children will start school ready to learn.
- The high school graduation rate will rise to at least 90 percent.
- U.S. students will be first in the world in science and mathematics.
- American students will be competent in core subjects.
- Every adult American will be literate.
- Every school in America will be safe and free of drugs.

- Parental involvement in schools will increase.
- Teacher development and professionalism will be enhanced.[7]

The Goals 2000: Educate America Act and the Improving America's Schools Act of 1994, which reauthorized the Elementary and Secondary Education Act, address the needs of children, particularly those in infancy and early childhood. The Head Start Bill, 1994–95, expanded Head Start Programs. The Improving America's Schools Act of 1993 discussed the importance of strong linkages between parents, schools, and community groups in raising our young.

Title I (formerly Chapter 1) was modified in 1994–95 to target schools with the highest concentration of poverty. Testing requirements were also made less generous to permit more time on teaching and learning.[8]

A wide body of research supports the fact that all later formal education is dramatically influenced by the learning experiences in the first year of life.

A Carnegie Corporation Report in 1994 called the birth-to-age-3 span the most critical period in a child's development, but the most neglected by policy makers.

Among the report's recommendations to spur "responsible parenthood" were expanding family-planning services and starting parenthood education in the elementary school. Better-quality childcare, child health, and safety were also suggested as well as more assistance from private groups.[9]

The following major recommendations were included in the Carnegie Report:

- Provide comprehensive programs to encourage planning for parenthood by all couples to avoid unnecessary risks and promote a healthy environment for child development.
- Expand family-leave policies and make the federal dependent-care tax credit refundable for low- and moderate-income families.
- Provide new federal aid to improve childcare for children under age three and encourage states to raise standards.
- Include comprehensive health services and immunizations for infants and toddlers in health-care reform.
- Offer home visits to all first-time mothers and more comprehensive programs for at-risk families.
- Strive to reduce unintentional injuries to young children, the leading cause of death among children ages one to four.
- Promote strategic community planning to provide comprehensive, coordinated services.

It is important to note that a generation after President Lyndon Johnson declared war on poverty, nearly one fourth of our youngest children grow up in poverty. In 1965, more of the poor were elderly than young. By 1995, 90 percent of the elderly poor were receiving significant benefits through Social Security cost-of-living adjustments, housing assistance, Medicaid, and other federal and state safeguards. Now, many child advocates believe we can, and should, do the same for our children.

The Importance of Early Education Programs

By 1994, only seven states and the District of Columbia had mandated kindergarten. Two other states have mandated the program if a child fails a specific test. However, most children do attend some type of kindergarten program in the United States although not all attend full-day programs.

Mandating two years of Head Start for those most in need, beginning at age three, has been suggested as one way to improve educational success for American students. Many of the problems are related to the breakdown of the traditional families. Because of divorce and births out of wedlock (the U.S. has one of the highest teenage-pregnancy rates in the world), one fourth of children live with one parent. Moreover, more than half of mothers of infants work outside the home, often having to struggle to find and afford quality childcare.

How best to teach young children has always been a source of debate. Most educators, however, endorse the idea of "developmentally appropriate practice." What does this term mean? Simply put, developmentally appropriate takes into account those aspects of teaching and learning that change with the age and experience of the learner.[10]

In 1994, the U.S. Department of Health, Education, and Welfare amended a contract to a Chicago-based research center to conduct the first longitudinal study to track children from the time they enter kindergarten. The study, known as the Early Childhood Longitudinal Study Kindergarten Cohort, will follow 23,000 kindergarten students as they progress through elementary school.

Ensuring that all students by 2000 start school ready to learn is the first of eight education goals state and national political leaders have set for the nation. The Early Childhood Longitudinal Study is aimed in part in providing a yardstick for measuring progress toward that goal. It will also provide data on children's key transitions through the primary grades, on their experiences in kindergartens and on how those experiences relate to later success in school.

The study will also take into account nonschool-related issues that affect learning success, such as health status, family, and economic background.

Shattered families and children living in homes without fathers have become an American crisis. With one third of births to unwed mothers in urban areas, most children are raised by a single woman. Broken homes have also led to an upsurge of violent crime, drug use, and failure in school.

CATEGORIES OF SPECIAL LEARNERS

If there is a single major difference between schools of the 1960s and 1990s, it would be that our increased knowledge of human development has caused specialization in designing educational programs. Schools of the 1990s are characterized by the labeling of learners according to special needs and the development of curriculum programs to accommodate individual differences. It is essential that supervisors master the many categories of students to help teachers understand and respond to the many needs found in schools.

As sensitive people, educators have a long history of working with students having special needs. Until 1975, most of these efforts in public schools were carried out in special rooms within school buildings or in special schools for categories of students such as those with physical handicaps. However, the diversity of learners with special needs and the expense of serving these learners sometimes caused service to be less than uniform. Three laws enacted at the federal level between 1965 and 1975 sought to organize all of the existing programs and spell out, legally, what the rights and obligations of special education were.

P.L. 89-313 (1965)—This law amended Title I legislation to provide funds to state agencies for supplementing education for handicapped children in state-operated schools.

P.L. 93-112 (1973)—This law (section 504) first provided that handicapped persons could not be discriminated against due to their handicap. Architectural barriers for handicapped persons were also eliminated by regulations under this law.

P.L. 94-142 (1975)—This law authorized a series of grants to state agencies to "initiate, expand, and improve" educational programs for the handicapped. The law also established the Bureau of the Handicapped in the U.S. Office of Education.

Unlike previous laws, Public Law 94-142 (Education for All Handicapped Children Act) promoted regular education for handicapped children at full public expense. The bill called for the identification of handicapped children, a thorough evaluation of their needs and a developed Individual Education Plan (IEP), free appropriate public education in the "least restrictive environment," and procedural safeguards for the process. The least restrictive environment clause (known as "mainstreaming") provided the greatest challenge to schools in implementing this benchmark legislation, but fifteen years after passage, the bill is fully implemented. Figure 4.4 outlines the major principles of the Public Law 94-142.

Inclusive Education

Some advocates for students with disabilities support "full inclusion," a concept that, in effect, does away with the option of placing students with disabilities anywhere but in regular classrooms in their neighborhood school. Advocates for students with severe disabilities, most notably, the Association for Persons with Severe Handicaps, have been among the most verbal proponents of opening up regular classrooms to students with disabilities. Organizations such as ASCD and the National Association of State Boards of Education—have also issued statements favoring inclusive education. The AFT and Council for Exceptional Children (the largest group of special educators) have stopped short of advocating full inclusion, stating that a continuum of services must be available to all children.[11]

P.L. 94-142 was enacted by Congress in November, 1975. Its major purpose, as stated in the act, is as follows:

> It is the purpose of this Act to assure that all handicapped children have available to them . . . a free, appropriate public education which emphasizes special education and related services designed to meet their unique needs, to assure that the rights of handicapped children and their parents or guardians are protected, to assist States and localities to provide for the education of all handicapped children, and to assess and assure the effectiveness of efforts to educate handicapped children. (Sec. 601(c)).

There are six major principles of P.L. 94-142:

1. *Principle of Zero Reject*

   This principle, simply stated, requires that *all* handicapped children be provided with a free, appropriate public education. States are required to provide full educational opportunities to all handicapped children in the age range of 3–18 by September 1, 1978, and to all handicapped children in the age range of 3–21 by September 1, 1980. The principle is implemented by conducting a child fund program on an annual basis to locate, identify and evaluate all handicapped children who reside in the jurisdiction of each public agency. If local agencies comply with this principle, they become eligible to receive federal funds based upon the number of handicapped children being served, not to exceed 12% of the school population.

   In addition to providing an educational program to all handicapped children, the public agency must ensure that handicapped children have equal opportunities with nonhandicapped children to participate in nonacademic and extracurricular services. In addition, physical education must be provided to every handicapped child.

2. *Principle of Nondiscriminatory Evaluation*

   A handicapped child must receive a full individual evaluation prior to placement in a special education program. A placement decision should be made by a group of persons knowledgeable about the child, the meaning of the evaluation data, and the placement options. The placement recommendation may be suggested by the evaluation team and finalized by a committee who has the responsibility for writing the Individual Educational Plan. All handicapped children must be completely re-evaluated every three years.

3. *Individualized Educational Programs*

   The legislative approach for ensuring that educational programs are tailored on an individual basis to the needs of handicapped students is through the requirement of providing individual educational plans for all handicapped students. The IEP must contain the following essentials:

Figure 4.4 Major Principles of Public Law 94-142

a. Current level of student's educational performance.

   b. Annual goals.

   c. Short-term objectives.

   d. Documentation of the special education services to be provided.

   e. Time the student will spend in special education and related services.

   f. Time student will spend in regular education.

   g. Dates for initiating service and anticipated duration.

   h. Evaluation procedures and schedules for determining mastery of the objectives.

   Members required to be in attendance at the IEP meeting must include the following:

   a. Representative of the public agency.

   b. The child's teacher.

   c. Child's parents.

   d. The child, when appropriate.

   e. Other individuals at the request of the parents.

   f. Individuals who provided the evaluation.

4. *Least Restrictive Environment*

   To the maximum extent appropriate, handicapped children should be educated with children who are not handicapped. The removal of handicapped children to special classes and separate facilities should occur only when the nature of severity of their handicap prevents them from successfully being educated in regular classes with the use of supplementary aids and services.

5. *Due Process*

   Due process is a procedure which seeks to ensure the fairness of educational decisions and the accountability of both the professionals and parents making these decisions. It can be viewed as a system of checks and balances concerning the identification, evaluation, and provision of services regarding handicapped students. It may be initiated by the parent or public agency as an impartial forum for presenting complaints regarding the child's identification, evaluation, and placement or for challenging decisions made by another party.

6. *Parent Participation*

   Each of the principles has either the direct or indirect implications for parental participation. At the local level, parents should be permitted to review any educational records on their child which are used by the agency before the meeting to develop the IEP and within a 45-day period after receipt of the request.

   These six principles of P.L. 94-142 provide the basis for the legislative definition of free, appropriate public education.

Figure 4.4 *Continued*

Others disagree with some of the ideas behind inclusive education—and especially with full inclusion. They argue that many students are pulled out of regular classrooms in the first place because they aren't served well there.

Working with Students Having Special Needs

The various laws and regulations concerning special students have resulted in some specific definitions of categories that are closely followed in today's schools:

Trainable mentally handicapped—A moderately mentally handicapped person is one who is impaired in intellectual and adaptive behavior and whose development reflects a reduced rate of learning. The measured intelligence of a moderately handicapped person falls approximately between three and four standard deviations below the mean (51–36 on the Stanford Binet and 54–40 on the Wechsler), and the assessed adaptive behavior falls below age and cultural expectations.

Severely mentally handicapped—A severely mentally handicapped person is one who is impaired in intellectual and adaptive behavior and whose development reflects a reduced rate of learning. The measured intelligence of a severely handicapped person falls approximately between four and five standard deviations below the mean (35–20 on the Stanford Binet and 39–25 on the Wechsler), and the assessed adaptive behavior falls below age and cultural expectations.

Profoundly mentally handicapped—A profoundly mentally handicapped person is one who is impaired in intellectual and adaptive behaviors and whose development reflects a reduced rate of learning. The measured intelligence of a profoundly handicapped person falls approximately five standard deviations below the mean (below 25 on the Stanford Binet), and there is limited or no adaptive behavior.

Educable mentally handicapped—An educable mentally handicapped student is one who is mildly impaired in intellectual and adaptive behavior and whose development reflects a reduced rate of learning. A student's performance on an individual psychological evaluation that indicated an approximate intellectual ability between two and three standard deviations below the mean (68–52 on the Stanford Binet and 69–55 on the Wechsler, plus or minus five).

Students with communicative disorders—Students with a communicative disorder may have trouble speaking, understanding others, or hearing the sounds of their world. They may have difficulty saying specific sounds or words, using words correctly, using the voice correctly, or speaking clearly and smoothly. Some students are unable to make muscles needed for speech work adequately. Other students may have a hearing problem that prevents them from understanding the teacher and others around them. Some students need help in learning words and in understanding how to put them together into sentences. To be considered for speech, language, or hearing therapy services, the student should be referred to the speech, language, and hearing clinician for testing, with written permission from parent or guardian. After all testing (speech, hearing, language, and any others as appropriate), a staffing committee meets to discuss the student's problem and to decide how best to help the student.

Hearing-impaired students—Students who are born with a severe hearing loss (70 dB or greater in better ear in speech frequencies), or who acquire a loss before learning language and speech, are considered deaf by state Department of Education definition. These students will be unable to learn language and speech unless they receive special education instruction. To be considered for enrollment in the Hearing Impaired Program, the student must have a medical evaluation that would include a general physical examination, an evaluation by an ear specialist (otologist), and a complete hearing evaluation by an audiologist. After all testing is completed, a staffing committee meets to discuss the student's problem and to decide how best to help the student.

Specific learning disabilities—A student with specific learning disabilities has a disorder in one or more of the basic psychological processes involved in understanding or in spoken and written language. These may be manifested in disorders of listening, thinking, reading, talking, writing, spelling, or arithmetic. They include conditions that have been referred to as perceptual handicaps, brain injury, minimal brain dysfunction, dyslexia, and developmental aphasia. They do not include learning problems due primarily to visual, hearing, or motor handicaps; mental retardation; emotional disturbance; or an environmental disadvantage.

To be considered for placement in a specific learning disabilities program, the student must have average to near average mental abilities, normal visual and hearing acuity, and no evidence of a primary physical handicap. Standardized achievement test scores would indicate difficulty in the basic academic areas of reading, writing, arithmetic, and/or spelling. Specialized test scores would show student difficulty in handling information received by sight and/or by hearing, in language, and/or in fine motor skills.

Emotionally handicapped—An emotionally handicapped student is one who exhibits consistent and persistent signs of behaviors that disrupt the learning process, such as withdrawal, distractibility, hyperactivity, or hypersensitivity.

Emotionally handicapped students show the following behaviors to the extent that they may not be served in the regular school program without at least part-time special placement or consultative services: learning problems that are not due primarily to mental retardation; severe behavior disorders that cannot be controlled or eliminated by medical intervention; inability to build or maintain satisfactory interpersonal relationships with adults and peers.

Physically handicapped—A student who has a crippling condition or other health impairment that requires an adaptation to the student's school environment or curriculum is considered physically handicapped. The student may have an impairment that interferes with the normal functions of the bones, joints, or muscles to such an extent that special arrangements must be made to provide an educational program.

The student may have a special health problem, such as cardiac disorders, diabetes, epilepsy, cystic fibrosis, hemophilia, asthma, leukemia, or nephritis, that would require special arrangements to provide an educational program.

Multi-handicapped students whose primary or most severe disability is a crippling condition or other health impairment may be included in this program.

The critical concern about all of these special groups of students is that they must be served by the school programs. On the other side of the coin is the danger of fragmenting the school program by placing all of the emphasis on exceptionality. A balance of general and specialized programs must be maintained. Figure 4.5 provides a checklist for identifying students who need educational therapy.

In addition to these many legal classifications and definitions, other special categories of students include gifted, talented, and creative students; disadvantaged and culturally different students; and non-English-speaking and bilingual students.

Gifted, talented, and creative—For years teachers have had the challenge of working with students who, because of superior intellectual development, are capable of high academic performance. In 1972, Congress acted to establish the Office of Gifted and Talented, an act resulting in the establishment of gifted programs in schools in all fifty states. Although funding for this office has been meager, identifying this special group of learners spurred research efforts that continue today. The result of such inquiry, however, has been to discredit many of the identification schema based solely on I.Q. (intelligence quotient) scores and to present a unique profile for gifted, talented, and creative thinking.

Disadvantaged and culturally different—By design, our schools are the melting pot of the American society. Court decisions, as well as federal and state laws, have mandated that children of different races and cultures be provided the opportunity to learn. In fact, the courts have even defended the rights of children who are not U.S. citizens to have a free public education. Among major legislation that has directly sought to aid these special learners in school are the Civil Rights Act of 1964, the Elementary and Secondary Education Act of 1965, and the Bilingual Education Act of 1968.

Cultural differences present a special challenge for supervisors due to the rapidly changing ethnic ratios in some parts of the country. Today

1. Gross motor and motor flexibility
   _____ incoordination and poor balance
   _____ difficulty with jumping/skipping/hopping (below age 9)
   _____ confusion in games requiring imitation of movements
   _____ poor sense of directionality
   _____ inept in drawing and writing at chalkboard
   _____ inaccuracies in copying at chalkboard
   _____ eyes do not work together
   _____ eyes lose or overshoot target

2. Physical fitness
   _____ tires easily
   _____ lacks strength

3. Auditory acuity, perception, memory/speech
   _____ confuses similar phonetic and phonic elements
   _____ inconsistent pronunciation of words usually pronounced correctly by peers
   _____ repeats, but does not comprehend
   _____ forgets oral directions, if more than one or two

4. Visual acuity, perception, memory
   _____ complains that he cannot see blackboard
   _____ says that words move or jump
   _____ facial expression strained
   _____ holds head to one side while reading

5. Hand-eye coordination
   _____ difficulty in tracing/copying/cutting/folding/pasting/coloring at desk
   _____ lack of success with puzzles/yo-yo's/toys involving targets, etc.

6. Language
   _____ has difficulty understanding others

Continued

Figure 4.5 Checklist for Identifying Students Who May Need Educational Therapy
Source: Reprinted with the permission of Simon & Schuster, Inc. from the Macmillan College text *Curriculum Development: A Guide to Practice,* 4th ed., by Jon Wiles and Joseph C. Bondi, © 1993 by Macmillan College Publishing Company, Inc.

_____ has difficulty associating and remembering

_____ has difficulty expressing himself

7. Intellectual functioning

_____ unevenness of intellectual development

_____ learns markedly better through one combination of sensory avenues than another

8. Personality

_____ overreacts to school failures

_____ does not seem to know he has a problem

_____ will not admit he has a problem

9. Academic problems

_____ can't tolerate having his routine disturbed

_____ knows it one time and doesn't the next

_____ writing neat, but slow

_____ writing fast, but sloppy

_____ passes the spelling test, but can't spell functionally

_____ math accurate, but slow

_____ math fast, but inaccurate

_____ reads well orally, but has poor comprehension

_____ does poor oral reading, but comprehends better than would be expected

_____ lacks word attack skills

_____ has conceptual/study skill/organizational problems in content areas

10. Parents

_____ seemingly uninformed about nature of learning problem

_____ seemingly unrealistic toward student's problems

Figure 4.5 _Continued_

sixteen states have over one million African-American citizens, and four states have over one million Hispanic citizens.

Non-English-speaking and bilingual—The United States has always been a country that receives and assimilates new citizen groups. Recent years have brought many such groups to our shores: the Cuban influx in the 1960s, Vietnamese refugees in the 1970s, Haitian "boat people" in the

1980s, plus a continuous influx of Mexican immigrants throughout the period. Accommodating these students who often do not speak English and honoring their native languages in schools has been difficult.

One other special group that presents cultural as well as language difficulties has been the mainstreaming of the Native American populations. During the 1970s and into the 1990s, Bureau of Indian Affairs schools have closed, and public schools have assumed the duty of providing a public education to Native American youths. In many districts of the West, preservation of language and heritage is a primary issue of curriculum development and teacher training.

The 1990 census documented that America was becoming a nation of increasing ethnic and cultural diversity. Increasing levels of immigration, especially among Hispanic and Asian populations, coupled with a lower birthrate among non-Hispanic white women has led to projections that Hispanics will outnumber blacks by 2010. The trend is clear that in the mid-twenty-first century, the United States will become a nation with no racial or ethnic majority. American society will shift from a society dominated by whites and rooted in western culture to a world society characterized by three large racial or ethnic minorities. The number of African, Asian, and Hispanic Americans and other minorities will continue to grow (at an even higher number in schools), while the still-significant white majority will continue its relative decline.[12]

Services for Special Students

In addition to the regular and special curricula provided for students in school, a large number of special services are provided that can be the concern of supervisors. Among these services are transportation, food provision, tutoring, and guidance. It is the area of guidance that illustrates the degree to which schools have become service industries. Here are some of the specialists who interact with supervisors each day to serve students:

Counselors—Deal with academic, vocational, and personal problems of students.
Psychometrists—Administer tests and make interpretations and diagnoses for instruction.
Psychologists—Administer special tests and give individual and group therapy.
Psychiatrists—Provide help to students with deep-seated problems.
Attendance personnel—Help enforce compulsory school attendance laws.
Social workers—Also known as visiting teachers; facilitate home–school communication about student needs.
Classroom teachers—Involved in low-level guidance functions such as advisor–advisee activities.

The supervisor must be aware of national organizations and agencies concerned with special needs students in order to provide the necessary services for such students (see Figure 4.6).

ACLU Juvenile Rights Project
22 East 40th Street
New York, NY 10016

American Academy for Cerebral Palsy
University Hospital School
Iowa City, IA 52240

**American Association for the Education of
Severely and Profoundly Handicapped**
1600 West Armory Way
Garden View Suite
Seattle, WA 98119

American Association for Gifted Children
15 Gramercy Park
New York, NY 10003

American Epilepsy Society
Department of Neurology
University of Minnesota
Box 341, Mayo Building
Minneapolis, MN 55455

American Foundation for the Blind
15 West 16th Street
New York, NY 10011

American Medical Association
535 North Dearborn Street
Chicago, IL 60610

American Psychological Association
1200 17th Street, NW
Washington, DC 20036

Association for the Aid of Crippled Children
345 East 46th Street
New York, NY 10017

**Association for Children with
Learning Disabilities**
2200 Brownsville Road
Pittsburgh, PA 16210

**Association for Education of the
Visually Handicapped**
919 Walnut
Philadelphia, PA 19107

Bureau for Education of the Handicapped
400 6th Street
Donohoe Building
Washington, DC 20202

Council for Exceptional Children
1920 Association Drive
Reston, VA 22091

**Institute for the Study of Mental
Retardation and Related Disabilities**
130 South First
University of Michigan
Ann Arbor, MI 48108

Muscular Dystrophy Association of America
810 7th Avenue
New York, NY 10019

National Association for Retarded Citizens
2709 Avenue E, East
P.O. Box 6109
Arlington, TX 76011

National Association of Social Workers
750 First St., NE
Suite 700
Washington, DC 20010

**National Committee for
Multi-Handicapped Children**
239 14th Street
Niagara Falls, NY 14303

National Institutes of Health
U.S. Department of Health, Education,
and Welfare
Washington, DC 20014

National Rehabilitation Association
1522 K Street, NW
Washington, DC 20005

**President's Committee
on Employment of the Handicapped**
U.S. Department of Labor
Washington, DC 20210

President's Committee on Mental Retardation
Regional Office Building #3
Room 2614
7th and D Streets, SW
Washington, DC 20201

Figure 4.6 National Organizations and Agencies Concerned with Special Needs Children

126

Finally, supervisors must make a special effort to learn of the various professional examiners who may be involved in the identification and treatment of schoolchildren (see Table 4.1).

ISSUES FOR INSTRUCTIONAL SUPERVISORS

This chapter has focused on the development of human beings in an institution called a school. All modern societies maintain some form of schooling to help young people develop and enter the society as productive members. The conception of a healthy and productive citizen, more than anything else, should define the program of the school and, consequentially, the role of the supervisor. Human development, and our recent knowledge of how it occurs, raises some serious issues for all instructional supervisors.

At the general level is the issue of scope of responsibility. For what is the school responsible? We have seen that children who come to school are vastly different. Do we wish to encourage those differences or reduce them? Is there a desired pattern of development? Can we expect the same performance of all students in school? What is a comprehensive program of education that will help children learn and mature? How can we maintain a balance in school programs? What is an adequate educational offering? The instructional supervisor, more than anyone else in school leadership, will answer these very important questions.

In addition, there are a host of instructional issues tied directly to human growth and development. They are, in a sense, dilemmas for the supervisor because they present value-laden choices that can only be answered in terms of a conception of the purpose of education. Following are some issues that are representative of the many other decision areas.

Table 4.1 Recommended Professional Examiners for Certifying Students for Special Education Programs

Classification	Recommended Professional Examiner
Crippled and Special Health Problems	Heart Specialists Orthopedist Pediatrician Neurologist Physician
Deaf and Hard-of-Hearing	Audiologist Otologist Otolaryngologist
Neurologically Impaired	Physician
Learning Disabled	Neurologist Psychologist
Visually Handicapped	Ophthalmologist Optometrist

Testing

In order to meet individual needs of students, it is first necessary to assess them in a meaningful way. Schools rely heavily on testing to achieve this insight, measuring everything from personality to intelligence. In schools throughout the nation, for instance, psychometrists regularly administer the Stanford-Binet, Wechsler (WISC), and Otis-Lennon tests to identify the "intelligence" of students. These scores are interpreted as in Table 4.2 and given to teachers as one source of information for planning instruction.

The problem with such scores is that they depend heavily on verbal skills, hearing, vocabulary, and syntax and can be culturally biased. They also can easily lead to a simplistic labeling of students—redbirds, bluejays, and buzzards. More recently, researchers have uncovered multiple forms of intelligence that can be measured and prove useful in determining student needs.[13]

How much testing should be done with students? How should testing and the results of testing be utilized? What safeguards can be built for error or rapid changes in the developmental pattern of the student? These are fair questions for any supervisor and possible sources of concern by classroom teachers.

Other Means of Assessment

Portfolio Assessment is one means of evaluating progress of students. It supplements test information with school examples of student work, provides a teaching tool, and serves as a means of alternative assessment in elementary school programs. A portfolio is a carefully created portrait of what a student knows and can do. Supervisors can help teachers develop this means of alternative assessment and also help teachers select the contents of portfolios.

Life Skills provide another means of assessing student progress in schools. The Wiles-Bondi Life Skills Program (see Table 4.3) has been implemented in a number of school districts to assess those skills identified as essential in the next century. Actual teaching for those life skills occurs with examples of student activities and skill mastery documented in student folders or portfolios.

Authentic Assessment is another means of measuring whether students are ready for the challenges of the next century. One use of authentic assessment is to measure whether students have developed a global consciousness. Global education has become a focus of study in many school districts. How can supervisors assist teachers to design more authentic assessments with regard to measuring students' understanding of global education? What sort of assessments might be used? These and other questions will pose challenges to supervisors as they prepare teachers to teach in the new century.

Grouping and Placement

In most elementary, middle, and secondary schools, teachers group students in order to provide more meaningful instruction. As a rule of thumb, for each year in school,

Table 4.2 The Meaning of I.Q. Scores (Stanford-Binet)

The Child Whose IQ Is:	Equals or Exceeds (percent)	The Child Whose IQ Is:	Equals or Exceeds (percent)
160	1 out of 10,000	101	52
156	3 out of 10,000	100	50
152	8 out of 10,000	99	48
148	2 out of 1,000	98	45
144	4 out of 1,000	97	43
140	7 out of 1,000	96	40
136	99	95	38
135	98	94	36
134	98	93	34
133	98	92	31
132	97	91	29
131	97	90	27
130	97	89	25
129	96	88	23
128	96	87	21
127	95	86	20
126	94	85	18
125	94	84	16
124	93	83	15
123	92	82	14
122	91	81	12
121	90	80	11
120	89	79	10
119	88	78	9
118	86	77	8
117	85	76	8
116	84	75	6
115	82	74	6
114	80	73	5
113	79	72	4
112	77	71	4
111	75	70	3
110	73	69	3
109	71	68	3
108	69	67	2
107	66	66	2
106	64	65	2
105	62	65	2
104	60	64	1
103	57	63	1
102	55	62	1

Source: Reproduced with the permission of the publishers from *Supplementary Guide for the Revised Stanford-Binet Scale* (L) by Rudolph Pinter, Anna Dragositz, and Rose Kushner. Stanford: Stanford University Press, 1944, p. 135.

Table 4.3 Wiles-Bondi Life Skills

Life Skills for Youth	Indicators
1. Achievement	a. Better grade averages in school b. Participation in honors programs c. Graduates from high school d. Continues education/training after high school
2. Organization	a. Attends school daily b. Completes homework c. Is punctual to class/meetings d. Keeps a personal calendar e. Completes tasks
3. Problem Solving	a. Can solve word problems b. Possesses analysis skills/synthesis skills/evaluation skills
4. Quest for Knowledge	a. Reads a variety of print for purpose or pleasure b. Enters training programs for purpose or pleasure c. Participates in cultural activities d. Is enthused about learning e. Will learn a new language
5. Good Mental and Physical Habits	a. Participates in exercise program b. Is aware of physical growth patterns c. Can make right choices about smoking/drugs/alcohol d. Can deal with stress e. Can reduce aggressive behaviors f. Practices safe sex or abstinence to reduce unwanted pregnancies and disease
6. Cooperative Behavior	a. Can work with peers/small groups to get tasks done b. Exhibits mannerly and courteous behavior c. Knows etiquette d. Serves as a peer teacher e. Has respect for others
7. Self-Concept	a. Can introduce self to others b. Can deal with strangers c. Volunteers for tasks d. Can handle increased responsibility e. Has empathy for handicapped f. Can interact comfortably with persons of different races and cultures
8. Open to Change	a. Can learn new tasks/jobs when there is a need b. Can adjust to changes in employer/employee status (e.g., shared decision making) c. Can re-tool for new jobs/skills d. Willing to employ new technology in getting jobs done e. Can adjust to travel and relocation when necessary f. Willing to change patterns of behavior that hinder work
9. Family Oriented	a. Enjoys children and willing to spend time with them b. Sees importance of a stable home c. Has allegiance to community
10. Future Oriented	a. Sees the internationalization of economics and interdependence of nations as important to the welfare of our country b. Practices positive consumer habits including saving for the future c. Envisions an education beyond compulsory schooling and first job d. Becomes a life-long learner

the range in a given class is one year (e.g., a sixth-grade class will have a six-year range in reading). Grouping is generally thought to be a sound educational practice.

There are, of course, real problems with grouping students. Most school schedules, for instance, are static. Once a student is grouped for two or more subjects, he or she is automatically sectioned for others. Grouping also fails to acknowledge change in students such as those proposed by Piaget for the middle years. Low achievement groupings can often cause disruptive and emotional behavior problems among students. Finally, the Federal District Court of Washington, DC, ruled in 1976 that ability grouping was unconstitutional because it was discriminatory against students of certain racial and socioeconomic backgrounds.

Obviously, the practice of grouping students found in over 80 percent of all districts in the United States is laden with issues. The validity of grouping students depends heavily on the supervisor's definition of education and the mission of the school in question.[14] Placing students by ability does not help students, according to evidence gained from studies conducted in the 1980s and 1990s by researchers such as Slavin, Oaks, and others.

Class Size and Student Achievement

The achievement effects of reducing class size has become a legal, as well as an academic, question. By 1995, 27 schools had legal challenges in which unequal funding among districts was an issue. Among the inequalities cited by poorer districts were larger class sizes.

Although advantages of smaller class sizes provide good arguments—teachers can focus on individual needs, students have more opportunities to actively participate in learning experiences, and so on—a review of studies on class size (many of which were poorly controlled, however) does not support better student achievement when class sizes are lowered. Effects of class size on achievement are extremely small.

If the expectation for its impact on achievement is realistically modest, reducing class size may be an appropriate policy. However, it cannot be seen as an adequate policy in itself for significantly accelerating student achievement.[15]

Pull-Out Programs

A phenomenon of the past twenty years has been the "pull-out" program—a special program superimposed over regular class time and characterized by students leaving and returning during the regular class period. Without question, pull-out programs for special students is one way to meet the real needs of those children. What concerns supervisors, however, is the effect of that program on those who remain.

If, for example, students are pulled out of a middle school class twice a week for a gifted program, should the teacher stall and await their return before introducing new material or simply hold the gifted students responsible for getting the new material themselves? This type of situation, incidentally, has done more to harm gifted education than any other we have witnessed.

The supervisor, in dealing with pull-out programs, is wrestling with the concept of the majority program—what every student should experience. If pull-outs are so frequent that they totally disrupt the continuity of the majority program, then there ceases to be a majority program. In too many schools today, there is no common denominator in the curriculum. Supervisors, as instructional designers, must confront this issue in meeting the needs of both special students and regular students.

Outcomes-Based Education

To professionals, outcomes-based education (OBE) makes great sense. If the outcomes of students are defined, the curriculum and instruction can be organized to attain those outcomes. The bottom line is that the product defines the process.

Opponents of OBE in the 1990s rallied in opposition stating that outcomes defined were often ill-defined, weren't measurable and, in many cases, were not really the mission of the school. One outcome receiving great attention was tolerance of others. Determining how to teach tolerance and for which groups were areas of contention.

The issue of outcomes-based education for the supervisor ultimately is, What is worth knowing and what is the purpose of schooling? Sharp disagreements on those issues have existed since public education began in the United States.[16]

Mainstreaming

Mainstreaming ceased to be an issue per se since the passage of P.L. 94-142, when it became law. Still, as supervisors attend staff meetings and develop I.E.P.'s (Individual Education Programs) for handicapped students, they do have a great deal of input in defining mainstreaming. Supervisors must have a larger concept of education in order to keep mainstreaming in balance and as a contributing factor in providing quality education.

The idea behind mainstreaming is to place a child into an environment that will be of most benefit to his or her educational experience. The "least restrictive environment" clause of P.L. 94-142 was intended to produce the most normal situation for any child who suffered a handicap. The definition of benefit to the student and normal condition for learning is widely open to professional interpretation. Mainstreaming is a good example of how our knowledge of human development directs our definition and design of classroom learning.

Inclusion, which carries mainstreaming to its greatest level, was discussed earlier in this chapter. Training of regular teachers, orienting parents, and preparing students for inclusion will challenge the skills of supervisors in today's schools.

Subsidized Care Programs

Few programs sponsored by the federal government in the 1960s received as much attention as the "free" breakfast and lunch programs for indigent children. These highly visible educational programs were begun because of the belief that a student with an empty stomach cannot be a good student. Although opponents argued that taxpayers were feeding children in the name of education, almost anyone who went to public school in the United States during the 1940s and 1950s was also subsidized every time he or she bought a school lunch.

At stake in all of these care programs—programs involving food, health care, school supplies, medical care, and other assistance—is the notion of the scope of the school's responsibility. If human development research tells us that children come to school unequal, it is not dishonest to treat them as equals? And if they are recognized as unequal, does the school have a responsibility to provide minimum assistance to them in their formative years? This question is very important to the design of curriculum and instruction and is one that all supervisors must satisfy prior to assisting other teachers in improving instruction.

Compensatory Programs

During the early days of school desegregation in the 1960s, a revolutionary concept was proposed that has since had a major impact on all school programming. The major theme was that some children would need more assistance from the school than others to compensate for environmental deficiencies in their home life. This idea resulted in massive federal programs such as Title I, Head Start, and Follow Through. From these legislated programs came a variety of novel initiates to compensate, including small teacher–pupil ratios, special materials, teacher aides, and parent helpers.

For supervisors, the notion of compensation and purposeful preference of some students over others, for whatever reason, is a powerful one. At issue is the notion of fairness, access to educational experience, and school mission. It may be easier to understand this issue by looking at programs for gifted students which obviously provide a superior learning environment, special materials, and highly trained teachers. Supervisors, because of their role, have the potential to define this balance between the regular offering and the compensated programs of the school.

Gifted Education

In the 1990s, no program in school is quite as controversial as gifted education programs. A positive side of these programs is the curriculum provided for an obviously superior group of students who would otherwise suffer in the regular classroom. A negative side is the use of superficial intelligence tests for identification, tremendous social pressure from parents to have their child in such programs, and the possible misuse of educational resources to favor a small minority of students.

The gifted education program raises questions about whether the public school is obligated to educate these students and what the core of the general program should be. Many parents of nongifted students have argued since 1972 that their children are also special and, if better instructional programs are offered for gifted students, their children should also have access to them. Although finance is a critical variable in this instance, supervisors must be able to rationalize the increased value of such experiences for a limited number of students at public expense.

Health and Sex Education

The AIDS problem has resulted in health education and sex education in some form in most school districts. Because of the controversy about the definition of morality, these programs are often masked by euphemisms: life education, family living, growing up in America. Schools teach this information to students because social statistics indicate it is sorely needed and because educational philosophy has generally accepted human development as a critical planning variable. This is also one of the most dangerous areas of the curriculum in terms of public opinion.

Supervisors regularly encounter citizen groups who oppose part of the school program. A label like "sex education" or even "humanism" can be a tinderbox for controversy. The "Rainbow Curriculum" in New York City in the 1990s resulted in the ouster of its school superintendent. Including topics such as understanding and tolerance of different races and ethnic groups and understanding life styles of homosexuals led to the controversy about such programs. The supervisor must be knowledgeable about human development and be able to rationalize health education programs to defuse potentially unpleasant encounters.

Punitive Discipline

There is widespread disagreement among teachers and educational theoreticians on the subject of discipline. In particular, the use of punitive discipline measures such as paddling and social isolation highlights questions about normal development and the influence of certain adult behaviors on child growth. Nationally, 4 percent of all students in public schools are paddled each year.

Arguments against paddling, offered by the National Center for the Study of Corporal Punishment at Temple University, include "increase in the amount of disruption and aggression, a decrease in genuine learning time, and a decline in school morale."[17] School supervisors should see all forms of student punishment in terms of the school program rather than historical precedent. A wealth of literature exists from which to form an educated opinion on this important question.

Grading Policies

In working with classroom teachers, school supervisors will find that grading is another subject over which there is a wide difference of opinion. Grades mean different things to different people, and school attempts to experiment with new grading patterns have not been widely successful. Ultimately, grading is a human development question because grades assess growth. At issue in the area of grading is the question of student capacity, fairness, and effect on subsequent student learning.

In many school districts, questioning grading practices may lead to a broader questioning of the entire program. Supervisors should be knowledgeable about what educational research says about grading in schools and should be able to clarify issues about grading for teachers. Ultimately, the supervisor's position on how grading should be handled will reflect his or her understanding of human development and the purpose of schooling.

Language Usage

A controversy that is not currently being addressed is the role of language in schools. We know that most school learning is directly dependent on the use of words to form thoughts and to communicate. Small children with big vocabularies, for instance, score higher on I.Q. tests and, therefore, receive preferred placement in learning groups. We also know that a degree of cultural bias exists in language use, since most school districts demand that only standard English be used to communicate in learning.

Supervisors must wrestle with this instructional problem because many students now do not speak standard English. In many parts of the United States in the 1990s, Spanish is the majority language. In addition, dialects and social class language patterns dominate some communication in certain school districts. The effects of language on school achievement and the role of language in learning can only be clarified in terms of the larger question of growth and development in students and the role of the school in providing an adequate education for the future.

Cultural and Sex Bias

Another issue related directly to human development is the question of cultural and sex bias found in schools. Traditionally, schools have taught students a set of values that are Anglo-Saxon, Protestant, and white in their orientation. Additionally, many of the values taught in schools possess a degree of sexism in defining roles and relationships. Supervisors should view these historical precedents critically to evaluate how they affect young people growing up today.

During the past two decades, progress has been made in removing obvious cultural and sex bias from school books and other learning materials. Less has been done to help teachers recognize and combat these conditions. Supervisors must first be aware of these human development questions before they can help teachers to improve instructional opportunities for students.

Retention

New studies have indicated that retention does nothing to increase student achievement and, in reality, results in lower self-concepts and greater failure rates. In the early 1900s, Florida and California introduced legislation to eliminate retention in lower grades.[18]

Acceleration

Educational acceleration as a curricular option has been a diverse issue among educators and parents since its first documented use in St. Louis in 1862.[19]

With computer programs and other technology providing new means of acceleration, this issue will demand attention of supervisory leaders. Students may not only accelerate beyond their normal grade level, but average students behind in grade level can now catch up through self-pacing computer programs.

With states experimenting with reducing four-year college programs to three years, high schools have also adopted acceleration practices. Advanced placement and early admission to college (including concurrent enrollment) have been available in high schools for some time, but other means of acceleration are now being used, including mentorship (studying with an expert or professional for credit) and curriculum compacting (testing out or passing previously mastered skills).

In the elementary and middle schools, nongraded classrooms, early entrance to schools, and grade skipping are used, but with an evaluation first of whether acceleration is developmentally appropriate.

DEVELOPMENT IN ADULTS

Although beyond the scope of this text, the role of the supervisor in promoting development in adults should also be mentioned. If the growth of teachers is the key to improved learning experiences for children, knowledge of adult development is a prerequisite for successful practice.

The literature on adult development is massive even though organized inquiry is relatively new (the study of gerontology, for instance, began in 1945). In the literature are various models, conceptions of adulthood, task stages, and implications for adult learning. We will address each of these separately in a brief form.

By far the best-known model of adult development is that of Erik Erikson in his Stages of Growth. This four-tier conception identifies the following:

1. *Role Identity*—Seeking to emerge from the role confusion of adolescence by projecting ideas found acceptable by other adults.
2. *Intimacy*—Committing to ongoing relationships as opposed to remaining isolated.
3. *Generativity*—Engaging in productive activity including helping to guide the next generation
4. *Ego integrity*—Accepting self and his or her lifestyle as an adult.[20]

A widely accepted definition of adulthood does not exist, although there are many conceptions of becoming an adult. In Muslim countries, for example, being an adult (Mukallaf) means accepting a moral and legal responsibility as well as physical maturity. The traditional Chinese way of viewing the process (Confucian) is a formal capping ceremony at age twenty and then marking milestones such as becoming a spouse, parent, scholar, public servant, and retiree. In the United States, an extended life expectancy makes age a poor criteria for adulthood. A better measure, and a more useful one for supervisors, is to view the tasks an adult must deal with in various stages of development.

In her classic book *Passages,* Gail Sheehy identifies numerous tasks that we must confront as we grow older.[21] For young adults (twenties to thirties), she identifies leaving the family, getting into the adult world, projecting an identity, and formulating a dream as major tasks. Events such as marriage, a first job, travel and exploration, becoming educated, and having children dominate this time. In this period, major life patterns are established. Young adults are confident and optimistic.

People in their thirties and forties, says Sheehy, develop an established pattern to their lives. The daily existence is more serious, more predictable, more responsible. Many question the patterns of their twenties. Jobs, marriages, and identity may reform. In the words of Proust, "The little boy in man dies hard. . . . sometimes it never does."[22]

In the late thirties and forties, people begin to view life from a different perspective. The dreams of their twenties may remain unfulfilled or have been overrun by circumstance. Reflection caused by the death of a parent injects a new time consciousness for future planning. For some individuals, a disassembly of self occurs, and feelings of aliveness or stagnation may dominate.

Finally, in the late forties and fifties, a "true adult" emerges who, by Erikson's model, becomes self-accepting and increasingly other-centered. If the tasks of the forties are not accomplished, the individual becomes stale and grows old. Those who have found a new acceptance and meaning may experience considerable personality growth and interest expansion.

In working with adults, supervisors will discover that there is no highly predictable plateau of development. It will be necessary to consider each teacher and ask, "What sort of tasks might be controlling this person's behavior?" From such an analysis should come a strategy for communication, assistance, and support (see Figure 4.7). Remember, the growth of each teacher affects the growth of many more children.

Some general principles for working with adults are outlined in Table 4.4. Further readings in this area are highly recommended.

THE ROLE OF THE SUPERVISOR

In concluding this chapter, it is important to review the role of the supervisor. We have defined supervision as a leadership role that is concerned with improving learning experiences for students. We have observed that this important educational role sits at the juncture of most communication and decision making in school settings. Supervisors link district offices with schools and classrooms. They also are highly educated professionals who can provide resources and knowledge of teachers and other leaders in the school system.

Supervision is first about helping people grow and develop. It is the job of the supervisor in education to work with others to provide an improved process for aiding the growth and development of students.

1. Have large experience bases and learn in terms of that background.
2. Approach adult learning based on needs.
3. Process information slower because there is more to contemplate.
4. Have a heightened fear of failure or self-esteem loss.
5. Learn better in a participative/sharing format.
6. Have time constraints—there are many competing events.
7. Have important reservoirs of experience.
8. Have developed their own reality and believe it.
9. Have different strengths and weaknesses as individuals.
10. Like children, have various learning handicaps.
11. Go through developmental stages which correlate with needs.
12. Are always interested in the interrelatedness of learning.
13. Sometimes use educational opportunities only to socialize.
14. Are anxiety prone and often need reassurance.
15. Are in charge of their own learning.

Figure 4.7 Principles of Teaching and Learning for Adults

Table 4.4 Strategies for Adult Learners Based on Age and Stage

	Age		
	18–20	**30–40**	**50–65**
Strategy	Lecture	Contract work	Peer instruction
Motivation	Needs credentials Has limited skills	Self-motivated Interested in self-expansion	Recreational/social learners Secure in career
Classroom	Normal	Mixture; use hotel conference room, etc.	Any location
Environment	Formal school	Less formal	Relaxed
Teaching Materials	As required by subject	Text and reference discussion	Whatever is needed
Evaluation of Students	Grading system using a scale such as A,B,C, etc.	Pass/fail	Pass/fail or audit
Techniques	Lecture	Small groups Short attention span Schedule breaks to serve as social activities	Instruction must be slower, louder Bigger print for written material Illumination must be brighter Easily bored, will not waste time Short attention span

To be effective in this role, supervisors must be generally knowledgeable about how humans develop. They must develop and possess a model or conception about growth and use that "big picture" in reviewing practice. Supervisors must be able to see student development in terms of physical, social, emotional, and intellectual maturation.

A special skill that the supervisor must possess is the ability to distinguish between normal and unique development in students. In cases of students with special needs, the supervisor must be able to design educational experiences that promote growth without undermining the basic program of schooling. A knowledge of resources to assist such students is a valuable asset for supervisors.

Supervisors must be aware of the issues in education that are directly tied to their conceptions of human development. A dozen such issues were provided to illustrate how knowledge about human growth can be interpreted in the public school classroom.

The role of the supervisor is to help teachers and other educational leaders understand issues and make wise decisions affecting student education. The force with which the supervisor pursues this role depends on his or her conception of leadership in education.

SUMMARY

The challenge of supervisors in the last decade of the twentieth century is to help teachers define educational experiences for their students. The area of human development is the base for all educational planning, since schools exist to assist learners in growing and developing. Supervisors must be knowledgeable and skilled in all facets of human development.

At no time in the history of this country have educational leaders faced more difficult problems in preparing programs for our young. The break-down of the family, health, and poverty problems of young tax our resources. Issues about what is appropriate to teach our young and how to do it are constantly debated in boardrooms, legislative meeting rooms, and the halls of Congress.

School supervisors must help educators, parents, and community leaders sort through issues that divide us and keep the focus on what we educators are all about—that is, helping young people grow and develop so they can become well adjusted, knowledgeable adults in the new century.

IMPLICATIONS FOR SUPERVISION

1. How many special children exist in your school district? What are the most dominant categories? What programs address their needs?

2. Does your district have a directory of resources for children with special needs? Is there a "network of specialists"?

3. How many teachers in your district are young? Mature? Quite senior? How are their various developmental needs addressed?

4. Can you describe "life's flow" from infancy to senility? How is your description organized? What are the implications for teaching and learning?

∾ CASE STUDY 1 ∾

Given the many social statistics about youth in America (crime, pregnancy, drugs), you, as the instructional leader, have decided to establish a new teacher-led guidance program in your school. By conducting an extensive need assessment, you are able to get teachers involved and motivated for this type of program. The program is scheduled and "ready to go" when, suddenly, you're in hot water. The parents in your community neither understand nor support this type of role for the school. One local church group discussed your program at length on Sunday and passed a resolution to "stop this usurpation of church and family rights." Over one hundred members of this church group have signed up to speak at Tuesday's school board meeting on this issue. On your desk is an urgent message from the assistant superintendent indicating that he needs to speak with you.

Questions
1. What is the proper relationship between the school and society in terms of addressing the growing needs of youth?
2. What moves would you make prior to speaking with the Assistant Superintendent?
3. How far would you be willing to go to defend the new instructional program being planned?

∾ CASE STUDY 2 ∾

It is unusual for a supervisor to be "summoned" by a building faculty, but that was essentially what was happening in this instance. Officially, of course, the building principal had requested that the supervisor come to a monthly faculty meeting to address the group about the new inclusion model for students with handicaps. Under this new program, most special students would be placed in a regular classroom under the direction of a regular classroom teacher, and the former special education teachers act as consulting educators for that teacher. A few phone calls prior to the meeting, however, confirmed for the supervisor that this meeting would be emotional.

For the regular faculty, these special students were an imposition. Each one required special attention, a task for which most teachers felt they were unprepared. Further, the presence of these students slowed down instruction and penalized the "normal" children in the classroom. Finally, some of these children with handicaps were disruptive and even physically dangerous to other children. Apparently, this was happening regularly in the new inclusion model, and the faculty was demanding another kind of program for special children in the school.

Questions
1. Why have schools moved toward an "inclusion" model with a consultative role for the previous special education teachers?
2. While students with handicaps are being mainstreamed and are protected under Public Law 94–142, what are the rights of the regular students in the school?
3. Outline the steps this supervisor should take to make this an orderly and professional discussion and review.

SUGGESTED LEARNING ACTIVITIES

1. Trace the development in the past thirty years of legislation and court decisions that protect and guarantee the rights of special students in school.
2. Outline a parent awareness program to help parents understand and support special programs in a school building.
3. Develop a set of procedures to assess the instructional contribution of special programs to the regular or general curriculum in a school.
4. Prepare a position paper on inclusion.
5. Prepare a list, with description, of assessment procedures that can be used in an elementary, middle, or high school.

ADDITIONAL READING

Apple, M. "The Politics of Curriculum and Teaching," *NASSP Bulletin* 75, 532 (February 1991): 39–50.

Apps, Jerold. *The Adult Learner on Campus.* Chicago: Follett, 1981.

Bennett, Kathleen P., and LeCompte, Margaret D. *The Way Schools Work: A Sociological Analysis of Education.* White Plains, NY: Longman, 1990.

Bergevin, Paul. *A Philosophy for Adult Education.* New York: Seabury Press, 1967.

Clinton, B. "President Clinton's Plan for Education," *Phi Delta Kappan,* 74, 131 (October 1992): 134–138.

Fine, Michelle. *Framing Dropouts: Notes on the Politics of an Urban Public High School.* Albany: State University of New York Press, 1991.

Fine, Michelle. *Notes on the Politics of an Urban Public High School.* Albany: State University of New York Press, 1991.

Finn, Jeremy D. *School Engagement and Students at Risk.* Washington, DC: U.S. Department of Education, 1993.

The Forgotten Half Pathways to Success for America's Youth and Young Families. Final Report, Youth and America's Future, The William T. Grant Foundation Commission on Work, Family, Citizenship, November 1988.

Giroux, H. "Curriculum, Multiculturalism, and the Politics of Identity," *NASSP Bulletin* 76, 548 (December 1992): 1–11.

Glatthorn, Allan A. *Alternatives in Education: Schools and Programs.* New York: Dodd, Mead, & Company, 1975.

Gross, Ronald. *The Lifelong Learner.* New York: Simon & Schuster, 1977.

Havighurst, Robert. *Development Tasks and Education.* New York: David McKay, 1972.

Holdzkom, D. "The Influences of State Agencies on Curriculum," *NASSP Bulletin* 76, 548 (December 1992): 13–23.

Kidd, J. R. *How Adults Learn.* New York: Association Press, 1973.

Knapp, Michael S., and Shields, Patrick M., eds. *Better Schooling for the Children of Poverty: Alternatives to Conventional Wisdom.* Berkeley, CA: McCutchan Publishing Corporation, 1991.

Knowles, Malcolm. *The Adult Learner: A Neglected Species.* Houston: Gulf Publishing Co., 1973.

Krueger, M. "Everyone Is an Exception: Assumptions to Avoid in the Sex Education Classroom," *Phi Delta Kappan* 74 (March 1993): 569–572.

LeCompte, Margaret Diane, and Dworkin, Anthony Gary. *Giving Up on School: Student Dropouts and Teacher Burnouts.* Newbury Park, CA: Corwin Press, Inc., 1991.

Lindeman, Edward. *The Meaning of Adult Education.* New York: New Republic, Inc., 1926.

Males, M. "Schools, Society and Teen Pregnancy," *Phi Delta Kappan* 74 (March 1993): 566–568.

Maslow, Abraham. *Toward a Psychology of Being.* New York: D. Van Nostrand, 1968.

McLagan, Patricia. *Helping Others Learn: Designing Programs for Adults.* Reading, MA: Addison-Wesley, 1978.

Miller, Harry. *Teaching and Learning in Adult Education.* New York: Macmillan, 1964.

Natriello, Gary; McDill, Edward L.; and Pallas, Aaron M. *Schooling Disadvantaged Children Racing*

Against Catastrophe. New York: Teachers College, 1990.

Nelson, F. "What Evangelicals Expect from Public School Administrators," *Educational Leadership* 45 (May 1988): 41–42.

Newmann, Fred M., ed. *Student Engagement and Achievement in American Secondary Schools.* New York: Teachers College Press, 1992.

Ravitch, D. "A Culture in Common," *Educational Leadership* 50 (December/January 1992): 8–11.

Robinson, Russell. *Helping Adults Learn and Change.* Milwaukee: Omni Books, 1979.

Rogers, Carl. *Freedom to Learn.* Columbus, OH: Charles Merrill, 1969.

Sadker, M., and Sadker, D. "Gender Equity and Educational Reform," *Educational Leadership* 47 (December 1989): 45–47.

Sheehy, Gail. *Passages: Predictable Crises of Adult Life.* New York: E. P. Dutton, 1976.

Slavin, Robert E.; Karweit, Nancy L.; and Madden, Nancy A. *Effective Programs for Students at Risk.* Boston: Allyn and Bacon, 1989.

Smith, Robert. *Learning How to Learn.* Chicago: Follett, 1982.

Tough, Allen. *Adult's Learning Projects.* Austin: University Press, 1979.

Vann, K., and Kunjufu, J. "The Importance of an Afrocentric, Multicultural Curriculum," *Phi Delta Kappan* 74 (February 1993): 490–491.

Wehlage, G. G. et al. *Reducing the Risk: Schools as Communities of Support.* London: The Falmer Press, 1989.

West, Lynda L. *Effective Strategies for Dropout Prevention of At-Risk Youth.* Gaithersburg, MD: Aspen Publications, Inc., 1991.

Zirkel, P. "Handicapped Parents," *Phi Delta Kappan* 72 (October 1990): 164–167.

Zirkel, P. "Home Schooling," *Phi Delta Kappan* (January 1991): 408–409.

Zirkel, P. "Special Education: Needless Adversaries?" *Phi Delta Kappan* 74 (June 1993): 809–810.

BOOKS TO REVIEW

Alexander, K., and Alexander, M. *American Public School Law.* St. Paul: West Publishing Co., 1992.

America 2000: An Education Strategy. Washington: U.S. Department of Education, 1991.

Elkind, D. *Parenting Your Teenager in the '90s.* Rosemont, NJ: Modern Learning Press, 1993. See also Elkind's *The Hurried Child* and *A Sympathetic Understanding of Children: Birth to 16.* Boston: Allyn and Bacon, 1974.

Giangreco, M. et al. *Choosing Options and Accommodations for Children (COACH).* Baltimore: Brookes Publishing Co., 1993.

Harmin, M. *Inspiring Active Learning.* Alexandria, VA: ASCD, 1994.

Joyce, B.; Wolf, J.; and Calhoun, E. *The Self-Reviewing School.* Alexandria, VA: ASCD, 1993.

CHAPTER 5

DESIGNING AND DEVELOPING CURRICULUM

Curriculum is the foundation upon which the practice of supervision rests. Without the direction and intent of a curriculum plan, there can be no anticipated effect from instruction. Since schooling is thought to be a purposeful activity, and teaching the act of imparting meaning, supervisors must be completely familiar with the process of curriculum development. Failure to understand the whole will make tinkering with the parts meaningless.

The word *curriculum* comes from the Latin word *currere,* which means to "run" or "run the course." With time, the "race" became the course of study or the learning path. In a school setting, the curriculum is the means by which the purpose of education is activated. Supervisors, by their role, are regularly in a position to give meaning to the curriculum by emphasizing or highlighting one thing over another; to suggest team teaching for an instructional pattern is skew the curriculum by its form of delivery. An understanding of this critical framework undergirds successful supervisory practice.

As a point of origin in understanding curriculum development, it is very important to acknowledge the value dimension of all curricula. Since a curriculum exists to teach, it also exists to change. The act of going from one state of knowing, or acting, or feeling to another means that values or preferences will be employed in designing curriculum. If formalized, we could say that all curriculum reflects philosophy and the values that support it.

THE HISTORY OF CURRICULUM DEVELOPMENT

Educators in public schools in America do not share a common philosophy, and this fact makes prescribing behavior for a teacher in a classroom difficult. Traditionally,

American education has promoted three major themes: (1) enculturation, including the passing of knowledge and heritage; (2) socialization, including preparation for participation in a democracy; and (3) liberation or the development of the individual person. The focus of the curriculum on any one of these, to the exclusion or diminution of the others, would redefine the role of the teacher. Teaching can be thought of as the art of making wise decisions from among a multitude of choices. Supervision is the process of assisting teachers in such decision making.

There are many philosophic labels to describe belief systems that might guide the schooling process. These names reflect differences in the degree of teacher control (structure) of the learning process and the degree to which the substance and process of education are fixed. Educators who believe that the "stuff" of learning is predetermined and unchallengeable and that the teacher should have absolute control of the process of learning would be called a "perennialist." By contrast, an educator who fully recognizes the uniqueness of the learner and who sees the teacher's role as that of a guide or facilitator might be called an "existentialist." In between these extreme definitions of education are "realists," "idealists," and "experimentalists." These five stereotypic philosophies and their beliefs are compared in Table 5.1.

Having established that supervision is dependent on curriculum and that curriculum is undergirded by philosophy and values, we can now proceed to the process of designing and developing curriculum, where supervisors help teachers make decisions about the learning act.

THE NEW SCHOOL LADDER

Over the past three hundred years, schools in America have changed their purpose and form numerous times, reflecting the sometimes coarse and dynamic nature of our society. By the late nineteenth century, a graded "ladder" of public schooling was established, ensuring passage from first to twelfth grade for those capable. In the twentieth century, the only adjustment to this graded hierarchy of learning was a modification of the intermediate grades from 7–9 (junior high) to a 6–8 arrangement (middle school), resulting from an awareness of human development and its impact on the schooling process.

By contrast, as we approach the twenty-first century, it appears that the ladder of education may be extended downward to birth and upward to death. Lifelong education, a conception in the middle of the twentieth century, may become a social necessity in the next century. Social concerns such as illegitimacy, youth crime, changing work conditions, and an aging population require an expanded role for schooling in the future.

American education has evolved into a four-tier ladder: early childhood (K–3), later childhood (4–5), preadolescent (6–8), and adolescent (9–12). Significant is the subtle change from a content-based curriculum found earlier in this century to a curriculum rationalized by stages of development in students. This larger reorientation over a forty-year period has caused schools and teachers to address student differences and specialness and to adapt the curriculum in many ways to individualize and

Table 5.1 Five Philosophies Compared

	Perennialism	Idealism	Realism	Experimentalism	Existentialism
Reality Ontology	A world of reason and God	A world of the mind	A world of things	A world of experience	A world of existing
Truth (Knowledge) Epistemology	Reason and revelation	Consistency of ideas	Correspondence and sensation (as we see it)	What works What is	Personal, subjective choice
Goodness Axiology	Rationality	Imitation of ideal self, person to be emulated	Laws of nature	The public test	Freedom
Teaching Reality	Disciplinary subjects and doctrine	Subject of the mind—literary, philosophical, religious	Subjects of physical world—math, science	Subject matter of social experiences—social studies	Subject matter of choice—art, ethics, philosophy
Teaching Truth	Discipline of the mind via drill	Teaching ideas via lecture, discussion	Teaching for mastery, of information—demonstrate, recite	Problem-solving, project method	Arousing personal responses—questioning
Teaching Goodness (Values)	Disciplining behavior (to reason)	Imitating heroes and other exemplars	Training in rules of conduct	Making group decisions in light of consequences	Awakening self to responsibility
Why Schools Exist	To reveal reason and God's will	To sharpen the mind and intellectual processes	To reveal the order of the world and universe	To discover and expand the society we live in to share experiences	To aid children in knowing themselves and their place in society
What Should Be Taught	External truths	Wisdom of the ages	Laws of physical reality	Group inquiry into social problems and social sciences, method and subject together	Unregimented topic areas
Role of the Teacher	Interprets, tells	Reports, person to be emulated	Displays, imparts knowledge	Aids, consultant	Questions, assists student in personal journey
Role of the Student	Passive reception	Receives, memorizes	Manipulates, passive participation	Active participation, contributes	Determines own rules
School's Attitude Toward Change	Truth is eternal, no real change	Truth to be preserved, anti-change	Always coming toward perfection, orderly change	Change is ever-present, a process	Change is necessary at all times

Source: Reprinted with the permission of Simon & Schuster, Inc. from the Merrill/Prentice Hall text *Curriculum Development*, 4/e, pp. 45–46, by Jon Wiles and Joseph Bondi. Copyright © 1993 by Prentice-Hall, Inc.

meet the needs of the school client. It is within this larger context that most school curriculum development has occurred in the 1960–1990 period, and it will be an extension of this new purpose for schooling (full-service, alternative, magnet) that will drive most curriculum work in public schools in the next decade.

As education leaders prepare to enter the new century, there are special and pressing concerns at each of the four levels of schooling presently activated. These concerns will directly influence supervision practice.

Early Childhood

The preschool and lower elementary experiences that make up early childhood education have a thirty-year history of program change and development. In the mid-1960s, with a focus on infant research, educators developed programs to stimulate growth and compensate for deficiency in development. Standard programs such as Head Start, *Sesame Street,* Chapter One, and school breakfast programs reflected that thrust. Social phenomena such as the complete breakdown of the family, rising numbers of illegitimate births, prenatal influences of drugs, child abandonment and abuse, and an increase in detectable defects requiring special treatments all point to change.

Certainly on the horizon are massive increases in parental education programs, earlier and longer school days for young children, a broader spectrum of services delivered through the school (full-service), a continuation of special academic programs such as Chapter One (reading and math), and the use of computers to overcome resistance to learning in a school setting.

Later Childhood

At the upper elementary level (grades 4–5), there is an awareness that foundational understandings of knowledge and social skills are not succeeding. An all-too-common pattern of curriculum redundance, and "holding" will give way to learning acceleration. Teaching basic life skills between ages 10–12 seems appropriate.

Of special importance is saving those students in this age group who have fallen behind and are threatened with continued failure. Dropout prevention programs using tutors, mentors, and other such bridges to the student's home environment will dominate. Also, the continuation of developing thinking skills and other self-directing strategies of learning seems promising at this level.

Preadolescence

The intermediate grades (6–8) have been dominated by the American middle school since the mid-1960s. Providing a broader educational experience for preadolescents, these schools sought to bridge the gulf between childhood and adolescence by slowing down social growth and attending to the emotional needs of learners through programs such as the advisory guidance and elective wheels.

Although we were deeply involved in this new form of intermediate education in its early stages, we now believe that a restructuring effort is again necessary. Compounding the problems are students who are much older than others in their grade, called "overagedness," which is now common in the middle grades. This has contributed to an explosion of youth crime and disruptive behaviors in schools. The issue of relevance, always buried in the sorting and selecting process, is now a pressing issue for intermediate school. Still unanswered is what alternative is appropriate for those not pursuing a serious academic track.

Projecting ahead, education at this level must address even more fully the social needs and behaviors of this developmental stage. Teen pregnancies, substance abuse, teen violence, and dysfunctional and overaged youth without a meaningful curriculum experience are all agendas for the near future.

Adolescence

Most unchanging, but still vital to the American society, is the high school program serving adolescent learners. The current system of graduation requirements and examinations of various sorts causes this institution to lose about one third of its students during the four years of attendance. The tradition of social experiences such as plays and sports events often masks the less-than-desirable social environment characterized by a teen culture featuring sex, drugs, vandalism, and a general purposelessness.

Among the agendas for curriculum development in the near future at this level are a meaningful experience for the majority of students who are not college bound, a significant increase in the access to the so-called "information highway" that is upon us, greater interface with the world of work, and the distinct possibility of a major home schooling movement.

Summary

The new school ladder of the 1990s points to continuing change in a vast number of arenas. All of these planned changes will be enacted through a curriculum development process, and supervisors will be the link between that process and the classroom teacher.

THE PROCESS OF CURRICULUM DEVELOPMENT

Regardless of which philosophy dominates education in the final years of this century, the actions leading to school improvement from within are predictable. Schools improve their state by a traditional cycle of planning that is credited to Ralph Tyler of the University of Chicago. The cycle consists of four steps or stages: analysis, design, implementation, and evaluation. Tyler suggested the cycle in asking these questions which undergird curriculum renewal:

1. What educational purposes should the school seek to attain?
2. How can learning experiences be selected that are likely to be useful in attaining these objectives?

3. How can learning experiences be organized for effective instruction?

4. How can the effectiveness of the learning experiences be evaluated?[1]

This last question, focusing on the evaluation of curriculum development work, suggested a cycle as opposed to a continuum or simple linear process. From this perspective, curriculum development, as a process, is value free, whereas curriculum, as a product, is value laden. Such an orientation allows the curriculum worker to carry out a renewal routine without worrying about a conflict of interest and, in many cases, without true conviction.

Steps in the Development Process

One of Tyler's best students, Hilda Taba, further defined the cycle with a series of practical steps that helped move the development process along:

1. Diagnosis of needs
2. Formulation of objectives
3. Selection of content
4. Organization of content
5. Selection of learning experiences
6. Organization of learning experiences
7. Determination of what to evaluate and the means of doing it[2]

The Statement of Purpose

Curriculum development begins with a statement of purpose or philosophy. John Dewey, America's best-known educational philosopher, saw such purpose statements as a "general theory of educating." One of Dewey's students, Boyd Bode, saw philosophy as a "source of relative consideration." Ralph Tyler, already mentioned for his contribution to the cycle of curriculum development, envisioned philosophy as a "screen for selecting educational objectives." Philosophies, or statements of beliefs, are useful to:

1. Suggest purpose or direction in program development
2. Clarify goals or objectives and learning activities
3. Guide the selection of learning strategies in the classroom
4. Provide direction for the roles of teachers and students
5. Assist in the evaluation of program components

A sample philosophy statement from the highly regarded Garden Hills school in Atlanta, GA, is presented in Figure 5.1.

We feel that the mission of the school is to have each child experience success in learning up to his or her potential.

We feel that each student has unique educational needs, and that the child, teachers, parents and community should work together to identify and establish curriculum to meet the needs.

We support the development of behaviors reflecting honesty, commitment, self-direction and responsibility. We feel that the school does a disservice if it emphasizes academic achievement and fails to teach responsible behavior.

We feel that the school prepares students for global citizenship. They should be able to perform as members of the family of mankind by showing responsibility and caring for people of cultures different from their own, acting as stewards of the earth and its resources and practicing the skills needed to settle differences by peaceful means.

Figure 5.1 Sample Philosophy Statement, Garden Hills Elementary School, Atlanta, GA
Source: *Phi Delta Kappan* 75, 2 (October 1993): 137.

Statements such as those of the Garden Hills faculty result from asking a series of questions that have many possible answers. John McNeil has posed eight questions that are useful in developing philosophical assumptions about our purpose:

1. Is the purpose of school to change, or adapt to, or accept the social order?
2. What can the school do better than any other agency or institution?
3. What objectives should be common to all?
4. Should objectives stress cooperation or competition?
5. Should objectives deal with controversial issues, or only those things for which there is established knowledge?
6. Should attitudes be taught? Fundamental skills? Problem-solving strategies?
7. Should teachers emphasize subject matter or try to create behavior outside of school?
8. Should objectives be based on the needs of the local community? Society in general? Expressed needs of students?[3]

The Statement of Goals

Following the identification of words that might guide decision making, the next step in the curriculum development process is to state broad or "platform" goals that might guide the development of program components. Some of these goals might reflect current problems being addressed by schools. For example, each year a Gallup poll is conducted to assess the public's concerns about schools. Table 5.2 shows the results of the most recent poll, in which the public was asked about the biggest problems for public education.

Another source for goals in school settings might be recommendations from professional bodies. For example, in the National Association for Elementary School

Table 5.2　Gallup Poll on Biggest Problems of Public Schools

What do you think are the biggest problems with which the public schools of this community must deal?

	National Totals %	No Children in School %	Public School Parents %	Nonpublic School Parents %
Lack of proper financial support	21	19	24	13
Drug abuse	16	17	14	9
Lack of discipline	15	15	15	19
Fighting/violence/gangs	13	12	14	17
Standards/quality of education	9	9	8	18
Overcrowded schools	8	6	11	10
Difficulty in getting good teachers	5	4	7	3
Parent's lack of support/interest	4	5	4	3
Integration/segregation, racial discrimination	4	4	4	4
Pupils' lack of interest, poor attitudes, truancy	4	3	4	4
Low pay for teachers	3	4	3	2
Moral standards, dress code, sex/pregnancy	3	3	3	9
There are no problems	1	1	3	2
Miscellaneous**	3	3	2	*
Don't know	14	17	10	16

*Less than one-half of 1%
**A total of 36 different kinds of problems were mentioned by 2% or fewer parents.
(Figures add to more than 100% because of multiple answers.)

Source: S. Elam, L. Rose, and A. Gallup, "The 25th Annual Phi Delta Kappan/Gallup Poll of the Public's Attitude Toward the Public Schools," *Phi Delta Kappan* 75, 2 (October 1993): 137–152.

Principals guide, *Standards for Quality Elementary and Middle Schools,* the following goals are suggested as basic:

- Developing a strong foundation in the fundamentals of reading, writing, and mathematics; and acquiring basic knowledge and understanding in science, social studies, fine arts, health, and physical education.
- Becoming competent verbal and nonverbal communicators—learning to express themselves well in speaking, reading, and writing; to be attentive listeners; and to be comfortable with information technology.
- Working in an environment of excellence marked by high expectations and persistent striving toward mastery levels of achievement.
- Becoming self-motivated, learning to take advantage of opportunities for personal development, and emerging with a lasting zest for learning.
- Respecting and demonstrating appreciation for their peers, their teachers, the staff, and the educational process itself; and practicing tolerance, flexibility, empathy, and equality.
- Developing positive self-concepts, recognizing and valuing their own uniqueness, and accepting both their capabilities and their limitations.[4]

These global goals could serve as organizers for programs with the curriculum, which might in turn be defined further as subjects or courses of study.

Goals may be defined in general or detailed terms, depending on the use of these statements. Stated broadly, they are guidelines for categories of concern. Stated more specifically, they give definition and form to school programs and documents. In their most specific form, behavioral goals and objectives translate intentions into prescriptions for teachers. Supervisors and teachers must be familiar with the behavioral objectives in order to translate district or school goals into classroom strategies.

Educational Objectives

A useful tool for supervisors in giving even more definition to goals are the learning taxonomies developed in the 1960s by Bloom, Krathwohl, and Harrow.[5] These classification systems present depth and complexity issues for the planner who must answer the question, "How much learning?" The Cognitive Domain of objectives is presented in Figure 5.2 and the Affective Domain in Figure 5.3. Using these constructs, a supervisor and a teacher can determine to what degree a goal has been attained by the student.

For example, if a goal for education is being a competent verbal communicator, the natural next question is, "How competent?" Do we want the student to "do as the teacher does" or to "act in this manner when the teacher is not present" or to adopt the school's version of competence to situations outside of the school environment? Do we want this behavior to be a basic response, or should the student value competent verbal communication? The taxonomies allow the supervisor and the teacher to discuss this matter with specificity and to translate the intent of the goals into lessons with prescribed student learning outcomes.

Curriculum Standards

Yet another tool available to supervisors to focus instruction, thereby closing the gap between the planned and experienced curriculum, is the curriculum standard. Standards can considered characterizations or benchmarks of quality in any program, and they may differ from goal and objectives in that they can be quantified and verified. If standards, observable standards, are present in each classroom for which the supervisor is responsible, there is a high probability that a minimum quality controlled program is in place. An example of a program standard in sixth-grade science is presented in Figure 5.4 (p. 154).

A Blueprint for Learning

Between the formal philosophy, the goals and guiding objectives, and the program standards, a blueprint for learning begins to emerge in the school setting. Clearly the "what" and "why" of planning are addressed, and perhaps even the "how" is coming into focus through this deductive reasoning. In some districts, however, goals are constructed in the absence of real data about the students being served. For this rea-

Levels of Cognitive Behavior

	Comprehension (ability to comprehend what is being communicated and make use of the idea without relating it to other ideas or material or seeing fullest meaning)	**Application** (ability to use ideas, principles, theories in new particular and concentrated situations)	**Analysis** (ability to break down a communication into constituent parts in order to make organization of the whole clear)	**Synthesis** (ability to put together parts and elements into a unified organization or whole)	**Evaluation** (ability to judge the value of ideas, procedures, methods, using appropriate criteria)
					Requires synthesis
				Requires analysis	Requires analysis
			Requires application	Requires application	Requires application
		Requires comprehension	Requires comprehension	Requires comprehension	Requires comprehension
Knowledge (ability to recall; to bring to mind the appropriate material)	Requires knowledge	Requires knowledge	Requires knowledge	Requires knowledge	Requires knowledge

Figure 5.2 The Taxonomy of Educational Objectives: Cognitive Domain

Source: From *Taxonomy of Educational Objectives: The Classification of Educational Goals. Handbook I: Cognitive Domain* edited by Benjamin S. Bloom et al. Copyright © 1956 by Longman, Inc. Reprinted with permission of Longman.

Levels of Affective Behavior

Receiving	Responding	Valuing	Organization	Characterization
Receiving (attending; becomes aware of an idea, process, or thing; is willing to notice a particular phenomenon)	**Responding** (makes response at first with compliance, later willingly and with satisfaction)	**Valuing** (accepts worth of a thing, idea or a behavior; prefers it; consistent in responding; develops a commitment to it)	**Organization** (organizes values; determines interrelationships; adapts behavior to value system)	**Characterization** (generalizes certain values into controlling tendencies; emphasis on internal consistency; later integrates these into a total philosophy of life or world view)
				Requires organization of values
			Requires development of values	Requires development of values
		Requires a response	Requires response	Requires a response
	Begins with attending	Begins with attending	Begins with attending	Begins with attending

Figure 5.3 The Taxonomy of Educational Objectives: Affective Domain

Source: From *Taxonomy of Educational Objectives: The Classification of Educational Goals: Handbook II: Affective Domain* by David R. Krathwohl et al. Copyright © 1964 by Longman, Inc. Reprinted with permission of Longman.

PROGRAM

Science

It is the concern of science education that the science program reflects the character of science, becoming a program exploratory in nature; fostering the development of scientifically and technologically knowledgeable citizens; furthering the students' general education; and providing content commensurate with the level of cognitive readiness of students. Further, it is highly desirable that the science program be composed of a variety of components, each designed to meet the varied needs and interests of the students.

PROGRAM STANDARDS

_____ Science is blocked with math at the sixth grade level.

_____ Scheduling options for math and science blocks are at the seventh grade.

_____ Science is taught as a separate discipline at eighth grade.

_____ A remedial program is offered at each grade level.

_____ An on-level program is offered at each grade level.

_____ An advanced level program is offered at each grade level.

_____ Every student has an opportunity to do some laboratory work as a part of his/her course of study.

_____ The science facilities include classroom and laboratory activity areas that adapt well for each course taught.

_____ Each laboratory area or each course taught is provided with adequate supplies and equipment.

_____ Supplementary books, reference books, printed materials, and audiovisual materials representing a considerable range of sophistication and diversity of student interest are provided.

_____ Adequate measures and devices are provided to maximize safety precautions for students and others working in the science classrooms and laboratories as specified in the safety guide.

Figure 5.4 Science Standards as a Checklist

son, another tool for the supervisor is a "needs assessment" that clearly identifies the type of learner being targeted and indicates, by inference, the relevance or appropriateness of the planned learning experiences.

Among the most important information to be made available about learners today is a general profile of the population, some data about the home and community, and information about the students' ability to learn. An outline of a quick needs assessment, by type of data, is suggested in Figure 5.5.

Following a redefinition of goals and objectives based on information about students, the curriculum development process proceeds to further define programs by

The Needs Assessment Framework

I. General Information
    a. Location of school district
    b. Demographic characteristics of immediate area
    c. Natural resources of region
    d. Commercial–industrial data
    e. Income levels of area residents
    f. Special social-economic considerations

II. General Population Characteristics
    a. Population growth patterns
    b. Age, race of population
    c. Educational levels of population
    d. Projected population

III. School Population Characteristics (Ages 3–19)
    a. School enrollment by grade level
    b. Birthrate trends in school district
    c. In-migration, out-migration patterns
    d. Race/sex/religious composition of school district
    e. Years of school completed by persons over 25 years of age
    f. Studies of school dropouts

IV. Programs and Course Offerings in District
    a. Organization of school programs
    b. Programs' concept and rationale
    c. Course offerings
    d. Special program needs

V. Professional Staff
    a. Training and experience
    b. Awareness of trends and developments
    c. Attitudes toward change

VI. Instructional Patterns and Strategies
    a. Philosophical focus of instructional program
    b. Observational and perceptual instructional data
    c. Assessment of instructional strategies in use
    d. Instructional materials in use
    e. Decision-making and planning processes
    f. Grouping for instruction
    g. Classroom management techniques
    h. Grading and placement of pupils
    i. Student independence
    j. Evaluation of instructional effectiveness

VII. Student Data
    a. Student experiences
    b. Student self-esteem
    c. Student achievement

VIII. Facilities
    a. Assessment of existing facilities and sites
    b. Special facilities
    c. Utilization of facilities
    d. Projected facility needs

IX. Summary of Data

Figure 5.5 The Basic Needs Assessment Framework

use of planning instruments such as course guides, syllabi, textbook selection, and computer software procurement. Here, too, the goals and objectives may be translated into subject matter by a series of deductive steps. The State of Florida Department of Education determines its program of studies by going from a series of goal statements, to a core of essential concepts, to a "scope and sequence" in grades K–12, to a final prescription. An illustration of this for a seventh-grade teacher is shown in Figures 5.6, 5.7, and 5.8 and Table 5.3. The so-called "engaging behaviors" show the introduction of behavioral objectives that become the basis of discussion between supervisor and teacher.

The Role of the Supervisor

The activities carried out in classrooms are vital to the success of the entire school program. The supervisor has the singular task of connecting curriculum planning and curriculum implementation. Armed with various structures (goals, syllabi, needs assessment data), the supervisor enters the classroom as a kind of "final filter" or quality control agent. At this level, the supervisor will be concerned with the learning environment, learning materials, lesson planning, teaching strategies, and instructional evaluation.

As discussed in Chapter 3, the environment of the classroom can range from bland to highly structured to colorful and flexible. To the degree that the teacher wishes to interact with the student or have the student take responsibility for his or her own learning (high levels on the taxonomies), the room must become more personal and flexible. Among variables to discuss with the teacher are room decor, seating arrangements, questioning techniques, pacing, and variety of instruction of materials. Research (see Chapter 2) can guide this discussion.

Learning materials need to be varied if the intent of the curriculum is to personalize and individualize. If the purpose of the curriculum is to engage the student, the more senses employed help ensure that the student will be reached in his or her learning modality. Along with this flexibility in materials are the alternative assessment methods used for meeting student needs.

Lessons at the classroom level need to be a subset of the curriculum planned; all teaching should be rationalized in terms of curriculum goals and objectives. The best way to ensure that what the teacher is teaching on Tuesday has something to do with the "grand plan" is to have the teacher construct simple curriculum maps outlining content, skills, and concept for the year or by grading period. Each weekly or daily lesson plan is then a subset of this simple planning tool (see Figure 5.9, p. 164).

Supervision's concern with learning strategies employed in the classroom is a reflection of the fact that the teacher is the key variable in the classroom. In most instances, the teacher acts, and the students react. Some teacher actions will reinforce high degrees of structure: lecture, textbook learning, drill, and forced-choice answers on tests will emphasize sameness or standardization. In contrast, strategies and methods such as cooperative learning, questioning with "wait time," and independent study increase the personalization of learning. The teacher can display any

This vision is designed to develop well-educated people who share a body of knowledge, preserve a set of values, understand common cultural allusions, and are prepared to participate with confidence in the dynamics of political, economic and social groups.

- Well-educated persons have a sense of where they are in time, in space and in culture. They have a sense of personal and social identity.

- Well-educated persons have minds that are well-stocked with information about people in time, in space and in culture. They share cultural allusions.

- Well-educated persons associate new experiences and events with the past. This association establishes a context in which they explain, sympathize, judge, decide and act.

- Well-educated persons participate in intellectual adventures. They willingly examine established knowledge and accept intellectual risks.

- Well-educated persons recognize conditions detrimental to human development and opportunity. They promote tolerance, understanding and acceptance.

- Well-educated persons possess a range of rhetorical skills. They can narrate, listen and persuade effectively.

- Well-educated persons possess a sense of personal, social and civic efficacy. They accept personal and social responsibility.

- Well-educated persons know how to create, share, shape and pursue visions. They can imagine times that are more just, spaces that are better used and cultures that are more humane.

Figure 5.6 Florida K–12 Social Studies Program of Study: A Vision for the Social Studies
Source: *Connections, Challenges, Choice—A Report of the Florida Commission on Social Studies Education: A Commitment to the Students of Florida.* Tallahassee: Florida Department of Education, 1991, pp. 1–126.

of the preceding methodologies according to the dictates of the learning objectives (knows, appreciates, applies).

Finally, the supervisor and the teacher can spend productive time talking about the type of evaluation employed in the classroom. Although most adults experienced only standardized assessments in school, the most recent thrust has been toward alternatives to standard assessment. Popular among these models that emphasize individual student performance are performance-based (portfolio, oral defense) or problem-solving models (scenario and applied theories) assessment (Figure 5.10, p. 165). Supervisors, as well as teachers, need to understand the great influence of this selection in an age of test-driven curriculum.

Curriculum Management Planning

Although it may appear that curriculum development is an orderly one-two-three process using deductive logic, in reality, the impurity of the work environment (dis-

MISSION STATEMENT

Social Studies is the integrated study of the social sciences and the humanities. Utilizing knowledge, skills and attitudes in an active learning environment, social studies promotes the development of well-educated students who have a sense of their place/role historically, geographically and culturally. Social studies enables students to make the informed, ethical, reasoned decisions required for effective participation as citizens of a culturally diverse, democratic society in a rapidly-changing, interdependent world.

CORE CONCEPTS

Interdependence

People interact within political, social and economic systems that are interrelated and reciprocal.

Related Concepts: causation, communication, community, exchange, government, group, individual, nation, society, transportation, democracy

Change

The process of the movement of people, ideas, values, behavior, goods, services and technology across time, space and culture is universal.

Related Concepts: adaptation, causation, evolution, development, revolution, location, communication, assimilation, migration, cultural diffusion, growth

Culture

People interact with their environments and create systems comprised of unique beliefs, values, traditions, languages, customs, technology and institutions as a way of meeting basic human needs.

Related Concepts: adaptation, religion, philosophy, art, music, literature, dance, drama, diversity, communication, norms, roles, values, ethics, assimilation, space-time, pluralism, homogeneity/heterogeneity

Figure 5.7 Florida K–12 Social Studies Program of Study: Core of Essential Concepts for Social Studies
Source: *Connections, Challenges, Choice—A Report of the Florida Commission on Social Studies Education: A Commitment to the Students of Florida.* Tallahassee: Florida Department of Education, 1991, pp. 1–126.

tortions) in school is extensive. Education is an open system, susceptible to influence from many sources, some of which are illogical. The goal of any supervisor should be to ensure, where possible, that such distortions are minimized and that the school develops the best imaginable program in a logical fashion. Failure to acknowledge this theory–practice gap, and to use sound management techniques to overcome it, dooms most curriculum work to failure.

We use a technique called Curriculum Management Planning (CMP) in our curriculum development work in schools. This approach sees schools as a system—related parts working together toward a common and predetermined end. If quality educational experiences are such an end, then all school functions (administration, teaching, parent involvement, and so on) should be geared toward that goal.

Scarcity

The condition of unlimited wants and limited resources necessitates the creation of systems for deciding how resources are to be utilized and distributed.

Related Concepts: conflict, exploration, migration, opportunity cost, policy, resources, specialization, production, consumption

Conflict

People and nations often have differing values and opposing goals resulting in disagreement, tensions and sometimes violence necessitating skill in coexistence, negotiation, living with ambiguity and conflict resolution.

Related Concepts: authority, collaboration, competition, power, interests/positions, justice, rights, rules, laws, equity, accommodation, democratic processes

Perspective

Perceptions, acquired through interaction with their environments, affect the way in which people understand the past, make sense of the present and prepare for the future.

Related Concepts: speculation, imagination, interpretation, introspection, bias, prejudice, causation, judgment, ethics, ethnocentrism, spatial relationships

Responsibility

Democratic societies depend upon the act of participation of citizens who recognize and accept the consequences of their economic, political and social behaviors.

Related Concepts: justice, choice, authority, rules, civic action, equality of opportunity, freedom, diversity, due process, decision making, dependability, self control, community, volunteerism, public welfare, civic virtue, citizenship, leadership, risk-taking, efficacy

Figure 5.7 *Continued*

The CMP can be envisioned from a systems diagram (Figure 5.11, p. 166) which shows a flow of activity from philosophy to evaluation. The linear flow from point to point is a variation of Tyler's curriculum cycle. What the Wiles-Bondi CMP does is move the process of improvement along and minimize distortion through management. Several premises of this approach have served us well and are highly recommended to supervisors in schools:

1. Involve people who will be affected by any changes. Committees serve as a vehicle for participation (both permanent and ad hoc committees).
2. Good decisions result from good information (needs assessment).
3. Goals should be obvious and attainable (standards and goal validation).
4. A scenario should unfold (long-range planning).
5. A history of "winning" should be established (reports and records).

GRADE LEVEL   Grade Seven
TOPIC   Immigration

CORE CONCEPTS

Interdependence — relationship among people from many nations of the world

Change — how various peoples adapt to new environment

Culture — study of European and African customs and values brought to the
          Americas during the 16th and 17th centuries

Scarcity — role of limited resources as a factor in decisions to immigrate

Conflict — the cultural conflict between Eastern and Western Hemispheres

Perspective — how groups view their surroundings

Responsibility — how political, economic and social decisions affect the quality of life

CONNECTION TO VISION

Students are well informed about people within a culture, understand the view-
points reflected in that culture, and believe that the quality of life for all groups can
be improved.

ENGAGING BEHAVIORS

During this unit, students, individually or in groups

- Read journals and diaries of European or African explorers and settlers
- Create maps showing area of European colonization in Western Hemisphere
- Compare the physical features of the European nation and its colonies
- Compare the physical features of West Africa and the Americas
- List the cultural characteristics of the major European colonial powers
- Recreate the journeys of several different groups to the Americas
- Research a famous explorer or settler of the Americas
- Write an imaginary journal of a typical colonist or slave in the Americas
- List the European/African cultural traits that survived the colonization period
- Create a visual presentation depicting life as an immigrant from West Africa
- Listen to native music of West African nations
- Design an oral or visual report about one of the European colonial powers

Figure 5.8 Florida K–12 Recommended Social Studies Program of Study: Classroom Blueprint
Source: *Connections, Challenges, Choice—A Report of the Florida Commission on Social Studies Education:
A Commitment to the Students of Florida.* Tallahassee: Florida Department of Education, 1991, pp. 1–126.

Table 5.3 Florida K–12 Recommended Social Studies Program of Study

	Course of Study	Theme	Link to Vision	Connections						
				Sociology	History	Geography	Economics	Political Science	Ethics	Humanities
K	My Family and Others	Observations of self and other families in the world	Begin to locate self in space	Variations in the human family	Songs/stories about other cultures	Basic physical geographic skills and concepts	Concepts of needs, wants, scarcity, choices	Personal responsibilities; rules at home and school	Codes of behavior followed by all people	Celebrations and expressions of creativity
1	Families Near and Far	Continued observations of self and other families in the world	Enrich personal and social sense of identity	Social interactions of diverse groups	Music, legends, stories about other cultures	Relationships between humans and environment	Choice, opportunity cost, specialization	Community rules and cooperation among groups	Characteristics of good citizens all over the world	Celebrations and expressions of creativity
2	Our Cultures: Past and Present	Ethnicity, customs, traditions and values of the United States	Associate new experiences with past; build allusionary base	Customs and values of diverse cultures	American heroes, holidays and symbols	Physical geography skills, map keys, symbols	Producer/consumer, property, risk-takers	Symbols of freedom; government for people	Role models who displayed traditional values	Expressions of diverse cultural heritages
3	Beginnings: People, Places and Events	Critical events from the past that helped shape our world	Personal and social identity; associate present with past	Interactions between cultures; spread of ideas	Narrative study of critical events from the past	Physical geography; influence on civilizations	Basic needs, trade, banking, specialization	Democracy, participatory gov't; codes of conduct	People who display universally valued traits	Developments, art, language, dance, music

continued

Source: *Connections, Challenges, Choice—A Report of the Florida Commission on Social Studies Education: A Commitment to the Students of Florida.* Tallahassee: Florida Department of Education, 1991, pp. 1–126.

Table 5.3 *Continued*

Course of Study	Theme	Link to Vision	Sociology	History	Geography	Economics	Political Science	Ethics	Humanities
						Connections			
4 U.S. and Florida History and Geography to 1880	Specific topics in the history and geography of the United States and Florida	Associate new experiences with the past: gather information about people in time, in space and in culture	Movement; interaction of people/ideas; relationship of events to present/future U.S. and Florida problems	Narrative/biographical history placed within a chronological/thematic frame of reference	Physical geography, exploration, settlement, transportation, expansion, migration, environment	Economic concerns related to exploration and trade; lifestyles, entrepreneurship and multiple work skills	Documents of democracy; levels/branches/purposes/functions of government; local and state study	Responsibilities of citizens for general welfare; ideals valued by Americans; group participation	American art forms; decoration, arts, literature, music, drama, and fine arts
5 U.S. and Florida History and Geography Since 1880									
6 Geography: Asia, Oceania and Africa	Systematic observation and analysis of people and their world using the geographic themes of location, place, human-environment interactions, movement and region	Expand personal sense of identity; provide additional information about people in space and in culture	Interaction of people/ideas; ways in which group dynamics influence norms and mores	Draws on relevant historical understandings related to each place	Human and physical geography placed within time and space	Interrelatedness of economics to the social and political order; concept of economic decision making	Connections between political institutions, the economy and society	Values and belief systems of many different cultures and how they can affect world views	Art, architecture, literature, music, language that display cultural differences and similarities
7 Geography: Europe and the Americas									

Table 5.3 *Continued*

Course of Study	Theme	Link to Vision	Connections						
			Sociology	History	Geography	Economics	Political Science	Ethics	Humanities
8 Florida: Challenges and Choices	Systematic analysis of contemporary Florida people and issues	Prepare students to explain, sympathize, judge, decide and act	Personal, social responsibility of individual/group	Study of events that created modern Florida	Five geographic themes as they relate to Florida	Personal/social/local/global decision making	Interconnectedness of political, economic issues	Value of ethical behavior in contemporary society	Art, literature, music, folk way of life in Florida
9 Eastern and Western Heritage	Chronological, topical study of civilization to the Renaissance	Expands common knowledge, values and cultural allusions	Interaction between cultures; spread of ideas		Influence on cities and cultural development	Division of labor; barter, banking, cash economy	Foundations for several forms of government	Universal nature of social order; responsibilities	Art, literature, music of past civilizations
10 Visions and Their Pursuits: An American Tradition	Chronological, thematic study of U.S. history to World War I	Identification in time, space, culture; aware of human condition	Social interaction; development of group norms	Narrative, cultural history placed within a chronological framework	Factors influencing development of certain regions	Economic concepts used to interpret history	Specific foundation of U.S. political system	Values affecting the treatment of specific groups	American art forms, music, folk/fine arts
11 Visions/Countervisions: Europe, U.S. and the World	Chronological, topical study of modern U.S. and world history	Awareness of cultural heritage of the U.S.; sense of time/space/culture	Interactions of people/society in modern world		Influence on political, economic world events	Comparing economic systems and effects	Emergence of political systems and their effects	Responsibilities of all citizens for ethical behavior	Art, literature, music as responses to events
12 The American Political and Economic Experience	Application of political and economic principles to the individual	Prepare for participation in social, political, and economic life	Development of norms. Interaction of people	Spread of political and economic ideas/systems	Influence on political, economic human behavior	Distribution and redistribution of resources	Relationship between people and their government	Ways to ensure ethical behavior	Examples of economic/political philosophies

Sample Curriculum Map in Social Studies

GRADE LEVEL: ___Third___   SUBJECT: ___Social Studies___

GRADING PERIOD: ___1st Nine Weeks___   TEACHER: ___Smith___

Content	Concepts	General Skills	Specific Skills/ Objectives	Texts/* Materials
1. National resources of the United States.	1. American culture is a composite of many cultures.	1. Collecting and organizing information.	1. The student names the states and water masses that border/ surround Florida.	*Florida Handbook* 1983–84
2. Major topographical classifications —desert, forest, ocean, river.	2. American cultures have shaped American behavior (freedom, individualism, equality).	2. Mapping. 3. Relating. 4. Thinking. 5. Comparing. 6. Communication. 7. Drawing conclusions. 8. Determining sequence.	2. The student locates the boundaries of the United States.	Rand McNally Atlas, 1983— Map of growing seasons
3. Climate regions of the United States.	3. People of different cultures have different points of view.		3. The student locates a specific geographical region of the United States.	*National Geographic Film, The United States,* U.S. Dept. of Interior
4. States and topographs in the United States.	4. Cultural ways are influenced by physical environment.		4. The student locates and names the state and geographic region in which he/she lives.	
5. Major water masses in the United States.	5. Florida and the United States are populated by people of different cultures and different points of view.		5. The student interprets information from a map legend.	
6. Peoples and cultures in the United States.				

*Textbook would appear in this column. Page and chapter numbers should be appropriate.

Figure 5.9 A Sample Curriculum Map for One Grading Period

What Is a Portfolio?

- Living and dynamic record of student progress over time
- Container of student work and accomplishments: drafts, journals, projects, logs, performances, exhibitions, sketches, writing samples, checklists, products, anecdotal records, "staged" and natural observations, oral examinations
- An instructional and assessment tool

Portfolio Stages

- Select learner outcome(s) to be evaluated and describe it
- Design tasks and instruments to measure cognitive and affective progress toward accomplishment of outcomes
- Conduct periodic, performance-based assessments
- Observe and systematically collect data on student progress
- Collect samples/examples of learner's work (teachers and students select) and describe reasons for the selection
- Collaborate, assess and evaluate learning progress with students through periodic, reflective interviews (use progress maps, performance criteria and discussion)
- Certify competencies and establish future learning goals
- Promote a classroom culture of high standards and quality work

Types of Portfolios

- Capstone Portfolio: verifies accomplishment of exit outcomes or may serve as an entrance portfolio to the next level
- Showcase Portfolio: students select works to showcase to others
- Working Portfolio: samples of current efforts toward a particular outcome
- "Process-folio": shows significant shifts in student growth related to a specific skill

Figure 5.10 Portfolio Evaluation

GOVERNMENT GOALS FOR PUBLIC EDUCATION

A number of new planning variables in the 1990s are influencing curriculum management planning including bureaucratic goal setting (Blueprint 2000), site-based management (decentralized decision making), site-based planning (school improvement plans), business/school interfacing, an on-rush of technology, and a multiplicity of curriculum designs. The emphasis on any of these would necessitate strategies for moving curriculum development forward.

In his last year as President, George Bush called together all of the state governors for an "Education Summit" (America 2000) with the expressed purpose of formulating some common national goals for public education. Soon-to-be-President

166

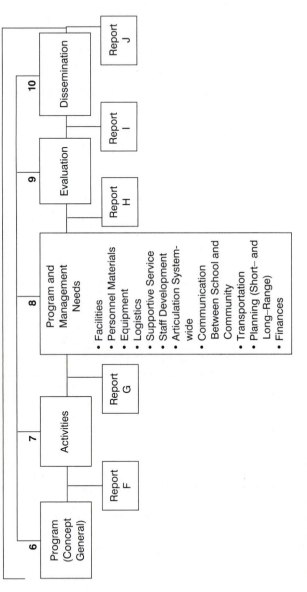

Figure 5.11 Comprehensive Management System
Source: Florida Department of Education, Tallahassee, FL.

Bill Clinton (Governor of Arkansas) chaired the body. The result of this historic meeting was the establishment of seven broad goals that might guide each state in the pursuit of educational excellence. Education, not being mentioned in the federal Constitution, is a state responsibility. Ultimately, each state acted to build these goals into their accountability plans (see Figure 5.12).

The use of the seven general goals to structure planning and curriculum work in many states was accomplished by requiring (statutory) schools to submit a school improvement plan indicating its progress in meeting the ascribed goals with a deadline of the year 2000. Many districts and schools formed S.I.T.'s (school improvement teams) who, funded by SIP (school improvement plans) monies, began the process of analysis and design of a new curriculum. Performance standards provided a structure for such committee work in a deductive manner. For instance, a preparation to enter the workforce (Goal 2) might have attaining standards such as communicating in English and other languages, interpreting information, and achieving literacy in computer operations. Schools would then prepare an action plan for attaining the standards such as that of Mayport Middle School (Figure 5.13).

Florida Education Accountability System

The accountability model proposed for Florida ultimately will establish appropriate goals and student outcomes. A set of transitional goals has been developed.

The proposed goals are:

- **Readiness to start school**—Communities and schools collaborate to prepare children and families for children's success in school.

- **Graduation rate and readiness for postsecondary education and employment**—Students graduate and are prepared to enter the workforce and postsecondary education.

- **Student performance**—Students successfully compete at the highest levels nationally and internationally and are prepared to make well-reasoned, thoughtful and healthy lifelong decisions.

- **Learning environment**—School boards provide a learning environment conducive to teaching and learning that includes sequential instruction in mathematics, science, reading, writing, and the social sciences and appropriate educational materials, equipment, and pupil-teacher ratio.

- **School safety and environment**—Communities provide an environment that is drug-free and protects students' health, safety, and civil rights.

- **Teachers and staff**—The schools, district, and state ensure professional teachers and staff.

- **Adult literacy**—Adult Floridians are literate and have the knowledge and skills needed to compete in a global economy and exercise the rights and responsibilities of citizenship.

Figure 5.12 State Education Goals—Florida Education Accountability System

For supervisors to capitalize on such mandated procedures would provide a driving force for promoting curriculum improvement. Goals for accountability, standards for performance attainment, and school-based plans tied to funding initiatives provide a framework for supervisory work. Throw in testing, the general push toward national assessment, and a standard achievement instrument, and a complete external curriculum cycle is in place.

The Stake of Business in Education

Driving this improvement train is a rather large interface between business and state and local government. With the reduction in the military–industrial complex, business has taken a strong interest in schools with their 45 million students. For business, standardization in curriculum means a target for products such as textbooks or computers in truly large numbers. Under the banner of "a competitive workforce," business has pushed government ever-closer to directing school operations. National goals, a fixed curriculum, consolidation of the publishing industry, and national testing would allow specification for business intervention. Some educators even see a concerted "privatization" movement in education that might have any number of forms: vouchers, private schools for hire, home schooling, and various test-out options such as the General Equivalency Degree (G.E.D.) diploma. From this perspective, media attacks on the schools form a frontline for discrediting these publicly-supported institutions.

Whether there is credibility to such notions, or whether these "thrusts" are simply random events, supervisors can see them as "tools" for improving instruction. If your district were going to spend $3.5 million for computers this year, a complete analysis seems appropriate.

The degree to which technology is affecting schools in the 1990s is hard to assess. Gone are the early computers and the drill programs in only math and reading. Replacing these are sophisticated hard sets and assembled stations and networks that allow a better diagnosis/prescription behavior by the teacher. In addition, telephones, new coaxial cable hookups, facsimile machines, on-line distance learning setups, and comprehensive learning stations all point to a very technological future in schools. These "tracks" into a new form of education should provide supervisors with ready-made avenues for curriculum improvement.

Finally, the curriculum materials themselves are constantly being reformed in the 1990s by both design and in response to social forces. Interdisciplinary curriculum, curriculum embedded in learning materials, "process curricula" teaching thinking skills, and new life skill programs designed to promote salient values are constantly being reviewed by schools. Just keeping up with such options and challenges should provide the supervisors with ready-made decisions for staff consideration.

LIFE SKILLS

Students today are evidencing a need for basic survival and life skills that will enable them to interact with others in our society. The onslaught of a technological future,

School Goal #2: Mayport Middle School will develop a technology plan that will provide students and staff with the skills necessary to be productive, successful members of our technologically advanced society.

Objectives
1. Each teacher in our school will be provided with a computer.
2. Our staff will work to develop a vocational technology lab.
3. Our staff will work to develop a comprehensive computer lab with equivalent computer and technology courses.
4. A network of computers will be developed so that they can be used by the instructional and administrative staff.

Strategies
1. Computer in-service training will be provided for all staff.
2. Proposals will be submitted to county, business/community partners and corporations (for grant purposes) to secure necessary funding and/or equipment.
3. Appropriate instructional materials will be secured to establish the technology curriculum.

Resources Needed
1. The school's technology committee will develop a technology plan and grant proposals to secure equipment and funds.
2. District staff will be needed to provide assistance in securing and developing grant proposals.
3. District staff and school-based staff will provide in-service training for the staff at Mayport Middle School.
4. Educational partnerships with business/community leaders will continue to be developed.

Timeline
1. Every teacher will be provided with a computer by June, 1995.
2. Phase 1 of vocational technology lab and appropriate curriculum operational by 1993–94 school year.
3. A computer lab will be operational by 1995–96 school year.
4. Technology and computer curriculum will be implemented by the end of the 1994–95 school year.
5. Networking capabilities for faculty and staff will be implemented by the end of the 1993–94 school year. Networking of existing computer labs will be completed by the end of the 1994–95 school year.
6. Progress will be assessed to determine success of this plan during the 1994–95 school year.

Evaluation
1. Monthly reports will be submitted by the technology committee to assess the progress of each objective.
2. School-based technology committee will meet on a regular basis to review progress and implement specific procedures needed to meet objectives.
3. SAC committee members will review by site visitations and staff surveys, to assess the progress of the technology plan.
4. Parent and employee responses on the Duval County Parent and Employee surveys will show an improved awareness of the school's technology.

Figure 5.13 Action Plan for School Goal #2
Source: Mayport Middle School, Duval County Schools, Jacksonville, Florida. Used by permission.

increased multiculturalism, and a soaring concern for juvenile justice programs all speak toward the inclusion of the "strand"(the section or area) within the regular school curriculum in the elementary, middle, and secondary programs.

The U.S. Department of Labor has developed a well-known set of skills, called "SCANS," to prepare workers of the future, but there are many such conceptions dating back to the 1960s. We have developed and implemented a group of ten life skills in a project funded by the Kellogg Foundation (refer to Table 4.3 in the previous chapter).

SUMMARY

The process of curriculum development, and the management of paths to instructional improvement, will accelerate during the 1990s. Forces beyond the school will push curriculum development into the twenty-first century. Guiding school faculties through these various means toward the end of improving school for children will be a major role for supervisors in the coming decade.

Curriculum is the foundation of supervisory practice. For teachers to impart meaning to students in their studies, there must be purpose. Such guidance is provided by the learning plan. Curriculum is always value laden, and supervisors and teachers will be faced with choices as they jointly decide to emphasize one thing over another in interpreting the curriculum.

Philosophies, goals, standards, objectives, and evaluation outcomes give structure to the process of curriculum development, a process that, by itself, is value free. In districts where the curriculum cycle is followed without ever seriously considering the values being promoted, supervision cannot be a serious pursuit.

In the 1990s, public education can be conceived of as a four-tier ladder of learning including early childhood, late childhood, preadolescent, and adolescent experiences. Superimposed on this human development framework is a series of pressing social problems that are the domain of the public school. Needs arising from occurrences such as the demise of the family, advances in technology, and a changing labor force suggest many adjustments will be needed by the year 2000. Full-service schools, life skill curriculums, better use of community resources, and accessing the high tech world of communication are a few of the more obvious changes on the horizon.

As districts wrestle with such developments, often through mandated processes such as Goals 2000, supervisors will represent the link between the planned experiences of youth and the actual experiences in a classroom setting.

IMPLICATIONS FOR SUPERVISION

1. What factors in your community distort the curriculum development process in schools?
2. How might schools and business best interface in planning for the future of the United States?
3. What sort of curriculum seems appropriate for the general education of a citizen in the twenty-first century?
4. Why shouldn't all students gain a formal education via a home computer as some "home schoolers" do now?

≈ CASE STUDY 1 ≈

There is increasing interest in today's schools for an applied curriculum that addresses real student needs. As a supervisor, you are committed to such a "life skills" component for students but are unable to gain much support for this addition to the curriculum from subject matter specialists in the district. Among the most common responses to your inquiries are: (1) there isn't room for anything else in the curriculum, (2) we can't afford to start any new programs, and (3) this role belongs to some other government agency.

Questions

1. Make a list of groups that you think would support or oppose a life skills curriculum in schools.
2. What strategy could be used to "force" this new area into an already-too-full curriculum?
3. What form would such a program take in today's schools? In the technological schools in the next century?

≈ CASE STUDY 2 ≈

As a new supervisor in this district, your immediate task is to organize the science textbook adoption procedure for the year. A plan for review and adoption was sent to each building principal along with a timeline and state-adopted list. Arrangements have been made for a district-wide display of texts that might be chosen. Then you receive the following memo from Benson, the most senior principal in the district and an opinion leader as well. Benson is straight to the point in his correspondence. "We have *always* selected our books at the building level in this district, and we would not like to see this local autonomy infringed upon." Additionally, Benson goes on to mention that the representatives from the book companies traditionally host little "wine and cheese" parties for the faculties and that these are very popular in the individual schools.

Questions

1. What are the major issues in this case?
2. If the supervisor finds that Benson is indeed very influential, for which items would you fight and which would you overlook?
3. Describe this process from a pure "curriculum" perspective.

SUGGESTED LEARNING ACTIVITIES

1. Write your own personal definition of curriculum development. Is it a dynamic or static definition?
2. Identify ways in which supervisors could be involved in the analysis, design, implementation, and evaluation of the curriculum.
3. Develop an outline of events that would lead a school district with no philosophy to one with a clear and consistent curriculum development process.
4. Develop a teacher evaluation instrument to be used by a supervisor that would reflect curriculum development at the classroom level.
5. Develop an operational definition of leadership in curriculum development.
6. Identify the five most important skills a supervisor must possess to be effective in school curriculum development efforts.

BOOKS TO REVIEW

Bottery, M. *The Morality of School: The Theory and Practice of Values in Education.* London: Cassell, 1990.

Centron, M. and Gayle, M. *Educational Renaissance: Our Schools at the Turn of the Twenty-First Century.* New York: St. Martin's Press, 1991.

Dewey, J. *Education and Experience.* New York: Macmillan, 1938.

Eisner, E. *The Educational Imagination,* 3rd ed. Englewood Cliffs, NJ: Merrill/Prentice Hall, 1994.

Elmore, R. *Handbook of Research on Curriculum.* New York: Macmillan, 1992.

Hill, J. *The New American School: Breaking the Mold.* Lancaster, PA: Technomic, 1992.

Keefe, J., and Jenkins, J. *Instructional Leadership Handbook.* Reston, VA: NASSP, 1991.

Longstreet, W., and Shane, H. *Curriculum For a New Millennium.* Boston, MA: Allyn and Bacon, 1993.

Rugg, H. *The Foundation and Technique of Curriculum Construction.* National Society for the Study of Education, Yearbook, 1926.

Taba, H. *Curriculum Development: Theory and Practice.* New York: Harcourt, Brace, Jovanovich, 1962.

Tanner, D., and Tanner, L. *History of School Curriculum.* New York: Macmillan, 1990.

U.S. Department of Labor. *Learning a Living: A Blueprint for High Performance, SCANS Report for America 2000.* Washington, DC: 1992.

Wiles, J., and Bondi, J. *Curriculum Development: A Guide to Practice,* 4th ed. Englewood Cliffs, NJ: Merrill/Prentice Hall, 1993.

Wiles, J. *Promoting Change in Schools: Ground Level Practices That Work.* New York: Scholastic, Inc., 1993.

Weiss, C. *Shared Decision-Making About What? A Comparison of Schools With and Without Teacher Participation.* Boston: Harvard University, Center for Educational Leadership, 1992.

CHAPTER 6 ≈

IMPROVING CLASSROOM
TEACHING

Any number of characteristics can contribute to the quality of a teacher's performance including the teacher's personality, knowledge of the subject matter, philosophical and psychological understandings, and pedagogy (the principles and practices of teaching). To be effective, the teacher must be able to organize and execute teaching strategies so that the intended goals are reached. In most cases, good teaching is a direct result of good decision making. The experienced teacher can transform the complexities of the classroom into a conceptual system that allows the interpretation of events and the anticipation (and direction) of classroom activities.

As early as 1904, John Dewey observed that too much emphasis in teacher preparation was placed on practice and the attainment of practical skills, rather than on concepts and analytical work that guide the teacher. Practical work, stated Dewey, should be pursued primarily to make the teacher more thoughtful rather than helping the teacher become immediately proficient. Teachers shouldn't "strike twelve too soon."[1] This theory versus practice argument is heard often among teachers and at universities. For practicing supervisors, the critical notion is how to get the novice classroom teacher beyond survival and to the master teacher level.

We prefer a program of teacher development that emphasizes both understanding and minimal competence. Understandings might include the purposes of teaching, self-awareness of practice, and critical decision areas that lead to consistency in the teaching pattern. Competencies would be drawn from both research and practices that have proven successful in schools and classrooms.

DIFFERENCES IN SCHOOLS AND CLASSROOMS

If a teacher is to grow toward excellence, he or she must first understand the purpose in education. In Chapter 5, the range of philosophies present in American education was introduced. The material in that chapter established that some educators seek to form the student's knowledge, behavior, and attitudes into a preconceived pattern by eliminating distortion and emphasizing high degrees of structure in the classroom. Such a path may assume that children are imperfect little adults or that the world is unchanging in many ways. This highly structured approach to educating children was contrasted with a personalized version in which the students are seen as unique individuals and the world today as experiencing steady and significant change. This teaching pattern attempts to be flexible in working with students in order to unleash their potential. The student-focused teacher believes that didactic (structured) teaching may even prevent student learning since it forces preconceived notions on the student (Figure 6.1).

Although these important ideas about the nature of humans and the focus of the curriculum are vital ingredients for purposeful teaching, most teachers early in their practice fail to understand how clearly their role is prescribed by the curriculum. These prescriptions—in the form of philosophies, goals, objectives, standards, and testing outcomes—direct the teacher in emphasizing one thing over another. Teaching, in most districts, is an extension of the curriculum.

New teachers, in particular, may see themselves as "free agents," who will close the classroom door and carry on the teaching act in a private way. Some experienced

---

The Nondirect Teacher

I have come to feel that the only learning which significantly influences behavior is self-discovered and self-appropriated learning.

Such self-discovered learning cannot be directly communicated to another because as soon as the individual attempts to communicate such experience directly, it becomes teaching.

When I try to teach, I find the results are damaging . . . it seems to cause the individual to distrust his own experience and to stifle significant learning.

As a consequence, I find that I am only interested in being a learner. I find the best way to learn is to drop my defensiveness and to state my own uncertainties. . . . *

The Direct Teacher

The curriculum should consist of permanent studies—rules of grammar, reading, rhetoric and logic, and mathematics, and the greatest books of the Western world.**

Figure 6.1 The Nondirect Teacher
*Carl Rogers, *Freedom to Learn* (Boston: Houghton Mifflin, 1969), p. 277.
**Robert M. Hutchins, *The Higher Learning in America* (New Haven, CT: Yale University Press, 1936), p. 82.

teachers, too, are guilty of disregarding the intentions of the system in which they teach. Their negligence is often revealed by poor test scores or an inappropriate foundation for later learnings.

Supervisors should work hard to develop a logic in the documents that guide teaching. The philosophy statements of the district and school, the state or district objectives, the curriculum maps, frameworks, or syllabi, and the textbooks selected and outlined all should provide this kind of guidance for the teacher (Figure 6.2). Such deductive logic, "*If* we measure a literate student by the CTBS scores, *then* we should address those skills measured by that test," or "*If* we desire a self-confident learner capable of making individual decisions, *then* the student should experience academic success," should be obvious. The overall game plan should clearly communicate that instruction is a subset of curriculum, that the curriculum is purposeful and directional and that the teacher's job is to impart meaning in the curriculum as intended.

There are numerous opportunities for supervisors to engage teachers in such an orientation; accreditation reviews, self-studies, goal setting through school-based management teams, reviews of practice, and establishing priorities. In too many cases, new teachers are not given that kind of orientation and direction. More experienced teachers may have to unlearn some of their assumed autonomy through various group processes.

Understanding may also break down in the area of classroom planning process. Although tremendous progress has been made over the last twenty years in requiring teachers to project their intentions through structured lesson plans, the process often fails to tie concepts and content together. Teachers need to see the school year in "chunks" where certain main ideas are communicated and lead to other main ideas. Where will we be by Halloween? By Christmas? By Easter? What content will be used to teach these understandings? How does your teaching this day or week contribute to that progress?

Figure 6.2 Structure Guiding Teacher Roles in the Classroom

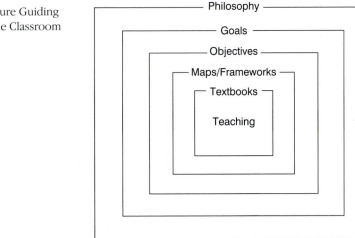

Supervisors can also help new and experienced teachers become more self-aware by observing and giving them feedback on the practices that characterize their classrooms. Observational instruments such as the Flanders (Figure 6.3), discussions of classroom practices following observation, or even action research projects in which a teacher tries two or more techniques to see which works best, can lead to an awareness of what is happening in that room. From such a growing awareness, assessment of how such teacher behaviors contribute or fail to contribute to the curriculum can evolve naturally. Where teacher skill deficiencies exist, a rationale for staff development emerges.

Finally, supervisors can assist teachers in becoming more aware of their practices by focusing on critical practice areas. These areas, such as discipline, grouping, and testing, tend to affect classroom teaching more than most teachers know. Not only does a discipline plan reveal the teacher's intentions in teaching, but classroom management can seriously interfere with classroom learning if the two are not congruent. We will discuss this later in the chapter.

CHARACTERISTICS OF EFFECTIVE SCHOOLS

It is difficult to be an effective teacher in an ineffective school. For a variety of reasons, some schools simply don't function well as a unit; some schools may just be a collection of individual teachers who do not share a common goal for the students they teach. In a review of major change projects in schools, one research identified common barriers to school development including:

1. An absence of theory or guiding principles about learning processes
2. No time for teachers to plan or learn new skills
3. A tendency toward quick-fix solutions and faddism in staff development
4. Management of all changes from the principal's office
5. Lack of technical assistance in areas requiring expertise
6. High turnover of teaching staff
7. An overload of competing demands on teacher time
8. Failure to consider the school structure in facing change
9. Failure to consider the school culture and site-specific differences in schools
10. Failure to clarify roles and relationships within the building[2]

We compare this type of school to a football team that has no positions, no plays, doesn't practice, doesn't know who they are playing, and who dump a team full of players onto the field for each game. Such a lack of organization and strategy is surely a formula for a losing team.[3] Yet, isn't this exactly what many schools do each August? Teachers arrive back from a summer break, attend a few general meetings, and go to their rooms to start the next year of teaching.

Description of Categories for a Thirteen-Category Modification
of the Flanders System of Interaction Analysis

Category Number	Description of Verbal Behavior
INDIRECT TEACHER	1. *Accepts Feeling:* Accepts and clarifies the feeling tone of students in a friendly manner. Student feelings may be of a positive or negative nature. Predicting and recalling student feelings are also included.
	2. *Praises or Encourages:* Praises or encourages student action, behavior recitation, comments, ideas, etc. Jokes that release tension not at the expense of another individual. Teacher nodding head or saying "uh-huh" or "go on" are included.
	3. *Accepts or Uses Ideas of Student:* Clarifying, building on, developing, and accepting the action, behavior, and ideas of the student.
	4. *Asks Questions*: Asking a question about the content (subject matter) or procedure with the intent that the student should answer.
	5. *Answers Student Questions (Student-Initiated Teacher Talk):* Giving direct answers to student questions regarding content or procedures.
DIRECT TALK	6. *Lecture (Teacher-Initiated Teacher Talk):* Giving facts, information, or opinions about content or procedure. Teacher expressing his or her own ideas. Asking rhetorical questions (not intended to be answered).
	7. *Gives Directions:* Directions, commands, or orders to which the student is expected to comply.
	8. *Corrective Feedback:* Telling a student that his answer is wrong when the correctness of his answer can be established by means other than opinions (i.e., empirical validation, definition, or custom).
	9. *Criticizes Student(s) or Justifies Authority:* Statements intended to change student behavior from a nonacceptable to an acceptable pattern; scolding someone; stating why the teacher is doing what he is doing so as to gain or maintain control; rejecting or criticizing a student's opinion or judgment.
STUDENT TALK	10. *Teacher-Initiated Student Talk:* Talk by students in response to requests or narrow teacher questions. The teacher initiates the contact or solicits student's statements.
	11. *Student Questions:* Student questions concerning content or procedure that are directed to the teacher.
	12. *Student-Initiated Student Talk:* Talk by students in response to broad teacher questions which require judgment or opinion. Voluntary declarative statements offered by the student, but not called for by the teacher.
	13. *Silence or Confusion:* Pauses, short periods of silence, and periods of confusion in which communication cannot be understood by an observer.

Indirect–Direct Ratio = Categories 1,2,3,4,5; Categories 5,7,8,9

Revised Indirect–Direct Ratio = Categories 1,2,3; Categories 7,8,9

Student–Teacher Ratio = Categories 10,11,12; Categories 1,2,3,4,5,6,7,8,9

Figure 6.3 Flanders Interaction Analysis Instrument
Source: John B. Hough, "A Thirteen Category Modification of Flanders' System of Interaction Analysis," mimeograph (Columbus: The Ohio State University, 1965), p. 4.

By contrast, some schools are highly organized and directional and seem to be successful whatever they do. Further, as the work of Ronald Edmonds demonstrated, some of these schools are located in the most unlikely places and still succeed.[4] Is there some secret to their success? Not really! In the educational literature called "effective schools," the common denominator of these "winners" is repeated time and again.

In most of the effective schools identified, there are clear goals and a strong instructional leader who might be thought of as a "coach." That coach, who could be a principal, supervisor, team leader, or any number of titles, helps to focus the program. The school mission is aligned with goals and objectives. The organization is constructed so that it facilitates mission accomplishment. Teachers and students are involved in the planning and operation of the school. Academics are stressed and high expectations are held for all students. Academic priorities are clear, and time and resources are allocated accordingly. Evaluation is continuous and provides feedback for regular change efforts. These and other similar characteristics form the framework for a successful school instructional program (Figure 6.4).

Naturally, a teacher in such a school is going to "look better" than a teacher operating in a dysfunctional program where confusion and error are commonplace. The instructional supervisor can do much to improve any individual teacher's performance simply by organizing the structure of the school so that all teachers are pulling together.

APPROACHES TO WORKING WITH TEACHERS

More than any other factor, the scope of the supervisor's role will determine how he or she will approach working with teachers (Figure 6.5, p. 181). In the nation's twenty-two largest and most bureaucratic school districts (100,000+ students), most supervisors are highly specialized and assist teachers primarily through organization and resource allocation. In medium- and smaller-sized districts (averaging 2,500 students) the approach is more interactive and personal. Here the supervisor may link school and district or work in school buildings as a coordinator of services. In very small or wealthy districts, the role of the supervisor may even be as a one-on-one teacher helper. These three roles and their liabilities are outlined in Table 6.1 (p. 181).

At the school site, supervisors must decide whether they will operate in a traditional line and staff role (serving the principal), or whether they will attempt to work directly with the staff. Developments in the 1980s and early 1990s have opened the door for this latter approach, and supervisors should be prepared to take advantage of this opportunity. A simple review of the characteristics of the effective school will indicate the dependence on teacher's involvement for a working unit.

Any number of levers can be used under this approach to access teacher input. Most widely used in the mid-1990s is the School Improvement Team (S.I.T.), an elected group that works with the principal to formulate instructional improvement. The role of the supervisor in this arrangement is as a communicator, resource-finder, and in some instances, knowledge expert. The supervisor works indirectly under this model to improve classroom instruction.

Brookover and Lezotte (1979)
- Improving schools accept and emphasize the importance of basic skills mastery as prime goals and objectives
- Staff of improving schools believe *all* students can master the basic skills objectives and they believe the principal shares this belief
- Staff of improving schools expect their students will go on with their education
- Staff of improving schools do not make excuses: they assume responsibility for teaching basic skills and are committed to do so
- Staff of improving schools spend more time on achieving basic skills objectives
- Principals at improving schools are assertive instructional leaders and disciplinarians, and they assume responsibility for the evaluation of the achievement of basic skills objectives
- Staff at improving schools accept the concept of accountability and are involved in developing (or using) accountability models
- Teachers at improving schools are not very satisfied or complacent about the status quo
- There is more parent-initiated contact and involvement at improving schools (even though the overall amount of parent involvement is less)
- The compensatory education programs in improving schools de-emphasize paraprofessional involvement and teacher involvement in the selection of Comp-Ed-bound students

Edmonds (1981)
- Clarity that pupil acquisition of the basic school skills takes precedence over all other school activities
- There is a climate of expectation in which no children are permitted to fall below minimum but efficacious levels of achievement
- Administrative leadership is strong and without it the disparate elements of good schooling can be neither brought together nor kept together
- A means is present by which pupil progress can be frequently monitored
- There is an atmosphere that is orderly without being rigid, quiet without being oppressive, and generally conducive to the instructional business at hand

Phi Delta Kappa (1980)
- Successful schools are characterized by clearly stated curricular goals and objectives
- The leaders' attitudes toward urban education and expectations for school or program success determine the impact of the leader on exceptional schools

continued

Figure 6.4 Summary of Effective School Research Findings
Source: J. Brookover and P. Lezotte, "Summary of Effective Schools Research Findings, *Educational Leadership,* December 1982, p. 18.

Other handles for the supervisor using a school-wide approach are to provide guiding resources (grants and programs), use evaluation as a source of direction (program, accreditation, or personal), facilitate communications in the school (between teachers and outside agencies, parents, and business), or engage teacher study groups in action research projects. Small-group leadership skills are a must for a supervisor working in this pattern.

Still quite common in smaller districts is a more personal and individual approach to instructional improvement. Serving as a helper, sometimes therapist,

- The behavior of the designated school or program leader is crucial in determining school success
- Successful urban schools frequently employ techniques of individualized instruction
- Structured learning environments are particularly successful in urban classrooms
- Reductions in adult/child ratios are associated with positive school performance
- Successful schools are often supported with special project funds from federal, state, and local sources
- Successful urban schools are characterized by high levels of parental contact with the school and parental involvement with school activities
- Successful schools frequently use staff development or in-service training programs to realize their objectives
- The greater the specificity or focus of the training program in terms of goals or processes, the greater the likelihood of its success
- Resource and facility manipulations alone are insufficient to affect school outcomes

Rutter and others (1979)
- Outcomes were better in schools where teachers expected the children to achieve well
- Outcomes were better in schools that provided pleasant working conditions for the pupils
- Outcomes were better in schools where immediate, direct praise and approval were the prevalent means of classroom feedback
- Outcomes were better in schools where teachers presented themselves as positive role models demonstrating punctuality, concern for the physical well-being of the school building, concern for the emotional well-being of the pupils, and restraint in the use of physical punishment
- Children's behavior was better in schools where teachers were readily available to be consulted by children about problems and where many children consulted with teachers
- Outcomes were better in schools where a high proportion of children held some kind of position of responsibility in the school system
- A school's atmosphere is influenced positively by the degree to which it functions as a coherent whole, with agreed ways of doing things that are consistent throughout the school and that have the general support of all staff

Figure 6.4 *Continued*

and instructional modeler, this supervisor attempts to improve the whole by improving the parts. The role of the supervisor under these conditions is almost always made more difficult by the requirement of evaluating the teacher in the process.

TEACHER DEVELOPMENT

Supervisors working with individual teachers to improve classroom instruction are at an advantage if they understand the evolution of teacher development. Numerous studies over the years have documented that teachers evolve through predictable pat-

Public school districts in the United States vary widely in size and in the diversity of their populations. New York City is the largest system with 940,000 students, but the average school district in the United States has 2,500 pupils and is comprised of five schools and 137 teaching units. Over 50 percent of the 15,363 regular school districts had less than 900 pupils.

Three states (Florida, Texas and California) have multiple large districts of over 100,000 pupils, and 10 percent of the school districts house nearly one-fourth of the 42 million public school students. John F. Kennedy High School in New York is the nation's largest school (4,600 students), but the average American school has only 488 students.

Racial and ethnic diversity varies widely in the United States. Some twenty-five large districts have a majority of black or Hispanic students.

These factors and others suggest that the supervisory role is often a function of the demography of the district where practice is occurring.

Figure 6.5 The Practice Environments in Public Schools
Source: U.S. Department of Education, Office of Educational Research and Improvement, *Characteristics of the 100 Largest Public Elementary and Secondary School Districts in the United States 1990–91* (Washington, DC: National Center for Education Statistics, 1993), pp. 124–125.

Table 6.1 A Typology of Supervisory Approaches

	Type I	Type II	Type III
Basic Description	Designer/manager	Linker/coordinator	Helper/therapist
Supervisory Focus	Organizational planning and execution	Integrating people and resources	Assisting individual growth and development
Supervisory Tools	Short- and long-range planning, budget control, performance evaluation	Assessment of organization processes	Need hierarchies, motivation theories, development profiles
Techniques Utilized	Systems management MBO, PERT/CPM, PPBS, ZBB	Organization development (O.D.) procedures	Structuring perception, manipulating climates, arousing needs, counseling
Strategy Employed	Structure the work flow by control of resources and plans	Diagnosis, assessment, and transformation of organization processes through inquiry/involvement	Upgrading of parts (individuals) contributes to improvement of the whole (school)
Problems Areas	Myopic leadership, obsolescence, member alienation	Planning overload, inability to be productive or humane	No "big picture" of organization, an appearance of disorder

◄—————————————————————————————————————►

High Organization
Emphasis

High Individual
Emphasis

181

terns. One study by T. M. Stinnert found that teachers start out in a highly defensive posture (textbook teaching), evolve into a master "coverage" teacher, experience a crisis of purpose, and then enter an "experimental" stage before taking one of these paths: quitting the profession, becoming a time-server, or evolving into an artist as a teacher.[5] These stages were parallel to the findings of Fuller[6] who identified a survival stage, a mastery stage, and an impact stage in learning to teach. One well-known model of adult growth by Erickson (see Chapter 4) would also support this evolution:

Role identity stage	Concern with image, self-analysis
Intimacy stage	Leave isolation and commit self to role
Generativity stage	Address productive activity, personal creativity
Ego identity stage	Acceptance of self and role[7]

If the teacher in the classroom could be seen through a developmental lens, supervisors could anticipate common needs and meet those needs more completely. For example, the supervisor might confront teachers-in-training, new teachers, experienced teachers, and very mature teachers in a classroom conference, and each would have predictable requests for assistance.

The student teacher or probationary teacher usually will not have had the training to understand all of the dynamics in the school. Patience, definition, and a lot of common sense is helpful with this teacher who is usually all-too-eager to learn about teaching.

The new hiree presents the supervisor with a different set of needs. The social–personal needs of the new teacher must be considered primary, but beyond those are logistical and pedagogical needs that are best met by organized sessions. A list of seminar topics by NASSP is indicative of such requirements (Figure 6.6).

The teacher who has gone beyond the survival stage and has mastered the basics of classroom organization is now ready to learn the art of teaching. If effective teaching is making appropriate teaching decisions, this individual who can now stand before a class and conduct business will possess a developing curiosity about the "art" side of the profession. In particular, learning about technique and acquiring new skills should be a part of every teacher's repertoire in the third to seventh year. A sample of the needs that teachers traditionally request can be found in one survey of 2,600 teachers reported in the *Journal of Teacher Education.* In order, those needs were the ability to:

1. Maintain order and help student with self-discipline
2. Motivate student achievement
3. Apply appropriate evaluative techniques
4. Individualize instruction to meet varying needs
5. Use audiovisual materials in teaching
6. Provide instruction at various cognitive levels
7. Facilitate development of self-concept in students

Getting Started	Motivation
Setting up the gradebook	Problem solving
Establishing rules and procedures	Direct instruction
Physically organizing the classroom	Guided inquiry
Using bulletin boards	Evaluation of instruction
Establishing policies for late work, attendance, etc.	
Writing letters to parents	**Diagnosis and Assessment**
Developing information packets	Teacher and student assessment
	Test construction
	Measurement devices
Classroom Management	Item analysis
Theories of management	
Managing groups, materials, instruction, time	**Purpose of Testing**
	NRT and CRT
	Writing objectives and essay tests
Instruction	Measuring attitude and social behaviors
Instructional models	
Long-range planning	**Parental Involvement**
Unit planning	Parent–teacher conferences
Lesson planning	Parents as resources
Goals and objectives	Parents as volunteers
Identifying resources	Parents as home tutors
Questioning strategies	

Figure 6.6 A List of Seminar Topics
Source: "Tips for Principals," *NAASP,* September 1990, p. 4.

8. Prepare teacher-made tests

9. Use observational techniques effectively in classroom

10. Understand the interaction of school forces such as decision making and communication.[8]

For the more mature, veteran teacher, supervision can often be seen as an inconvenience at best. Holding tenure or a continuing contract and having survived many seasons in the classroom, this teacher may wonder about the qualifications of the supervisor who has just arrived to provide assistance. The supervisor should be prepared for a standard list of excuses (Figure 6.7) and view such token resistance as an "art form" rather than a serious impediment.

It is important in working with such a teacher to determine whether he or she has developed beyond the survival stage. To confront an experienced teacher who is playing out the first year for the twentieth time is depressing. Much more likely, however, is to discover a teacher whose development has been "arrested" somewhere along the line and most often by the organization in which they work.

Figure 6.7 Table of Excuses

To save everyone time, give your excuse by number.

1. That's the way we've always done it.
2. I didn't know you were in a hurry for it.
3. That's not in my department.
4. No one told me to go ahead.
5. I'm waiting for an O.K.
6. How did I know this was different?
7. That's his job, not mine.
8. Wait until the boss comes back and ask him.
9. I forgot.
10. I didn't think it was very important.
11. I'm so busy I just can't get around to it!
12. I thought I told you.
13. I wasn't hired to do that!

We believe that the supervisor should see each teacher as a bright person who liked people enough to become credentialed and go to work knowing full well that the extrinsic benefits would be less than other parallel work. If that person has failed to become the teacher that we all wish for our children, it is up to the supervisor to invest the time to find out why development stopped. Although such counseling (therapy model) is painfully slow, it is vital; such a teacher sees between 30 to 180 students a day, year in and year out, and will affect the lives of thousands of children during a full career.

Particularly helpful with such a teacher is the new role of "teams" in schools and the possibility of either differentiating instruction or conducting a job analysis to see where this teacher might best contribute. Each supervisor will have to search their conscience to determine if they will want to invest heavy staff development dollars on this "horse still in the barn."

SKILLS OF INSTRUCTION

Beyond an understanding of the purpose of education and the persona of the teacher is a set of skills and practices that can be categorized as pedagogy. Pedagogical knowledge enables the teacher to do the following:

1. Set up the classroom for instruction, establish routines, and organize student groups for a variety of learning activities and purposes
2. Conduct lessons in an efficient manner, asking appropriate questions, establishing an effective pace, avoiding disciplinary problems, and managing various forms of misbehavior

3. Adapt subject matter so that it can be understood in the intended form; making it appropriate to student needs and background, coordinating content with concepts, skills, and attitudes at desired levels, and using media and methods effectively

4. Encourage active learning through interactive teaching; develop adequate self-concepts in students and teach critical thinking skills

Two trends over the past thirty years make pedagogy even more important than ever. First, during this period the role of the classroom teacher has evolved from a solitary craftsperson who was characterized by knowledge and autonomy to a learning manager who operates within a clearly defined system of educating. This change in the condition of teaching makes it essential that the individual teacher possess and use the appropriate skills to deliver the curriculum in the form that it is intended. To do otherwise is to be dysfunctional.

The second trend during this same period has been the development of a major base of research knowledge about teaching (see Chapter 3). This knowledge base has progressed to the point where researchers can forecast that a teacher using certain techniques under certain conditions will get predictable results in learning. The critical question for today's instruction is, "What kind of teaching skills should the teacher employ to get the job done?"

Undergirding these two major changes in teaching is a science and art basis for instruction absent thirty years ago. At the science level is a prescription for traditional instruction that may be best represented by the teacher evaluation instrument used in the State of Florida. This twenty-step prescription follows closely the research bases for "direct" instruction and serves as a legal mandate for teacher behavior in the classroom in that state (see Chapter 3, Figure 3.2).

As discussed in Chapter 3, the research base for education has evolved beyond direct teaching only. Several texts on teaching now provide categories such as direct teaching, indirect teaching, and self-directed teaching with appropriate sets of teaching skills to meet the prescription.[9]

Beyond the basic science of teaching being provided by numerous studies of teaching effectiveness is the "art" side of the equation where supervisors and teachers make choices from among many options to gain the desired effect. Interactive teaching is more indirect, providing more input from, and autonomy for, the learner so that the pattern of teaching becomes more complex. Rather than standardizing instruction, the teacher now attempts to personalize or individualize the learning act. Here, selection of technique, method, and media become a sort of art form because the teacher realizes that the process chosen in teaching will influence the act of learning itself. Teaching strategies become all important.

TEACHING STRATEGIES

As the supervisor works with the teacher within the context of guiding documents and instructional purposes, numerous instructional decisions will have to be made to tailor teaching to the instructional objectives. Teaching strategies such as lectures, field trips, films, small-group discussions, cooperative learning, laboratory work, conferencing, use of computers, or salient reading all are means to some end. For example, a whole-group lecture may serve to give all students necessary information, demonstrate a technique, or build listening and note-taking skills. Small-group work, by contrast, may enable students to share ideas, learn planning skills, or practice leadership behaviors.

Discipline

Discipline involves many choices (see Table 6.2). Some experts prescribe a teacher-directed pattern that uses behaviorism to shape, encourage, or discourage student behavior. The use of group rules and consequences, as in Assertive Discipline, for example, will have one effect on the student. By contrast, a faculty following Glasser's Reality Therapy models will involve the student in the setting of such behavior targets and rewards. The philosophy of the district, by determining whether the long-run intent of the educational process is to standardize or individu-alize behavior, indicates which discipline approach is most appropriate. Are we con-taining the student during schools hours, or is this a life skill we are teaching?

Testing

Teachers who test and grade need to know whether we are seeking to "grade and sort" students or whether our philosophy indicates that we think all students can succeed. The decision to use a standardized or curriculum-embedded test (from text), to use true–false, multiple choice, or essay exams makes a great deal of differ-ence in *how* learning will occur. Are we teaching to a narrow cognitive focus (the facts) or a broad cognitive focus (concepts)?

Determining the Instructional Focus

With instructional choices, the supervisor and the teacher can construct an "instruc-tional logic" that guides the selection of strategies, methods, and media. A series of questions can form the basis of an intellectual discussion about teaching: What am I expected to teach? Why am I teaching this to my students? Whom am I teaching? What is the appropriate level of instruction? What is the expected outcome or product? What can I do to get my students to learn in the intended manner? The questions are answered by philosophy and goal statements, curriculum maps and frameworks, con-ceptual organization of materials and texts, needs assessments and student academic records, test scores, and the selection of appropriate methods media and strategies.

A series of questions can assist the teacher and supervisor in assessing the desired pattern in the classroom:

Twenty Questions Before Teaching
1. Is the room prepared? Is furniture arranged to promote desired learning? Is the environment conducive to what I intend to teach?
2. Do I have a plan for getting students into the room and settled in their seats?

Table 6.2 Comparing Discipline Approaches

Authority	To Know What Is Going On	To Provide Smooth Transitions	To Maintain Group Alertness	To Involve Students	To Attend to Misbehavior
Skinner	Realize value of non-verbal interaction, i.e., smiles, pats, and handshakes to communicate to students that you know what is going on.	Realize that smooth transitions may be part of your procedures for awarding reinforcers, i.e., points and tokens, to reward appropriate behavior.	Set rules, rewards, and consequences; emphasize that responsibility for good behavior rests with each student.	Involve students in "token economies," in contracts, and in graphing own behavior performance.	Provide tangibles to students who follow the class rules; represent tangibles as "points" for the whole class to use to "purchase" a special activity.
Canter	Realize that the student has the right to choose how to behave in your class with the understanding of the consequences that will follow his or her choice.	Insist on decent, responsible behavior.	Set clear limits and consequences; follow through consistently; state what you expect; state the consequences, and why the limits are needed.	Use firm tone of voice; keep eye contact; use nonverbal gestures as well as verbal statements; use hints, questions, and direct messages about requesting student behavior, give and receive compliments.	Follow through with your promises and the reasonable, previously stated consequences that have been established in your class.
Dreikurs	Realize that the student wants status, recognition, and a feeling of belonging. Misbehavior is associated with mistaken goals of getting attention, seeking power, getting revenge, and wanting to be left alone.	Identify a mistaken student goal; act in ways that do not reinforce these goals.	Provide firm guidance and leadership.	Allow students to have a say in establishing rules and consequences in your class.	Make it clear that unpleasant consequences will follow inappropriate behavior.
Ginott	Communicate with the student's feelings about a situation and about his/herself.	Invite student cooperation.	Model the behavior you expect to see in your students.	Build student's self-esteem.	Give a message that addresses the situation and does not attack the student's character.

continued

Source: J. McNeil and J. Wiles, *The Essentials of Teaching* (New York: Macmillan, 1990), Chapter 10.

Table 6.2 *Continued*

Authority	To Know What Is Going On	To Provide Smooth Transitions	To Maintain Group Alertness	To Involve Students	To Attend to Misbehavior
Glasser	Realize that the student is a rational being; he/she can control his/her behavior.	Help the student make good choices; good choices produce good behavior and bad choices produce bad behavior.	Understand class rules are essential.	Realize that classroom meetings are effective means for attending to rules, behavior, and discipline.	Accept no excuses for inappropriate behavior; see that reasonable consequences always follow.
Kounin	Develop "with-itness", a skill enabling you to see what is happening in all parts of the classroom at all times.	Avoid jerkiness which consists of thrusts (giving directions before your group is ready); of dangles (leaving one activity dangling in the verbal air and starting another one and then returning to the first activity); of flip-flops (terminating one activity, beginning another one, and then returning to the first activity you terminated).	Avoid slowdowns (delays and time wasting) that can be caused by overdwelling (too much time spent on explanations) and by fragmentation (breaking down an activity into several unnecessary steps); develop a group focus through format (active participation by all students in the group); through accountability (holding all students accountable for the concept of the lesson) and by attention (seeing all the students and using unison responses as well as individual responses).	Avoid boredom by providing a feeling of progress for the students, by offering challenges, by varying class activities, by changing the level of intellectual challenge, by varying lesson presentations, and by using many different learning materials and aids.	Understand teacher correction influences behavior of other nearby students (the ripple-effect).

3. Have I thought of a "motivational opener" to make the transition from the last class they attended to this one?

4. Can I give the students a preview (advanced organizers) of what we'll be doing during the period so they'll know what to expect?

5. Have I estimated the time required for each activity this period?

6. Are the major concepts for this lesson covered by my planned activities?

7. Are the essential facts I want taught in the materials to be used?

8. Have I planned for the appropriate level of affect desired?

9. Have I planned to allow each student to participate at an appropriate level of learning?

10. Are the necessary and appropriate materials present in the room?

11. Do I have a plan for discussion? Have I clarified what kind of discussion will contribute to the lesson objectives?

12. Have I planned for relevance? Do I have some real-life examples?

13. Have I considered handout procedures and steps for collecting homework?

14. How will I involve special students in this lesson?

15. What is my plan for grouping? What directions will I give?

16. Do I have a plan for possible deviant behavior today?

17. Do I want to emphasize a certain format/standards for today's homework or assignment?

18. What kind of test questions would I ask about today's material? Do I want to share these expectations with students?

19. What kind of technique will I use for closure of today's class?

20. What is my procedure for dismissal of the class?

As the supervisor and the teacher enter into a dialogue about the effect of teaching strategies in the individual classroom, the roots of a theory of instruction will emerge. "That theory grows from the process of experimentation as investigators 'play around' with new data in light of earlier conclusions."[10] Hunches become hypotheses, which can be validated and invalidated by "action research" in the individual teacher's room. The validated hunches (about teaching practices) become systems of propositions (if–then) or theories. Such theories can be modified, and probably will be, under varying circumstances. As the theory changes, the teacher (and the supervisor) grow in their ability to assess their effectiveness.

In the 1990s, new and exciting work has occurred in the area of teaching with a cognitive focus. Not only have we come to realize the impact of our "props" on learning, but also to begin to understand how students think and process teacher behaviors. In particular, the area known as Schema Theory opens up new understandings of the teaching act.[11]

According to this theory, students possess a background that at all times influences the reception of all teaching. This background, or schemata, is made up of general and specific knowledge that will interpret and form the way the teacher's input is received. As teachers teach, and that schemata is activated, learning occurs. Teachers can learn to activate this student background in different ways for different purposes:

1. Linking old information to new information (semantic mapping, coaching student inquiry)
2. Reconstructing the student's background (creating cognitive dissonance)
3. Teaching students how to learn (metacognition, scaffolding, thinking skills)
4. Making learning purposeful (interest development, attribution, attitude formation)
5. Organizing knowledge in new ways (guides and outlines, mental imagery, advanced organizers, creative use of student questions)

The level of sophistication in discussions about teaching between the supervisor and the teacher can reach high levels of complexity and sophistication. This is because the act of learning, and the act of teaching, are among the most complex human behaviors. To arrest the development of a teacher, who employs only the strategies of a direct model (lecture, didactic questions, multiple-choice tests), is close to a crime in education.

THE EVALUATION OF INSTRUCTION

Along with the task of improving instruction for students, the supervisor is often asked to be an evaluator as well. The behaviors in the past that caused teachers to use the derogatory term "snoopervisor" do not have to be invoked in the 1990s. Professionalism is alive and well in most school districts, and there is a professional knowledge base that can make the supervisor an asset to most teachers. The key to successful evaluation experiences is to establish a professional "set" and maintain a close client relationship.

Most evaluation sessions in today's schools will be conducted with a guiding instrument (such as the Florida model) and using the clinical supervision techniques developed by Goldhammer in the 1960s. Such conferencing is important since it may represent the only opportunity the supervisor will have to engage the teacher in professional dialogue.

In the clinical supervision model, both supervisor and teacher are assumed to be knowledgeable about the teaching act and to communicate as colleagues. The role of the teacher is to identify concerns; the role of the supervisor is to provide assistance. The clinical supervision model usually employs a five-step process:

1. Preobservational conference for orientation
2. An observation by the supervisor, sometimes using an instrument such as the Flanders
3. Assessment by supervisor and selection of area of emphasis
4. The conference featuring an exchange of views and feedback
5. A post-conference analysis by the supervisor

Variations in this procedure over the past thirty years have included attempts to plan micro-teaching sessions for the teacher, to define teaching in terms of competencies, to employ peer supervision sessions among teachers, to make supervision a "team" function, and to place the responsibility for evaluation in the hands of other teachers in a center.

Whatever the form, there are several common purposes to most conferences:

1. To enhance the relationship between the supervisor and teacher

2. To provide the teacher with feedback about his or her performance

3. To promote further understanding of the act of teaching

4. To stimulate exploration of new strategies of teaching

5. To encourage personal teacher growth in skills, behaviors, and attitudes

The actual evaluation conference can be "scripted" by imagining the steps necessary for a successful conclusion. First, a comfortable and quiet location will be needed where the total attention of both parties can be focused upon the conference itself. Second, a social period should proceed the business of the conference since most teachers will be slightly uncomfortable. Third, the supervisor should set the stage for the session by outlining the purposes and procedures. Fourth, the teacher should be drawn into the session with some involving technique. Finally, the supervisor should conclude the conference only when it is clear that the teacher understands, agrees, and is committed to whatever course of action is determined.

A checklist may help the supervisor guide the conference to a successful close (Figure 6.8). Finally, a complete evaluation form is included (Figure 6.9).

SUMMARY

A teacher's performance in the classroom is the result of a number of contributing factors including the personality of the teacher, his or her knowledge of philosophy and psychology, the teacher's understanding of subject matter, and the skills of teaching possessed. Supervisors must work with all four of these areas to improve classroom teaching.

A beginning point for improving instruction is to make the teacher aware of the goals and objectives of the program within which they are teaching. Tied closely to this understanding is the actual planning process by which the teacher prepares to instruct.

Effective schools have certain things in common including high degrees of organization, a clear mission, and teacher involvement in the operation of the school. Effective teachers are most often found in effective schools; they, too, have high degrees of organization and direction.

Supervisors should work with teachers in ways compatible to the environment. The role for the teacher in a bureaucracy will not be the same as a supervisor in a small and personal work environment. Regardless, supervisors should try to view teachers as individuals on a continuum of development and provide assistance accordingly.

The actual skills of instruction can be drawn from both practice and research. They should, where possible, be coordinated with the goals of instruction. The ability to selectively apply the many teaching methods, media, and strategies to meet curricular goals represents the artistry of teaching. In the 1990s, skills to increase student cognitive

---

Planning

Analyze the data—be prepared to discuss performance and provide specific feedback.

Identify the focus of conference, the building blocks and growth areas. Decide on the decision level (delegate, suggest, recommend, or direct).

Determine the best approach to use, based on purpose and the other person.

Plan for the best time, location, and environment.

Interaction

Clarify the purpose of the conference.

Explain the conference process—what will happen.

Explore the other person's expectations for the conference.

Involve the other person through questions and discussion.

Encourage active participation in discussion through nods, smiles, listening, and encouraging remarks.

Provide specific feedback about performance.

Check for understanding of concepts and feedback.

Clarify areas of confusion or misunderstanding.

Enhance or maintain the self-esteem of the employee.

Listen and respond with empathy if the other person appears to be discouraged.

Ask for help in solving the problem.

Promote a positive climate through eye contact, body lean, attentiveness, nods and smiles, and positive voice tone.

Encourage the other person to identify strategies to improve performance and how and when to use them.

Check for agreement by listening and/or asking questions.

Check for commitment to change by listening and/or asking questions.

Close by identifying key points, enhancing self-esteem, and arranging for follow-up.

Figure 6.8 A Checklist for Guiding Conferences
Source: "The Practitioner," *NASSP,* October 1989, pp. 6–7.

efforts represent a fertile area for staff development with experienced teachers.

Finally, the evaluation of teachers should be tailored, where possible, to their progress and personal development. New teachers may respond to a direct identification of desired skills in evaluation, whereas the mature teacher may need a more indirect approach to assessment.

There are nearly as many evaluation instruments as there are teachers, and the supervisor may have to select one that best fits the purpose of the evaluation being conducted. It is unlikely that one instrument would be appropriate for all teachers. For the new teacher trying to learn the fundamentals, an instrument similar to Figure 3.2 might prove beneficial. This instrument identifies the parts of teaching and provides teachers with a rating of their preparation in each of eight areas.

For a more experienced teacher, such an instrument might impede real communication about classroom events. A more appropriate approach may be to place this teacher on a school-based improvement team and have that team view the instructional practices in the school in terms of goal areas. The opportunity to visit other classrooms may also provide the same teacher with insights into his or her own practices.

Indicators have been identified which relate to each of the eight teacher competencies identified on the Evaluation of Professional Growth of Teacher form. For each of the indicators rate yourself on the scale as indicated below. Place your rating in the blank beside the indicator. To assist you in determining a rating, look at the percentages for how often you do the item. For example, you may want to rate yourself a 7.5 on an item. At the end of each area, complete your overall rating on each competency area.

Rating Scale

10–9	8–7	6–4	3–2	1–0
Almost always	Most of the time	Frequently	Rarely	Almost never
(100–90%)	(89–70%)	(69–30%)	(29–10%)	(9–0%)

I. **Demonstrates the ability to plan and deliver instruction.**

____ 1. My lesson plans reflect a coordination with the team, *other teachers of the same subject*, the department, and county objectives so that courses will have similar skill focus and content, similar expectations for student performance on tests, projects, and other assignments.

____ 2. My long-range lesson plans and student evaluation procedures are developed at least nine weeks in advance.

____ 3. At the beginning of each week, I give my students in writing the homework assignments, test dates, and other due dates. (Placing this information on the chalk board or a bulletin board meets this requirement.)

____ 4. My lesson plans are available prior to instruction and organized along with nine weeks' grading procedures, and tests, quizzes, and handouts to date.

____ 5. My lesson plans focus on skill development in communication, math, physical development, and/or social skills. Course content is organized to teach skills and lesson plans identify the specific skill(s).

____ 6. I use advanced organizers, reviews, clear directions at the beginning and end of each lesson and when activities change.

____ 7. I give homework that reinforces the day's lesson at least three times a week. This should not be confused with seatwork that can be completed before the bell.

____ 8. I organize and present information in logical sequence. The instruction moves from beginning to end with smooth transitions between at least two different activities.

____ 9. I use supplemental materials, a variety of activities, and labs to enhance instruction.

____ 10. I design my instruction to actively engage students in the learning process.

____ 11. I use effective questioning techniques which include high order questions, wait time, amplification, extension, and corrective feedback.

____ **Total points divided by 110 gives a rating on Area I of ____**

II. **Demonstrates knowledge of subject matter.**

____ 12. I model correct usage of standard English when writing and speaking.

____ 13. I give correct information during lecture/discussions, on tests, and other written materials.

____ 14. I focus instruction on use of content to develop and demonstrate understanding of skills related to the course including communication and math skills.

____ **Total points divided by 30 gives a rating on Area II of ____**

continued

Figure 6.9 Evaluation of Professional Growth of Teacher Self-Evaluation Form
Source: Michael Walker, Director General, Duval County Schools, Jacksonville, Florida. Used by permission.

III. Demonstrates the ability to utilize appropriate classroom management techniques, including the ability to maintain appropriate discipline.

___ 15. I begin instruction with the bell and end with the bell; increasing time on task is an instructional priority.

___ 16. I organize class administrative details so that they do not take away from maximizing instructional time. Example: roll call, paper distribution, and progress reports are done only when students have a seat work activity related to the lesson/skill for the day.

___ 17. I consistently use the school discipline plan to manage student conduct.

___ 18. I supervise students in the hall or classroom.

___ 19. I circulate about the classroom to provide individual assistance and to monitor off-task behavior.

___ 20. I check roll each period and in homeroom or A/A and complete attendance forms.

___ 21. My students know my expectations for classroom operations and comply with my expectations.

___ **Total points divided by 70 gives a rating on Area III of ___**

IV. Shows sensitivity to student needs by maintaining positive school environment.

___ 22. I actively engage students in meaningful Advisor/Advisee activities designed to promote students' sense of self-worth.

___ 23. I have established a climate of courtesy and respect.

___ 24. I demonstrate non-verbal behavior that shows interest.

___ 25. I find ways on a daily basis to specifically compliment/praise/reward students for appropriate academic and social behavior.

___ 26. I seek opportunities on a daily basis to speak with students, parents, and teachers outside of classes.

___ 27. My students, within a short period of time, respond to both academic and non-academic directions. (In other words, students do what I expect them to do.)

___ 28. I desist off-task/disruptive students individually so as not to distract the class.

___ 29. I avoid the use of sarcasm, a harsh and/or loud/screaming voice, and personal put downs.

___ **Total points divided by 80 gives a rating on Area IV of ___**

V. Demonstrates the abilities to evaluate instructional needs of students.

___ 30. My evaluation/grading is based on student's ability to master specific skills and content.

___ 31. I have designed my grading criteria so that grade distributions tend to reflect the school's population as measured on standardized tests.

___ 32. I design my planning and instruction to give students of all ability levels an opportunity to be successful in meeting both course performance measures and tests.

___ 33. I design student evaluations to measure and give feedback on both process/skills as well as the correct answer. (Checking only for the correct answer and scantron tests [a machine that scores tests on "bubble" sheets] cannot do this.)

___ 34. I give students feedback on the *quality* of their homework.

___ 35. I discuss individual student instructional problems at team meetings.

___ 36. I periodically evaluate the effectiveness of test items.

___ **Total points divided by 70 gives a rating on Area V of ___**

Figure 6.9 *Continued*

VI. Demonstrates a willingness to assume non-instructional responsibilities.

____ 37. Before/after school and during the change of classes I am in the halls and/or outside my door actively supervising students by enforcing school rules.

____ 38. I sign up to chaperone schoolwide activities (not team) at least two times a year.

____ 39. I am punctual and on duty when and where assigned—to classes before and after school, pep rallies, intramurals, etc.

____ 40. I meet weekly and work with my team for planning and for carrying out non-instructional team activities.

____ 41. My contacts with parents focus on what students have done behaviorally or academically, not what I have or have not done.

____ 42. I sponsor, co-sponsor or am involved in a student activity on an on-going basis.

____ **Total points divided by 60 gives a rating on Area VI of ____**

VII. Demonstrates a commitment to professional growth.

____ 43. I am a member of a content area professional organization.

____ 44. I update and extend my training through professional reading, working on advanced degrees, working on committees, attending workshops and/or conferences.

____ 45. I revise and improve instructional planning yearly so as to keep up with latest in educational research and curriculum development.

____ **Total points divided by 30 gives a rating on Area VII of ____**

VIII. Shows evidence of professional characteristics.

____ 46. I adhere to the code of ethics for educators as enacted by the Florida legislature.

____ 47. I act to promote the profession by speaking positively about the school and its staff.

____ 48. I model the behaviors that are expected of students, staff, and parents.

____ 49. I am actively involved in bringing about needed change and improvements in the school by regular involvement in decision making by regular attendance at meetings.

____ 50. I promptly turn in requested reports, i.e., attendance information, homework and assignments for ISSP, class list.

____ **Total points divided by 50 gives a rating on Area VIII of ____**

Overall Rating

Directions: Place the scores and the ratings for each of the eight areas in the space provided. Then total your *points* for each section score and divide by 50 to get an overall score. Then look at the ratings for each section and determine which you rated highest and which you rated lowest.

Points Each Section	Rating Each Section	
____	____	I. Ability to plan and deliver instruction
____	____	II. Knowledge of subject matter
____	____	III. Classroom management
____	____	IV. Maintaining a positive school environment
____	____	V. Evaluation of instructional needs
____	____	VI. Assumes non-instructional responsibilities
____	____	VII. Commitment to professional growth
____	____	VIII. Professional characteristics
____	**Total points divided by 500 gives an overall rating of ____**	

Figure 6.9 *Continued*

IMPLICATIONS FOR SUPERVISION

1. This chapter presents teacher development as a staged evolution. Can you identify reasons why teacher growth is arrested in many districts?
2. At what point does the "science" of teaching become the "art" of teaching?

3. Using Figure 3.2 from Chapter 3, can you identify an underlying philosophy of evaluation? Can you modify this instrument to fit the needs of your district? What are the major differences between Figure 3.2 and your instrument?

≈ CASE STUDY 1 ≈

For the past five years, you have been working as a supervisor in one of America's larger school districts. An opportunity to practice supervision in a suburb presents itself, and you are offered a position with an increase in salary. Your inclination is to accept this new opportunity, but a colleague in your present district warns you that it is dangerous to be a supervisor in the suburbs.

Questions
1. How does the role of supervisor differ in an urban, suburban, or rural district?
2. If you do accept this new position, is there any retraining that you should seek to increase your competence on the job?

≈ CASE STUDY 2 ≈

The supervisor had to admit that the meeting with the teacher had been less than satisfactory. If this conferencing was supposed to lead to better classroom instruction, something was missing! The supervisor had followed the state-mandated process, step-by-step, but the teacher hadn't responded in the "textbook" manner.

The whole evaluation program was based on teacher effectiveness research that identified key skills of teaching like "advanced organizers" and "questioning techniques." Following several observations, the supervisor and the teacher were to sit down and analyze the performance of the teacher and to set goals for improvement. Instead, the teacher had challenged the validity of the skills observed, saying they were based on composite studies drawn from a skewed population of effective school characteristics. The teacher had sounded very knowledgeable and was known to be taking a research course at a nearby university.

Questions
1. What should the supervisor do, given this communication impasse?
2. How would the supervisor's behavior be affected if it was found that the teacher was correct in her observations about the evaluation tool?

SUGGESTED LEARNING ACTIVITIES

1. Visit a local public school and request to see the teacher evaluation criteria. What sort of teaching (direct, indirect, self-direct) is being promoted?
2. List the kind of events that might interrupt the development of a classroom teacher in the first seven years.

3. Describe how the concept of "discipline and classroom management" differ as the teacher's philosophy of education changes.

BOOKS TO REVIEW

Bernstein, B. *The Structuring of Pedagogic Discourse.* New York: Routledge and Kegan, 1990.

Blase, J., and Kirby, P. *Bringing Out the Best in Teachers: What Effective Principals Do.* Newbury Park, CA: Corwin Press, 1991.

Cangelosi, J. *Evaluating Classroom Instruction.* New York: Longman, 1991.

Curry, L. *Learning Styles in Secondary Schools: A Review of Instruments and Implications for Their Use.* Madison, WI: National Center on Effective Secondary Schools, 1990.

English, F. *Deciding What to Teach and Test.* Newbury Park, CA: Corwin Press, 1992.

Glatthorn, A. *Supervisory Leadership: Introduction to Instructional Supervision.* Glenview, IL: Scott Foresman, 1990.

Glickman, C., ed. *Supervision in Transition.* Alexandria, VA: Association for Supervision and Curriculum Development, 1992.

Goldhammer, R. et al. *Clinical Supervision: Special Methods for the Supervision of Teachers.* Orlando: Harcourt, Brace, Jovanovich, 1993.

Keefe, J., and Jenkins, J., eds. *Instructional Leader Handbook.* Reston, VA: National Association of Secondary Principals, 1991.

Lieberman, A. *The Changing Context of Teaching.* Chicago: National Society for the Study of Education, 1992.

Olivia, P. *Supervision for Today's Schools,* 4th ed. New York: Longman, 1993.

Pajak, E. *Approaches to Clinical Supervision: Alternatives for Improving Instruction.* Norwood, MA: Christopher-Gordon Publishers, 1993.

Rosenholz, S. *Teachers' Workplace: The Social Organization of Schools.* New York: Teachers College, Columbia University, 1991.

Sergiovanni, T., and Starrett, R. *Supervision: A Redefinition.* New York: McGraw-Hill, 1993.

THE EFFECTIVE USE OF TECHNOLOGY

George Jimenez, a high school junior, is supposed to be in school today, but he's not. No, George is not playing hooky, and he is not another dropout. Today, George is attending his computer tutorial program at the center near his home and is interacting with the U.S. Army in a premilitary training program. The year is 1997, and George's school district has finally arrived in the age of high technology.

Technology has had a pervasive influence on American society during the past twenty years. In the early and mid-1970s, Americans marveled at the direct and instantaneous coverage of a war 12,000 miles away. In an era predating accessible personal computers, VCRs, coaxial cable television, facsimile machines, car telephones, price scanners, interactive video, teleconferencing capacity, and a host of other miracle consumer products, the age of technology was just beginning.

Schools in the 1970s had not yet entered the age of technology, and in the 1990s some schools still have not joined what will be seen as a distinctive watershed in modern history. A challenge to all schools in the early years of the twenty-first century will be to use technology to its full advantage. Failure to meet this challenge will make any school obsolete and dysfunctional to the process of learning.

In the later years of the 1970s and the early years of the 1980s, educators began to see the value of the changing technology about them. "Computers" became a synonym for technology, and many districts began crash buying programs to become "modern." Over an ten-year period, a variety of computers—Texas Instrument, Tandy, Commodore, Apple, IBM, and others—were purchased by school districts like collector items, only to be discarded when the software accompanying the machines proved shallow and nontransferable. The standard machine of this era was the Apple

IIe, a durable computer with a drill-focused software format. In the 1990s, the Apple Macintosh or the IBM PS/1 is generally used.

By the late 1980s, most schools and districts realized the folly of buying machines without a coordinated plan for adapting the computer to the existing curriculum. During the early 1990s, computer labs with upgraded software packages dominated purchasing efforts. Purchases during this era amounted to billions of dollars, making technology in schools a very large business venture for vendors. As this text is written, schools possess new software systems designed to cover a mandated curriculum and accelerate instruction speed for each student. Paralleling this adoption of computers in schools is a continuing effort to search out other applications of new technologies.

TECHNOLOGY IN SCHOOLS—A TWENTY-YEAR PERSPECTIVE

All schools pay lip-service to becoming technologically advanced, but few schools have demonstrated an ability to use the power of technology to redefine education and the schooling process. For many districts, the difference between being "high tech" and saying "oh heck" is a matter of grasping the meaning of technological change. Going beyond the confines of the school curriculum and creating new teacher–student relationships and new social structures in the classroom has rarely occurred in public schools in the mid-1990s.

Twenty years ago, in the midst of a telecommunication revolution focused on the home television set, the computer was simply a large thing that processed data "somewhere." Early versions of the personal computer, although stimulating for consumers, were often just adaptations of early programmed instruction technology, selecting and advancing through a predetermined software path. By the early 1980s, however, personal computers were available that could manipulate as much data as the original industrial computers could but at a fraction of the cost. For example, a 1965 IBM 1401 model industrial computer cost $55,000. By 1975, the same capacity computer (TICCIT) had fallen to $4,000. In 1986, a personal computer with essentially the same capacity cost $3,000. In the mid-1990s, the PC setup is about two thirds the 1986 cost.

These falling prices and rising market competition meant that schools could, for the first time, aspire to enter a world of electronically manipulated information after centuries of dependence on humans to do this task. Naturally, all schools aspired to become "space-age" in their instructional delivery, and many began buying personal computers with image as the sole criteria. According to a survey conducted by Johns Hopkins University in 1989–90 (N=1000), 96 percent of all schools had computers in some rooms.[1] The study did not mention that "many schools had lots of discarded equipment, often adding to the prestige of the school, but with little educational value."[2]

Like much of the technology in the past, schools tried to use computers without considering their meaning for instruction. Instead of taking advantage of what the computer could do, teachers reported that they used the computer for drill, as word processors, and for remediation in subjects such as math and English. Failure to come to grips with the issue of "control" of learning continues to bedevil school districts today.

By the early 1990s, the long-awaited marriage of the curriculum software with the existing curriculum requirements for students began to occur. Companies such as Jostens Learning Corporation, using IBM delivery units, were able to promise schools a technology with payoff; students who studied via the computer would score well on standardized achievement tests. Although such claims have not been substantiated in the many federal programs using such systems,[3] school districts rushed to invest in this "inevitable" future. The cost of computerized instruction for schools and districts accelerated geometrically.

The 1990s have been a time of new investment for schools and districts in Integrated Learning Systems (ILS's) or Integrated Instructional systems (IIS's). These package "labs" usually consist of a network of thirty personal computers with a file server that both delivers software and keeps records on the progress of individual students. The coverage of the basic curriculum offered by the school or district integrates the various learnings of the student. Sufficient to accommodate an entire class at once (thirty stations), such labs begin at about $200,000 per package. With 100,000 schools, and possibly fifteen classrooms per school, it is easy to see that this is a major business venture. Federal funds for disadvantaged youth have been the most common avenue for new consumers.

Not all schools have been arrested at the level of buying a computer setup and rotating students through the lab. Many schools have been able to place remote terminals in individual classrooms where teachers are able to use them for supplemental learning or rewards. Retarding a more creative use of these in class stations is the software format of the host terminal which requires students to address predetermined facts or procedures and to progress through these items in a predetermined order. The good news is that teachers and students don't have to know much about computers to operate like this. The bad news is that the computer is not fulfilling its promise; it is only a substitute teacher (Figure 7.1).

An exception to this sort of mindlessness warned of by Silverman twenty-five years ago,[4] is the Earth Lab project in New York City.[5] Operated in a Harlem elemen-

---

Drill and practice on concepts already mastered

Tutorial modes using a branching program

Gaming modes that motivate students, introduce procedures, or are used for recreation

Simulation used to teach scaled-down versions of complex operations

Discovery learning through inductive or problem-solving formats

Clerical uses such as generating tests and record storage

Figure 7.1 Most Common Uses of Computers in Schools
Source: J. C. Lockard, *Microcomputers for Teachers* (New York: Harper & Collins, 1990), p. 12.

tary school over a six-year period and funded by the National Science Foundation, this project seeks to decompartmentalize instruction by stressing the connections between subjects. Students in this school work on collaborative projects, much as real scientists do, and these small-group inquiries are not "programmed" to a predetermined conclusion. The key to understanding the promise of this project is the full involvement, and major investment, by students in the learning process. Control of knowledge and learning is shared, as it must be, if the computer is to deliver on its promise of better learning.

Another school of interest in terms of technological application is the Thomas Jefferson High School for Science and Technology (Magnet) in Fairfax County, Virginia. Cited in *Redbook Magazine*[6] (1994) as one of America's best 134 schools, it features eleven technological laboratories including:

Life Science and Biotechnology

Computer Systems

Energy Systems

Prototyping and Engineering

Telecommunications/Television Production

Computer-Assisted Design

Microelectronics

Industrial Automation and Robotics

Chemical Analysis

Optics and Modern Physics

Aerospace and Geoscience

Another serious problem with the adaptation of technology to schools, in particular the computer, has been the role of the teacher in the mix. Schools, for all time, have involved a knower (the teacher) and a learner (the student). With the introduction of the computer (as with the other technologies and equipment), the teacher has been pushed into a technician's role. Because teachers are unable to develop or modify (program) instructional materials delivered by a computer, they are literally prisoners of the commercial system and its programmers.

Since traditional curriculum decisions such as the worth of material, its appropriateness for the population, the rate of coverage, and the method of delivery are all predetermined, the teacher is restricted to monitoring the student's physical interaction with the machine. Said another way, the "art" of teaching, making those hundreds of little decisions that give flavor to instruction, is eradicated in the present form of computer use. The same could be said of most videotapes, television programming, and prescribed long-distance learning opportunities, which may partially explain their limited usage.

This conception of curriculum as "stuff" and students to be "filled" is the most traditional and rigid definition of curriculum and represents a disservice to a century of curriculum work and to the capacities of most teachers. Teachers are not like foremen in a factory, and many teachers would argue with the assumption that teaching is simply covering a set of facts for a standardized examination. Until administrators, with the help of alert supervisors, understand this problem, technology and computers will be blunted on the classroom door.

What technology, including computers, can do is free the teacher and the learner from the rigid and prescribed curriculum of the old days. Searching and researching, discovery, sharing ideas, manipulating data, and cooperating in inquiry are the strong suit of technology in the next century. Computers and technology will allow students new access to knowledge and new ways of sharing and communicating with the world about them. In order for this promise to be fulfilled, however, supervisors will have to bring a new context to the schooling experience. Technology is, and will continue to be, severely limited if it is a means of standardizing learning. Schools must ask, repeatedly, "How can these technologies help to individualize instruction for our students?" If this means abandoning the computer lab approach that has absorbed so many educational resources in the 1990s, so be it.

We now move on to how technology impacts learning. The new technologies have the capacity to do things impossible twenty years ago; to transcend time and distance and link each child to a world-wide curriculum. For twenty years we have been attempting to "put radar on the stagecoach."[7] As we enter the next century, this revolution in delivery options can free us from the narrow confines of the schoolhouse.

It is time for supervisors to abandon the posture of "consumer" of technology and move toward the more appropriate role of instructional design leader. Instead of responding to the host of new technologies, we must begin to guide it. This means making wise cost–benefit decisions in the context of a clear definition of the purpose of educating our children.

STATE-OF-THE-ART TECHNOLOGY IN THE MID-1990S

Technology in the mid-1990s is largely an unplanned consumer experience in which choices outweigh our ability to assess novelty. Prior to this decade, most technology was introduced as single events; the television of the 1950s, the transistors and early computers of the 1960s, the video recorders and compact discs of the 1970s, and the car telephones and fax machines of the 1980s were individually acclaimed and absorbed by a starry-eyed consuming public. In the 1990s, unlike previous decades, we are viewing the integration of all of these technologies into systems for communication and learning. Schools, like individuals, struggle to absorb the meaning of these systems.

Integrated systems of technology, combining previously available technological items, have produced interactive learning systems—a combination of computer technology, transmission technology, television technology, and optical technologies. These interactive technologies can respond appropriately and rapidly to students or teachers using new forms of communication. They promise to match student learning styles to media and are not bound by the four walls of a classroom. As such, integrated learning systems pose a challenge to formal education programs in schools.

Does such instantaneous and world-wide linking of learners portend an age in which all students are reduced to ultraviolet key-punching zombies whose ability to massage data with disc-direct lasers, frame-freezing, slow-motion blow-ups and reverse angle capacity is realized? Not hardly! For educators, the new and integrated technology of the 1990s promises freedom from the impossible task of trying to make children alike in terms of thoughts, behaviors and feelings. These changes will allow educators to accommodate a rapidly changing environment by contending with a shifting database and delivering learning to students through an unlimited variety of mediums.

Schools in the 1990s, and beyond, will be a mixture of traditional teacher-focused instruction and some kind of technological supplement. The difference from the past is that these technologies will be interactive, rather than strictly teacher controlled. In education, "interactive technology" refers to technologies that can respond appropriately and quickly to students or teachers. This interaction can be either between person and machine or among people linked by applied technology.

The key motivators for pursuing technological learning, other than getting on the bandwagon, is that technology is superior to conventional teaching in a number of ways. First, technology can store and retrieve information faultlessly, allowing, for instance, the instant recognition of student knowledge and previous education. A second plus for such technology is that it allows the integration of direct instruction with inquiry learning; students can digress and apply learning without disrupting other students. Third, technology may allow for a better understanding of knowledge by presenting the student with a simultaneous auditory, visual, and tactile presentation, thereby increasing the odds of a learning "reception." Finally, such technology can put the teacher in the role of instructional designer, thereby reversing a thirty-year trend of encroachment by publishing companies using comprehensive learning packages.

Among the new technologies now used in schools are various uses of television, the computer, compact discs, and telephone/fax adaptions. Each of these have an impact on public and private schoolchildren.

Television

In 1952, the federal government set aside 252 television channels for the exclusive use of education. In 1953, the first educational television stations began operation. Millions of young persons benefitted from ETV shows such as *Sesame Street* and *Electric Company.* This media was distinct from previous projected media (overhead projectors, movies, slides, and opaque projection), however, in that it was "live" and less controlled by the teacher. In its freest form, it could broadcast a disaster live (such as the *Challenger* explosion) to the dismay of the classroom teacher.

Throughout the 1970s and 1980s, educational institutions experimented with various kinds of deliveries of television, including cable-delivered, look-down systems (beamed from airplanes), satellite-delivered, and subscription delivery via satellite. For example, TI-IN, the San Antonio-based company delivers general instruction throughout the United States to subscribers as well as specific instruction (advanced chemistry) to school districts with insufficient staff resources. Another example, Channel One, delivers a twelve-minute news broadcast daily to subscribing schools throughout the nation.

A third example of television application just now becoming available is the super-high-frequency microwave approach to delivery that will challenge traditional cable and fiber optics. Copying cellular telephone technology by using multiple transceivers, existing service by Cellularvision can deliver forty-one channels of television, telephone, video conferencing, and interactive video communications "through the wall." By the summer of 1994, 489 local service areas were available around the nation. Lowered cost is a significant advantage of this new development.

The power of television use by schools is not yet realized although technology exists to make this one of the best learning mediums. For example, two-way interactive television, instantaneous, has been technologically possible for thirty years from the most remote sites. Although distance learning generally features institution-to-institution learning, the possibility of special educational networks using the 282 channels remains untapped. Few home viewers realize, for example, that their cable channels have two-way capacity (upstream and downstream in cable jargon) for broadcast. Since 96 percent of all American homes have TV, the combinations for learning are almost unlimited.

Computers

Computer technology has advanced remarkably in the past decade, and schools have struggled to keep up with these changes. Even in the mid-1990s, many districts are still focusing on keyboard skills and drill-type instruction in computer rooms. For example, the ten most popular software packages in math in public schools are most exclusively "coverage" programs (Table 7.1).

It has been estimated that by the year 2000, 80 percent of American schoolchildren will technologically manipulate information in their schoolwork.[8] This projection presents a challenge to schools, as pointed out by Apple Computer founder Steven Wozinak:

> There is no point in having to solve the problems over and over again every day. It's a waste of time . . . machines can do that stuff and leave us to think about more important things . . . personal computers are going to free people from the mundane things . . . they will allow people's minds to work at a higher level.[9]

One of the great advantages of computers is that they allow networking between prospective learners. Two rather exciting applications of this idea are the LAN (local area network) and the BBS (bulletin board services). Both of these concepts allow both teacher-to-teacher and student-to-student sharing of information and are particularly appealing for research projects.

The LAN connects computers to a master console (the teacher) that will allow the teacher to direct an individualized program of learning for up to sixty pupils at

Table 7.1 Top Ten Mathematics Software Applications

Name	Distributor	Cost
1. The Geometric Supposer™	Sunburst	$154
2. Graphing Equations™	Sunburst	59
3. Appleworks™	Apple	180
4. Apple Logo™	Apple	100
5. muMath-80™	USC Educational Technology Center	40
6. Graph Primer and Graph™	MECC	88
7. Survival Math™	Sunburst	59
8. The King's Rule™	Sunburst	59
9. Algebra Series™	Microcomputer Workshops Courseware	89
10. Golf Classic™	Milliken	40

Source: Pamela McLaughlin, *Computer Applications in Education. The Best of ERIC, 1991* (Syracuse, NY: Clearinghouse on Information Resources, August 1992).

once. Computerized lessons (software) will automatically adjust to an individual student's pace and interests. In such a classroom, a teacher may face a three-tiered student body (*Hollywood Squares*-style) and easily maintain eye contact with whomever he or she is speaking via a headset. Private tutoring by the teacher is available to any student in the LAN. Roll call will be handled as the students "log on," and a record of all student learning will be available at all times for teacher review. Grades will, of course, be calculated automatically and could be available for parental review if the network were extended.

The BBS is a more exclusive, nontraditional form of communication that promises great things for schools in the late 1990s. The BBS, accessed through the personal computer, allows two or more persons to communicate about anything, world-wide. All BBS's have a host or lead computer (main hard drive) operated by a systems operator. In schools, the host machine is normally found in a library since security (intrusion by hackers) is a threat to any serious communication and software originates with the host.

Operating out of a "chat mode" (keyboarding), for instance, a student in California can communicate with a student in Japan about earthquakes, access a library collection in Denver, or write to a pen pal in South Africa. This is called a "bulletin board" because messages are left, gathered into "bundles," and travel at night to distant places where they are exchanged and returned to the sending party. There are special "nets" like the Earthlab in Massachusetts, the National Geographic Kids Net in Washington, DC, and the TREKNET (for Star Trek fans), to mention a few. Most computer systems have their own version of the BBS (for example, Proline for Apple Computers). The granddaddy of all nets is called "Internet," which enables users to change nets and search nets with one command. Three million users are now on Internet, and the number grows daily.

Although the equipment required to be a systems operator may be considerable, the user only needs a computer, monitor, and a modem to access the electronic message board. Businesses have been using such networks for a long time (CompuServe® or America Online®, for example); schools, on the other hand, are just now exploring the true possibilities. For example, one school (Twin Lakes, West Palm Beach, Florida) uses a Tandy 3Com system to call a parent when the child is absent or if they need for the parent to contact the school.

Telephone/Fax

One last example of "standalone" technology in school is the use of telephone/fax capabilities to exchange information. This medium is easily accessible, cheap, and instantly gratifying to the participant. In one example of this technology, we created WIN (The World Instructional Network) connecting international schools in Colombia, Taiwan, Singapore, Malaysia, Japan, and Korea. Students in this net produced a daily newspaper, conducted environmental research projects, and produced a book of international poetry (Figure 7.2).

Scheduled to be available in late 1995 in the United States are the so-called "fifth generation" computers. These computers will use artificial intelligence (AI) and can program themselves to respond to human voices in command form. Imagine your students saying, "Write a paper on the Constitutional Convention, NOW!"

In the early 1990s, new and exciting learning resources that combined technologies were becoming available for school use. Combining, for instance, a videodisc, computer, and projection devices, teachers employed CD-ROM (computer disc read-only memory). Such machines allowed teachers to access banks of information (such as slides on European art) and display them as they taught, just like the evening news. The standard CD-ROM stores the equivalent of 550 million characters (or 1000 floppy discs); the average school library could be contained on only two of these.

The videodisc was quickly superseded by the interactive video which allowed an individual student to interact "almost personally" with the machine. By branching to new interest areas, incorporating films, slides, and music, by simulating mechanical, organic and interpersonal processes, as well as providing drill and tutorial services, the machine is a master at individualizing. Particularly impressive, although at a $70,000 price tag, is the EMG Acceleration Station 2000 that can be used with groups as well as individuals.[10] Equipment specifications for the new station are shown in Figure 7.3.

We could continue in a description of the miracles of technology but would probably only succeed in "dating" our text as each new wave of technology makes the last offering obsolete. This new era has ushered in an age in which individuals anywhere in the world can be linked by various communication mediums to other persons and resources in an unlimited number of ways. More than ever before, learners (students and teachers) can *communicate*. However, still to be determined is about what they will be communicating—which brings us back to the supervisor who is ultimately the learning designer in any school system.

Goal:
Wiles, Bondi and Associates seek to link together schools of excellence for the purpose of promoting instructional quality and communication among teachers and to promote programs for youth.

Description:
The World Instructional Network (WIN) will tie together schools of excellence throughout the world by existing and inexpensive technology to demonstrate the feasibility of such linkage and to improve the quality of instruction in American education. Among the possible products of this network will be sharing of instructional resources, research and consulting services, worldwide teacher-to-teacher contacts, worldwide student learning projects, and information cataloging of quality instructional practices.

Step 1: Communication
In early May, 1991, a site visit was conducted at the Taipei American School (Taiwan) and the Hong Kong International School in order to determine instructional needs and requirements of teachers. A decision was made to develop a world instructional network using as pilots American schools overseas and schools of excellence in the United States. A decision was made to limit the demonstration of such service to no more than 10 schools initially, but with a long-term goal of servicing between 100–250 schools worldwide by 1995 on a subscription basis. Expenses incurred during the demonstration period will determine subscription rates in subsequent years.

A proposal was shared with the above-mentioned schools as well as the United States Department of State and selected schools in Asia and South America. To date, commitments to participate have been received from Taipei, Hong Kong, Malaysia (Kuala Lumpur), with interest expressed by Ecuador, Venezuela, and the Dominican Republic American school. All commitments will be finalized by agreement by July 1, 1991.

Step 2: Sharing
During the period September 1, 1991 and January 1, 1992, the pilot schools will demonstrate a sharing of resources and practices under the coordination of Wiles-Bondi. Among those events projected are a common needs assessment, a newsletter of instruction practices, research services and updates in identified areas, common student learning projects, and planning future instructional conferences. In the spring of 1992, pilot schools will assess this project at a conference of international schools or electronically, and the service will be promoted on a cost-share basis to other schools throughout the world. Membership on a cost-share basis will be limited to schools demonstrating innovation and academic excellence.

Step 3: Projected Activities of the Network
While the exact roles and relationships of these schools of excellence will be determined in 1991–92, possible projects might include the following:
   a. Student projects (environmental research studies, linguistics comparisons, historical research)
   b. Student competitions (brain bowls, world essay contests)
   c. Teacher-to-teacher in-servicing/dissemination of ideas
   d. Tailor-made conferencing for teachers throughout the world or by teleconferencing
   e. Teacher exchanges/visitation studies for educators

Step 4: Assessment and Activation
In the spring of 1992, pilot schools will share information about their experience in participating in the project and make recommendations for the activation of the world instructional network. A report will be presented to a conference of administrators from overseas American schools and information about the fall 1992 activation date disseminated. Selected schools in the United States will be invited to join as members as early as 1992. A report will be forwarded to the funding agency supporting this project.

All services by Wiles-Bondi and Associates, Inc., during the pilot phase of this project will be provided without charge to participants or the funding agency.

For further information, contact Dr. Jon Wiles, Wiles-Bondi, Inc., P.O. Box 16545, Tampa, Florida 33687.

Figure 7.2 World Instructional Network
Source: Wiles, Bondi & Associates, Tampa, FL, 1990.

WORLD INSTRUCTIONAL NETWORK

WILES BONDI
AND ASSOCIATES, INC.
EDUCATIONAL CONSULTANTS

October, 1991 Issue

TEACHERS AND ADMINISTRATORS IDENTIFY NEEDS
INSTRUCTIONAL NEEDS ASSESSMENT COMPLETED BY INTERNATIONAL SCHOOLS

Teachers in the seven pilot schools in Asia made quick work of identifying instructional problems they face. One, two and three in most schools were culturally and linguistically diverse pupils, lack of current instructional resources, and the mobility of their students. Shirley Geiss of ISSH wanted access to current software, books, and periodicals. Humoresque Smothers of IS Seoul wanted to know about trends in teaching students with diverse backgrounds. Karen Pearson of Taipei observed that mobility of students was having a temporary effect on performance.

The teachers responding went on to identify other instructional problems such as living in a foreign culture, accessing instructional aids, the number of ESL students, problems of receiving transferring students, becoming obsolete, not having access to current trends and research in their subject areas, keeping up with technology, and being able to purchase instructional materials from the United States.

Asked what the Wiles Group might do for them, the teachers stated they needed help retrieving materials and getting in touch with colleagues in other schools. Services desired include the procurement of instructional resources, helping teachers stay current, receiving new books and publications in a timely manner, assisting in teacher-to-teacher projects, and putting them in touch with influential educators in the United States. As a group, the teachers seemed to endorse the expansion of the network and the inclusion of some stateside schools.

Three projected ideas were endorsed to the degree that they will be activated. A network editorial group will be formed, helping to coordinate this newsletter or other publications. The Columbus Project will commence in October. Finally, critical thinking and creative thinking activities will begin to flow between teachers in various schools.

Administrators in seven international schools in Asia have completed an assessment of needs to determine if a World Instructional Network could benefit them in their jobs. Asked why he was interested in this unique program for international schools Glenn Gerber, Principal at Hong Kong replied, "We want to keep current." Catherine Funk, Principal in Taipei said, "We want to increase our resources... to access information and up-to-date research." Dorothy Loveland, Dean at Sacred Heart School in Tokyo observed, "International schools are a bit isolated as far as the exchange of new ideas. A network could be useful for exchanging samples of work and new ideas."

The administrators responding identified the problems that might be addressed by the WIN as more information about school programs, retrieval of critical instructional resources, and helping each other discover good staff development opportunities for their faculties.

The administrators identified the areas in which they could use research information as ability grouping, advisory guidance programs, use of interdisciplinary units in teaching, and the use of strategies for teaching diverse students. The administrators said they could use materials in all of these areas plus some specific areas such as team formation, supervision models, and environmental education.

Administrators generally shunned the idea of outside consultants except in a conference format. Problems with which they could use assistance were dealing with small teams, scheduling, ability groups, environmental education, and staff development. If an administrator's conference were held for those in the World Instructional Network, favorite places would be Bali, Thailand, and Malaysia.

Please Xerox on Colored Paper and Distribute To Your Teachers

Figure 7.2 *Continued*

209

The Acceleration Station 2000 is a dynamic tool for teachers combining strategies, information, and resources to enhance and accelerate group instruction. Using a large television monitor to display the information from the Macintosh screen, the comprehensive, interactive research information may be accessed as a group activity. Activity structures are provided for higher order thinking skills and study skills instruction.

The cooperative learning component of the Acceleration Station 2000 outlines projects for students to complete in groups. The Macintosh serves as a research, organization, and writing instrument. The activities are designed to take the accelerated teaching and accelerated learning activities to a synthesis/evaluation level in a cooperative learning environment.

Equipment Specifications

The following is a list of equipment required for one (1) Acceleration Station 2000*:

1 Macintosh II CI (5 meg/1 floppy)	1 Speaker Phone
1 Standard Keyboard	1 AFX-1000 Fax Machine
4 Memory Simms, 1 Meg 80 ns	1 CC-04 Serial Interface Cable
1 STV-24 Video Board	1 T-1 Audio Interface Kit
1 4 Port Serial Board	1 RGB VideoCable
1 650 Meg External Hard Drive	1 SCSI Terminator
1 LD-V8000 Laser Player	2 Surge Protector/Strip
1 DM-2710 Color Monitor 27"	3 208 Phone Net Kit
1 A/V Serial Switcher	1 Custom Computer Desk
1 Scanjet IIc, Color Flatbed Scanner	1 Printer Table
1 Set Interactive Keypads	1 Big Book Easel
1 Personal Laser Writer NT	1 CD ROM Player
1 Paintwriter XL	1 Tripod
1 Mitel Smart-1 Dialer	1 Cam-Corder
1 PDF-2 Phone Fax Switch	

*For more information contact the Education Management Group (EMG Corporation)

Figure 7.3 Acceleration Station 2000

With all of these Disney-like capacities (holograms, anyone?), what can we do to improve learning opportunities for our youth? Equally important, how can we help citizens of the twenty-first century to manage tech/knowledge? Isn't it fun to be in education!

THE EFFECTS OF TECHNOLOGY ON LEARNING

The various technologies mentioned in the previous section are like all other media in that they serve to link teacher and student in some manner. And, as Gagne has observed, "Learning is limited by what the learner perceives, and that can be directly influenced by the designer."[11] Supervisors must begin to see technology as more than a thing; it is a tool to shape learning. Supervisors must also view technology from the perspective of a probable future, rather than from their own experiences in the past.

A widely accepted principle of learning theory holds that the more senses that are employed in learning, the greater the chance that learning is reinforced. The use of multimedia, particularly electronic technology, also goes hand-in-hand with emerging understandings of learning styles in students. Finally, as Marshall McLuhan observed nearly thirty years ago, the medium will "color" the learning experiences; "The medium is the message."[12]

Supervisors of instruction must move from the somewhat passive role of consumer of technology to the role of designer of instruction using technology. This will not be easy because it calls for an understanding of how learning occurs (a theory of instruction) and an ability to judge the impact of a certain technology on a learning activity. As Anderson has observed,

> There is no generally understood rationale as to why some information is presented by motion pictures rather than programmed instruction in print, or by textbooks rather than by slides or audiotapes . . . the problem of media selection has been further complicated by a tendency for course developers to consider media selection as an isolated and independent function that is undertaken at some point well along in the instructional development process.[13]

It may be helpful to think about some old technology and some new technology and how that medium would affect learning. If, for instance, students in an eighth-grade classroom were studying the Constitutional Convention, how would a 16mm film, a distance learning experience with an expert, or a programmed computer experience affect the meaning of the lesson?

As a simple point of origin, it might be stated that the purpose of teaching defines the appropriate medium or technology. Thus, we can ask ourselves, Is this a mastery learning experience? Will students benefit from interaction with others? Is student background and experience important to this learning? Is this a relatively fixed knowledge base, or are we teaching a process for future use? Using these and other traditional instruction questions, we can begin to characterize various technologies and "plug them in" to the curriculum.

With the new technologies (videodiscs, interactive television, and so on), it is not so simple. These technologies create a curriculum of experience on their own. How can the teacher know what the student is experiencing and learning if the media (technology) is creating meaning just through delivery? How can any teacher monitor a room full of students using expansive learning tools such as those now available? It would be like every child being on a different television channel and the teacher being responsible for all content.

In this thought, then, is the emerging reality of the new technology; it will produce a kind of learning not experienced before and certainly quite divorced from a fixed knowledge base that has been ordered in advance. Technology will free the student from the confines of "school learning" and will lessen the control of the teacher in terms of student thought, feeling, and perhaps behavior. This is neither good or bad; it is just true!

Taking these ideas one step further, the traditional school has always reinforced teacher control through high degrees of structure. A textbook, teacher lectures, the test, rows of chairs—all of these focus attention on the teacher. More recent methods, such as team-teaching, cooperative learning, or even computer-assisted instruction still retained the teacher's choice of the curriculum or program. Advanced and interactive technology will restructure the teacher–learner relationship and necessarily alter the role of the teacher forever. Schools that try to maintain strict teacher control while applying interactive technology will be increasingly frustrated and will become increasingly dysfunctional and irrelevant to real learning.

We have arrived at a point in which learning becomes an individual activity and the teacher's input into the process is to set up experiences (hopefully, in a pattern to establish meaning) for the learner. In this sense, technology and its application in today's schools is a philosophical thing. It is also political.

THE POLITICS OF TECHNOLOGY

The new technology in schools also presents supervisors with a political problem. David Easton has defined politics "as the authoritative allocation of scarce resources."[14] Certainly, all school persons recognize that resources are always limited, but this definition also suggests that they are allocated by an authority. Said in different terms, the supervisor of instruction will make definite cost–benefit decisions in purchasing new and expensive technology, and those hard choices may spell the difference between a quality education and a mediocre one for students.

Beyond the normal in-school decisions among various products available lies a business sphere with which many supervisors are unfamiliar—a world of fierce competition for sales. Schools, even more than the military, are a new target for business. The fact that 45 million children attend school each day makes any item (lunchroom trays, textbooks, school pictures) a massive market. New technology, with its mystique, is the granddaddy of all educational markets.

Supervisors must sharpen their skills of consumer comparison, and they must carry specifications into such discussions to ensure that what they purchase will support what their district needs. They must also become familiar with the retrieval and assessment of studies of the new technologies.

HELPING TEACHERS ACCEPT TECHNOLOGY

Perhaps the toughest part of moving a school district into the new technological world of the twenty-first century is gaining teacher acceptance. Classroom teachers may actively or passively resist technology for obvious reasons:

1. Lack of familiarity with new technology
2. Lack of competence in using new technology

3. Lack of understanding of the role of the new technology in instruction
4. Fear of comparison with technology in instructional acts
5. Love of the traditional role of teaching

Most teachers now possess or have access to a computer, but such experience does not mean that they are comfortable with computers and other electronic hardware. In a world of chalk, printed handouts, textbooks, and teacher-evaluated tests, knowing what a computer or CD-ROM is doesn't qualify as being familiar with it.

Even more foreign for many teachers is competence with such machines. Although teachers are regularly encouraged to attend computer awareness training, many learn only low-level, time-consuming activities that fail to suggest the time-efficiency or labor-saving capabilities. More important, the teacher who attends such a session without a perceived need often views any new learning as an additional task.

As stated earlier, the real meaning of technology in schools is that teachers can now be the true curriculum designers of learning experiences for students. To engage in interactive technology of the 1990s is to remove teacher "control" of the learning act, while empowering teacher influence over the process of learning. Too many teachers see only technology as a new form of the old act of teaching. Somehow, we must be able to put "old wine in new bottles."

With good reason, many teachers fear technology as an unfair competitor in the learning process. A teacher who allows his or her best lecture to be placed on videodisc is a teacher who never has to produce that best lecture again. Likewise, a teacher who is asked to join in a research study matching CAI versus the live teacher in teaching math skills is a teacher who should be suspicious. In fact, in many ways, technology is a superior medium for traditional forms of knowledge transmission.

Finally, many classroom teachers just simply love their role as "the teacher." Supervisors should understand this basic human need for being adored and possessing god-like powers over others. Teaching remains one of the most satisfying occupations available, and we suspect that most teachers "model" their behaviors as opposed to "learning" their behaviors. If teaching is not the traditional set of behaviors we all associate with the classroom, what is it?

It is clear from the five points of resistance listed that a strategy must be employed to gain teacher acceptance of technology. First, technology must be made available to teachers in the school environment. Teachers should be encouraged to use fax machines and computers in daily tasks. For some schools that treat telephones as a sacred object of administrative power, this will be quite a change.

Second, teachers will have to be rewarded for becoming competent in the use of targeted technology. Although the rewards may vary, we must communicate to each teacher that remaining a dinosaur is no longer an option in the late 1990s. When students possess more technological knowledge than their teachers, a lack of respect in teaching and learning must follow.

Third, and perhaps most important, teachers must begin to see technology as a device to free them from dependence on others in teaching and learning. For nearly thirty years, teachers have had to choose from among unacceptable and often irrelevant textbooks, and supervisors have been asked to buy technological software packages "lock, stock, and barrel." Once a technological medium has been established, teachers and supervisors can regain the "designing" role in selecting curriculum (Figure 7.4).

Supervisors must move forward with all deliberate speed to ensure teachers that they are not in a race with technology for their jobs! By contrast, we view the massive need for qualified classroom teachers looming on the horizon as an opportunity for technology to upgrade the profession. If, for example, we do achieve those *Hollywood Squares*-LANs with sixty to seventy students under the direction of a teaching manager, can't we envision that TM making twice as much money as today's teacher? Technology may soon professionalize some school districts like nothing has ever done in the past.

Finally, supervisors will have to gently wean teachers from the traditional self-centered role of the "source of knowledge." Actually, teachers haven't been the source of most learning since television arrived on the scene fifty years ago, and perhaps we need to confront any number of outdated assumptions that we still seem to hold about knowledge in a technological world. Fixed knowledge, contained in courses and credits, and dispensed by credentialed teachers may simply be an obsolete concept. Perhaps the excitement of learning new ways and new mediums can take the sting out of losing the cherished role of purveyor of knowledge.

SUMMARY

Technology has had a profound influence on American society during the past thirty years. Although many schools and districts have become a part of a new technological future, many have not. Schools and districts that fail to adopt the on-rush of technology in this decade may become hopelessly dysfunctional as a learning institution in the twenty-first century.

Supervisors, by their position, can influence the role of technology in schools. We believe that schools must cease to be mere consumers of the technology and must begin directing the flow of technology. The supervisor, in the role of instructional designer, can be instrumental in helping his or her district to make crucial cost–benefit decisions.

The new interactive technologies are beginning to redefine the teacher–student relationship, by making learning a more independent event and by freeing the student from the control of a "school" in learning. Being no longer dependent on a teacher to define learning and direct learning experiences, the student can transcend time and distance alone. Teachers must be assisted in understanding this change.

Specifically, teachers will need to overcome a number of obstacles to the full utilization of technology. Among these are becoming more familiar with the latest technologies, becoming competent in the use of technology, understanding the meaning of technologically-driven learning, overcoming fear of competing with technology, and the letting go of the traditional role of the teacher.

Finally, technology brings political problems for the supervisor because, in allocating scarce resources, the supervisor must be authoritative. Not only will very costly decisions be made by supervisors or at the recommendation of supervisors, but those decisions will have lasting impact on the quality of the educational experiences of students for years to come.

Teachers will:
- Be comfortable using technology
- Be adequately trained on available multimedia educational technology and strategies for implementing technology in and out of the classrooms
- Receive ongoing training for emerging technologies and educational uses of this technology
- Integrate technology throughout the curriculum
- Effectively use technology to accomplish schoolwide outcomes as defined in our school improvement plan
- Communicate with parents using available technology

Each classroom will have:
- A teacher technology workstation which includes computer, printer, CD-ROM, modem with telecommunications capability, telephone, access to file server and grade-appropriate software, large screen video monitor, closed circuit television, laserdisc player, LCD panel, overhead projector, appropriate school-wide networking, and emerging hardware and software
- Additional computer workstations (one per three students)
- Supporting furniture

Our school will have:
- A total telecommunications network including a phone messaging system (call-in bulletin board, voice mail, and outbound dialing capabilities) and purchased telecommunications access (CompuServe and Prodigy)
- Satellite dish
- School-wide network for six stations in each classroom plus additional stations for administration and media center
- A powerful high-speed file server
- A minimum of 15 laptop computers for checkout for home and classroom use
- A scanner
- Two laser printers—one each for administration and teacher use
- Two video cameras and appropriate accessories
- Adequate wiring for schoolwide networking and telecommunications
- One facsimile machine
- Computer workstations for media center (2), administrative offices, and guidance counselor
- A curriculum/technology specialist

Our community will have:
- The ability to use technology for clear two-way communication between home and school
- Opportunities to assist students' learning through technology
- Access to technological training
- An invitation to share a partnership role in our technology plan

Figure 7.4 Specifications for Using Technology

IMPLICATIONS FOR SUPERVISION

1. Can you develop a list of assumptions that undergird traditional instruction? How many of these assumptions are questioned by the onrush of technology?
2. How can your district ensure that its expenditures on technology in the late 1990s won't be "throwing good money after bad"?

3. Outline a strategy for rehabilitating a teacher trained prior to 1990 who sees technology as an inconvenience.

❧ CASE STUDY 1 ❧

"What does it take?" Jack simply couldn't comprehend the wastefulness of this situation. The district has made a commitment to high technology after an extensive review of those electronic learning systems best thought to produce learning gains in reading and math. Through sacrifice, two EMG Acceleration Station 2000 units had been purchased. The company had come to the site and trained ten teachers to operate the units. A classroom had been dedicated to the system. Yet, this was the third time this week Jack had passed by and found the room unused. "What is wrong with these teachers?" he wondered. "How will the district ever be able to enter the age of technology?"

Questions
1. Provide an explanation for why teachers are not using this technology in their school.
2. Provide a strategy for overcoming this resistance to supplemental instructional technology.
3. Which of the five areas of concern in teacher resistance cited in this chapter does your strategy address?

❧ CASE STUDY 2 ❧

During an inventory of program software in the district, Sandy was becoming increasingly nervous about the technological thrust of the district. It appeared that teachers were ordering games for children rather than sound instructional software. Not only was the cost of these items significant, but the purchases seemed to underscore a lack of strategy in the use of computers in the district. "Are we," she wondered, "simply entertaining the kids with these computers, or are such purchases an educationally sound investment in student motivation?"

Questions
1. How would you explain, as instructional supervisor, that "Golf Classic" (see Table 7.1) is one of the top ten software packages in schools?
2. Under what conditions should teachers be allowed to identify and requisition software for their classroom computers? List your guidelines.

SUGGESTED LEARNING ACTIVITIES

1. Visit a local elementary school and inventory the kinds of technology currently in use. Ask to see the plans for addressing technological changes in the future.
2. Make an inventory of the kind of technology available to you in your home and everyday life. Try to determine how such common technology can be adapted to the school. Give examples.
3. Identify and list the ways in which technology might intersect the lives of students and their families in the future. Which of these seem most promising for future school–parent/community contacts?

ADDITIONAL READING

Barron, Ann E. "Optical Media in Education,"*The Computing Teacher* 20, 8 (May 1993). Published by the Journal of the International Society for Technology in Education.

Berenfeld, Boris. "Linking East-West Schools Via Telecomputing, "*Technological Horizons in Education* 20, 6 (January 1993).

Bosch, Karen A. "Is There a Computer Crisis in the Classroom?" *Schools in the Middle* 2, 4 (Summer 1993).

Galbreath, Jeremy. "Multimedia: Beyond the Desktop," *Educational Technology* 33, 5 (May 1993).

Greenleaf, Cynthia. "Technological Indeterminacy: The Role of Classroom Writing Practices in Shaping Computer Use," Tech. Report No. 57, Center for the Study of Writing, 1992.

Hadley, Martha, and Sheingold, Karen. "Commonalities and Distinctive Patterns in Teachers' Integration of Computers," *American Journal of Education* 101, 3 (May 1993).

Tierne, Drew. "Exploring the Effectiveness of the Channel One School Telecasts," *Educational Technology* 33, 5 (May 1993).

BOOKS TO REVIEW

Bork, A. "Is Technology-Based Learning Effective?" *Contemporary Education,* 63 (Fall 1991): 6–14.

Bracy, G. "Computers and Learning: The Research Jury Is Still Out," *Electronic Learning,* 7 (October 1988): 28–30.

Flavell, E. "Do Young Children Think of Television Images as Pictures or Real Objects?," *Journal of Broadcasting and Electronic Media,* 34 (Fall 1990): 399–419.

Hadley, M., and Shiengold, K. "Commonality and Distinctiveness Patterns in Teacher Integration of Computers," *American Journal of Education,* 101, 3 (May 1993).

Heinich, R., Molenda, M., Russell, J., and Smaldino, S. *Instructional Media and New Technologies in Instruction,* 5th ed. Englewood Cliffs, NJ: Merrill/Prentice Hall, 1996.

Julyan, C. "National Geographic Network for Kids: Real Science in the Elementary Classrooms," *Classroom Computer Learning,* 10, 2 (1989): 30–41.

Lockard, J. *Microcomputers for Educators.* New York: Harper and Collins, 1990.

Toch, T. "Homeroom Sweepstakes: Education and Commercialism Proving a Tough Mix at Chris Whittle's Channel One," *U.S. News and World Report,* November 9, 1992, pp. 86–89.

Tolman, M., and Allred, R. "The Computer and Education: What Research Says to the Teacher," ERIC ED 355 344 1991.

CHAPTER 8 ≈

ENCOURAGING HUMAN RELATIONS

Of all the skills of supervision, none is cited as often in the literature as human relations. In fact, most supervision activity is just that! Supervisors are communicators and connectors in the human network of the school. Most supervisory activity is face to face. Supervision is not a role for someone who is shy or unwilling to relate to others in a positive and outgoing manner. Supervisors, as people, should be humane, "self-actualized" individuals who establish a cooperative climate by their very presence.

THE SUPERVISOR AS A SELF-ACTUALIZED PERSON

Because supervision is a "people position," it is helpful if the individual in that role relates naturally to others with an outgoing personality. The supervisor should be self-actualized, which means that he or she should hold a positive view of self, have the capacity to identify with others, and have a rich experience base from which to provide an understanding of events in which he or she is involved. If these characteristics do not come naturally to the supervisor, he or she must master these behaviors as quickly as possible on the job.

Supervisors must strive to be humane in their work because they often serve as the linkage between the goals of the organization and the needs of the individuals in it. A task-directed supervisor is unable to bridge the sometimes enormous gap between the job to be done and the persons who must do it. Qualities that contribute to a humanized organization are:

1. Permitting free expression
2. Placing the individual above the organization
3. Seeing each person as unique
4. Providing for the right to make mistakes
5. Allowing individuals to assume responsibility

Supervisors should become familiar with the concept of a work climate, which is often a critical factor in teacher motivation. The climate is a perceived reality that is shared by all those working in a school. Although this "reality" is not necessarily factual, it is the basis for teachers' behavior. Research has identified nine organizational variables that make up the climate or feeling of an institution.

1. *Structure*—The feelings that employees have about the constraints in the group; how many rules, regulations, procedures there are. Is there an emphasis on red tape and going through channels, or is there a loose and informal atmosphere?
2. *Responsibility*—The feeling of being your own boss. Not having to doublecheck all of your decisions; when you have a job to do, knowing that it is your job.
3. *Reward*—The feeling of being rewarded for a job well done. Emphasizing positive rewards rather than punishment; the perceived fairness of the pay and promotion policies.
4. *Risk*—The sense of riskiness and challenge in the job and in the organization. Is there an emphasis on taking calculated risks, or is playing it safe the best way to operate?
5. *Warmth*—The feeling of good fellowship that prevails in the work group atmosphere. The emphasis on being well-liked; the prevalence of friendly and informal social groups.
6. *Support*—The perceived helpfulness of the managers and other employees in the group. Emphasis on mutual support from above and below.
7. *Standards*—The perceived importance of implicit and explicit goals and performance standards. Emphasis on doing a good job; the challenge represented in personal and group goals.
8. *Conflict*—The feeling that managers and other workers want to hear different opinions. Emphasis placed on getting problems out in the open, rather than smoothing them over or ignoring them.
9. *Identity*—The feeling of belonging to a company and being a valuable member of a working team. Importance placed on this kind of spirit.[1]

ORGANIZATIONAL CULTURE AND CLIMATE

Such research has also led to a series of hypotheses about the relationship between a person in an organization and the climate:

1. Individuals are attracted to work climates that arouse their dominant needs.

2. Such on-the-job climates are made up of experiences and incentives.

3. These climates interact with needs to arouse motivation toward need satisfaction.

4. Climates can mediate between organizational tasks requirements and individual needs—it is the linkage.

5. Climates represent the most powerful leverage point available to managers to bring about change.[2]

Collectively, these research observations suggest that the way a supervisor acts and how he or she works with others have a major influence on the effectiveness of any organization or school.

Although organizational culture and climate are terms that educators of the nineties have found intriguing, these terms have long been in the literature. The work of Elton Mayo and others with the Western Electric research of the twenties was important not in what the studies set out to answer, but rather what occurred in the workers' studies. Attending to such issues as the workers' attitudes and human needs on the job brought about changes in the workers' behavior on the job at Western Electric seemingly only because the workers were themselves being examined. This phenomenon later became known as the "Hawthorne Effect." That work, along with the work of Chester Barnard relating formal organization to informal organization and attending to both the needs of the worker and the organization, helped form the basis of the human relations movement. It was this intervention between people and organization that became known as "climate."[3,4]

Even though the concepts of organizational culture and climate had been around for years, it took the Japanese economic miracle to show the value to Americans. Their system used theories such as "Theory Z" of Ouchi[5] to emphasize the whole person, the human concern, and the realization that there just might be a link between how the whole person is treated and how he or she performs. The stories about Sony, Toyota, and others seemed to give a causal relationship between how workers were treated and how they did on the job for the good of the company.

However, scientifically establishing a link between this human force and increased productivity or, in the case of schools, better teachers and learning, is difficult because of the human variables. Because most variables are difficult or impossible to control, it is hard to determine if a staff or community functions a certain way because of the actions of a leader (such as the school principal or supervisor). Any effort to relate organizational culture or climate to effectiveness confronts this difficulty of assessing effectiveness of educational organizations. We can only say that there is an association between the culture of the school and the effectiveness of certain organizational functions. The lack of pure scientific research here cannot be ignored, but it should not inhibit speculations.[6]

In schools today, the principal, as the single most influential leader, initiates, inspires, or discourages change. In order to nurture an environment conducive to growth of individuals and the organization, the principal is dependent on several major tactical functions. These tactical functions can be categorized according to Likert's six characteristics of the organization:

1. Leadership processes
2. Motivational forces
3. Communication processes
4. Decision-making phases
5. Goal-setting processes
6. Control processes[7]

Leadership Processes

If a school today is to maintain a collaborative culture, transformational leadership (a term first used by James McGregor Burns in 1978)[8] can be a powerful tool. Transformational leadership simply involves staff in collaboration, goal setting, and shared leadership with others by delegating. When we alter the power relationship, however, we must stay focused on teamwork and comprehensive school improvement and not simply take charge to get things done.[9] Shifting from a "Type A" to a "Type Z" organizational approach emphasizes participative decision making and manifests itself through other people rather than over them. A leader's (e.g., school principal) management skills are particularly needed so that the team concept approach does not get lost in the process of delegating. Thus, through collaboration, an entire staff is empowered to accomplish the mission at hand.

Leadership in a collaboration culture is rooted in several important factors. The first is emphasis on the priorities Henri Fayol emphasized many years ago: planning, organizing, coordinating, commanding and controlling.[10] These can be classified as initiating structure and task orientation. Scheduling, organizing, supervising, and monitoring are all essentials if a school is to function well.

The second crucial factor in leader behavior revolves around the human factors of consideration for others, mainly conflict management, motivation, and decision making.

Finally, there is one other leadership function that must be noted. School leaders have to be more than just competent managers. They have to be knowledgeable of curriculum and other school matters. They must link staff improvement to instructional improvement and vice versa. As school leaders, they must be "teachers of teachers," constantly diagnosing educational problems, counseling teachers, and evaluating and remediating the pedagogical work of teachers. Leadership, then, is multidimensional, involving managerial, human, and educational skills.

Motivational Forces

There are a number of theoretical approaches to motivation, including Douglas McGregor's Theory X, Theory Y Model; Abraham Maslow's Hierarchy of Needs; and Frederick Herzberg's Two-Factor Theory of Motivation. William Ouchi's Theory Z approach in 1981, although focusing on organizational behavior, did suggest that humanizing every condition not only increases productivity and profits for the company, but also self-esteem for its employees. Ouchi, a Japanese-American, found that while Japan was emphasizing human factors, the United States was emphasizing technology as a key to increased production. Theory Z called for a redirection of attention to human relations in the corporate world.

In 1982, Thomas Peters and Robert Waterman published *In Search of Excellence,* which described management characteristics that sixty-two American companies had in common. The consistent theme throughout that book was that climate or culture was more important than procedures or control systems.[11]

Why did it take so long for American companies to discover the human factor in increased productivity? Was it because of the years of bureaucratic behavior (both management and union), or was it the belief that organizational structure, rules, and regulations have to be hard? Peters and Waterman showed that Ouchi's organizational culture was important in the American corporations that were considered "excellent."

What are the implications for schools? One certain assumption is that simply mandating democratic procedures, such as site-based decision making, does not change schools. Culture develops over a period of time. It is an accumulation of philosophies, values, beliefs, attitudes, and norms that knit a school together. Leaders expecting a "quick-fix" for American schools will find that the status quo will remain until those beliefs, attitude levels, and so on are ingrained into the organization. The real test of leadership in the nineties and beyond will be whether American education can produce the kind of visionary school leaders who can and will stay in an organization long enough to really change the organizational culture of a school.

Communication Processes

Just as Max Weber stressed vertical communication as a cornerstone of a well-run organization,[12] others have emphasized that active communication of the culture is an opportune strategy for school leaders, especially school principals. Informing, counseling, visiting classrooms, and persuading are all forms of communication that will result in greater collaboration and desired behavior. There are some estimates that principals spend 75 percent of each day in some type of school communication. If that estimate is anywhere near correct, this large investment in time spent conveying the message better result in a more efficient, more functional organization.

As American businesses have confronted the recession of the eighties and deregulation, technological upheavals, and foreign competition of the nineties, so must American schools confront shrinking finances, special interests faltering public support, and challenges of educational companies for profit. Communicating the purposes of American public education can best be done by those with the most vested interests: students, teachers, and parents. A culture with open communication, pride, and a feeling that people are truly important will communicate the value of schools much better than newsletters and press releases coming from school administrators. Worker-owned companies, worker commercials, and labor–management agreements all indicate that American businesses and industries are building a "we" climate of communication to the public. Will America's public schools learn the same lesson?

HUMAN RELATIONS SKILLS

Because most supervisory work is face to face, the practicing supervisor must master the skills of organizing people to work on problems. Supervisors spend an enormous amount of time in group meetings, holding conferences, and generally working with individuals in the organization to improve communication. A beginning point for the study of these many roles is with the nature of communication.

Communication among individuals in organizations is a delicate art requiring, among other things, self-discipline and a cooperative spirit. Spoken English is a complex language full of subtleties. Superimposed on these language patterns are a host of nonverbal cues that can alter the meaning of speech. Add to these dimensions an environmental context, and the result is a communication system that operates at varying levels of effectiveness.

Various social sciences have developed entire languages to describe the intricacies of communication in the American culture and have provided a model of foci in three such social sciences:

Anthropology	**Sociology**	**Psychology**
Cultural behaviors	Role behaviors	Personal behaviors
Acculturation	Interaction	Personality
Implicit meanings	Empathetic meanings	Inferred meanings

Collectively, social science inquiry in the area of interpersonal communication has added immeasurably to our understanding of this complex and important dimension of curriculum improvement.

In any pattern of communication among humans there are at least the following nine elements:

1. What the speaker wants to say
2. What the speaker wants to conceal
3. What the speaker reveals without knowing it
4. What the listener wants or expects to hear
5. What the listener's perception of the speaker will let him hear
6. What the listener's experiences tell him the words mean
7. What the listener wants to conceal
8. What the emotional climate of the situation permits the persons to share
9. What the physical structure of the situation permits the persons to share[13]

Various models have shown communication to be a process of encoding and decoding. A source encodes a message and tries to transmit it to a receiver who tries to receive it and decode the message. Such a transmission between sender and receiver is often distorted by various barriers to communication and by defensive behaviors. Gibb has defined such communication defense:

> Defensive behavior is defined as that behavior which occurs when an individual perceives a threat or anticipates threat in the group. The person who behaves defensively, even though he gives some attention to the common task, devotes an appreciable portion of his energy to defending himself. Besides talking about the topic, he thinks about how he appears to others, how he can be seen more favorable, how he may win, dominate, impress, or escape punishment, and/or how he may avoid or mitigate a perceived or an anticipated attack.[14]

Berlo, in a study of human communication, has identified the following four major predictors of faulty communication that can be used by curriculum leaders to anticipate possible communication breakdown:

1. The amount of competition messages have
2. The threats to status and ego which are involved
3. The uncertainty and error in what is expected
4. The number of links there are in the communication chain[15]

Other barriers to effective communication among people might include any of the following:

1. People use words and symbols that have differing meanings.
2. People have different perceptions of problems being discussed.
3. Members of communication groups possess different values.
4. People bring to discussions varying levels of feeling or affect.
5. Words are sometimes used to prevent real thinking.
6. A lack of acceptance of diverse opinion is present in some communication.
7. Vested interests can interfere with genuine communication.
8. Feelings of personal insecurity can distort communication.
9. Tendencies to make premature evaluations are a barrier to communication.
10. Negative feelings about situations block effective communication.

UNDERSTANDING DIVERSITY

The United States has always been a diverse nation, and American schools have always been charged with educating children from different nationalities in the skills and knowledge they will need to be successful.[16] In the last half of the twentieth century, immigrants fleeing war, dictatorships, and poverty entered the U.S. in large numbers. The Korean War, the Vietnam War, and later upheavals in Central America,

Mexico, Cuba, and the Middle East all contributed to the influx of refugees. America's schools were heavily affected by minority students. The increasing diversity led to programs being mandated in first language of minority students (most notably, Spanish in ESL, and English as a Second Language programs). ESL training for teachers was also mandated by court action in several states. Multicultural education was also a response in school districts. The large numbers of minority students had an enormous impact on urban districts. Miami (Dade County) during the 1980s had almost twelve hundred students from Nicaragua alone entering the district each month. That is the equivalent of building a new school a month just for one minority group. By the end of the 1980s, foreign-born Nicaraguan students outnumbered foreign-born Cuban students in Miami.

Other areas of the country also felt the effects of minority students. During the 1980s, Minnesota's population of blacks, Asians, Native Americans, and Hispanics increased by 72 percent. In St. Paul, a commission was appointed in 1994 to study diversity and equality in its schools where half that district's students belonged to minority groups.[17] The panel recommended that the district build in accountability for minority-student achievement, hire more minority teachers, and overhaul its curriculum to address the needs of a racially and socioeconomically diverse student body. It also recommended improvements in explaining and enforcing the district's racial-harassment policy.

The previous example is only one of many that have implications for supervisory leaders. Challenges to the teaching of a Eurocentric view of American history and demands of minorities for greater representation in policy-making groups pose additional challenges for supervisory leadership in the next decades. Projections that numbers of black minority students will be surpassed by Hispanics and Asians in the United States will change the way Americans view minorities. By mid-century (2050), there will be no majority population in the United States, thus giving new meaning to the term "pluralistic society."

MEN AND WOMEN AS LEADERS IN EDUCATION

In the past, supervisors were largely white males; however, today increasingly more women and minorities are emerging into leadership roles. In 1994, the Census Bureau reported that the youngest women today are better educated than their male peers, reversing a long-term trend. Twenty-four percent of women 35 and older have college degrees, compared with 31 percent of men in the same age group. Among the youngest generation, 32 percent of women 25 to 34 have college degrees versus 31 percent of men. Men still have an edge in advanced degrees, but women are rapidly narrowing the gap.

WORKING WITH PARENTS AND THE COMMUNITY

Parents and community leaders became extremely active in defining the curriculum of our schools in the nineties. Conservative challenges were no longer aimed just at individual books or programs, but at all as aspects of the curriculum.[18]

Until the late 1980s, educators did not take such challenges very seriously because the courts consistently backed school boards in resisting censorship efforts. Christian fundamentalist groups in the 1990s became more vocal and stronger in exerting political influence. Charter schools, looking like private religious schools, became a vehicle in the mid-nineties for gaining control over curriculum issues and instructional strategies. Because such schools carefully avoided the appearance of combining religion and schooling and admitted minorities and those not of the Christian faith, they avoided the separation of church and state challenge.[19]

"Secular Humanism" as a target for the religious right was replaced by a new term, "New Agers." New Agers were accused of seducing America away from its Christian heritage. New Agers were also accused of being antichrist, atheistic, and anti-God and determined to spread their philosophy in the public schools. Among those labeled as New Agers were the American Civil Liberties Union, Alcoholics Anonymous, the Catholic church, *Reader's Digest, Newsweek,* the Muppets, Ralph Nader, Yale University, and Boris Yeltsin. A massive literature base had evolved in the 1990s that carried the message of Christian fundamentalism.

Supervisors must respect the views of all persons and deal with the concerns raised by parents and community members in a professional manner. Public schools are not value free; neither are they value neutral. Policy matters and educational leaders cannot appease all groups. There are times when supervisory leaders must take a stand against extremist views. Understanding human relations and having the skills to deal with diverse groups and ideas will be essential skills for school leaders as they guide schools into the next century.

TECHNIQUES FOR PRACTICING HUMAN RELATIONS IN SCHOOLS

Group Work

Although relationships exist at the dyad, organizational, community, and societal levels, most curriculum development work proceeds at the small-group level. For this reason, curriculum leaders need to be particularly attentive to group work as a means of promoting better school programs.

Groups can generally be described as two or more people who possess a common objective. As groups interact in pursuit of an objective, their behavior is affected by a number of variables, including the background of the group, participation patterns, communication patterns, the cohesiveness of the group, the goals of the group, standards affecting the group, procedures affecting the group, and the atmosphere or climate surrounding the group.

Groups perform various tasks that are important to the development of school programs. Among these group tasks are:

1. *Initiating activities*—Suggesting new ideas, defining problems, proposing solutions, reorganizing materials
2. *Coordinating*—Showing relationships among various ideas or suggestions, pulling ideas together, relating activities of various subgroups

3. *Summarizing*—Pulling together related data, restating suggestions after discussion

4. *Testing feasibility*—Examining the practicality of feasibility of ideas, making reevaluation decisions about activities

Group work in educational environments is often ineffective due to various types of nonfunctional behaviors. Leaders should be aware of some of the more common forms of nonfunctional actions:

1. *Being aggressive*—Showing hostility against the group or some individual, criticizing or blaming others, deflating the status of others

2. *Blocking*—Interfering with the group process by speaking tangentially, citing personal experiences unrelated to the problem, rejecting ideas without consideration

3. *Competing*—Vying with others to talk most often, produce the best idea, gain favor of the leader

4. *Special pleading*—Introducing ideas or suggestions that relate to one's own concerns

5. *Seeking recognition*—Calling attention to oneself by excessive talking, extreme ideas, or unusual behavior

6. *Withdrawing*—Being indifferent or passive, daydreaming, doodling, whispering to others, physically leaving the discussion.

As a group leader, the curriculum specialist should be able to differentiate between those roles and actions that contribute to group effectiveness and those roles that are basically negative and do not contribute to the effectiveness of the group. The following personal characteristics are regarded as productive and contributing to group effectiveness:

1. Brings the discussion back to the point

2. Seeks clarification of meaning when ideas expressed are not clear

3. Questions and evaluates ideas expressed in objective manner

4. Challenges reasoning when the soundness of logic is doubtful

5. Introduces a new way of thinking about topic

6. Makes a summary of points

7. Underscores points of agreement or disagreement

8. Tries to resolve conflict or differences of opinion

9. Introduces facts or relevant information

10. Evaluates progress of the group

Roles that are regarded as negative or nonproductive are:

1. Aggressively expresses disapproval of ideas of others

2. Attacks the group or the ideas under consideration

3 . Attempts to reintroduce idea after it has been rejected

4 . Tries to assert authority by demanding

5 . Introduces information which is obviously irrelevant

6 . Tries to invoke sympathy by depreciation of self

7 . Uses stereotypes to cover own biases and prejudices

8 . Downgrades the importance of group's role or function

Sensitivity to such roles allows the group leader to analyze the flow of group work and head off potential distractions to group progress.

Group Leadership

While working with groups, the curriculum leader does not have to restrict his or her role to that of passive observer. It is possible to take steps that will encourage greater group productivity (see Figure 8.1). In any group discussion, the leader has at least six roles which, if pursued, will lead the group toward accomplishment of its objectives. These areas are presentation of the topic, the initiation of discussion, guiding the discussion, controlling discussion, preventing side-tracking, and summarizing the discussion.

In presenting the topic to be discussed, the leader should suggest the importance of the problem, place the general purpose of the discussion before the group, suggest a logical pathway for the discussion to follow, and define any ambiguous terms to remove misunderstanding. It is useful, where possible, to relate the current discussion to previous meetings or other convenient reference points.

In initiating the discussion, the leader should provide advanced thinking for the group. Major questions to be answered are identified, and relevant facts and figures are cited. A case in point may be drawn for purposes of illustration. In some cases, it may even be useful to purposefully misstate a position to provoke discussion.

The leader's job in guiding the discussion should involve keeping the discussion goal directed, assisting members in expressing themselves through feedback, and providing the transition from one aspect of the discussion to another. In fulfilling this role, the leader may use direct questions, stories, illustrations, or leading questions to maintain the flow of interaction.

In controlling the discussion, the leader should be concerned with the pace of progress and the involvement of the participants. Among techniques that can be used to keep discussion moving are purposeful negative statements, drawing contrasts between positions of participants, and regularly calling attention to the time remaining.

The discussion leader in a small group can deal with sidetracking in a number of ways:

1 . Restating the original question or problems

2 . Securing a statement from a reliable group member to head off a rambler

3 . Requesting that side issues be postponed until main issues are settled

If a group is to be productive, the individuals in question must first become a group in a psychological sense through acquiring the feeling of group belongingness which can come only from a central purpose which they all accept.

If a group is to be productive, its members must have a common definition of the undertaking in which they are to engage.

If a group is to be productive, it must have a task of some real consequence to perform.

If a group is to be productive, its members must feel that something will actually come of what they are expected to do; said differently, its members must not feel that what they are asked to do is simply busywork.

If a group is to be productive, the dissatisfaction of its members with the aspect of the status quo to which the group's undertaking relates must outweigh in their minds whatever threats to their comfort they perceive in the performance of this undertaking.

If a group is to be productive, its members must not be expected or required to attempt undertakings which are beyond their respective capabilities or which are so easy for the individuals in question to perform that they feel no sense of real accomplishment.

If a group is to be productive, decisions as to work planning, assignment, and scheduling must be made, whenever possible, on a shared basis within the group, and through the method of consensus rather than of majority vote; in instances in which these decisions either have already been made by exterior authority or in which they must be made by the group leader alone, the basis for the decisions made must be clearly explained to all members of the group.

If a group is to be productive, each member of the group must clearly understand what he is expected to do and why, accept his role, and feel himself responsible to the group for its accomplishment.

Figure 8.1 Productivity in Group Work
Source: Reprinted with the permission of Simon & Schuster, Inc. from the Merrill/Prentice Hall text *Curriculum Development,* 4th ed., by Jon Wiles and Joseph Bondi. Copyright © 1993 by Prentice Hall, Inc.

Finally, the leader should summarize the discussion. This involves knowing when to terminate discussion reviewing the high points that have been addressed.

Three situations in particular are troublesome to persons new to leading discussions in small groups: the dead silence, the overtalkative member, and the silent member. Any of these three conditions can sabotage an otherwise fruitful discussion period.

A most anxiety-producing situation is one in which there is a complete absence of participation resulting in an awkward silence among group members. Although the natural response in such a situation is to speak to fill the conversational vacuum, the leader must do just the opposite. Silence in discussions sometimes means that real thinking is occurring, and this assumption must be made by the leader. Another common impulse is to seek out a member of the group and prod him or her for a contribution. Such a tactic will surely contribute to less participation. When the silent period is convincingly unproductive, the leader should try an encouraging remark such as, "There must be some different points of view here." Failing

If a group is to be productive, its members must communicate in a common language.

If a group is to be productive, its members must be guided by task-pertinent values which they share in common.

If a group is to be productive, it is usually necessary for its members to be in frequent face-to-face association with one another.

If a group is to be productive, its members must have a common (though not necessarily a talked-about) agreement as to their respective statuses within the group.

If a group is to be productive, each of its members must gain a feeling of individual importance from his/her personal contributions in performing the work of the group.

If a group is to be productive, the distribution of credit for its accomplishments must be seen as equitable by its members.

If a group is to be productive, it must keep on the beam and not spend time on inconsequential or irrelevant matters.

If a group is to be productive, the way it goes about its work must be seen by its members as contributing to the fulfillment of their respective issue and social-psychological needs, and, by extension, of those of their dependents (if any) as well.

If a group is to be productive, that status leader must make the actual leadership group-centered, with the leadership role passing freely from member to member.

If a group is to be productive, the task it is to perform must be consistent with the purposes of the other groups to which its members belong.

If a group is to be productive, the satisfactions its members expect to experience from accomplishing the group's task must outweigh in their minds the satisfactions they gain from their membership in the group per se.

Figure 8.1 *Continued*

response, the leader should turn to the process involved with a comment such as, "Let's see if we can discover what's blocking us."

Another situation that can ruin a group discussion is an overtalkative member. Such a person, if permitted, will monopolize discussion and produce anxiety among group members. The best strategy in these situations is to intervene after a respectful period of time with a comment such as, "Perhaps we can hear from other members of the group." In the event that the dominating member still doesn't get the message, the leader can initiate an evaluation of the process and propose finding a way to gain input from all members.

A final situation that can be awkward occurs when a member of the group is regularly silent. The leader should recognize that some persons are fearful of being put on the spot and will resent being spotlighted. The leader can, however, observe the silent member and look for signals that he or she is ready to participate. If the member seems to be on the verge of speaking, an encouraging glance or nod may be all that is needed.

If the leader becomes convinced that a member's silence is the result of boredom or withdrawal, he or she may need to confront the member away from other group members with a provocative or challenging question. Whether a member should be forced into a discussion, and whether such an act is productive for the entire group, is a matter of judgment and discretion.

Leaders of small groups should regularly evaluate their own performance following a discussion by asking themselves a series of questions such as the following:

1. Did members contribute to the discussion?
2. Did some people do more talking than others?
3. Are you receiving contributions from all parts of the group?
4. Do members talk mostly to the leader or to each other?
5. Was there evidence of cliques or interest groups in the discussion?

Group leaders can sometimes retard creative thinking by regulating discussions in nonproductive ways. Among the most common errors in this respect are:

1. A preoccupation with order throughout the discussion
2. Stressing too often "hard evidence" or factual information
3. Placing too much emphasis on history or the way things have been done
4. Using coercive techniques to insure participation
5. Suggesting that mistakes are not acceptable

Two skills that are useful for all small-group leaders to possess are paraphrasing and brainstorming. In paraphrasing, the leader attempts to restate the point of view of another to his or her satisfaction prior to continuing discussion. This technique is especially useful in argumentative situations and often sets a pattern followed by other group members.

In brainstorming, the leader introduces a technique that frees the group discussion from previous barriers to speaking. Here the leader sets ground rules which include the following:

1. No criticism of others is allowed.
2. Combining of ideas is encouraged.
3. Quality ideas are sought.
4. Wild ideas are encouraged.

In introducing a brainstorming session, the leader hopes to have members "spark" each other and have one idea "hitch-hike" upon another. Brainstorming, as a technique, is recommended when discussions continually cover familiar ground and little or no progress toward a solution to problems is forthcoming.

Finally, leaders of small groups should work to become better listeners. Numerous studies have identified poor listening skills as the biggest block to personal communication. Nicholas has identified ten steps to better listening:

1. While listening, concentrate on finding areas of interest that are useful to you.

2. Judge the content of what is said rather than the delivery.

3. Postpone early judgment about what is being said. Such a posture will allow you to remain analytical if you favor what is being said or to keep from being distracted by calculating embarrassing questions should you disagree with the speaker's message.

4. Focus on the central ideas proposed by the speaker. What is the central idea? What are the supporting "planks" or statements?

5. Remain flexible in listening. Think of various ways to remember what is being said.

6. Work hard at listening. Try to direct all conscious attention on the presentation being made.

7. Resist distractions in the environment by making adjustments or by greater concentration.

8. Exercise your mind by regularly listening to technical expository material that you haven't had experience with.

9. Keep your mind open to new ideas by being aware of your own biases and limited experiences.

10. Capitalize on thought speed. Since comprehension speed exceeds speaking speed by about 3:1, the listener must work to keep his concentration. This can be done by anticipating what is to be said, by making mental summaries, by weighing speaker evidence, and by listening between the lines.[20]

Group Evaluation

Group evaluation is necessary to help assure that the work of a group does not deteriorate. When all members of a group feel responsibility for the group and can evaluate its effectiveness without being defensive, the evaluation will be most useful to the group. There are a number of group processes one might examine in evaluating group effectiveness. Figure 8.2 illustrates eight of these processes.

As a reference to good group work, Figure 8.3 provides a planning checklist for conducting an effective meeting.

Conferences

Much of a supervisor's day is spent in conferences that help alleviate the problems. Supervisors see parents, teachers, and other district personnel to iron out communication difficulties and solve genuine problems. We treat each of these three primary groups separately because of the nature of communication with each group.

Parents are the primary clients of the school; they pay for education by their taxes and entrust their children to educators. For this reason, parents often contact the school to voice concerns to the principal. Supervisors are regularly asked to look

GOALS

Poor   1 2 3 4 5 6 7 8 9 10   **Good**
Confused, diverse, conflicting,   Clear to all, shared by all,
indifferent, little interest.   care about the goals, feel involved.

PARTICIPATION

Poor   1 2 3 4 5 6 7 8 9 10   **Good**
Few dominate, some passive;   All get in, all are really
some not listened to; several talk   listened to.
at once or interrupt.

FEELINGS

Poor   1 2 3 4 5 6 7 8 9 10   **Good**
Unexpected, ignored, or criticized.   Freely expressed, empathic.

DIAGNOSIS OF GROUP PROBLEMS

Poor   1 2 3 4 5 6 7 8 9 10   **Good**
Jump directly to remedial proposals;   When problems arise, the situation
treat symptoms rather than   is carefully diagnosed before
basic causes.   action is proposed; remedies
                                    attack basic causes.

LEADERSHIP

Poor   1 2 3 4 5 6 7 8 9 10   **Good**
Group needs for leadership not met;   As needs for leadership arise,
group depends too much on single   various members meet them
person or on a few persons.   ("distributed leadership"); anyone
                                    feels free to volunteer as
                                    he/she sees a group need.

DECISIONS

Poor   1 2 3 4 5 6 7 8 9 10   **Good**
Needed decisions don't get made;   Consensus sought and tested;
decision made by part of group,   deviates appreciated and used
other uncommitted.   to improve decision; decisions
                                    when made are fully supported.

Figure 8.2 Group Evaluation Form

into these concerns and to work out an amiable solution with the parent. Some typical concerns are as follows:

The curriculum	Discipline at the school
Dress codes	Out-of-school problems
Request for a specific teacher	Changes in class assignments
Grades and evaluation practices	Other students picking on my child

Essentials of Effective Meetings

A. Convene on time
B. Good opening/warm-up exercise
C. Well-planned agenda (prioritized)
D. Clear roles (leader, recorder, participants)
E. Appropriate environment (comfortable)
F. Materials/equipment
G. No outside interruptions
H. Define adjournment time

I. Pre-Meeting Checklist [   ]
   A. Precise purpose—objective
   B. Written announcement (time, purpose, location, etc.)
   C. Tentative agenda distributed with vital backup materials
   D. Predetermined adjournment time
   E. Identify audience
   F. Identify materials (visuals, equipment) needed
   G. Who can help? Advise in advance
   H. Plan ingredients—all points to be made
   I. Estimate time for each agenda item
   J. Plan opening
   K. Integrate impact features
   L. Examine texture (variety)
   M. Dry-run visuals/equipment

II. Role of Chairperson [   ]
   A. Begin on time
   B. Provide overview
   C. Keep on target
   D. One agenda item at a time
   E. Cut off redundant debate
   F. Neutralize "dominator"
   G. Draw out the "timid/perplexed"
   H. Encourage full discussion
   I. Keep climate relaxed/wholesome
   J. Use rules for brainstorming
   K. Use rules of order
   L. Tap resources of audience
   M. Delegate to "volunteer"
   N. Serve as negotiator, arbitrator, neutral, compassionate listener—shift role
   O. Keep calm
   P. Adjourn on time

Figure 8.3 Checklist for a Meeting Leader

Continued

III. Role of Meeting Participant [   ]
    A. Do advance preparation
    B. Be on time
    C. Raise questions for clarification—"Gate opening for expertise"
    D. Demonstrate responsible (attitude/behavior) good manners
    E. Accept share of work—offer to help
    F. Stick to point
    G. Help others to stay on topic
    H. Be sensitive to others' feelings (particularly chairperson)
    I. *Listen actively—listening with warmth is contagious*

IV. Post-meeting Checklist [   ]
    A. Minutes or record distributed—24 hours
    B. Clear follow-up assignments and timeline
    C. Evaluation
    D. Next meeting (date/time)
    E. Location
    F. Tentative agenda
    G. Responsibilities

V. Meeting Record [   ]
    A. Purpose—to provide
        1. Minutes of meeting to participants
        2. Concise, right-to-the-point notes
        3. Opportunity for recorder to be active participant
        4. Basis for summarizing the meeting
        5. Critical elements and decisions made
        6. Immediate dissemination

    B. Objective—to provide
        1. Date, time convened, and time terminated
        2. Name of recorder
        3. Names of participants
        4. Specific topics covered
        5. Time spent on each topic
        6. Decisions reached and actions to be taken
        7. Responsibilities for followup
        8. Deadlines for action to be taken
        9. List of handouts distributed at the meeting

Figure 8.3 *Continued*

Figures 8.4 and 8.5 provide some general information about possible topics to discuss with parents and obvious do's and don'ts for parent conferences.

Supervisors should think through a parent conference before it occurs because the results of a mismanaged conference can be damaging to the school and the district. In setting up the conference, the following questions should be asked:

1. How will I use body language (a smile, eye contact, leaning forward to show approval)?
2. How can I greet the parents so that anxiety will be reduced?
3. What message does my appearance send (businesslike, professional, friendly)?

During the conference, the supervisor needs to be aware of the parents' feelings. Most parents come to such conferences feeling unequal and, perhaps, defensive. They may fear learning something about their child they don't want to know. The supervisor should not take it personally if parents display anger. The supervisor is a representative of the school.

Supervisors should be careful of their language. Jargon is plentiful in schools (IEP, affective, and so on). Messages should be sent to the parents in small doses and in familiar language. It may help to remain slightly vague (seems, appears, may be) to smooth the communication.

The supervisor should consider the timing and order of the conference. A "we-ness" must be established to have real communication. Advanced thinking about topics and the supervisor's reaction to those topics will help. Some possible solutions may be formulated before the conference.

Finally, the supervisor must give thought to closure of the parent conference. Many parents will be reluctant to terminate a discussion with a school official. Four common ways to close a parent conference are:

1. Mention a "pressing appointment."
2. Inform the secretary to interrupt at a predetermined time.
3. Send body language that the conference is ending (stand up, change tone of voice).
4. Press a buzzer near your desk that signals the secretary.

Conferences with teachers differ from those with parents in that the supervisor must, under all circumstances, maintain an open and professional communication with the teacher. Reasons for teacher-supervisor conferences include:

1. Evaluation or review
2. Curriculum or instructional concerns
3. Parental complaint or an administrative concern
4. Union contract or grievance procedures

It is important for supervisors to remember in conferring with classroom teachers that the ultimate object is to improve instruction for students. Teachers are profes-

Family Living and Home Background
Learning about normal or other conditions
Learning about adults other than parents living in the home
Learning about child's place in family in relation to other children
Making use of leisure time
Having some definite responsibilities
Learning to dress and undress self
Understanding parents' interest, plans, hopes for the child
Understanding parents' influence on child's attitudes
Learning about parents' ideas of acceptable behavior
Learning about parents' methods of discipline
Learning about child's attitude and behavior at home

Emotional and Social Development
Getting along well with others
Having friends his/her own age
Enjoying group games
Enjoying school
Exhibiting self-control
Accepting criticism
Acting subdued and unresponsive
Being over-aggressive
Feeling secure at home, at school, and to and from school
Exhibiting nervous manifestations
Considering the rights of others
Protecting and respecting property—personal, school, and community
Working and playing well with others
Accepting responsibility
Observing school rules
Displaying leadership qualities

Child's Health
Noting significant illnesses and accidents from infancy on
Noting physical defects—progress in correction
Developing health habits
Exhibiting food idiosyncrasies
Developing proper sleeping habits
Learning about sleeping facilities
Developing recreational habits
Developing muscular coordination
Maintaining good attendance

Figure 8.4 Conference Topics for Discussion

Do's	Don'ts
1. When there are several children in the family, consult other teachers in planning conference.	1. Don't talk "down" to parents.
	2. Don't embarrass or offend parents.
2. Create an atmosphere of friendly informality.	3. Don't argue.
	4. Don't show your personal reactions.
3. Show by your attitude that you are sincerely interested.	5. Don't listen to complaints about other members of the faculty.
4. Try to understand how the parents feel about their child.	6. Don't listen to gossip about other pupils or their families.
5. Remember that parents are people who have problems, too.	7. Don't lose your sense of humor even when parents lose theirs.
6. Be prepared to understand that there may be more than one solution to a problem.	8. Don't pass over parents' suggestions for a plan of action.
7. Encourage the parent to tell his/her side of the story. It releases tension.	9. Don't appear as one who is passing judgment on the parents' way of life.
8. Answer questions directly and in a straightforward manner.	10. Don't assume that the parents want advice. Wait until you are asked.
9. Admit that you do not have all of the answers.	11. Don't make parents feel that you think that they have failed in the upbringing of their child.
10. Explain the philosophy and objectives of the school.	12. Don't discuss anything told to you by the parents in confidence.
11. Find commendable things to tell parents about their children.	13. Don't ever give parents I.Q. figures. Instead, give them an idea of the group into which their child falls. ("He is a little slow" or "His intelligence is above average.")
12. Maintain the "we" relationship to remind the parent that home and school work together.	
13. Offer plans on a trial basis.	
14. Keep the conference on the question at hand to avoid digression.	
15. Keep your voice quiet and relaxed.	
16. Summarize the conference.	
17. End the conference on a note of confidence and optimism.	

Figure 8.5 Conference Do's and Don'ts

sional, highly educated individuals who practice one of the most difficult roles in our society. In schools, because of the interpersonal nature of the organizations, traditional supervisory practices do not work. Supervisors must approach any teacher conference from the standpoint of establishing a professional relationship and improving practice for students. To become bogged down in power/compliance issues or interpersonal hostility is counterproductive to the ultimate objective of supervision.

In working with teachers through conferencing, supervisors should be aware of the following variables:

1. *Body language*—Are gestures, facial movements, eye contact conveying a different message than the words?.
2. *Time*—Does the scheduling of the meeting reflect its importance?
3. *The use of space*—Is the supervisor sitting down as an equal or is a desk being used to separate and identify the roles?
4. *Word usage*—How many times does the supervisor use the word "I"? Is he or she overusing superlatives? Is jargon used to mask the real concerns?
5. *Written follow-up*—Is the communication dull, third-person messages that communicate a bureaucratic tone?

Conferencing with other district personnel requires some planning by the supervisor because of line and staff relationships and the changing nature of the supervision position. When preparing to hold a one-on-one conference, the supervisor should ask, "What is the relationship of this individual to the supervision function?" If the relationship is a "line" relationship (one of authority with a direct power connection to a superior), the communication will usually be task directed. If, on the other hand, the relationship is "staff" (an assisting role without authority), the communication will be more of an interpersonal nature.

We make this distinction to reflect the changing nature of supervision in a school setting. Even a decade ago, the position of supervisor was an extension of teaching. Today, because of unionization and collective bargaining, supervision is more an extension of management or administration. The modern supervisor must acknowledge this distinction or risk being placed in a compromising position during conferences with either line or staff associates.

To test this distinction, think about the following situations:

1. You have had a luncheon meeting with your immediate superior. Upon returning, a friend and staff member in another department wants to know all about what happened.
2. You are in the middle of a conference with a teacher and a call comes in from your superior. The secretary says it is important.
3. You are meeting with staff members about a project and one of the staff members continually interrupts your presentation.

4. A staff member from your unit meets with you to complain about the work habits of another staff member.

5. You are writing an article for publication about your school district and its programs. Should you consult with your superior?

SPECIAL PROBLEMS IN HUMAN RELATIONS

In Chapter 1, we mentioned that supervision in education is different from supervision in other kinds of organizations because schools deal with a human product. The real measure of the effectiveness of schools cannot be immediately seen or measured. This condition presents some real problems in human relations—problems that must be addressed by the supervisor. Two such special problems are teacher motivation and stress.

Motivation

Teachers confront the problem of motivation in a number of ways during their careers. One problem is that, until recently, there has been no career ladder in the field of teaching. A teacher entered the profession as a teacher and remained in that role years later. In general, experience was neither rewarded nor acknowledged from one year to the next. The old adage that familiarity breeds contempt has some application if the daily teaching routine is allowed to become an insipid routine that stretches out endlessly.

A related problem for many teachers is that most staff development or training opportunities do not discriminate among the inexperienced and experienced teachers. Rarely do school systems design in-service experiences to reflect the growing maturity of the teacher. Said another way, most school districts do not have a model of teacher growth toward excellence, and teachers have no accurate method of assessing their abilities or needs for self-improvement.

A final part of the motivation picture for many classroom teachers is their perception of the position of teacher. A visit to any teacher preparation program will reveal highly curious and eager students who want to teach. However, after three years of teaching, those students often reveal a slightly cynical attitude about teaching and its requirements. The new teacher is quickly socialized by older teachers, and whatever vision, mission, or curiosity he or she possessed prior to teaching is absorbed by the environment and requirements of the job.

These and other factors contribute to an overall motivation problem in teaching staffs throughout the nation. This problem is a direct responsibility of the school supervisor. Helping teachers perceive teaching as a long-term process of growth, building meaningful in-service experiences commensurate with individual needs, and looking for ways to diversify and enrich the teaching role are all challenges to the human relations skills of the supervisor.

Stress

A related and serious problem affecting teachers is that of stress buildup and burnout. The burnout syndrome strikes disproportionately in helping professions such as teaching. It involves physical, emotional, and attitudinal exhaustion generated by excessive demands on an individual's energy, emotions, or resources. The degree of stress buildup in the teaching profession is reflected by an extensive literature that documents the condition. The actual cause for such burnout seems to be a result of substantial imbalance between environmental demands and the individual's response capability. Common symptoms diminishing the pleasure of teaching include increased drug or alcohol use, greater use of scheduled sick days, fatigue, depression, insomnia, and susceptibility to minor sicknesses.

Historically, our society has associated teaching with low income and limited prestige. Accordingly, the profession has associated a "service orientation" with motivation, and teachers have relied on intrinsic rewards rather than material benefits for job satisfaction. Teachers who believe that they are making a significant impact on the lives of their students find it much easier to sustain a high degree of job satisfaction than teachers who receive little positive reinforcement. Unfortunately, the social message in the media has been that schools and teachers are failing in their role. This lack of appreciation and understanding on the part of the public, plus the miserable extrinsic rewards offered to career teachers, took its toll on the profession in the 1980s and 1990s.

Supervisors must confront this human relations problem, if for no other reason than to foster instructional quality control. An organization, such as a school, must have fully functioning people if it is to be effective in its mission of developing students. Three different checklists are shown in Figures 8.6 and 8.7. These lists may help diagnose teachers who are susceptible to stress buildup, teachers actually experiencing high degrees of stress, and symptoms of teacher burnout. How a supervisor responds to this growing problem in teaching will be dictated by consideration such as environmental factors, school organization, and the degree of supervisory authority at the school building level.

SUMMARY

Human relations skills are foundational skills in school supervision. Because supervisors tend to be communicators and connectors in the human network of the school, such skills are essentials for practice. As a "people position," supervision calls for an individual who is self-confident and skilled in relating to others.

Three general tasks for supervisors in school are to create a humane atmosphere, set a positive work climate, and establish an appropriate image for supervision. Supervisors learn quickly that others react to how the supervisor talks, dresses, and works. The supervisor establishes the "feel" of supervision by his or her behavior.

The many human relations skills of supervision include promoting effective communication, working with small groups, and holding conferences with parents, teachers, and district personnel. Special problems in the 1990s include motivating career teachers and the phenomenon of "teacher

Rate yourself as to how you typically react in each of the situations listed below. There are no right and wrong answers.

4 Always   3 Frequently   2 Sometimes   1 Never

_____ 1. Do you try to do as much as possible in the least amount of time?
_____ 2. Do you become impatient with delays or interruptions?
_____ 3. Do you always have to win at games to enjoy yourself?
_____ 4. Do you find yourself speeding up the car to beat the red light?
_____ 5. Are you unlikely to ask for, or indicate you need, help with a problem?
_____ 6. Do you constantly seek the admiration and respect of others?
_____ 7. Are you overly critical of the way others do their work?
_____ 8. Do you have the habit of looking at your watch or clock often?
_____ 9. Do you constantly strive to better your position and achievements?
_____ 10. Do you spread yourself "too thin" in terms of your time?
_____ 11. Do you have a habit of doing more than one thing at a time?
_____ 12. Do you frequently get angry or irritable?
_____ 13. Do you have little time for hobbies or time by yourself?
_____ 14. Do you have a tendency to talk quickly or hasten conversations?
_____ 15. Do you consider yourself hard-driving?
_____ 16. Do your friends or relatives consider you hard-driving?
_____ 17. Do you have a tendency to get involved in multiple projects?
_____ 18. Do you have a lot of deadlines in your work?
_____ 19. Do you feel vaguely guilty if you relax and do nothing during leisure time?
_____ 20. Do you take on too many responsibilities?
_____ 21. Are you constantly volunteering for things without the ability to say "no"?
_____ 22. Are you constantly making excuses or apologies for yourself and your actions?
_____ 23. Do you tend to carry your domestic stresses to work and vice versa?
_____ 24. Do you feel stress from having the dual responsibilities of family life and a full-time job?
_____ 25. Do you tend to feel under pressure about things which you have little or no control (i.e., state of the economy, nuclear war, family illness, etc.)?
_____   TOTAL

Interpretation

If your score is between 25 and 35, chances are you are nonproductive or your life lacks stimulation.

A score between 35 and 60 designates a good balance in your ability to handle and control stress.

If you tallied a score ranging between 60 and 70, your stress level is marginal and you are bordering on being excessively tense.

If your total number of points exceeds 70, you may be a candidate for heart disease.

Figure 8.6 How to Tell If You Are a Stress-Prone Personality

243

Check boxes for listings that describe your behavior or feelings

[ ] Increased food, cigarette, and/or liquor consumption.*
[ ] Tiredness not alleviated by a night's sleep.*
[ ] Increased frequency of colds, flu, or allergy episodes.*
[ ] Absenteeism for generalized or vague ailments.*
[ ] Elevated blood pressure.*
[ ] Grinding or clenching of teeth.*

3 × ____ = ____

[ ] Sensations of déjà vu with work/personal situations . . . the "I've been here before" or "Here we go again" feeling.
[ ] Complaints about the sameness of tasks, strong craving for greater uniqueness, variety.
[ ] Reduced ability to see uniqueness when it is present.
[ ] Language shift to jargon or "labeling" of people.
[ ] Lumping consumers/clients/coworkers/public into large undifferentiated groups, e.g., "those taxpayers."
[ ] Suppression of feelings resulting in mask-like expressions.
[ ] Cynical comments about the agency/company/system/department.
[ ] Reduced physical or time involvement with consumers/coworkers.
[ ] Belief that clients/consumers deserve their problems.
[ ] Diffusion of responsibility through staff/neighborhood gripe sessions.
[ ] Strong need to conserve energy because "everyone wants a piece of me and there's not enough to go around."
[ ] Increased intellectualization of situations, elaborate "explanations" for minor incidents.
[ ] Rationalizations of actions (e.g., following gripe sessions, hastily identifying it as a "conference").
[ ] Obesity—exceeding healthy weight by more than 20%.

5 × ____ = ____

[ ] Cynical or negative feelings toward clients/consumers/coworkers/public expressed in contemptuous or derogatory language, sometimes followed by an attempt to cancel the message (e.g., "Women are dense! . . . Only joking, girls.").
[ ] Laughing at clients/consumers/coworkers and their problems.
[ ] Cynicism about new worker's optimism (e.g., "He'll learn!").
[ ] Frequent gallows humor about self, work, consumers, colleagues.
[ ] Exaggeration of the border between work and social/personal life.
[ ] Exaggerated "going-by-the-book" to short-circuit personal involvement with clients/consumers, public, changing into petty bureaucrat.
[ ] Serious doubting of effectiveness ("Do I make any difference here?"), or values ("Is there any point in my life?"), or even the morality of efforts ("Have I helped him/her or just set someone up to get hurt?").

9 × ____ = ____
TOTAL ____

SCORING: Multiply number of boxes checked in each group by 3, 5, or 9 as indicated. More than 3 items in any one category indicates danger of overstress. A total score exceeding 100 indicates a strong need for action.

*Check with a doctor . . . cause may be chemical or physical.

Figure 8.7 Are You Burning Out?

burnout." As we move toward a new century, schools will be challenged to do more to help students cope with a technological society unlike any we could have envisioned twenty years ago. In addition, schools have taken over many of the functions once led by the family and other institutions. Questions as to how well schools are functioning may be posed by both those inside and outside the school building. The challenge by those holding extremist views will continue to test the human relations skills of supervisors. Also, the growing diversity of our population will necessitate new understandings and skills of educational leaders.

There have been other strong challenges for supervisory leaders in the past. Public dissatisfaction with schools, fewer economic resources, deteriorating social and economic conditions in large urban school districts, growing teacher stress and the push for a free-market choice system in education are issues that have faced education leaders before. In dealing with these problems we must not lose sight of our ethical responsibility as leaders to do what is right for students and to maintain the moral compass needed to improve our democratic society.

IMPLICATIONS FOR SUPERVISION

1. Most individuals find meetings tiresome and avoid them when possible. Construct a list of those things you find bothersome about meetings. For each one, think of a strategy to overcome this problem.

2. What special communication problems exist when a teaching team holds a parent conference?
3. How might staff development be structured to address the problem of teacher burnout?

⧼ CASE STUDY 1 ⧽

Never in her wildest dreams had the supervisor expected a full auditorium for a school-sponsored meeting. How could people get so excited about textbooks? At issue was a proposal from the Parents for Decency group to remove approximately fifty books from the school library because they were felt to be pornographic. Other parents came out of the woodwork to react to this proposal.

The frightening thing about the meeting had been that rather than opposing the proposal, each group of parents seemed to want to remove other books for other reasons. One group was concerned with sexism in textbooks. Another group thought that the library had too many books insensitive to

the needs of minority children. Still another group was anxious to review all books for "humanism."

The principal and superintendent attended the meeting but refused to engage the people, stating that books were an instructional concern and that the staff (supervisor) would develop a procedure for getting people together to air their concerns.

Questions
1. What is the best way to get people to communicate about controversial issues related to schooling?
2. Outline a plan of attack for developing this procedure.

≈ CASE STUDY 2 ≈

It was surely a case of discrimination if she had ever seen one. Prior to becoming a supervisor, she had heard that schools were a man's world. True, most administrators were men, but who could ever have guessed how invisible a woman supervisor could be in a meeting among men? It was just as bad trying to speak out in a face-to-face conversation with the administrator. Whenever she said something, the administrator just looked away. It was infuriating!

The worst part was that, when she raised the issue with the superintendent, he acted genuinely surprised and said, "I doubt that he was doing it on purpose."

Questions

1. What are some of the more common snubs that men give women supervisors in a school setting? Members of minority groups such as blacks?
2. How might a woman supervisor in a school setting bring this behavior to the attention of her male counterparts in a meaningful way?

SUGGESTED LEARNING ACTIVITIES

1. Develop a list of characteristics of a "people person."
2. Using the information given in this chapter, profile a person skilled in human relations. What skills are most important in this role?
3. Prepare a report on groups challenging school programs today. Cite issues.
4. What are the five most important things to know about effective group leadership?
5. What are some strategies that a supervisor might employ to decrease stress buildup in the teaching staff?

ADDITIONAL READING

Adler, Louis, and Tellez, Kip. "Curriculum Challenges from the Religious Right: The Impressions Reading Serves," *Urban Education*, July 1992, pp. 152–73.

Buehrer, E. *The New Age Masquerade.* Brentwood, TN: Wolsemuth and Hyatt, 1993.

"The Rainbow Curriculum, Fernandez Ousted as School Chief in New York City," *Education Week* 17 (February 1993): 1, 14.

Reichman, Henry. *Censorship and Selection.* Chicago: American Library Association and AASA, 1988.

Simonds, R. *President's Report.* Costa Mesa, CA: NACE/CEE, 1992.

BOOKS TO REVIEW

Cawelti, Gordon, ed. *Challenges and Achievements of American Education,* 1993 Yearbook. Alexandria, VA: ASCD, 1993.

Elmore, Richard, and Fuhrman, A. eds. *The Governance of Curriculum,* 1994 Yearbook. Alexandria, VA: ASCD, 1994.

Glickman, Carl, ed. *Supervision in Transition,* 1992 Yearbook. Alexandria, VA: ASCD, 1992.

Joyce, Bruce; Wolf, James; and Calhoun, Emily. *The Self-Reviewing School.* Alexandria, VA: ASCD, 1993.

Land, G., and Jarman, B. *Breakpoint and Beyond: Mastering the Future—Today.* New York: Harper Business, 1992.

Noll, James. *Taking Sides,* 8th ed. Guilford, CT: Dushkin Publishing, 1994.

Pratt, David. *Curriculum Planning: A Handbook for Professionals.* Fort Worth: Harcourt Brace, 1994.

Spring, Joel. *Conflict of Interest—The Politics of American Education,* 2nd ed. New York: Longman, 1993.

CHAPTER 9 ∾

PROVIDING EFFECTIVE STAFF DEVELOPMENT

Staff development represents perhaps the greatest challenge of supervisors today as they help prepare professional educators for leadership roles in the next century. Most of the teachers hired in the growth era of the 1960s and early 1970s will retire. Veteran staffs, who experienced the top-down management leadership styles of the 1980s, are being asked to assume greater leadership roles in schools.

Colleges of education are not producing enough new teachers to fill the needs of school districts and the ranks of teaching staffs are being filled with retooled professionals squeezed out of other professions. Many of those teachers enter the profession lacking the traditional courses found in teacher education programs.

The need to rejuvenate mature staffs, prepare new teachers to deal with increasing numbers of diverse youth, and train teachers to work collegially dictate a new approach to staff development.

American industry and business have learned many lessons in the past quarter century about improving employee performance. A new global economy, increasing levels of technology, internationalization of business, and interdependence among nations have resulted in the retooling of mature workers. New forms of employer–employee relationships have been developed as well as innovative training programs to prepare new workers and those already on the job for an ever-changing economic world.

American educators have always been enamored with industrial or business models, especially training models. Not having the luxury of closing plants, eliminating great numbers of workers, or reorganizing to get "leaner and meaner" as business does to gain a competitive edge, schools have just tinkered with improvement plans for its workers.

249

Faced with mounting pressure to reshape American schools, educational leaders have found that business and industrial training models do not provide all the answers for retooling educational staffs. In education, we rely heavily on people to carry out the required tasks of school improvement, unlike industry which can improve through robotics, increased technology, and modernized equipment. Technology can facilitate improved instruction, but it is staff development that cultivates teacher knowledge and skills to improve schools.

At the beginning of the 1990s, a new realization about staff development began to emerge. Changing the individual through staff development or in-service was long regarded as a significant approach to organizational improvement. Little and others, studying staff development activities in California, found attempting to change organizations by changing individuals resulted in little change.[1] Little et al. found that school districts spent an average of about $1700 a year per teacher and administrator. Although those efforts consumed about 1.8 percent of California's educational funding, those staff development activities did little to change teaching performance. In fact, the resources were allocated in ways that generally reinforced traditional patterns of teachers and conventional structures of schools.

Merely adding staff development activities directed toward improving individual teaching performance was not enough. Clearly, those activities had to be in conjunction with changing school structures.

Many of the school reform reports called for restructuring schools through site-based or school-based management. "Teacher empowerment" became a rallying cry. New ways of communicating and making decisions were used to plan school activities including staff development. Training was needed for both teachers and those in supervisory positions on how to make the new democracy work. Processes, rather than products, became the foci of staff development activities. For instance, workshops dealt with ways of improving techniques of decision making, group processes, and communication between supervisors or principals and teachers.

The goals of structural modification, which include integrating all functions of school organizations (curriculum, instruction, staff development), must not be forgotten while teachers and supervisors focus on the processes of school-based management. Building an organizational structure that facilitates improved teacher performance is more likely to result in positive changes in schools than simply focusing on individual improvement of teachers.

This chapter will examine the history of staff development as well as provide examples of successful staff development programs. We will examine leadership roles in staff development and outline role expectations and skills needed by supervisors to meet the challenges facing schools today. Particular emphasis will be given to the changing roles of supervisors in staff development. One important change is moving school leaders from all-knowing managers controlling all of the instructional activities of teachers to facilitators who work collaboratively with teachers in decisions about self-improvement.

We can gain a better understanding of the evolution of today's new approaches to improving performance of its professional educators by reviewing the history of staff development. The next section provides a look at a century of staff development.

HISTORY OF STAFF DEVELOPMENT

To understand better the problems and challenges of planning and developing staff development programs, it will be useful for supervisors to review the history of staff development.

From the early 1900s to the 1930s, educators believed that improving public schools could be best achieved by having teachers meet certain quantitative standards (teacher certification). The formal concept of instructional program improvement and teaching began with an emphasis on meeting certification requirements. That concept still prevails in public education today. Meeting certification requirements became the primary objective of both teachers and teacher-education institutions. Efforts to help professional educators adjust to social changes and new problems gave way to teachers enrolling in traditional courses required to complete degrees.

During the Depression of the thirties, lack of work opportunities for youth caused many who would have dropped out to remain in high school. Other youths who might have attended college in better times knew high school would be their last chance at a formal education. These students believed the curriculum irrelevant to their needs and interests and, indeed, to society in general. Pupil unrest caused educators to review the methodology used by teachers and administrators. Progressive educators were beginning to develop new teaching-learning procedures, new and expanded content, and new organizational patterns. Each innovation required practicing teachers to upgrade their knowledge and skills. Because most teachers and administrators had completed all of their certification requirements, colleges and universities shifted the focus of staff development to these new-found needs. Thus, activities designed to improve teacher performance were now being offered independent of certification programs.

Although this development was exciting and offered new insights into the improvement of educational opportunities, it proved to have little success in improving teaching and the curriculum.

Educational leaders such as Ralph Tyler and Hilda Taba reported much later that little impact had been made on improving the educational program for youth. Their findings are summarized in three major generalizations:

1. When programs, systems, strategies, and materials are developed in isolation of the educational practitioner, they are likely to become the end rather than the means.

2. When teachers and administrators do not understand the need to change or the basis for change, new programs, strategies, and so on will not occur in the school regardless of the validity of the research and the soundness of the design.

3. If an educational institution, higher, elementary, or secondary, develops and implements programs as ends, clients will be sought to fit the programs rather than continually altering programs to meet the needs and the interests of the clientele.[2]

From the end of World War II into the early fifties, the focus of teacher education once again was on meeting certification standards. An increased birthrate coupled with a teacher shortage forced school districts to employ teachers who were not certified. The lack of long-range planning by both local school districts and colleges of education resulted in a low priority being set for the professional development of teachers already certified.

It was not until the Sputnik years and our entrance into the space age that continuous education of teachers, apart from certification status, became a major thrust. Because the United States feared it was lagging behind Russia in producing highly skilled scientists and technicians, new teaching programs in science and mathematics became a priority. High school science programs were being upgraded, and training of teachers followed. With help from the federal government and state legislatures, local school districts became responsible for planning and implementing teacher improvement programs. Universities and colleges provided on-site courses and workshops in school districts.

The experience gained from the science and mathematics (and later, social studies and language arts) in-service programs was not lost. Local districts, and more specifically, the practicing educators in those districts, became the focus for staff development. This marked the beginning of staff development. For the first time, educational leaders were asking practitioners three important questions:

1. What does a pupil need to become a successful learner?
2. What programs and services are needed to assure pupils they will be successful learners?
3. What knowledge and skills do teachers need to implement fully the programs and services?

It cannot be implied from the experiences of the late fifties and early sixties that all planners used the results of the questions asked to the best advantage. It does say that planners were more concerned with the product of staff development as well as involving teachers and administrators in the development of the product than before. However, both behaviors are considered important to staff development as it is now known.

The 1960s saw professional improvement activities called "in-service education." Universities and colleges continued to serve as the primary resources of in-service education with workshops and courses being conducted on campuses and in school districts. During the next two decades, in-service education was considered more and more important by educators and state legislators. The number of school days in a school year was increased to give teachers and administrators more time to plan and participate in in-service activities. In addition, some states began to fund teacher education centers to increase in-service opportunities for teachers.

Specific needs of students were given more consideration during this period by professional educators and lawmakers at both the state and national level. Student needs were identified by category, and funds were provided. Examples include programs such as Title I of the Elementary and Secondary Education Act, which was aimed at helping pupils from low-income homes overcome academic deficiencies; Headstart, which focused on school readiness for preschool students from low-income homes; and P. L. 94–142 (Federal Handicapped Act), which mandated individualized educational programs for schoolchildren with handicaps. These and other programs, with a requirement for teacher and administrative training, caused local school districts to become more active and independent in in-service training activities.

The 1970s saw a decrease in student enrollment and an oversupply of qualified teaching personnel. Certification was no longer a major focus of in-service activities. However, many states increased teacher certification mandates through such measures as periodic recertification. These new mandates led to the states encouraging local school districts to provide staff development for recertification. Florida, for instance, allows teachers to select an option of recertification through completing a certain number of workshop hours at the district level or college hours taken through extension courses held in districts or at a university.

Many educational leaders believe the concept of staff development as we know it today began when local school district planners (responsible for improving performance of teachers and administrators) accepted the mandate to initiate and implement educational change. In turn, local school districts were encouraged to provide training activities for the purpose of teacher recertification.

Another development in many states was the elimination of the category of life certificate from the state certification laws that required all teachers to be periodically recertified. Georgia, for example, required all teachers with a bachelor's or master's degree to be recertified every five years after 1981. Those with specialist or doctoral degrees were required to be recertified every ten years.

Beginning teacher programs in a number of states have added even more mandates for staff development. Some states, for example, require all first-year teachers to pass both written and performance tests before they are given regular teaching certificates.

A majority of states have legislated that all school districts must file staff development plans with the state as part of mandated comprehensive plans.

Staff development emerged at a time when society demanded immediate changes in public schools. As the problems and complexities of society increased, local school districts were called on to deliver more and more services formerly provided by the home and community. Because local school districts assumed these major responsibilities, curricula changes and the upgrading of the skills and knowledge of its teachers became immediate priorities.

Most studies of staff development efforts reveal that the link between staff development and school achievement (both for student and teachers) has failed to materialize. Teachers who are likely to change behavior and use new ideas do the following:

1. Become aware of the need for improvement through analysis of their own behavior.
2. Make a written commitment to try new ideas in their classrooms the next day.
3. Modify workshop ideas to fit their classrooms.
4. Try out ideas, observe each other, and report successes or failures to their group. This requires follow-up in-service where ideas can be shared.

5. Learn by doing—try, evaluate, try again.

6. Use a variety of techniques: modeling, observations, and simulations.

The decade of the 1980s continued the conservative trend of the 1970s with many states imposing teacher tests on new teachers entering the profession. Some states tied merit pay to teacher examinations, and some attempted teacher tests for teachers already in service. However, almost all states dropped such programs in the early 1990s.

Lack of teacher time away from students continued to plague staff developers during the 1980s. Contract negotiations often resulted in higher pay for teachers at the expense of reducing in-service days. With funding tight in many districts, paying stipends for summer training was often eliminated or reduced. In many districts, trading pay for in-service days resulted in teachers receiving as little as three to four days of training a year. That training was often spread out over the year with little continuity involved.

In 1991–92, the average teacher was likely to be a white female slightly over forty years of age with a graduate degree and fifteen to twenty years of service, earning about $33,000 a year (National Center for Educational Statistics, 1993). Compared with the general population of professionals with college degrees, teachers are older, earn less money, and are more likely to be female.[3]

With a dwindling supply of teachers and an increasing demand for new teachers (about 250,000 new teachers a year were needed each year of the 1990s) and about 60 percent of the number provided by colleges of education, teacher hires in the 1990s are coming in greater numbers from those whose choice of teaching was a second choice. Shortages also continue in critical areas such as foreign languages, the sciences, guidance, and special education. In addition, if salaries remain low, younger teachers will be hard to retain. Mature teachers hanging on until retirement, less qualified individuals, and older persons filling the ranks of a profession that wasn't their first choice, all combine to make the last decade of the century one of the great challenges to supervisors leading staff development activities.

BELIEFS AND MYTHS ABOUT STAFF DEVELOPMENT

Beliefs About Staff Development

A philosophical base should be established for all staff development programs. A set of procedural guidelines should be built on concepts, values, and theories that professional educators hold to be valid and important to staff development. Examples of belief statements for staff development follow:

1. All teachers and administrators have a desire to be successful and respected professional educators.

2. The knowledge, attitudes, and performance of teachers and administrators have the greatest impact on the effectiveness of educational programs and services.

3. Professional educators should continuously search for more effective methods of meeting the needs and interests of pupils.

4. The improvement in the proficiency (awareness, knowledge, and skills) of teachers and administrators should be a continuous process.

5. Staff development at the local school district level is the combined responsibility of the district and the individual educator.

6. To be effective, a staff development program must be guided by a systematic plan of action and an integral component of a comprehensive plan for improving the school system.

7. To accurately identify the priorities for staff development programs, the needs of individual teachers and administrators must be considered.

8. Teachers and administrators will show a greater commitment to programs that they help plan.

9. The success of a staff development program will depend heavily upon the amount teachers and administrators are involved in the planning process.

10. Each local school district has needs, priorities, and characteristics that are not common to all other school districts.

11. Staff development programs should be individualized by school district and by school employees insofar as possible.

12. Each local school district should have the autonomy to plan and implement its own staff development program.

13. Certification renewal for local school personnel should be integrated into the staff development program, and should be a by-product of the program, rather than a programmatic entity or prime product.

14. Local staff development programs should be a high priority concern as evidenced by financial resources, time to plan and implement, personnel resources, and verbal and physical support from the leadership at both the state and local levels.

15. If staff development is to be explored, planned, and managed effectively, it must be clearly articulated among all parties having interest and/or an investment in staff development.

16. Teachers and administrators profit most from staff development experience when they are respected, their expertise is valued, their ideas used, and their problems taken seriously.

17. The underlying purpose for staff development is to improve the instructional and service programs of a school district.

18. Staff development should have a direct correlation with the school district's philosophy, goals, and programs.

19. Curriculum development and professional growth through staff development should share a common ground.

20. A systematic program of staff development must be developed in which in-district and out-of-district resources can collaborate to provide leadership and assistance.

21. Educators in designated leadership positions (superintendents, principals, etc.) should have a definite plan for improvement of teaching as one of their primary responsibilities.[4]

Myths About Staff Development

Effective teaching is not a set of generic practices, but instead a set of context-driven decisions about teaching.[5] We cannot train teachers to use the same set of practices for every lesson. Teachers do *not* automatically review a previous day's lesson, formulate objectives, present, model, check for understanding, provide guided practice, and have closure in a set of teaching steps. Rather, they constantly reflect, observe student learning, and adjust learning activities accordingly.

Unfortunately, the work of Madeline Hunter, David Berliner, and others have been presented by others (not the method) as simple-minded prescriptions of uniform criterion for evaluating teaching. To train teachers in such lock-step prescriptions really separates teachers from reality. To identify "good teaching" as a set of prescriptions is ludicrous.

A second myth is that teachers engage in staff development activities for incentives such as greater pay, merit pay plans, or career ladders. External incentives don't drive teachers to improve teaching performances. What does is the joy of teachers seeing new practices having positive effects on students.

We have long been engaged in training teachers in schools. In follow-up sessions after workshops, teachers love to share stories about what works with students. The pleasure of seeing students achieve, rise to new heights, and reach breakthroughs in learning new tasks far outweigh any monitoring or career gains teachers receive.

Duval reported that elementary teachers spent up to $2000 a year out of their own pockets for supplies, materials, and trips for students.[6] Interviews of state and national teachers of the year reflect the joy of teaching and overcoming bureaucratic processes to help students.

We know that excellent teachers are motivated by control over time, instruction, resources, and teaching strategies. They are not motivated by conforming to teacher evaluation systems such as those adopted by many states. A 1990 Carnegie Foundation Study found that 70 percent of all teachers in the United States are not involved deeply in decisions about curriculum, staff development, school budgets, grouping of students, or promotion and return policies.[7] Hopefully school-based decision-making of the 1990s will change that unhealthy situation.

Other myths about staff development include:

- *Teachers are the only people who need to improve their performance.* Teachers remain the key group in staff development, but others need staff development or in-service just as much. These include supervisors, administrators, support personnel, district personnel, school board members, parents, and even students who are student tutors or aides. Often, administrators decide on what teachers need, schedule the in-service, and go about other duties. Administrators not only need specialized training but also need to participate *with* teachers in in-service activities. In fact, administrators should be sitting in the front row of every in-service activity scheduled at their school.

- *Motivational and inspirational speakers really get teachers excited about changing practices or improving performance.* These sessions, usually a one-shot affair, do little to change teacher behavior. Inspirational speakers are usually witty (many borrowing comedy club one-liners and applying them to schools), charming, and, most of all, expensive. They leave town with a grin and a pocket full of cash while teachers usually have follow-up to help them with the real world of the classroom.

- *Teachers and administrators who need staff development will be the first ones to take advantage of staff development activities.* Unfortunately, those who need training the most are often the ones who will opt out of in-service activities. Questionnaires asking teachers or administrators what they need in in-service training must be followed by guidance from their supervisors to get those needing help into the right types of training. For instance, a teacher needing help in classroom management shouldn't have the option of turning down assistance. Effective leaders will work with those needing assistance to get the persons to "buy in" to training.

- *Teachers will automatically transfer what they pick up in in-service workshops into the classroom without assistance.* Follow-up clinical assistance is absolutely necessary if teachers are to implement what they have learned. Consultants who can't provide follow-up in-service in the classroom shouldn't be hired. Also, in-service workshops that last two or three days without any follow-up do little to change teacher behavior.

- *Staff development can really take place with little cost.* Too often, districts will invest heavily in computers or materials while leaving little for in-service training. Staff development does cost money, not only for consultants but also for substitutes to allow teachers to participate in training. For instance, many districts now allow students to leave early one day a week, thus allowing teachers and administrators time for training.

- *Staff development activities should be geared to immediate needs of the district, not to long-range needs.* Immediate needs do have to be addressed, but if staff development is only reacting, then little long-term growth occurs in a district. Curriculum development and organizational changes require systematic, long-range in-service plans. Workshops scheduled two or three times a year do little good.

- *Only outside consultants have the expertise to deliver effective in-service.* As with cooperative learning among students, teachers have much to offer peers. The same goes for administrators assisting administrators. Examples of such programs as the Teachers Teaching Teachers (TTT Model) and Administrators Assisting Administrators (AAA Model) are found in later sections of this chapter. Teachers and administrators who are released to assist peers at other school sites are very effective delivery agents for staff development.[8]

MODELS OF EFFECTIVE STAFF DEVELOPMENT

Although there is a rich research base to guide the selection of topics for staff development, there is much less research to guide the design of the training process. Critical decisions need to be made about training schedules, activities, and group sizes. We know that long-term training efforts are more likely to succeed than short-term ones. Also, presentation, demonstration, practice, and feedback have been found to be valuable components of staff development delivery systems.

A goal for staff development should be to create a program that enables teachers to share their problems, solutions, and expertise; to put teachers in touch with research on teaching; and to provide teachers with a way to become aware of and to consider the effects of their teaching on students.

The following sections represent successful delivery systems of staff development.

Clinical Methods of Staff Development

MICROTEACHING.   Microteaching is a process that makes it possible for teachers to participate in an actual teaching situation and receive immediate feedback on their performance. Teaching behavior is defined in terms of specific skills or techniques so that a specific lesson might focus on a single skill. Often, observational systems are utilized to help identify particular teacher behaviors. Other systems are used to look at such teaching skills as the effective use of classroom questions and classroom management.

Microteaching, as a procedure, gives teachers and supervisors the opportunity to identify, define, describe, analyze, and retest certain teaching skills in a lab setting. Teachers can try out lessons on students, other teachers, and supervisors. Through the use of such aids as films or videotapes, teachers can teach and reteach until a skill is mastered.

CLINICAL SUPERVISION.   The aims of traditional supervision and clinical supervision are the same—to improve instruction. In traditional supervision, however, the supervisor is the instructional expert. In clinical supervision, both the supervisor and teacher are assumed to be instructional experts. The teacher and the supervisor communicate as colleagues, with the teacher identifying concerns and the supervisor assisting the teacher in analyzing and improving teaching performance.

In the 1950s, Morris Cogan and colleagues initiated a study of supervision that led the process of clinical supervision.[9] Through a study of graduate students, Cogan found that suggestions on improvement of teaching coming from supervisors often fell on deaf ears. Students were not listening to supervisors because they felt supervisors were not concerned with the same problems the graduate students were experiencing in their classrooms.

In the clinical approach, the teacher is not the passive recipient of supervision but is an active partner whose participation and commitment are critical to the success of the supervisory process. Clinical supervision emphasizes teacher growth and assumes teachers possess the drive and personal resources to improve their teaching. The system is "clinical" because it depends upon direct, trained observation of classroom behaviors.

As a process, clinical supervision helps the teacher to identify and clarify problems, receive data from the supervisor, and develop solutions to problems with the help of the supervisor. Clinical supervision involves more supervisory time than one or two visits to a classroom.

Clinical supervisory techniques offer a number of advantages over traditional methods of supervision. They include:

1. Supervisors and teachers work together toward common objectives.
2. Supervisors can influence teaching behavior to a greater degree.
3. Teachers and supervisors have positive feelings toward the supervisory process.

Clinical supervision involves the following five-step process:

1. *Preobservational conference*—The preobservational conference between supervisor and teacher helps establish rapport between the two, allows the supervisor to get an orientation toward the group of students to be observed, and provides an opportunity for the teacher and supervisor to develop a contract outlining on what aspects of teaching he or she would like feedback.
2. *Observation*—The supervisor enters the classroom quietly and tries to avoid eye contact with students or teacher. The observer takes notes during the observation, particularly noting behaviors or teaching methods discussed during the preobservational conference. After the observation, the observer slips out of the classroom as quietly and unobtrusively as he or she entered.
3. *Analysis and strategy*—At this step, the supervisor reviews her or his notes in respect to the contract, analyzing the teaching patterns and crucial incidents observed during the lesson. Often if an observational system has been used, the supervisor can refer to specific verbal behaviors, levels of questions, or classroom management techniques.

   After the analysis, the supervisor must consider how to approach the teacher with the suggestions he or she may have developed. The supervisor must consider how defensive the teacher is and how best to approach the conference with the teacher.
4. *Supervisory conference*—During the supervisory conference, the teacher obtains feedback on those aspects of teaching that concerned her or him. Specific contract items are reviewed first, with additional feedback on other behavioral patterns later. As a final step in the observational conference, the supervisor may help the teacher plan the next lesson. The new lesson will incorporate the improvements identified during the conference.
5. *Postconference analysis*—The final step in the clinical supervision process is a postconference analysis of the total clinical process. This step is really an in-service

process for the supervisor. The supervisor can check to see if the teacher's professional integrity was respected during the conference, if the teacher had time to fully discuss specific contract items reviewed, and if the contract was satisfactory.

The combination of microteaching in a lab setting with clinical analysis of a live classroom holds promise for improving teaching. There are limitations in both the clinical and microteaching designs. The one-to-one relationship between supervisor and teacher is time consuming and expensive; videotaping equipment is costly. There are also valuable group interaction opportunities that may be lost. Finally, the focus on self found in the clinical design may retard looking outward for new ideas and advice.

Competency-Based Staff Development

Another approach to professional development with a focus on the individual is the competency-based staff development model. In this approach, no attempt is made to impose one particular instructional strategy or technique for everyone. There are five characteristics of the competency-based model:

1. All staff development efforts focus on the learner (teacher or administrator). Each learner is involved in designating the strategy necessary to develop a specific competency.
2. Instructional modules are prepared to help the teacher or administrator reach his or her professional objective. The instructional objectives are criterion referenced so that the competence attained by a particular participant is independent of reference to performance of others. Competencies are developed or assessed on three types of criteria: knowledge, performance, and consequences.
3. Each participant sets a target date for attainment of a particular objective viewed as essential to the achievement of a stated competency.
4. Developmental activities occur in a field setting. Simulated conditions are sometimes used to reduce the risk element.
5. Emphasis is placed on exit rather than entrance requirements. Objectives are clearly defined so that all parties know when the objective has been attained.

There have been a number of approaches for identifying both pre- and in-service teacher competencies. Depending on what study is reviewed, the competencies may be listed as general, specific, or sometimes "critical."

Many states have moved toward competency-based certification for initial certification as well as recertification of teachers. Florida has been a leader in developing competency tests for teachers and demanding mastery of identified teaching competencies. Applicants for initial regular certification must pass a comprehensive written examination. A growing criticism of "too many tests" and the need to fill teaching positions in critical areas is forcing a reexamination of such requirements.

In making the transition from staff development for renewal credits to staff development for professional growth, one would assume that all teaching personnel would be motivated to acquire new competencies or refine present ones. Unfortunately, some teachers do not want to disrupt the status quo. They see change as a threat. Other teachers simply do not have the time or energy to spend time in developmental activities. Teachers are busy people. Primary teachers work an average of 43.9 hours a week; intermediate teachers, 47.8 hours; middle school teachers, 47.1 hours; and high school teachers, 51.1 hours per week. With family and other out-of-school obligations, there remains little time for professional development.

Clinical supervision and other supervisory processes, where informative (not judgmental) feedback is provided participants, are helping teachers and administrators become more supportive of professional development.

Those who work with clinical supervision and competency-based staff development recognize that good human relations are the key to the success of both processes. Supervisors must spend considerable time establishing rapport with teachers and administrators.

School-Based Staff Development Programs

School-based staff development programs operate on the following premises:

1. Teachers should be involved in the identification and articulation of their own training needs.
2. Growth experiences for teachers, as well as for children, should be individualized. If such growth experiences are to be meaningful, they should belong to the learner, not be imposed by someone else.
3. The single school is the largest and proper unit for educational change.

Florida has been a leader in legislating school-based staff development programs. Gordon Lawrence, in a paper prepared for the Florida Department of Education, presented many findings that support the establishment of school-based staff development programs. Nine of his findings are listed here:

1. Teacher attitudes are more likely to be influenced in school-based than in college-based in-service programs.
2. School-based programs in which teachers participate as helpers to each other and planners of in-service activities tend to have greater success in accomplishing their objectives than do programs that are conducted by college or other outside personnel without the assistance of teachers.
3. School-based in-service programs that emphasize self-instruction by teachers have a strong record of effectiveness.
4. In-service education programs that have differentiated training experiences for different teachers (that is, "individualized") are more likely to accomplish their objectives than are programs that have common activities for all participants.

5. In-service education programs that place the teacher in active roles (constructing and generating materials, ideas, and behavior) are more likely to accomplish their objectives than are programs that place the teacher in a receptive role (accepting ideas and behavior prescriptions not of his or her own making).

6. In-service education programs that emphasize demonstrations, supervised trials, and feedback are more likely to accomplish their goals than are programs in which the teachers are expected to store up ideas and behavior prescriptions for a future time.

7. In-service education programs in which teachers share and provide mutual assistance to each other are more likely to accomplish their objectives than are programs in which each teacher does separate work.

8. Teachers are more likely to benefit from in-service education activities that are linked to a general effort of the school than they are from single-shot programs that are not part of a general staff development plan.

9. Teachers are more likely to benefit from in-service programs in which they can choose goals and activities for themselves, as contrasted with programs in which the goals and activities are preplanned.[10]

Peer Supervision

Peer supervision as a concept implies that teachers can supervise each other and provide observation, analysis, and feedback to their peers. Peer supervision is still a disturbingly slippery concept for many leaders in the field. It is difficult to know whether it describes a system in which teachers are organized into helping teams under the direction of a supervisor or a system in which the total teacher team has the responsibility for the improvement of instruction.

Teacher militancy in recent years has led teachers to demand greater control over their own teaching. Unions have pressed for responsibility for teachers in providing in-service education, evaluation, and other supervisory tasks. Teacher education center councils, where teachers have majority voting rights, have given rise to renewed efforts to give teachers more control over their destinies. Indeed, teacher organizations have lobbied for controlling access to the profession, selection, and retention of staff members. Because of confusion about the roles of supervisors, evaluation of teachers has become a dilemma for teachers and supervisors. For instance, teachers do not know whether a supervisor's visit is for instructional improvement, administrative evaluation, or both.

There are several drawbacks to peer supervision. As it is defined in many districts, teachers do not know if peer supervision is designed for improvement of instruction, evaluation, or both. Supervisors are also reluctant to share part of their domain of teacher evaluation with teachers. Finally, teachers must have an openness and trust among peers that exists in few places. Tenure laws and declining enrollment mean the prospect of increased numbers of senior teachers. With the security of tenured positions, such teachers may be resistant to supervisory efforts to upgrade instruction. Will peers be able to effect changes on those persons?

Peer supervision does hold promise as an adjunct to a broadly based program for instructional improvement. It is clear that the influence of supervisors in the instructional improvement process can be enhanced by the legitimate involvement of teachers in that process. However, supervisors must provide the linkage necessary between self-directed improvement and improvement that results from formal, organizationally directed supervision.

Coaching

Coaching is a structured adaptation of peer supervision. It is a method in which teacher teams of two or more members work together to improve their teaching.

Several models of coaching have evolved. In a *collegial* coaching model, pairs of teachers observe and critique each other on strategies designed by the teacher to be observed. A *technical* coaching model involves two teachers or consultants with teachers who work on a specified teaching skill. *Challenge* coaching works through a group to solve an instructional problem.

Mentoring

Mentoring also employs a collegial strategy but utilizes the assistance of a more experienced person with a less experienced or less knowledgeable person.

Mentors of teachers often have released time. Lead or master teachers often are used in supportive roles to help teachers one-to-one in the classroom.

Instructional supervisors train mentors and monitor the mentoring process. Supervisors often team with the mentor and person receiving assistance to form a collegial working group.

Teacher Education Centers

The teacher education center concept is a unified approach to the study of teaching and supervision. It is a coordinated program of pre-service and in-service experiences planned and administered cooperatively by universities, unions, private firms, governmental agencies, and public school systems.

The teacher center is an approach to in-service education, but not the only approach. Teacher centers supported by federal funds must be governed by a board composed of a majority of classroom teachers. In 1978, the federal government appropriated $8.25 million to create and support teacher centers. Fifty-five local school districts and five universities were awarded grants. Additional funding for teacher centers continued in the years after 1978.

Both the National Educational Association (NEA) and American Federation of Teachers (AFT) have received National Institute of Education (NIE) grants to assist members with teacher center projects. NEA took a different approach than AFT in establishing teacher centers. NEA began teacher center projects in 1977 at fifty-two sites in twenty-five states. AFT did not select sites and develop programs but chose instead to work through its local affiliates providing help and assistance when requested.

In 1975, a national clearinghouse for teacher centers, the Teachers' Centers Exchange, was funded by NIE and housed in the Far West Laboratory for Educational Research and Development in San Francisco.

Teacher centers can be placed in one of five categories: school district, independent, consortium, legislative, or union. Even though many centers have elements of more than one of these categories, there are unique characteristics of each of five.

School district centers usually avoid accepting funds from sources outside the district. They remain close to the teachers and conduct workshops, offer graduate courses, and help develop materials for teachers in the district.

Independent teacher centers until recently comprised over 50 percent of all teacher centers; today less than 10 percent are independent. Independent centers receive funds from foundations, business donations, and earned income including that from workshops and sale of teaching materials.

Consortium teacher centers are based on cooperation of a number of groups both in and out of education. Consortium centers operate on the premise that professional growth of teachers involves pre-service, in-service, and the surrounding community, and all of those elements are incorporated in consortium teacher centers.

Legislative teacher centers are those established by legislation in a state. Florida is unique in that the Florida Teacher Center Act of 1973 mandated that each of Florida's sixty-seven school districts help sponsor a teacher center. The state legislative set aside five dollars per student to be spent on staff development, with three of those dollars going directly into teacher centers. Several legislative acts after the 1973 Teacher Center Act provided further aid and direction to teacher centers including the sharing of a portion of funds between colleges of education and teacher centers. The sharing with colleges of education was eliminated in 1990.

Union teacher centers are supported and controlled by an organization representing teachers in collective bargaining. In New York City, 95 percent of teachers belong to the AFT and participate in the David Wites Education Lounge. This center is supported by union dues, and policy is dictated by the union.

Workshops, pre- and in-service courses, studies of teaching and supervision, special programs for paraprofessionals and teachers, development of materials, developing programs for children with special needs, bookmobiles, libraries, and personal tutoring are some of the services provided through teacher centers. Through centers, teachers are being offered a chance to take an active role in decisions affecting their professional growth. Teacher education centers offer a promise for professional growth and improvement of teachers, as well as a challenge to those in supervisory positions to provide new kinds of services in different settings.

Teachers Teaching Teachers (TTT) Model

The Teachers Teaching Teachers (TTT) Model has been widely adopted by large school districts in middle school transitions. By training teacher trainers who work at school sites, outside consultant costs and travel time have been eliminated or greatly reduced in districts using the TTT Model.

In 1989–90, the Dade County (Florida) School District implemented an additional planning period during each day for in-service training by staff trainers. Staff training time increased thirty full days a year using this model. Training by peers is not only cost effective but also relevant, since it allows for immediate feedback at the classroom level. The Duval County (Jacksonville, Florida) TTT Model in 1993–94 was used to train all middle school teachers in effective teaching strategies.

In-service for Supervisors

The focus of this chapter has been on the leadership roles supervisors assume in developing effective in-service programs. However, supervisors themselves need professional development. Supervisors have assumed responsibility for their own development by attending seminars, conferences, summer programs, and graduate classes. Professional associations, state departments, and school districts have established supervisory development programs to help supervisors improve their own performance.

Without feedback, supervisors may feel they are providing the services teachers desire. Surveys of teachers often reveal supervisors are not perceived as being useful to teachers where it counts the most to them—in the classroom helping with discipline, conducting teaching demonstrations, or helping with student evaluation.

As supervisory roles change, supervisors must be keenly aware of the leadership roles they must play in the professional growth of teachers. To be effective leaders, supervisors must have both the knowledge and skills necessary to change the behaviors of others.

A SYSTEMATIC VIEW OF TEACHER DEVELOPMENT

Since the quality of student learning is directly related to the quality of instruction, a major role of supervisors is to help teachers develop the competence to provide improved instruction. Although staff development in a school district may take on many different forms, those programs must nonetheless focus on the requisites needed by school personnel to advance the goals of the organization and to enhance staff competence.

Through the 1990s, there has been a growing interest in school organizations to improve student performance. National and state reports have focused on student achievement as measured by national tests or state assessment tests. In the early 1980s, the emphasis in schools was on minimum competence of students. In the mid-1980s, the emphasis changed to standards of excellence in which average and above-average students were challenged to excel in the science, mathematics, and communication skills. "Brain Bowls" and "Academic Decathlons" were organized, pitting the brightest students from one high school against those of another high school. Quality of instructional programs seemed to be measured by the number of students in advanced courses and the number of computers at school sites. Lost in the shuffle was the need to develop teacher renewal activities to enhance teaching quality. Other than state efforts (strongly resisted by teacher unions) to implement merit pay plans for teachers and to implement beginning teacher programs to measure competencies of first-year teachers, little has been done to improve the art and science of teaching.

Supervisors today must wrestle with a growing resistance of veteran staffs to "learn new tricks." Union agreements have narrowed full in-service days to as little as three days per year in many school districts. Computers, like their predecessors—teaching machines and educational television—have been seen as one more imposition on teachers' time to teach in the didactic fashion with which they are so comfortable. Often, computers mean more record keeping for teachers who are already overburdened with diagnostic-prescriptive programs requiring extensive record keeping.

Teacher shortages in critical areas such as mathematics and science have brought about state programs to hire teachers with no formal training in teaching institutions. Many school districts are using out-of-field instructors to teach courses mandated by new graduation requirements in states. These developments, along with the others stated earlier, pose serious challenges for supervisors as they develop staff development programs in their school districts.

If educational organizations are to continue to grow, members of their professional staffs must also continue to grow. Since a prime purpose of supervision is to provide the leadership necessary to promote a continuing climate of improvement, it is vital that supervisors possess the knowledge base and practical skills to carry out the critical function.

Staff Development and In-service

The terms "staff development" and "in-service education" are often used interchangeably. The distinction between the two is a conceptional one. Some would say that while staff development is in-service education, not all in-service education is staff development. Other authors see staff development as basically growth oriented whereas in-service education assumes a deficiency in the teacher and presupposes a set of appropriate ideas, skills, and methods that need developing.

We, however, feel that the term "staff development" can encompass all activities leading to professional growth. Our definition of staff development is based on the premise that the professional growth of an educator begins on entry into a teacher education program and continues until employment ends.

Experiences leading to professional growth (knowledge, skills, attitudes, and so on) can be divided into two categories:

1. *Pre-service education*—Formalized teacher education programs designed to help the individual meet employment requirements.

2. *In-service education*—Programs designed to improve the proficiencies of the practicing educator, which may be under the auspices of the employing school district or at the full discretion of the individual.

With a growing emphasis on alternative certification programs and induction programs, the distinction between pre-service and in-service education is beginning to blur.

Teacher Induction

Although the selection of new teachers is often a process external to the school site, the actual induction of the new teacher should be an active process at the building level. The induction of a new teacher into the system represents the best overall opportunity to influence subsequent professional behavior.

Induction can be envisioned as a five-step process which includes community adjustment, personnel adjustment, system adjustment, personal adjustment, and establishment of expectations. Until these five sets of tasks are completed by the inductee, the teacher will not be able to direct full attention to the teaching act.

COMMUNITY ADJUSTMENTS. This category would include such basics as finding housing, finding schools or child care for children, locating physicians or other special need groups, and a basic "scouting" of the new environment. The school can help in this process by assigning a "buddy" for all new teachers much as the military has done overseas for years for new personnel.

PERSONNEL ADJUSTMENT. High on the priority list of all new teachers is getting on the payroll and receiving benefits for their labor. Often this requires significant time filling out papers and making visits to designated offices. A simple school check-off list for new teachers and a couple of advance telephone calls to coordinate a visit can make this mundane process personal rather than institutional.

SYSTEM ADJUSTMENT. Many new teachers enter the school system oriented only on how to find their room and how to get their texts and supplies. A very natural and important question in the mind of any new teacher is, "How do I fit into the bigger picture?" If you want to orient the new teacher to district goals and philosophy, discipline procedures, or extracurricular duties and expectations, this is the time. What is delivered to the new teacher during induction will influence the individual's perception through the years.

PERSONAL ADJUSTMENT. Like moving into a new neighborhood, the new teacher will be anxious to establish relationships and become known to others. Perhaps the schools should invest more on arrival parties than on "going away" parties for teachers. A "buddy" appointment can facilitate this very important task for the new teacher.

ESTABLISHING EXPECTATIONS. Setting expectations for teacher performance can best be accomplished during induction when the new teacher is curious and seeking such information. Sharing evaluation criteria, assessment or visitation schedules, and the role of the supervisor in improving instruction are all relevant topics at this stage of development.

In summary, induction of a new teacher is an opportunity for the supervisor to establish contact, bond with the new teacher, set perceptions of performance expectations, and accelerate the improvement of a teacher's performance in the classroom.

EVALUATING STAFF DEVELOPMENT

A number of studies of staff development in the past fifteen years have identified factors that have resulted in changing teacher behavior and instructional practice.[11] Yet relatively few studies have determined if staff development activities have led to improved student outcomes.

There are many student outcomes that can be measured including cognitive as well as affective achievement. Factors such as attendance, graduation rates, and other outcomes, can be selected when determining whether staff development has been effective.

Since many factors influence student outcomes, it is difficult to say that staff development alone will bring about significant improvement. Thus a multi-faceted approach to measuring improvement needs to be developed. Such an approach would help identify the role staff development may have had in improvement of teaching and student learning.[12]

Recent practice of instructional supervisors leans toward prescriptive, systematic forms of staff development and school improvement. However, the focus of teacher development places teachers in a new role as leaders in educational change.[13] Collaboration, collegiality, peer assistance, Teachers Teaching Teachers (TTT) Model, and school culture are processes found in schools. Teachers are trying out new ideas, sharing those ideas with peers, and exerting a new independence as they improve their teaching and grow professionally.

The old role of the supervisor determining what is best for teachers (a top-down model) has been replaced by empowerment— teachers making decisions about what is best for them. The supervisor thus becomes part of a collaborative team providing expertise and resources to help teacher development take place. An interdependent collegiality helps teachers develop their craft through a process of reflective inquiry. The belief that only supervisors have a scientific knowledge of teaching, and only they can help teachers improve, has been replaced by a belief that teachers may have many of the answers themselves gained from their own practice.

WHO ARE STAFF DEVELOPERS AND WHAT DO THEY DO?

In 1992, the National Staff Development Council (NSDC) surveyed its 5,900 members to gather information about the status of staff developers and staff development in North America.

As reported in the *Journal of Staff Development,* a profile of staff developers was presented.[14] That profile revealed some interesting information. Nearly 75 percent of staff developers are in the age range of 41 to 55. They are not only mid-career, but overwhelmingly white and female. Over one half of staff developers have a post-masters degree with 25 percent holding doctorates.

Staff developers who work for school districts spend their time assisting individual staff members, conducting in-service training, managing staff development programs, and developing training programs or courses. The majority of time is spent managing staff development programs.

Another interesting fact is that most persons who fulfill staff development responsibilities in their school systems and agencies do this only a portion of their time. In fact, less than one half of staff developers spend more than one half their time fulfilling staff development responsibilities.

In examining career paths of staff developers, over 90 percent have been teachers. Another 50 percent have been administrators. More than one third have been staff developers, consultants, or supervisors. When asked to identify present positions, about one half of staff developers identify themselves as administrators rather than staff developers. Fifty percent also identify their positions as staff developers. Many identify more than one position such as administrator and staff developer or supervisor and staff developer.

Over 8 percent of those responding to the survey indicated they worked in school districts of less than 10,000 students.

Nearly one half of staff developers in school districts report directly to the superintendent. One third report to the curriculum director or assistant supervisor in charge of curriculum.

Teachers remain the largest group served by staff development. Seventy-five percent of clients served are teachers. Other professional staff including principals, assistant principals, counselors, and support staff make up the other groups served the most. Parents and district office staff make up less than 5 percent of clients served by staff development.

Financial support for staff development follows economic conditions, and districts in the late eighties and early nineties continued to cut staff development funds. Over 80 percent of districts report less than 3 percent of their budget is allocated to staff development.

Organizational development interventions tend to be curriculum development, team building, and strategies planning. Workshops in conflict management are increasing in number.

Topics most often covered in staff development programs include generic instructional strategies, curriculum implementation, classroom management, subject-specific instructional strategies, learning styles, motivation, and multicultural themes. Workshops are the most frequently used delivery system, and most staff development takes place on-site at the school. Over 60 percent of districts have no separate training site or resource center.

LEADERSHIP ROLES IN STAFF DEVELOPMENT

Supervisors can improve teachers' competencies in a number of ways, but they must be perceived by teachers as a valued resource. Studies have shown that instructional supervisors believe what they do has high value, although the teachers with whom they work find instructional supervision to be of little value. Principals can improve teacher performance but need to spend more time in the classroom providing direct assistance to teachers.

Thus, those closest to teachers, either in the minds of teachers or in reality, seem to provide little leadership in improving teachers' instructional performance.

Teachers are touched only briefly by pre-service training. When they find themselves placed in a school setting, they often learn their craft in unbelievable solitude inside their cells in the honeycomb of a school. They may get help from a department chair or mentor next door, but often those persons are too busy to be of much help. It is no wonder that teachers see teaching as an individualistic act since they often learn teaching tasks by their own ingenuity.

Leadership in most schools is directed at the daily problems of logistics and management. Record keeping and reporting brought on by accountability mandates leave but precious bits of free time for teachers. In any given year, teachers, on the average, participate in only three days of in-service work, and these often include isolated topics and little or no follow-up.

The challenge facing supervisors today in planning for and delivering staff development activities is not insurmountable but does require skills of building a synergistic environment in which a collaborative enterprise is both normal and sustaining. Teachers must see a need for staff development activities, be a part of the planning for those activities, and feel a sense of growth and competency by participating in them. Teachers, even veteran staff members, can be good learners. They can master just about every teaching technique and are willing to implement any new instructional program or curriculum they feel is sensible—if the conditions are right. The following sections outline skills and tasks supervisors can use to achieve high quality staff development.

Influencing Teacher Education Training

Although supervisors are not responsible for teacher in-service training, they can and should influence the training. Supervisors can, for example, collaborate with teacher training institutions by teaching courses at a university or college, serving on college committees, working directly with university supervisors in internship programs, and by serving on teacher education center committees.

Teacher education programs have been under attack for a number of years. Newspapers, magazines, and professional journals have been filled with articles criticizing the state of education in general and teacher training in particular. In 1983, the National Commission on Excellence in Education issued an unprecedented denunciation of the quality of American education. Various state commissions echoed the national report. In teacher education programs, low academic standards and the relevance of such preparation programs for the practical needs of the public schools have been debated.

From a teacher surplus to a teacher shortage, schools have faced a continuing crisis in getting properly trained teachers into the classrooms. Declining enrollments have meant a decreasing need for teachers. However, the number of graduates in education has not kept pace with the need for more teachers, especially in the critical areas of mathematics and science. Compounding the problem of teacher shortfall in the 1990s are increased requirements for high school students. Many of those requirements include additional courses in science and mathematics, thus exacerbating the overall shortages in those two areas.

Other than increasing field experiences and the length of time in teacher preparation programs to include a fifth year, teacher education institutions have done little to change the organization and procedures of such programs. Those programs continue to communicate the misconceptions of teacher education:

Misconception No. 1.   *The business of teaching is transmitting knowledge.*   This must be the case because the average teacher education program consists of three years of disciplined coursework followed by one year of professional preparation.

Misconception No. 2.   *The best way to prepare for teaching is to be told about it.*   This must be true, or we would round up teachers-to-be and run them through a string of courses beginning with a survey and ending with methods.

Misconception No. 3.   *Mastery of the skills of teaching is best gained through reading and writing reports.*   The incredible procedures found in endless education teacher preparation courses are reading about reaching processes and writing papers about topics such as open education and learning center operation.

Misconception No. 4.   *Regardless of their destination, all teachers should be trained the same.*   Like the patient described by Mager in *Goal Analysis,* we line up student teachers for the treatment without ever inquiring about their destinations. A footnote to this condition is that although nearly half the kids in school live in eight states and most of them in sixteen metropolitan areas, most teachers are trained in rural land-grant institutions.

Misconception No. 5.   *Children are all alike.*   Although your individual judgment would tell you this is untrue, we deal with that unitary figment, the average child, most exclusively. Only recently have we noted a few exceptions such as the mentally and physically handicapped, underachievers and overachievers, the culturally deprived, delayed and nondelayed learners, gifted, dyslexic, emotionally disturbed, disruptive . . . but when we plan for instruction, these "exceptions" seem to evaporate from discussions.

Misconception No. 6.   *Most kids you teach will be interested in you and your message.*   How quickly university professors and teachers in training forget those we left behind. Of every 100 ninth-graders in school, 75 finish high school, 48 enter college, and 23 will graduate from college.

Motivation is an elusive commodity to the 75 percent of those who are put out by the system along the way. Many will teach students who have already mentally checked out. Yet, we treat such motivation as a "given" in most courses.

Misconception No. 7.   *Most schools are innovative and exciting places.*   Many education courses experienced by teachers in training would lead them to believe that the average school is an orgy of innovativeness—open, electric, fluid. To the contrary, as Silverman's survey pointed out . . . and Joseph Mayer Rice's identical accounts at the turn of the last century . . . most schools are conservative and mindless.

Misconception No. 8.   *Good teaching is an absolute quality.*   Surely this must be so because no one ever mentions that a strict disciplinarian can also be a good teacher. Good teaching is not an absolute quality. Like leadership itself, good teaching is a situational phenomenon. Teachers are delivery systems for a curricular program.

Misconception No. 9.   *Teaching is really pretty simple.*   All that is required is to know your subject, know your methods, and plug in. That may have been true thirty years ago—today the requirements for existing are staggering.

Misconception No. 10.   *Teacher training ends at graduation.*   After all, many teachers have five-year, ten-year, or even lifetime certificates. This must mean that they will need little support again from teacher training institutions.

Teacher education programs thus provide contradictions between what teachers learn in presented programs and what is required of them in schools where they teach. Such contradictions reveal fundamental differences about the knowledge teaching requires, about the process of learning to teach, and about the nature of teacher's work.[15]

As schools continue to restructure in the 1990s, the dominant view of supervision and restructuring is that teachers' professional development be encouraged and enhanced through collaboration with other professionals in the school workplace. Yet, most present programs continue to prepare teachers to be isolated craftspersons in the classrooms, masters of their discipline or specialty, existing in a hierarchy of top-down management.

That view is being challenged today by modern supervision and those engaged in school restructuring. Peer coaching, team teaching, collaboration between supervisor and teacher—all require skills and attitudes necessary for adults to be colleagues.

Another contradiction found between pre-service and in-service programs is the notion that there are a set of teaching methods that are uniformly applicable in the school setting. Unfortunately, teacher education models posing as instruction supervision reinforce the false premise that teaching requires only technical knowledge that can be measured by some performance assessment system.

As the national debate over the quality of teachers and teaching heats up, many policy makers and legislators will be seeking answers to the critical questions of whether teacher education programs can attract quality students and whether we can keep them in the field once they graduate. Supervisors can individually and collectively begin to exert an influence on teacher education programs. They must insist on becoming partners in the process of planning and carrying out teacher preparation programs. They must be master teachers themselves, willing to enter a classroom and work with students and teachers. Finally, they must work to become the premier leaders in their field so that their voices will be heard and respected.

Assessing Staff Development Needs

Staff development activities should be directly related to instructional problems and interests of teachers. To learn about those problems and interests and plan in-service activities, a needs-assessment process should be used. Surveys of teachers and administrators can be used as well as collecting other data available at a school in the school district. Staff development activities should be based upon documented need, be highly organized, be sustained beyond one workshop session, and lead to direct improvement of instruction in the classroom level. Staff development activities should be a part of an ongoing curriculum management plan that is a comprehensive plan for managing a school or district curricular and instructional program.

A major point is that staff development activities should lead to the improvement of student learning. Staff development for the sake of staff development leads to nothing except a waste of precious dollars.

Listening to teachers is important. Too often staff development leaders assess content needs but fail to ask teachers how and where staff development should occur. Figure 9.1 illustrates how a survey of in-service needs can allow for both.

Preparing a Staff Development Plan

Since a prime purpose of supervision is to provide the leadership necessary to promote a continuing climate of improvement, it is vital that supervisors be able to plan and conduct effective in-service programs.

Preparing a staff development plan should include teachers, students, administrators, parents, and supervisors. Local school districts can improve student learning opportunities by improving the educational system and the performance of those who implement it.

There are essential steps in developing an in-service plan. Figure 9.2 outlines these steps.

Staff development in school districts may occur at four levels in a school district. Planning staff development at these four levels is more successful when the programs are coordinated with the comprehensive plan of the district. A model for a comprehensive plan, the Wiles-Bondi Curriculum Management Plan (CMP), is found in Chapter 10. Figure 9.3 illustrates those four levels and describes those affected by the staff development.

```
                                                    _____
                                                            Name

    I.  I would be willing to participate in the following (check one or more):

        _____  Workshops on listening skills/interpersonal relations
        _____  Interdisciplinary teaming
        _____  Curriculum development in my subject area/scope and
                 sequence/skills checklists/writing a base or life skills curriculum
        _____  Classroom management/motivational techniques/classroom interaction

    II. I would like to participate in clinical in-service sessions (consultant in the class-
        room with me) where I could get help in the following areas:

        _____

        _____

        _____

        _____

        _____

        _____

        _____

   III. I would like to visit certain programs such as:

        _____

        _____

        _____

    IV. I would be willing to participate in workshops (check one or more):

        _____  After school hours and evenings
        _____  Friday evening/Saturday morning
        _____  In-service days only
        _____  During released time when provided substitute
        _____  1–2 weeks in summer

    V.  I'd like to receive the following if possible:

        _____  In-service points
        _____  Course credit
        _____  Released-time substitutes
        _____  Trade-off time
        _____  Stipends for summer writing
```

Figure 9.1 Survey of In-service Needs

Intro

Conduct an Assessment of Need

a. Identify the target learners.

b. Determine a strategy for learner needs assessment—goals and objectives, test data, survey data, nature and degree of involvement in in-service project.

c. Conduct learner needs assessment.

d. Assign priorities to identified learner needs/tasks.

e. Collect baseline data regarding target learners.

Make Policy Decisions to Initiate an In-service Project

a. Involve target learners, administrators, supervisors in identifying program objectives.

b. Designate supervisory personnel (leadership agents) and support personnel to provide leadership for the project.

c. Develop budget and process guidelines.

d. Set a time frame for the project.

e. Design in-service activities, materials, resources.

Develop Evaluative Measures to Assess Developed In-service Program Objectives and Related Activities

a. Design evaluative measures to assess competencies of leadership staff.

b. Institute monitoring and formative evaluation regarding in-service project objectives and activities.

c. Develop evaluative measures to assess support elements, resources.

d. Conduct summative evaluation of in-service objectives, activities, leadership and supportive staff.

Figure 9.2 A Model for In-service Education

Facilitating Human Development in Staff Development

Supervisors must realize that if a better school program is desired, an environment in which teachers can be creative and improve teaching must be facilitated.

Promoting a willingness to try new ideas and techniques in the classroom is an essential step in sparking creativeness in teachers. Supervisors should demonstrate new procedures and provide security for teachers who are willing to try new ideas even if they fail. Constructive experimentation can result in better teaching. Finally, supervisors should be willing to share the heat when experimental programs do not succeed.

Societal demands on public education have resulted in the consolidation of small schools and school districts. As a result, schools and school districts have become complex organizations. Bigger schools and school districts have become further and further removed from classroom teachers. At the same time, teachers' pro-

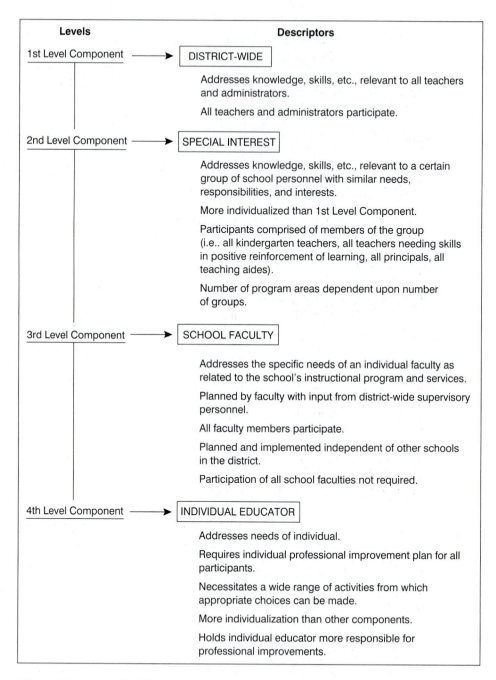

Levels	Descriptors

1st Level Component ——→ DISTRICT-WIDE

Addresses knowledge, skills, etc., relevant to all teachers and administrators.

All teachers and administrators participate.

2nd Level Component ——→ SPECIAL INTEREST

Addresses knowledge, skills, etc., relevant to a certain group of school personnel with similar needs, responsibilities, and interests.

More individualized than 1st Level Component.

Participants comprised of members of the group (i.e.. all kindergarten teachers, all teachers needing skills in positive reinforcement of learning, all principals, all teaching aides).

Number of program areas dependent upon number of groups.

3rd Level Component ——→ SCHOOL FACULTY

Addresses the specific needs of an individual faculty as related to the school's instructional program and services.

Planned by faculty with input from district-wide supervisory personnel.

All faculty members participate.

Planned and implemented independent of other schools in the district.

Participation of all school faculties not required.

4th Level Component ——→ INDIVIDUAL EDUCATOR

Addresses needs of individual.

Requires individual professional improvement plan for all participants.

Necessitates a wide range of activities from which appropriate choices can be made.

More individualization than other components.

Holds individual educator more responsible for professional improvements.

Figure 9.3 Levels of Staff Development

fessional organizations have become larger, the leadership of those organizations have become larger, and the leadership of those organizations has become further removed from the needs of the individual teacher. All of these developments, along with an accountability movement, have resulted in school leaders being viewed by teachers as bureaucrats. To help prevent political competition and encourage cooperative behavior between school leaders and teachers, supervisors should encourage a network of educational partnerships between teachers to help solve problems of greater educational significance. Supervisors who can form those partnerships and are really perceived by teachers and others as willing to share in decision making will help ensure their survival as supervisors. What educational partners are saying to each other is, "I can't be successful without you."

"Doing to" rather than "doing with" teachers has been a focus of supervision for the past thirty years. Even clinical supervision, which was originally conceived as a collaborative process, has become a sophisticated mechanism of teaching inspection and instructional surveillance.

Prescriptive forms of staff development and school improvement are being replaced by a focus on teacher development in which a culture of interdependent collegiality allows teachers to transform reflectively the classroom experience. In such a process, teachers can examine the classroom context and their role in becoming a facilitator of student learning.[16]

In a culture of collegiality, teachers learn from taking risks and trying out new ideas. Collaboration among teachers allows an exchange of ideas about what works with students and, in many cases, what doesn't work. A school culture in which supervisors help develop a climate in which collaboration practices can occur represents an "idea factory" in which educational change can flourish. Those in leadership roles must work with school and district administrators to loosen bureaucratic control. Often this involves changing fundamental beliefs of administrators about leadership. Also, teachers who have lived in an environment where top-down decisions about staff development is the norm must seize the opportunity to make decisions, work with colleagues, and become "teachers of teachers" as well as "teachers of children."

SUMMARY

Staff development is a primary role of the supervisor. Supervisors must provide the leadership necessary to promote a continuing climate of improvement. The 1990s have seen a shift in staff development from a bureaucratic, top-down model to a focus on teacher development which places teachers in a collaborative role with supervisors in developing improvement programs. The new view of supervision and restructuring of schools is that teachers' professional development is encouraged and developed in a culture of interdependent collegiality.

In recent years, teacher evaluation models, masquerading as instructional supervision, have extended the view that teaching requires only technical knowledge. Although performance-based evaluation systems such as the Florida Beginning Teacher Program (Florida Performance Management System) give a good illusion that a uniform set of teaching practices can be prescribed, taught, and evaluated, teachers and supervisors today recognize that such systems neither evaluate a teacher's overall practice nor provide information that teachers can use to meet individual teams' needs of a student.

Supervisors can use their knowledge and skills to work in collaboration with teachers and other professionals to plan staff development activities. The old assumption that instructional supervisors had a scientific knowledge base and set of analytical skills beyond the orbit of the classroom teacher has been dispelled by a new sense of teaching efficiency and professional empowerment on the part of teachers.

Supervisors are by no means left out of a leadership role in teacher development in the new work of teacher empowerment. They, too, are teachers and can work in a peer relationship to form a learning support group among teachers. That relationship requires interpersonal skills on the part of the modern supervisor that are quite different from those needed in the hierarchical power role of the past.

IMPLICATIONS FOR SUPERVISION

1. Can you identify a "pattern" of in-service opportunities in your district?
2. Can you outline the steps that would convert district staff development from "top-down" to a Teachers Teaching Teachers (TTT) model?
3. How can districts provide a better in-service for the beginning of the year to replace a now standard "motivational" speaker?

✎ CASE STUDY 1 ✎

The superintendent and board have decided that the present grades 7–9 junior high school will be converted in two years to a grades 6–8 middle school. The conversion is one of necessity to cope with declining enrollment rather than developing a needed program for middle grades students. The faculty and community have already raised questions about a middle school. The faculty is a veteran staff that likes the junior high school and sees little need to change their secondary teaching styles to accommodate the younger middle school students.

Over the years the community has changed. There are a number of single-parent homes, and the mobility rate of students in the middle grades (students entering and leaving during the school year) exceeds 35 percent. In addition, there are a number of students who are over-aged for their

grade and an even greater number who are below grade level in achievement.

Your assignment, as supervisor, is to develop and implement a staff development plan to carry out a successful middle school program.

Questions

1. Outline a two-year staff development plan for the middle school faculty. What tasks and timelines would you use?
2. What sources of information would you use as a needs assessment of faculty in-service needs?
3. What strategies would you use to get the "old dogs" to learn the new instructional tricks necessary for middle school teaching?

᪥ CASE STUDY 2 ᪥

It was surely a case of discrimination if she had ever seen one. Prior to becoming a supervisor she had heard that schools were a man's world. True, most administrators were men, but who could ever have guessed how invisible a woman supervisor could be in a meeting among men. It was just as bad trying to speak out in a face-to-face conversation with the administrator. Whenever she said something, the administrator just looked away. It was infuriating!

The worst part was that, when she raised the issue with the superintendent, he acted genuinely surprised and said, "I doubt that he was doing it on purpose."

Questions

1. What are some of the more common snubs that men give women supervisors in a school setting? Members of minority groups such as blacks?

2. How might a woman supervisor in a school setting bring this behavior to the attention of her male counterparts in a meaningful way?

SUGGESTED LEARNING ACTIVITIES

1. The superintendent has asked you to begin an extensive staff development plan to "improve teaching skills." Many teachers resent the implication that their teaching skills need improvement. You, as a supervisor, have the task of carrying out the superintendent's order in the face of open teacher dissatisfaction. What steps would you take to overcome hostile teacher feelings?

2. Develop an assessment of needs for a staff development program at your school.

3. Work with a colleague in a clinical supervision setting going through the five steps outlined in the chapter.

4. You are a member of a school improvement committee that is developing a staff development program to improve teaching at your school. What collaborative teaching programs and activities would you propose?

ADDITIONAL READING

Brandt, R. "On Teachers Coaching Teachers: A Conversation with Bruce Joyce," *Educational Leadership* 44 (February 1987): 13.

Brooks, J., and Brooks, M. *In Search of Understanding: The Case for Constructivist Classrooms.* Alexander, VA: Association for Supervision and Curriculum Development, 1993.

Daresh, John. *Supervision as a Proactive Process.* Prospect Heights, IL: Waveland Press, 1989.

Darling-Hammond, L. "Teacher Professionalism: Why & How?" In *Schools as Collaborative Cultures: Creating the Future Now,* ed. A. Lieberman. New York: The Falmer Press, 1993.

Davidson, N., Henkelman, J., and Stasinowsky, H. "Findings from a National Staff Development Council Status Survey of Staff Development and Staff Developers," *Journal of Staff Development* 14, 4 (Fall 1993): 58–62.

Ellis, S. Putting It All Together: An Integrated Staff Development Program." In *Staff Development: A Handbook of Effective Practices,* ed. S. D. Caldwell, pp. 58–69. Oxford, OH: National Staff Development Council, May 1994.

Fullan, M. "Invention, Reform, and Restructuring Strategies." In *Challenges and Achievement of American Education,* 1993 ASCD Yearbook. Alexandria, VA.: Association for Supervision and Curriculum Development, 1993.

Garnston, R. "How Administrators Support Peer Coaching," *Educational Leadership* 44 (February 1987): 13.

Glickman, C. *Supervision in Transition,* 1992 ASCD Yearbook. Alexandria, VA.: Association for Supervision and Curriculum Development, 1992.

Goldhammer, R., Anderson, R., and Krajewski, R. *Clinical Supervision: Special Methods for the Supervision of Teachers.* New York: Holt, Rinehart and Winston, 1969.

Gordon, S. "Paradigms, Transitions, and the New Supervisor," *Journal of Curriculum and Supervision* 8, 1 (Fall 1992): 64–76.

Hammond, L., and Sclar, E. "Policy and Supervisor." In *Supervision in Transition,* 1992 ASCD Yearbook. Alexandria, VA: Association for Supervision and Curriculum Development, 1992.

Joyce, B., and Dower, B. "The Coaching of Teaching," *Educational Leadership* 40 (October 1982): 4–10.

Joyce, B., Wolf, J., and Calhoun, E. *The Self-Renewing School.* Alexandria, VA: Association for Supervision and Curriculum Development, 1993.

Leinhardt, G. "What Research on Learning Tells Us About Teaching," *Educational Leadership,* April 1992, pp. 20–25.

Lieberman, A., and Miller, L., eds. "New Demands, New Realities, New Perspectives," *Staff Development For Education in the 90s,* 2nd ed. New York: Teachers College, Columbia University, 1991.

Marburger, C. *School-Based Improvement.* Columbia, MD: National Committee for Citizens in Education, 1988.

National Commission on Excellence in Education. *A Nation at Risk.* Washington, DC: National Commission on Excellence in Education, 1983.

National Governors' Association. *A Time for Results.* Washington, DC: National Governors' Association, 1984.

Oliva, P., *Supervision for Today's Schools,* 4th ed. White Plains: Longman, 1993.

Pajak, E. "Change and Continuity in Supervision and Leadership." In *Challenges and Achievements of American Education,* 1993 ASCD Yearbook. Alexandria, VA: Association for Supervision and Curriculum Development, 1993.

Schlechty, P. "On the Frontier of School Reform with Trailblazers, Pioneers, and Settlers," *Journal of Staff Development* 14, 4 (Fall 1993): 46–51.

Sizer, T. *Horace's School.* New York: Houghton Mifflin, 1992.

Sleeter, Christina. "Staff Development for Designated Schooling," *Phi Delta Kappan,* September 1990, pp. 33–40.

Streshly, W. "Staff Development in a Site-Based Curriculum Development Model," *NASSP Bulletin,* January 1992, pp. 56–59.

Wood, F., and Thompson, S. "Assumptions About Staff Development Based on Research and Best Practices," *Journal of Staff Development* 14, 4 (Fall 1993): 52–56.

Books to Review

Cawelti, Gordon, ed. *Challenges and Achievements of American Education.* 1993 ASCD Yearbook. Alexandria, VA: Association for Supervision and Curriculum Development, 1993.

Daresh, John C. *Supervision as a Proactive Process.*. Prospect Heights, IL: Waveland Press, 1989.

Glickman, Carl, ed. *Supervision in Transition.* 1992 ASCD Yearbook. Alexandria, VA: Association for Supervision and Curriculum Development, 1992.

Joyce, Bruce; Wolf, James; and Calhoun, Emily. *The Self-Renewing School.* Alexandria, VA: Association for Supervision and Curriculum Development, 1993.

Oliva, P. *Supervision for Today's Schools,* 4th ed. White Plains, NY: Longman, 1993.

Patterson, Jerry L. *Leadership for Tomorrow's Schools.* Alexandria, VA: Association for Supervision and Curriculum Development, 1993.

CHAPTER 10 ≈

ADMINISTRATIVE FUNCTIONS

Because school supervisors are staff persons, they are often required to fulfill administrative functions as part of their responsibilities. Such functions range from little jobs in support of superordinates to professional tasks dictated by their unique knowledge base and perspective. This chapter will provide a sampling of this range of administrative functions and the critical nature of these competencies.

Since school supervision is a highly mobile role, moving from one school to another and between the district office and other agencies, the supervisor should seek to view administrative tasks systematically. As Robert Katz once observed:

> The conceptual skill is the ability to see the organization as a whole; it includes recognizing how the various functions of the organization should depend on one another, and how changes in any one part affect all others. Recognizing these relationships and perceiving the significant elements in any situation, the administrator should be able to act in a way which advances the overall welfare of the organization.[1]

In viewing the school system as a series of programs designed to produce an effect on student learning, the supervisor can ask a number of generic questions that will help structure the many seemingly unrelated tasks:

1. Does this program meet an identified need?
2. Does this program support the goals and objectives of the district?
3. Does this program fit within the existing curriculum?
4. Can this program be carried out within the existing instructional organization, or will new programs be required?
5. Can this program be carried out by existing staff, or will new staff or training be required?

281

6. Are facilities and resources adequate to carry out this initiative?

7. Do we possess a method to assess the effectiveness of this decision?

Within each program, there are many activities where similar questions can be constructed; for example, Is this meeting contributing to an existing goal of the district?

SYSTEM TASKS TO IMPROVE INSTRUCTION

Using such a systems perspective, the supervisor will be faced with constructing a way of working to improve instruction. Among the global activities found in every school or district would be:

1. To develop a decision-making database

2. To form and activate an administrative team that builds on school-based management

3. To catalog and coordinate all ongoing activities

4. To review various goals for priority in order to focus efforts

5. To arrive at a procedure for making critical value-laden decisions

6. To develop a planning format

7. To determine job responsibilities and spheres of accountability

8. To develop an action plan format.

Let's look at each of these in more detail.

Developing a Decision-Making Database

This step can be thought of as a four-step process including collecting information, analyzing this data for meaning, making professional judgments about the value of this information, and connecting such decisions to resource allocation. According to management expert Peter Drucker, "Such information is the manager's main tool."[2] In a previous chapter, we addressed the need for an ongoing needs assessment in which critical data is gathered systematically for analysis. This could be birthrates, test scores, analysis of grades awarded, or any number of available data. At the school level, one of the major functions of the school office is to serve as a record center and information processing center. Figure 10.1 outlines such a management system.

Organizing such data is a major task, and one suggestion for classifying is:

1. Program design information

2. Program monitoring information

3. Program impact information

Regardless of what main categories are used, the supervisor will need to determine what information is needed, find reliable and appropriate sources of such

A. Goal
    1. Maintain permanent historical student records
    2. Be able to provide statistical reports as required
B. Keeps track of:
    1. Student information
        a. Student directories
        b. Student body analysis reports
        c. Bus and route reports
        d. Homeroom assignment reports
        e. Counselor assignment reports
    2. Course information
        a. Seating statistics
        b. Teacher schedules
        c. Room assignments
    3. Student course assignments
        a. Student schedules
        b. Class lists
    4. Student grade and attendance rosters
        a. Attendance reports
        b. Grade reports
        c. Rank
        d. Exception grade analysis reports
            1. Honor roll/dean's list
            2. Punitive grades (Ds, Fs, Is)
C. Updates:
    1. Cumulative academic permanent records
        a. Grade promotion
        b. Progress toward graduation
    2. Year-end (or semester-end) reports
        a. Grade distribution reports
            1. By course
            2. By teacher
            3. By department
            4. By grade
            5. By class
D. Other responsibilities/concerns
    1. Records backup—re-creation ability
        a. Hard copy
        b. Computer
        c. Microfiche
    2. Confidentiality
        a. Buckley amendment
            1. Private information/release permission
            2. Directory information
    3. Accuracy of clerical personnel
        a. Check systems
            1. Conflict checks in scheduling (esp. for computer systems)
            2. Grade points per grade roster (esp. for computer systems)

Figure 10.1 Student Records Management at the School Site

information, collect and analyze the data, use the data to make key decisions, and present the information to those others who need to be familiar with its meaning.

The actual application of the data to school issues presents the supervisor with something of a dilemma because he or she will have to decide what information to share. Even the collection and dissemination of the data provides opportunity for the mismanagement or misuse of information. In analyzing and making judgments, the supervisor should establish criteria for identifying the important elements of the problem and the applicability of data. Steps such as categorizing, separating the relevant from the irrelevant, and confirming data should be clearly thought out.

Finally, a process should be established to tie information analysis and decision making to the allocation of resources. Resources are the gasoline of the local school engine, and it is imperative that good decisions lead to proper allocation of resources by priority. The connection between resources and school goals should be clearly defined and widely disseminated. The search for additional resources should follow the same pattern.

Forming and Activating an Administrative Team

At the supervisory level, coordination is needed among the various decision makers and the multitude of committees found in most schools. Because the past ten years in public schools have seen the evolution of school-based management teams (also called "school improvement teams"), the supervisor must act through these groups whose roles, in many cases, are undergirded by law. Cutting vertically from community to district to school to classroom, and horizontally across subjects and programs, the supervisor is perfectly positioned to serve as a communicator. To be effective in this role, however, the supervisor will need to be highly organized.

Organization to make intended goals happen comes from good planning skills. Supervisors will need both long-term plans (strategic) and short-term plans (operational). In the strategic plan, the school or district looks ahead to situations that it might confront (technology, budget shortage, new officers) and prioritizes these anticipated events of perceived importance in terms of organizational objectives. Having done that, the organization considers ways to pursue or avoid those events. In the operational plan, by contrast, activities are specific to each targeted objective.

It should be noted that one characteristic of an exemplary school is that it looks ahead, anticipates, and capitalizes on opportunities. As the supervisor focuses on future problems and opportunities, rather than current or past problems, the role of the supervisor takes on a visionary quality; supervision becomes an organizational brain.

Cataloging All Ongoing Activities

Cataloging is an important step for a supervisor because of the many roles and responsibilities in any school or district. Few persons in the district possess the perspective of a supervisor who interacts with many role groups and sees many district documents on a daily basis. On the other hand, the supervisor has many opportunities to overlap and even contradict the efforts of other groups. We believe the best way to deal with this recurring problem in many districts is for the supervisor to regularly describe all ongoing activities and send copies of this information to other role groups on a "should know" basis.

This potential problem area might arise, for instance, when two agencies in the same district are pursuing a foundation or business for a grant. By initiating communication about supervisory activities, the supervisor will discover that his or her office will become a clearinghouse for information, like a hub on a wheel with many spokes.

Reviewing Goals for Priority

Both upward and downward communication in the chain of command is necessary to determine which goals have priority. Naturally, supervisors should be aware of board goals and objectives as well as special projects of the district officers. Equally important, the supervisor must be aware of conditions at the school level and in the classroom that might place limitations on such priorities.

If the supervisor finds that such goals and priorities are not clear to all, a meeting should be held so that everyone can respond to the planned instructional improvement activities. Again, in this role, the supervisor may serve as a catalyst for discussion and assume further leadership roles.

Arriving at Decision-Making Procedures

Setting up procedures for decision making presents a challenge to the person in a leadership role in a staff capacity. The difficulty in many districts is that the organizational chart that depicts line and staff does not always reflect reality when it comes to real decision making. For instructional decisions, the supervisor should seek to create a committee where all decisions are reviewed. In our Curriculum Management Planning model, used in many school districts in the past decade, the true decisions are made by a coordinating committee that oversees other committees (Figure 10.2). This arrangement begs the question of who really made a decision or how it got to the final step. The CMP structure is always predictable concerning the final decision.

Developing a Format for Planning

The format selected for planning should be a personal choice for the supervisor. Although many planning software systems available are now available for the personal computer, the supervisor should construct a self-serving model that meets local conditions. It should be remembered that the format selected will be used for presenting all data and planning of projects.

Figure 10.3 illustrates an example of a planning format. In this case, we were attempting to monitor comprehensive change in twenty Orlando, Florida, schools simultaneously and were being overwhelmed with detail. The process of storage and retrieval of information from nine planning areas reminded us of a library system.

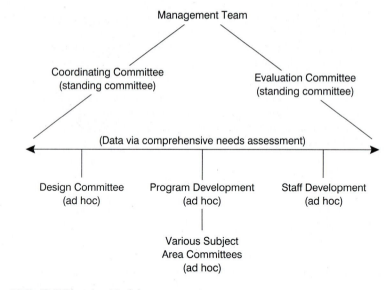

Figure 10.2 CMP Planning Model
Source: Wiles, Bondi & Associates, Inc., Tampa, Florida.

The result was a fairly simple grid that assigned numbers to both topic and time resulting in an orderly place for everything. In addition, when stored in a computer program, events could be retrieved by type, time, or sequence.

Identifying Job Responsibilities

Supervisors may find that explaining job responsibilities may be their toughest assignment. The straightforward way that supervisors in industry tell workers what their jobs are is not part of the education scene in America. We have found, however, that people will self-select job responsibilities when they are informed about the task, can see it in relation to the whole, and find that the task meets their personal needs in some way.

In many school districts, teachers are not fully informed about the "what and why" of decision making and often are asked to contribute to projects that they don't understand. If, as part of the planning process, reports could be issued and widely disseminated, then those persons who will be asked to assume responsibility will have a better idea of the "big picture" and what their contribution should be.

Developing an Action Plan Format

Some sort of communication document must be constructed that tells each participant what they are to do. Usually, these documents include the date, who is responsible, what is to be done, the product, and the due date in some kind of flow of

INVENTING A PLANNING SYSTEM BASED ON LIBRARY MODEL

Fall 1993
140—Facility modifications identified, scheduled 1994/95, 1995/96
240—Complete curriculum delivered to all teachers
340—Begin seminar series for potential middle school leaders
440—PR emphasis on curriculum (target parents) design
640—Teachers assess own school by new curriculum
740—Resource assessment by building against curriculum needs
741—Total resource budget developed for 1994/95, 1995/96
840—Data processing pilots new student evaluation in one school
940—Board Report V delivered by Coordinating Committee

The 40 Series Fall 1993

CALENDAR OF EVENTS

	Summer 1992 0–9	Fall 1992 10–19	Spring 1993 20–29	Summer 1993 30–39	Fall 1993 40–49
Facilities and Special Programs Placement (100–199)	100			130	140
Curriculum (200–299)	200 201 202	210 211 212	220 221 222 223 224	230	240
Administrator/Supervisor Training (300–399)		310	320	330 331	340
Public Relations (400–499)			420		440
Transportation and Redistricting (500–599)				530	
Teacher Training (600–699)			620 621 622		640
Instructional Materials (700–799)					740 741
Evaluation (800–899)	800 801	810 811 812	820 821 822		840
Board Reports (900–999)	900	910	920	930	940

Figure 10.3 Example of a Planning System
Source: Wiles, Bondi & Associates, Inc., Tampa, Florida.

events chart. In some manner, the "job sheet" for a teacher should be tied to a more general form that includes the work of a number of teachers on a task. Such a task sheet should be one of several attached to a project sheet. If constructed in this manner, each job contributes to a task, each set of tasks to a project, and each project is tied to some goal or objective of the school or district.[3]

PROMOTING CHANGE IN EDUCATIONAL SYSTEMS

Supervision, if it is to improve instruction, must seek change. Change is not bad, but it must be purposeful and must improve the condition of those affected by it. Change in schools is different from change in other walks of life, and supervisors must give extensive thought to this important part of their work.

A beginning point is to understand the conservative nature of the school. Since schools operate in a world of values, they are cautious, and most seek stability. Because any alteration destabilizes the institution, schools will accept it only under very special circumstances.

Change in schools, unlike other institutions, is almost always a social event and is rarely an isolated event. People in schools consider change in a social context, considering what other people think. When one part of the school is modified, other parts are also affected. Change in schools, because of the normative nature of the action, takes time; anything major will realistically require between three to five years to implement. Most of the successful change in schools is at the building level, which is also the most stable unit of organization.

Both understanding and a commitment are required since any change will depend on people for implementation. The purpose for a reorganization or modification should be rational, supported by data where possible, and seen in context. Any language, strategies, or techniques used should be tailored to the local culture of the school. Change, to be permanent, must be institutionalized and cannot survive as an extension of a personality.

Money and politics are the stream in which change flows in education. The application of money always brings innovation (not to be confused with lasting change), and any new or outside money is always tied to a value or norm of the supporting source.

Creating a context for change in schools often means borrowing the influence of outsiders (business, government, politicians). Ideas from other walks of life (outside) are almost always an untapped source of ideas for innovation and renewal in public schools. The supervisor should never forget that education is big business, and the larger the district, the larger the business implications for any change.

Additionally, in schools, there is a very special "show-and-tell" orientation in introducing anything new. Innovations that reduce a workload are almost always embraced in schools. All districts and schools have limits to the amount of alterations they can tolerate, but this level is often underestimated in schools.

Finally, the supervisor can expect that board members will not often grasp the educational implications of change that are proposed. The information given to a board will produce a "set" toward the proposed innovation. Superintendents and principals will accept change if they possess a philosophy or are a bit bored. Teachers are the final filters of change and must be courted; they have not been rewarded for adapting to improvements during the past thirty years. Consultants to schools always have agendas but can be used to introduce ideas and make transitions less painful.

Control Devices for Changing

Supervisors have ten mediums through which they can direct and control the change process. An understanding of these "levers" and how they influence the organization as a system is critical for improving schools. These devices are budget, committee membership, evaluation, public relations, technology, resource assignment, training, curriculum development, document formats, and reports. Following are descriptions of each:

1. Number one among the control items is budget, which was already noted as the "fuel" of change. A district with no money is a district without momentum. If various tasks and worksheets are given a fiscal value, a planner can easily promote priorities by making the item essential or peripheral, early or late. Items not really critical to the project that have been forced into the scheme (standards) can be abandoned on the spot.

2. A second variable allowing for the control of change is membership on committees. The planner will quickly realize that some committees are primary, even pivotal, to the change effort, and others are supportive; the titles are irrelevant. Persons thought to be supercompetent, possessing special knowledge, or even loyal can be placed on certain committees in leadership roles. By contrast, others can be diluted in their influence by assignment. This observation is not meant to suggest manipulation, but rather to observe the reality that committee structures can actually rewire the organization's operation.

3. Another major handle is evaluation, a topic covered in greater detail in the next section. Evaluation is often judgment (although we prefer a validation model), and the person who judges determines the final form of work. In every plan for change, there is a "report-to" section that determines the form and meaning of activity.

4. Yet another handle for controlling change is public relations. Public relations activity forms public opinion. Just as researchers can slant results, so can public relations people by putting the spotlight anywhere they choose. Especially in large districts, it is vital that the desired change be promoted in the best possible light for low-level communication and reference.

5. A fifth area that provides a means for controlling changes is technology. In any large-scale project, the storage and accessibility of information are critical. The establishment of special communications nets, the design of "tickler" files, the coded access to planning data, and the format of reporting driven data all provide leeway and control.

6. The assignment of facilities for meetings, work areas, access to equipment, or any function can influence the work to be done and the form of that work.

7. Training is a key control device. As teachers (who are the ultimate target of any change) are provided staff development opportunities, they are allowed access to information that can change their behavior. The person who designs those experiences influences the actions of the implementing instrument.

8. Design development and dissemination of instructional materials can be a control device. Ultimately, the tools that students use will shape how students respond to the ideas and how well they are able to learn.

9. Documents, such as assignment sheets, notes, reports, records, and particularly the standards, enable planners to interpret current and past processes.

10. Finally, board reports can also be a source of control since some items are highlighted while others are excluded in the name of efficiency. Of particular importance in board reports is the format by which actions to be taken (for review, for vote, and so on) are set up.

OVERCOMING COMMON OBSTACLES IN SCHOOL CHANGE

The literature on school change is extensive and identifies numerous predictable impediments to successful change. The task for supervisors promoting an innovation is to identify what is desired, set a course for that target, and overcome or neutralize these obstacles. Among the dictates to overcome these problem areas, translated into a prescription for the supervisor, are to set a way of thinking about change, establish a legitimate leadership role, define the change, gain buy-in from teachers and others, selectively apply the control devices, and sustain the change until complete. Each of these steps is reviewed in terms of what the supervisor must accomplish to be successful.

Creating a Vision

In order to lead, educators must have a vision about what needs to be changed. Without this perspective, the numerous distractions of an "open" system will inhibit progress. This vision will at first be concerned with "what," but it will also include thinking about "how." In particular, thinking about priorities, relationships, and sequencing prior to suggesting changes will pay dividends. Any educational group being led will want specific ideas about how change will occur.

Becoming Legitimate

Whether the leader is an insider or an outsider, he or she must be seen as legitimate in order to lead change. There are a number of ways to do this. The most direct means is to wrap it in the law, which gives it irrefutable legitimacy in schools. Another method is to find the true decision makers and borrow their influence and authority. A third way is to gain an endorsement from those in authority (by letter, videotape, or whatever). A fourth possibility is to make your efforts the board's effort by pursuing policy that will govern change. A final method is to promote a media image that, with time, becomes a truth.

Followers in education will demand to know what the expected outcome is if change is being promoted and they are to be affected. The first task is to establish a "set" for this change. Why are we changing? How does this fit into the past? How will it affect the future? What is this change like? The leader should try to paint any change as an extension of the past and to identify it with positive themes such as "good for kids" or "lighten the workload."

In addition, the planner must quickly provide a long-term outlook and reinforce the notion that quality improvements (not innovation) take time. The notion of a distance-rate-time problem will communicate that the time period depends on many things and, in particular, on the application of resources.

A third concern for setting expectations is to establish a shared reality among those being affected. We do not recommend talking philosophy or using jargon since these imprecise vehicles will encourage conflict and obstruction. Conducting a comprehensive needs assessment and talking about the "meaning of numbers" are more productive.

Finally, we believe that most educators underestimate how much teachers and fellow educators want to be recognized. We have never worked in a district that wanted to be second-best.

Providing Definition

If we can identify, in a general sense, what we want to do with school programming, we can continue to define and refine the concept until everyone is contributing to that end. In my process this begins with a model, continues with a general plan, and is further defined by standards and then reports that detail what, who, when, and how these things will be accomplished. Including cost estimates will assist in prioritizing and connecting events.

Giving regular and scheduled reports to the board allows the definition of the change process to become more detailed and more legitimate with each month. The key to a meaningful definition of the effort is to establish a system in which each player can understand how his or her part fits the whole. Sharing the planner's bird's-eye view with all involved will further this end.

Attaining "Buy-In"

People are open to change to the degree that they understand its intent, are involved in its conception and implementation, and see it as benefiting them personally. The method outlined in this book stresses the importance of opening up the change process to anyone wishing to be involved. We believe that this orientation makes it easier to communicate tough messages and to unfreeze overly stable areas.

The control of media releases, even the active pursuit of media image by systematic release of information, can foster a certain kind of communication about change. Again, educators constantly underestimate the capacity of schools to do great things, and the challenge of "being number one" or "second to none" consistently brings full effort. Educators want to be successful, and they want to be recognized. "Showing and telling" is a successful change strategy.

Finally, planners of change should use existing communication networks where possible. Find those persons who are influential and use them as conduits to others who respect their opinion. Since we can never be sure who these people are, don't burn bridges or be needlessly confrontational.

Gaining Control

Positive change in schools results from gaining control of the process and eliminating or overcoming natural and unforeseen barriers. The process outlined in this book is nothing more than a strategy to get control of the process of change.

The key to taking charge is found in the very first acts of this change strategy. Initially, the change leader must seek the endorsement of those with authority. We go to the board and the superintendent and ask permission to pursue a logical set of steps and, as quickly as possible, overlap the change process and their authority. We also gather the management team (the important functionaries) and secure their commitment to implement ideas blessed by the board. This communication among the leadership team of most school districts is less than perfect, and the early requests create a decision-making network.

The second early step to control is to move from philosophy (everybody has one) to analysis of numbers resulting from a needs assessment. Although conducting a needs assessment may seem like a perfunctory act, it isn't. The individual or group that designs the questions determines the answers. As they say about research: the researcher can prove anything he or she desires. (It is a byproduct of the scientific orientation of our nation that facts beat opinions.)

This book has identified many of the handles for controlling the process of change. Included in this long list of available actions are:

1. Establishing committees and communications networks
2. Promoting budgetary patterns for priority
3. Planning and "staging" systems of changing
4. Using public relations for image enhancement
5. Using evaluation to constrain actions toward ends
6. Designing certain priorities into training
7. Using reports to establish patterns and priorities
8. Using special committees (ad hoc) to separate and buffer
9. Loading committee appointments
10. Using enhancement projects to give direction to change

The "short list" suggests that each and every action taken by the promoter of change can be used to control or direct the process of changing. Advanced thinking about any step in the analyze-design-implement-evaluate cycle will help eliminate most classic failures of the change process in education.

The recommended process is *not* proposed to take over the change process, but rather to protect the process from interference and intrusion in our open system of education. *Rather than wresting control of change from the district, we are attempting to give control to the district.* It is the objective of this process to institutionalize change (remove personality, money, or other forms of influence) as soon as possible. We can only hope that a trained professional will do his or her best to guide the process in the best interest of schoolchildren.

The long-range objective of any change process such as the one outlined in this book is to institutionalize a process in a school or district that continues over time. Lasting change is not only one measure of our success or failure as planners but also of whether the institution can learn and remember how to address future change. What we ultimately desire in any school or district is to establish a history of successful change.

Sustaining Momentum

Most failed change in education results from lost momentum. Since most change in schools originates from the idea of an individual or a source of funding, the driving force behind it is personality or money. Take away either of these items, and most times the process grinds to a halt. Most educational innovations last eighteen months, and our school culture is characterized by continuous unsuccessful change.

One of the keys to sustaining momentum is keeping people informed and involved in the process. Individuals resist change when they don't know what is happening and don't feel involved in change; therefore, the prescribed change process should meet such needs. Involvement is the key to this approach and can be accomplished through reports, projections of activity, evaluation summaries, news releases, and even regular "tickler file" contacts.

Another key to momentum is keeping the project from getting bogged down or stretched out. The unfolding design of reports and the developmental staging concept that takes us from point to point are responsible for the feeling of constant movement toward goals. Using the ad hoc problem-solving committees provides a way of addressing issues without holding up the entire process. This approach helps since committees tend to lop off the extreme ends of any position on any question.

Tactics Within the Change Process

Finally, we see the change process as a series of strategies within the traditional curriculum development cycle. It is the administration of these strategies that makes change "move." Tactics that will accelerate the process of change include:

Analysis Stage

Set the stage by introducing the change within a context.

Introduce change as an extension of the past.

Give positive outcomes such as promising a reduced workload or better way of working.

Where possible, borrow inside or outside authority to endorse the concept.

Design Stage

Institutionalize the change event (no personalities).

A clear theme makes buy-in easier.

Always define the change in terms of the system.

Make the language of change appropriate to the local culture.

Present the change in distinct stages.

Implementation Stage

Be sure to provide a destination and a duration for the change.

Keep the planned change visible through the life of the process.

Borrow freely from other walks of life in promoting the change.

Present change in a logical sequence so that it appears manageable.

Evaluation Stage

Clearly identify the target so that the change can be seen as positive.

Remember that counting is always more productive than debating.

Determine the board orientation to changing.

THE PROCESSES OF MANAGEMENT

To be effective in administrative functions, the supervisor must have a way of organizing the many daily tasks related to the job. Having already noted that a systems perspective is useful, the supervisor must then think about the various functions in their day-to-day office. The key to effectiveness is to establish routines within each function area. Examples of such function areas are a center for commanding (leading), for communicating, for keeping records, for servicing, and for finance.

The command function consists of providing directives so that each part knows its role and relationship to the whole. In addition to the various reports already noted, various specifications for committee work, curriculum development, staff development, and other tasks should be given definition.

The information function includes tasks such as mail handling, routing of information for review, handling invoices for purchasing, creating style specifications for external communication (letters, reports), telephone routing and management, and other related items.

The record center maintains critical information in a form that can be retrieved and applied. Reports, research, needs assessment data, various committee assignments, and other documents are filed and catalogued for access. Computers play a big role in this function area.

The service area includes tasks such as public relations efforts, contact with community, staff development operations, office janitorial service, and procedures for visitors.

Finally, the financial function or center addresses budgetary procedures, grants, equipment renewal, personnel serving in a staff relationship, and related areas.

These function areas, once organized, represent the skeleton of a working supervisory unit. Without such administrative preparation, the supervisor will spend a vast majority of time putting out fires and responding to new situations for which there is no procedure.

Special Concern Areas

Three special concern areas in administration prove bothersome for school supervisors and heavily influence their effectiveness on the job. These areas are budget administration, personnel administration, and dealing with politics in the workplace.

Budgets in schools have changed significantly during the past twenty years as local funds have been supplanted by state funds (about 60 percent comes from the state today), and federal contributions have become increasingly categorical. Today, the backbone of most local school district budgets is the state foundation program: a distribution formula that guarantees a floor (foundation) of funding for all districts regardless of their capacity to raise monies.

States disperse funds in three forms: general appropriations, categorical units, and equalization grants. Although each state funding pattern is unique, most contributions from the state to the local district are either flat grants based on a formula (average daily attendance) or equalization grants (by teaching unit or weighted student approach). In addition, states may award grants to local districts for items such as construction, busing, or maintenance. Most federal funds are passed through to the local district with strong categorical regulations.

Finally, local districts sometimes raise monies through instruments of indebtedness called "bonds." Bonds allow local districts to raise money for immediate needs while at the same time obligating taxpayers to repay the amount, with interest, in the future. States set limits on how much bonding a local school district can have.

At the local district and school level, such monies are kept in budgets with very specific record-keeping mechanisms. These classifications of the budget provide a basis for grouping and analyzing expenditures. School systems throughout the United States use a fairly uniform coding system in budgetary matters. Series numbers are assigned to indicate the destination of a budget item: for example, instruction is usually a 200 series, and capital outlay is generally a 900 series (see Figure 10.4). Within these series, specific functions are identified.

School districts use "object codes" to indicate what service or commodity is being received as a result of an expenditure. These codes are numbered from 0 to 1,000, in increments of 10, to allow the addition of items as they are procured, for example, 010 may represent regular salaries and 020 overtime pay.

Finally, district budgets contain special funds that are often designated by state accounting systems. Fund 01 may be an incidental fund; Fund 04, a debt service fund; and Fund 12, a lunchroom fund.

The supervisor, new or on the job, will inherit a budget that looks a lot like the local school budget (Figure 10.5), showing object and function codes and projects attached to special funding sources. An early task for any new supervisor would be to

Figure 10.4 Budgeting Codes
Instruction—The 200 Series

210. *Salaries*
    211. *Principals*
    212. *Consultants or Supervisors*
    213. *Teachers*
    214. *Other Instructional Staff*
        214-a. School Librarians
        214-b. Audiovisual Personnel
        214-c. Guidance Personnel
        214-d. Psychological Personnel
        214-e. Television Instructional Personnel
    215. *Secretarial and Clerical Assistants*
        215-a. Principal's Office
        215-b. Consultants or Supervisors
        215-c. Teachers
        215-d. Other Instructional Staff
    216. *Other Salaries for Instruction*
220. *Textbooks*
230. *School Libraries and Audiovisual Materials*
    230-a. School Library Books
    230-b. Periodicals and Newspapers
    230-c. Audiovisual Materials
    230-d. Other School Library Expenses
240. *Teaching Supplies*
250. *Other Expenses*
    250-a. Supplies
    250-b. Travel
    250-c. Miscellaneous Expenses

spend time in the district finance office receiving instruction on local procedures for accounting. The ability to manage within the budget will be a primary basis for judging competence for new supervisors.

PERSONNEL ADMINISTRATION

Because supervisors attempt to improve instruction by working directly with classroom teachers, personnel administration represents the strongest path to better schools. Failure to understand that recruiting and inducting good teachers leads to great schools is an all-to-common error in supervision today. Three thoughts summarize the importance of this area:

1. People are the most important asset in education.
2. People represent the largest single controllable variable in the organization.
3. People are the source of most performance problems in schools.

SCHOOL *Hometown Elementary* NO. 6101 EST. FTE 610.95 EST. W/FTE 744.68
Expenditure Budget by Object Staffing

Object No. Description	Instruction Function 5000	Instr. Support Function 6000	General Support Function 7000	Total Budget 1980–81
100 Salaries	$507,223.57	$33,443.03	$98,681.35	$639,347.95
200 Benefits	91,986.20	6,508.63	22,202.07	120,696.90
300 Purchased Services	313.00	662.83	3,456.03	4,431.86
3XX Utilities	-0-	-0-	49,652.25	49,652.25
511 Supplies	6,349.97	594.01	2,616.54	9,560.52
512 AV Supplies	-0-	96.55	-0-	96.55
520 Textbooks	18,296.85	-0-	-0-	18,296.85
530 Periodicals	-0-	303.42	-0-	303.42
620 AV Materials (New)	-0-	703.84	-0-	703.84
640 Furn., Fixt., & Equip. (New)	506.22	96.96	900.00	1,503.18
737 Prof. Dues	-0-	-0-	-0-	-0-
794 Field Trips	845.91	-0-	-0-	845.91*
810 Library Books (Repl.)	-0-	818.52	-0-	818.52
840 Furn., Fixt., & Eq. (Repl.)	732.02	300.00	1,489.00	1,056.98
	$624,789.70	$43,527.79	$178,997.24	$847,314.73

1980–81 Staffing	Units
Certificated	
Classrm. Tchrs.	31.70
R.O.T.C.	
Occup. Spec.	1.01
Guid. Coun.	1.00
Media Spec.	
Deans	1.00
Principal	
Asst. Princ.	
Curr. Coord.	1.00
Sub-Total	35.71
Non-Certif.	
Library Clerk	.50
Secretary	1.00
Bookkeeper	1.00
Office Clerk	
Custodial	3.52
Sub-Total	6.02
Aides	
Instr.*	2.00
Guidance	
Media	
Instr. Supp.	
Sub-Total	2.00
SCHOOL TOTAL	47.73
Summer	3.00
Supplements	1.00

* Instructional Aides (Teacher units converted)

Figure 10.5 A School Budget by Object Codes

A supervisor's personnel functions can be broken down as follows:

1. *Planning*—The supervisor reviews the organizational charts and studies the demographics of the school or district to determine the needs of the future. The supervisor establishes a process for long-range and short-range planning. The various positions desired are defined and described.

2. *Recruitment*—A process to find good people is established by policies and various activities. Data is used to guide a screening and selection process. During the interview stage, standard guidelines and team ratings are used to diminish bias. Equal Employment Opportunity (EEO) guidelines are followed to the letter of the law. During interviews, the supervisor should pay particular attention to conflicting information.

3. *Induction*—Few districts recognize the importance of this step in which a general orientation to the purpose of the job is transmitted. The initial purpose of the induction process is to focus on adjustment (housing, medical, payroll), but the long-range purpose is to shape and reinforce a view of performance expectations. In particular, the inductee will face four problems: adjusting to the community and environment, becoming knowledgeable about the system, performing the assignment, and overcoming personal problems. The time to address obvious personal problems (alcoholism, absenteeism) is in the first two weeks.

4. *Appraisal*—As quickly as possible, performance targets should be set and transmitted to the teacher. Ineffective performances should be noted and deficiencies scheduled for remediation or retraining through staff development. Benchmark expectations for all new employees should be clear during the first year. Mentoring should be encouraged.

5. *Information*—During the first five years, staff development should be perceived as an opportunity to give the teacher as much information as possible about the organization: goals, programs, problems. The reason for encouraging a broader perspective of the task by the teacher is that, by the fifth year, the individual will need to transfer from an extrinsic reward orientation to an intrinsic reward orientation (defining the job by purpose, not pay).

6. *Retention*—All businesses suffer from the problem of training employees only to have them leave. Schools make important contributions to the professional competence of teachers through staff development, and maintaining a high-quality instructional program often means retaining highly trained teachers. Teachers leave a school or district because of job dissatisfaction, inadequate pay, and work conditions. Supervisors should focus on the job and its tasks and seek creative ways to make teaching more interesting.

Among the nonfinancial incentives supervisors can employ are cross-function training, continued formal education, career development training, task force assignments, self-improvement grants, and special recognition awards.

Work conditions can be improved by providing alternative environments, getting teachers more involved in planning and decision making (site-based management), giving teachers an assistant, increasing resources for teachers, improving the comfort and appearance of spaces, and building in discretionary time.

The financial incentives for teachers, while improving, are still not an adequate base for motivation or retention. Among the most popular ideas are increasing base pay, loan forgiveness, increased retirement security, better health packages, promotion or advancement bonuses (team leaders), and quasi-administrative roles with pay (teacher on leave to the district office).

POLITICS ON THE JOB

Probably the biggest surprise for many new supervisors is the degree to which their job is political. Schools are political because there is competition for scarce resources. Since the supervisor is constantly processing the allocation of these resources by scheduling tasks, it is easy to understand why the job is influenced by forces ranging from teacher unions to salespersons to angry parents. Acknowledging this political dimension, and planning for it, is an important task.

A first step for the new supervisor is to understand that the nature of the organizational hierarchy will determine how pressure will be applied for resources. In Figure 10.6, Kimbrough identifies four stereotypic power configurations found in public schools. The primary difference between the four types is the degree of stability that will be found in each. Stability equals predictability, and in very stable organizations, pressure on the supervisor will come from very predictable sources. Among the pre-

---

Monopolistic Elite

1. Single pyramid of pervasive power
2. Issues contained, 80%-100% overlap
3. Communication up and down within group

Multigroup Noncompetitive

1. Two or more pyramids which share power
2. Minor issue competition, 70–80% overlap
3. Communication to guarantee consensus

Competitive Elite

1. Two or more pyramids in competition for power
2. Major competition on issues, 50% or less overlap
3. Communication with satellites, little with competitors

Segmented Pluralism

1. No stable pyramids of power
2. Issues determine power arrangements, no overlap
3. Little communication, function of issue

Figure 10.6 Types of Power Structures
Source: Adapted from Ralph Kimbrough, *Political Power and Educational Decision Making* (Chicago: Rand-McNally, 1964), pp. 83–106.

dictable forces are school board members, central office staff, various community group representatives, and the teacher union. Not so predictable are political action committees (pressure groups) from the Far Right and the Far Left who will try to influence supervisory decision making for a special purpose.

As Wildavsky has observed,

> Human nature is never more evident than when people are struggling to gain a larger share of funds or to apportion what they have among myriad elements. If politics is regarded in part as conflict over whose preferences will prevail in the determination of policy, the budget records the outcome of the struggle.[4]

In general, political activity for the supervisor (budget struggles) will be greater at the district level, since at the local school level only 5 percent of the budget is discretionary; the rest being predetermined by category or fixed charges (salaries, maintenance, telephone). For this reason, the supervisor should be easygoing at the school level but more aggressive in various interactions at the district level. Being responsible for improving educational experience for students gives the supervisor the ultimate "card" in any such game.

In districts where resources are slim and competition fierce, the supervisor will have to adopt a congressional model of give-and-take to be effective in improving instructional programs. Knowing priorities and understanding the relationships between the parts in the school system will help the supervisor bargain for resources. Since, theoretically, everyone is on the same team in a school district, directing resources to mutually advantageous causes will quickly gain support.

The supervisor must remember that the political dimensions of any school district are quite complex, and the new supervisor should become a student of the system before getting involved in any tradeoffs. The lessons learned about the process of change are particularly important in this respect.

GUIDELINES FOR REALISTIC PRACTICE

The message a supervisor should gain from this chapter is to understand the organization in which he or she is working, to build both a conceptual model of how things work and a series of procedures in key areas, and to begin to steer the organization toward better practice. The difference between an average district and an excellent district is often the vision and decision-making pattern of a supervisor.

SUMMARY

Administration functions for the supervisor are what makes the organization work. In most instances, supervision will be a "do-it-yourself" kind of operation, but the supervisor who is organized can do more than the supervisor who fails to share and delegate. Supervisors have a unique freedom to maneuver within the school organizations.

The beginning point for practice for any supervisor is to develop the conceptual skill of seeing how things work. Sometimes things work by the book, and sometimes activities are more political. Making an organization as stable as possible through establishing routines will help control politics in decision making.

Creating a system of procedures includes tasks such as developing a way to gather decision-making data, forming a decision-making team, coordinating the many activities attempting to improve instruction, clarifying goals and targets, formatting all planning efforts and action plans, and assessing progress regularly.

An indispensable knowledge area for supervisors is the process of change. School improvement, however defined, means change. Understanding the culture of schools and the perceptions of teachers will help the supervisor formulate workable strategies. Change can be controlled or steered using devices such as budget, committee membership, evaluation, public relations, technology, resource assignment, staff development or training, curriculum development, document formatting, and formal reports. Management of change at the school site can be coordinated by focusing on specific functions such as command, information, records, and finance. Once organized, these functions form a skeleton for all supervisory behaviors in the school.

Finally, three special areas of concern should receive attention from the new supervisor: budget administration, personnel administration, and school politics. These areas are of special importance because they are often used to judge the basic competence of the novice supervisor.

IMPLICATIONS FOR SUPERVISION

1. Identify the three most important changes, other than those mandated by law, that have occurred in your district in the last decade. What do they have in common?
2. Explain what ethical problems might arise from a supervisor operating under the congenial needle of "give and take."
3. What simple rule or premise will help you prioritize the many administrative tasks each day?

๑ CASE STUDY 1 ๑

As a supervisor, you have been engaged in long-range planning for your subject area for a number of years. Recently, the superintendent asked you to chair a committee charged with developing a comprehensive plan for the entire district for the next five years. Curriculum revision, building needs, staff development, and budget needs as well as others to be identified by your group are to be addressed in your plan. The superintendent has requested that timelines and persons responsible for carrying out tasks be identified in the comprehensive plan. She has also suggested that community persons be actively involved in the development of the comprehensive plan.

Questions
1. What aspects would you include in the comprehensive plan?
2. Whom would you suggest as members of the planning committee?
3. What planning techniques and management tools would you employ in developing the comprehensive plan?

❧ CASE STUDY 2 ❧

An unsettling feeling came over Sylvia as the superintendent continued his budget report to supervisors and administrators. So this was what a conservative board meant. They were really serious about cutting 15 percent of the local district budget by next year. Never had anyone in the room thought that a basic budget could mean this. Sylvia leaned forward to catch the superintendent's summation, "And so I'm asking for the assistance and cooperation of each of you in meeting this contingency. You will be asked to assess the drop of enrollment last year and adjust your staff patterns and material budget accordingly."

The following week Sylvia received the district's much-dreaded envelope that showed her fair share of budget cuts to be $79,000. Material reductions would not cover the deficit. Teaching positions would have to be eliminated.

Sylvia now knows that any cut in staff will necessarily affect the curriculum available to students. She plans to visit principals and the assistant superintendents for business and curriculum. She is tempted to see the superintendent and some friends on the board to try to get some relief from the budget reduction mandate.

Questions
1. With what information does Sylvia need before pleading her case?
2. What risks will Sylvia take if she makes an "end run" to the superintendent and board members to gain relief from budget cuts?
3. What contingency strategies should Sylvia use in case budget figures are amended at the last minute to give her back funds?

BOOKS TO REVIEW

Argyris, C. *Overcoming Organizational Defenses: Facilitating Organizational Learning.* Boston: Allyn and Bacon. 1990.

Blase, J., ed. *The Politics of Life in Schools: Power, Conflict, Cooperation.* Newbury Park, CA: Sage, 1991.

Block, P. *The Empowered Manager: Positive Political Skills At Work.* San Francisco: Jossey-Bass, 1991.

Campbell, R. et al. *The Organization and Control of American Schools,* 6th ed. New York: Macmillan, 1990.

Carlson, R., and Ackerman, G. *Educational Planning: Concepts, Strategies, Practices.* New York: Longman, 1991.

Cuban, L. *The Managerial Imperative and the Practice of Leadership in Schools.* Albany: State University Press of New York, 1988.

Finchbaugh, R. *The 21st Century Board of Education.* Lancaster, PA: Technomics, 1993.

Harris, B., and Monk, B. *Personnel Administration in Education: Leadership for Educational Improvement.* Needham Heights, MA: Allyn and Bacon, 1992.

Hoy, K., and Miskel, R. *Educational Administration: Theory, Research and Practice.* New York: McGraw-Hill, 1991.

Joyce, B. et al. *The Self-Renewing School.* Alexandria, VA: ASCD, 1993.

National Policy Board for Educational Administration, *Principals for Our Changing Schools.* Fairfax, VA: 1993.

Owens, R. *Organizational Behavior in Education,* 4th ed. Englewood Cliffs, NJ: Prentice Hall, 1991.

CHAPTER 11 ≈

ORGANIZING FOR EVALUATION

For most school supervisors, evaluation is an essential tool. As supervision moves toward a knowledge-based leadership role, an awareness and competence in evaluation technology can make the supervisor distinctive. Supervisors are regularly involved in evaluation efforts as they assess the success of programs, processes, and people. Evaluation is the "bottom-line" activity in all school improvement.

Although it appears obvious that evaluation is crucial to both school and classroom improvement efforts, it is surprising how many teachers and administrators display a disinterest in the subject. Why evaluate? This question strikes at the very heart of any supervisory behavior. If schools exist to aid humans in their development, if the curriculum is the plan for such improvement, and if the teacher is the primary delivery mechanism for such a plan, then we *must* determine if the plan is working. Evaluation is the basic means by which we measure our success. Additionally, evaluation is often the moving force in educational improvement.

ORGANIZING FOR EVALUATION

Supervisors are generally involved in evaluation activities in four areas:

1. *Programs*–Reviewing the design of school programs to see if they meet, conceptually and structurally, the intentions of planning groups.
2. *Process*–Overseeing operational techniques to assess efficiency and effectiveness of organization.
3. *Products*–Summarizing the performance of school programs in terms of predetermined expectations.
4. *Personnel*–Analyzing the contribution of people to the planned programs of the school.

These four areas are directly related although, in practice, many supervisors act as if they are isolated dimensions of evaluation. A common evaluation problem in schools, for instance, is the assessment of classroom teachers (personnel) without thorough consideration for instructional design (programs).

Certain evaluation activities are built into the routine of most school districts in the United States. Most districts and schools, for instance, seek accreditation through either a national accreditation association or state accreditation. In many states, certain accountability measures have been mandated, requiring schools to report data to state agencies in areas such as testing. Most school districts require the annual evaluation of personnel and, in some case, programs. But, although such requirements may keep a school supervisor busy making reports and conducting evaluations, they rarely improve instructional experiences.

What the supervisor needs to be effective in evaluation is a thorough grasp of the knowledge base of evaluation plus a way of organizing its many dimensions. A starting point is to ask, "What is the purpose of evaluation activity in my school?" A second question might be, "What is the connection between the various evaluation activities in my school?" A third question might be, "How can I as the supervisor begin to tie together these evaluation efforts so that they begin to improve classroom learning?" These questions may lead the supervisor to other questions about learning that become the basis for inquiries into educational research.

Evaluation has at least five general purposes that contribute to the judgment of the effectiveness of a school program:

1. To make explicit the rationale of the instructional program as a basis for deciding which aspects of the program should be evaluated for effectiveness and what types of data should be gathered

2. To collect data upon which judgments about effectiveness can be formulated

3. To analyze data and draw conclusions

4. To make decisions based on such data

5. To implement the decisions to improve the instructional program

Following is a more specific outline of this general evaluation function, provided by Daniel Stufflebeam:[1]

A. Focusing the Evaluation
   1. Identify the major level(s) of decision making to be served (e.g., local, state, or national).
   2. For each level of decision making, project the decision situations to be served, and describe each one in terms of its focus, focus timing, and composition of alternatives.
   3. Define criteria for each decision situation by specifying variables for measurement and standards for use in the judgment of alternatives.
   4. Define policies within which the evaluation must operate.

B. Collection of Information
   1. Specify the source of the information to be collected.
   2. Specify the instruments and methods for collecting the needed information.
   3. Specify the sampling procedure to be employed.
   4. Specify the conditions and schedule for information collection.
C. Organization of Information
   1. Specify a format for the information which is to be collected.
   2. Specify a means for coding, organizing, storing, and retrieving information.
D. Analysis of Information
   1. Specify the analytical procedures to be employed.
   2. Specify a means for performing the analysis.
E. Reporting of Information
   1. Define the audiences for the evaluation reports.
   2. Specify means for providing information to the audiences.
   3. Specify the format for evaluation reports and/or reporting sessions.
   4. Schedule the reporting information.

These efforts to define the purpose and roles of evaluation should lead to a second step in which the supervisor attempts to see the overall pattern of evaluation as a design. In Table 11.1, the purposes of evaluation are stated. In Table 11.2, the goals of education are tied to basic data and information sources gathered by a sample district.

A third step in further defining evaluation would be to spell out how these findings or data are to be translated into action steps for improving instruction. In many schools, such a translation is the primary work of supervision, and the choice of a medium for reaching classroom teachers is a critical variable for supervisors.

Table 11.1 Purposes of Evaluation

Approach	Focus	Procedure	Questions
Program Design	Conceptual/structure	Validation of goals/purposes	Do we have the kind of program intended?
Program Process	Operational/technique	Program analysis/checklists	Is the program we have efficient in delivering services?
Program Product	Structured feedback	Testing and survey	Does the program work? Are there desired outcomes?
Program Personnel	Observation/analysis	Review/redesign	Are personnel making a direct contribution to the planned program?

Table 11.2 Connecting Goals and Data

Goal	Data and Information Sources
I Communication	Educational Quality Assessment Comprehensive Test of Basic Skills Individual Reading Assessment Placement Tests from Reading Series Woodcock Reading Tests Stanford Diagnostic Test
II Mathematics	Educational Quality Assessment Comprehensive Test of Basic Skills California Achievement Test District Mathematics Tests
III Self-Esteem	Educational Quality Assessment Teacher Observations Parent/Teacher Conference Tennessee Self-Concept Scale
IV Analytical Thinking	Educational Quality Assessment Comprehensive Test of Basic Skills Teacher Observation
V Understanding Others	Educational Quality Assessment Teachers Observation
VI Citizenship	Educational Quality Teacher Observation

THE ROLE OF RESEARCH IN EVALUATION

One of the important contributions of evaluation in school planning is that it introduces the element of rationality into the decision-making process. Said another way, evaluation can minimize the degree of random or superfluous change in schools. Evaluation can reduce some theoretical issues to a decision-making level, clearly identify desired outcomes, and measure progress toward those ends. Evaluation cannot, however, establish basic principles or assumptions that guide school planning. Answering basic questions about school is the role of research.

Research, unlike basic evaluation or validation efforts, is concerned with discovering basic educational principles. The research seeks to develop lawful relationships among a class of problems with a high degree of generalizability. The researcher hopes to establish rules (explanatory statements) about process that govern common educational activities. Research is called into play in schools when essential differences of opinion exist about a perceived reality.

In terms of our knowledge about teaching and learning in a classroom, our research efforts are primitive. Only in the past twenty years have researchers conducted sound empirical studies that isolate variables and consider teacher behaviors and student behaviors in an environmental context. Some of the major research areas that have emerged are:

1. The impact of context on the teacher's behavior
2. The impact of the student's background on learning
3. The individual differences among students in a classroom
4. The relationship of subject matter to teacher effectiveness
5. The problem of establishing a cognitive match between teacher and student
6. The causal impact of student behavior on teacher behavior

Even something as well researched as human development continues to produce leads for educators. Consider the following finding of a major research project at Johns Hopkins University:

> Researchers have gathered evidence suggesting that there is a biological basis for mathematical ability in children. The researchers found that children who are exceptional in math are more than twice as likely to be left-handed, six times as likely to have allergies, and five times as likely to be near-sighted as the population at large.[2]

It is obvious that such research, whatever its validity, has overwhelming implications for planners of teaching and learning. The problem that supervisors face is that there are literally hundreds of studies available that give leads or hypotheses about learning, but few whose principles of learning are universally accepted. This leaves the supervisor the task of gathering, interpreting, and finding research patterns to pass on to teachers and others involved in planning.

Action Research for School Improvement

Perceiving research and evaluation as the vehicle by which schools measure forward progress in school improvement helps define the relationship of the supervisor and teacher. In the school, the successful education supervisor will engage the teacher in a reflective practice position. Teachers who question their own practices will possess a disposition to improve.

The authors have spent years in learning how to engage teachers in the evaluation of their own practice. This experience tells us that, initially, the classroom teacher will resist such introspection out of ignorance of pedagogy. The direct teaching pattern, characterized by lecture and tests from the text, is so pervasive that many new teachers aren't aware that other patterns exist. Transforming this "can't see" posture into one of "what if" is made possible by introducing a research perspective. Going from "cocksure ignorance to thoughtful uncertainty" results when the teacher gains an "if-then" perspective.

Supervisors can engage a teacher, or faculty of teachers, by addressing information of interest in their areas of greatest need. How do we best maintain a disciplined learning environment? How do we motivate students to learn? How can we best engage learners with a wide range of ability? Why do girls become less proficient at mathematics after the fifth grade? What color, temperature, noise, and light level facilitates the most learning? Any such question will open up discussion which, as a byproduct, will lead to inquiry.

Only after the supervisor and teacher begin such a discussion can the subject be broached of how one might "control" some classroom level action research to find the answers. At first, the sophistication of such inquiry should be limited to an awareness of intervening variables (student home life, I.Q., gender) and use of an experimental and control population in any study. Only later, when the school becomes more introspective, should the concept of "significance" and the statistical control of data be introduced.

A simple example of a study by one teacher might involve the use of homework. Although most educators believe that homework reinforces learning in school through a "practice effect," little research exists to support this widely-held belief. A teacher might easily set up a study in which a population of students is given homework to reinforce in-class study for two weeks (and then tested) and then followed by two weeks without homework. Regardless of the outcome, the supervisor and teacher could then begin a serious discussion about what practices (delivery, materials, testing, grouping, grading) facilitate achievement.

We have found that most teachers are truly dedicated professionals who want to be as good as they can be in teaching. Although the initial act of questioning practices may be mildly threatening, the rediscovery of interest in personal improvement can be highly stimulating. The key to the introduction of action research for school improvement is to be objective at all times. Action research is not a judging activity, but rather a professional search for workable and successful practices.

SCHOOLWIDE EVALUATION PLANNING

Evaluation in any school must be comprehensive if it is to serve its primary purpose of improving student learning experiences. Since the operation of a school should be based on the objectives of the curriculum, it makes sense that evaluation, too, should be tied directly to the goals and purpose of the program. This means that all aspects of the school program should contribute to the major concepts that are found in a program design.

One way of viewing evaluation is a corrective mechanism or feedback loop in the curriculum cycle. The goals of the school are represented by objectives which, in turn, create the basic program design. Student learning experiences, for instance, are structured into activities that have clear objectives and expectations. As the program is implemented, these expectations are either met or not met. Evaluation helps clarify any discrepancies between the expected outcomes and the actual performance.

At that point, evaluation guides the adjustments to the program to allow a fuller correspondence between expectations and outcomes. In some cases, feedback may suggest a revision of basic goals and purposes.

Another way to approach school evaluation would be to use evaluation as a means of validating program goals and objectives. In this approach, evidences are gathered to justify specific facets of the program, and these facets or subsystems collectively comprise the evaluation program. Examples of such subsystems are student performance, teacher effectiveness, program design, resource utilization, facilities usage, policies and regulation, parent and community feedback, and staff development programs.

Using this approach, a concern for any one area of the program would trigger a review of other areas. For example, if student study skills proved deficient in testing, other areas could be explored for probable cause; for example, deficient materials, additional teacher training, or inadequate facilities.

By combining these two ways of viewing evaluation, the supervisor can develop a system of assessing the school program and taking corrective action where necessary. Following are some guiding questions in each of these areas:

Program Design

1. Is the program concept consistent with the overall philosophy of the district and its leaders?

2. Does the program articulate (fit) with preceding elementary, middle, or secondary programs? Is there a consistent follow-through in other programs?

3. Are resources dedicated to this program commensurate with other programs found in the curriculum?

4. Is there an internal consistency to this program such as a set of objectives that provide structure?

Facilities Usage

1. Does the physical location and allocation of space reflect this program's priority in the curriculum?

2. Are learning areas within the space consistent with the instructional intent in delivering this program to students?

Policies and Regulations

1. Are some policies and regulations essential in allowing this program to function fully?

2. Are there rules or policies that, in fact, contradict the spirit of this program?

3. Is there a better way to handle policy formation and enforcement in operating this program?

Resource Utilization

1. Is there a clear relationship between the allocation of resources and funds and the curricular objectives of this program?

2. Are resources available to support innovative instructional approaches or to promote desired changes?

3. Is there an established procedure for assessing future resource needs and planning for their acquisition?

Student Performance

1. Is student evaluation in this program both systematic and continuous?

2. Is student evaluation perceived by teachers as a measure of the program's success?

3. Are parents involved in the evaluation of the student and program?

4. Is student evaluation directional, indicating where improvement is needed?

Teacher Effectiveness

1. Is program improvement based on input by the instructional staff?

2. Is teacher evaluation tied directly to program improvement?

3. Have the talents and abilities of teachers been fully explored in terms of contributing to this program?

4. Are there any unplanned organizational or administrative constraints on teaching styles in this program?

Staff Development

1. Are monies budgeted for staff development tied to the needs and goals of this specific program?

2. Do teachers have the opportunity to critique current staff development efforts?

3. Can it be shown, through evaluation, where staff development in the past has improved this program?

Parent-Community Feedback

1. Are members of the community involved in the formation and maintenance of this program?

2. Are members of the community kept informed about any major changes contemplated or implemented in this program?

3. Does a communication vehicle exist that effectively shares the accomplishments of this program with parents and community?

Each of these components of a schoolwide evaluation system is important to both program improvement and program performance. Each major area is interrelated and crucial to other areas.

TESTING—A SPECIAL PROBLEM AREA OF EVALUATION

Of all of the areas of evaluation that need to be addressed by the supervisor, the use of tests by teachers is a "high-need" area. The reliance upon tests, both standardized and teacher-made, is unquestioned by most classroom teachers. These practitioners need to know the limitations of testing and to work to control error in student evaluation.

For example, most teachers believe that the S.A.T. (Scholastic Assessment Test), the C.T.B.S. (Comprehensive Test of Basic Skills), C.A.T. (California Achievement Test), the Iowa Test of Basic Skills, and other standardized and nationally normed tests truly measure student achievement. It therefore comes as a surprise to learn that the S.A.T., for instance, was normed in 1941 on a population of 11,000 white, male, and mostly middle-class students who were college bound. Today, over a million students (including 25 percent of minority students) take this test each year.

Teachers might also be surprised to learn that, according to a 1988 Gallup Poll, one person in seven in the United States could not identify the United States on a map of the world. Such persons have always been with us, and knowing that such a large segment of the population is so unable to perform might give a new interpretation of classroom testing efforts.[3]

The Purposes of Testing

TEACHER'S PURPOSES

Teachers use the results of testing to make a range of decisions. Each decision is associated with a different kind of test or evaluation information, as indicated in the following list:

1. *Diagnostic tests, observations, and interviews* are used to collect information useful in answering these questions: What learning difficulties are students experiencing? What requisite skill, knowledge, or attitude is missing?

2. *Readiness and placement tests* as well as *interest inventories* are appropriate in addressing these questions: What instructional materials are best for particular students? In what level of textbook or group should individual students be placed?

3. *Mastery tests* are typically used to verify that students have attained a predetermined standard of performance from a unit and a course of instruction: Have students acquired mastery of the essentials taught in a given course? Are students ready to proceed to a new unit of instruction within a course?

4. *"Pop" and periodic quizzes, class assignments, challenging puzzles and problems* are among the testing activities that teachers generate for their instrumental value: How can tests best be used to motivate students, to stimulate their participation in the learning process, and to maintain class control?

5. Data from *mastery, achievement, and competency tests* form only a partial basis for the grading of students: What course grade or mark should be given each student? Should the grade reflect the growth, effort, and interests of the individual student or the interests of uniformity and a larger concern for accountability?

Teachers use testing for other purposes as well, such as to help them determine which aspects of the instruction are most effective and which need improvement.

Political Purposes

Although this chapter focuses on testing as an aid to teachers' decision making, it is necessary to summarize the testing exercised by those outside the classroom–those who mandate testing for their own purposes–because of their influence on the work of teachers.

Colleges and universities use tests for selection and admission, such as the Scholastic Aptitude Test (S.A.T.). Counselors and administrators use tests to place students in special education and accelerated instructional programs. The federal government demands standardized testing to accompany instructional programs funded by federal money. The accountability movement has spawned a plethora of tests. State legislators have mandated competency examinations for high school graduation as well as achievement testing in such academic subjects as math, English, and science. Local school districts employ standardized testing for monitoring the achievement of individual schools in basic subjects and are increasingly creating their own grade-level tests of essential skills in reading, writing, and arithmetic so they can have more influence in directing teacher activity within the classroom.

The primary purpose of mandated tests is political and controlling. These tests act as constraints on the autonomy of the teacher and can be misleading in that they often fail to give a comprehensive picture of the effects of schooling. Madaus reports that mandated tests create only an illusion of meaning to the high school diploma and students' competency to function in society.[4] In fact, good performance on imposed competency exams guarantees nothing at all, much less real-life success. Teachers help most low-achieving students–chiefly poor white and minority students with academic problems–pass these exams through coaching and practicing with comparable test items, but it is doubtful that the students are any better in reading, writing, and arithmetic as a result of the tests.

TYPES OF TESTS

Norm-Referenced (NR) and Criterion-Referenced (CR) Tests

As indicated earlier, tests that are external to the schools are standardized "norm-referenced" (NR) tests designed to "spread test scores," thereby making it easier to differentiate schools and individuals along a continuum. One exception is found in mandated competency tests, which focus on particular competencies. These clearly specified tests quiz students on their comprehension of the meaning of safety warnings such as those commonly found on medical bottles, on mechanical equipment, and items of public hazard. In "criterion-referenced" (CR) tests, the student's performance is not compared with the performance of others but is evaluated in terms of

Table 11.3 Norm-Referenced Versus Criterion-Referenced Tests

Norm-Referenced Test	Criterion-Referenced Test
Best for showing how a student's performance compares to that of other students	Best for showing whether a student can perform a specific task
Best for maximizing differences in student performance	Best for showing the effects of classroom instruction

whether he or she demonstrates a predetermined level of mastery of the task. Table 11.3 contrasts the advantages of the two types of tests.

Norm-referenced tests are designed to rank students in order of achievement, from high to low. Thus, a key feature in their construction are test items that provide a wide range of scores. Items that all students are likely to answer correctly are discarded. Those who prepare NR tests aim to achieve a normal curve, with one half of the students taking the test falling below the mean. (In standardized norm-referenced tests, the normed group used to establish the average scores was pulled from a national sample.) In contrast, criterion-referenced tests are not concerned with the relative achievement of students but with whether the student can perform a particular task or a specified domain of tasks (for example, maps—physical, road relief, vegetation, political, weather, and their interpretations). In constructing a CR test, the test developer selects items that match the content and the performance called for in the task and does not discard items that all students are likely to answer correctly. Because the NR test developer alters item difficulty to obtain a range of scores, NR test items tend to discriminate on the basis of students' prior backgrounds and aptitudes. Thus, the CR test is a more sensitive measure of the effects of classroom learning; that is, the items students answer correctly on the CR test reflect what they have been taught in the classroom, whereas students' prior backgrounds and aptitudes affect their performance on the NR test.

There is tension between those who impose standardized tests and classroom teachers. The National Council of Teachers of English, for example, argues that standardized testing perpetuates the separation of evaluation from learning and limits the curriculum to only those skills measured by the tests.[5] Thus, testing becomes an end in itself–a substitute for teacher–student interaction–and causes teachers to spend valuable time preparing students for external assessment. Students' quick, correct answers are appreciated, not their evaluation or interpretation. The time taken to figure something out leaves less time for filling in answers; so, the more one thinks, the poorer the test results will be. Imposed testing has mostly negative effects, such as reduction in time for teaching and fragmentation of the curriculum.

In an assessment of testing in American public schools, Herman and Door-Bremme found that externally imposed tests provide little information of value to teachers' decision making as compared to information available through interacting with students and data from locally developed tests.[6] Matching standardized tests and a particular teacher's curriculum is problematic. The results from external standardized tests, competency tests, and district objective-based tests often seem remote and irrelevant to teachers.

Teacher-Made Tests

As an alternative to tests designed by test specialists and administered, scored, and interpreted under standard conditions, "teacher-made" tests are used for placement, diagnosis, assessment of learning progress, and end-of-course achievement. These informal tests provide information that is highly valued by teachers in making routine classroom decisions. In constructing their own tests, teachers can match what is tested with what is taught, design the test format, determine how to administer and score the test, and control the timing of the test.

In reviewing teacher-made tests, Fleming and Chambers found that teachers use more questions of the short-answer type and rarely devise essay examinations. For the most part, teacher-made tests require students to recall facts and terms; only rarely do they demand learners to translate, apply, or otherwise use knowledge. The investigators discovered a general tendency "to omit test directions, to use illegible test copies and to omit the point values to be assigned to test questions."[7] Other studies support these findings. For example, Stetz and Beck found that students fault teacher-made tests for requiring most memorization, for not testing many important ideas, and for not giving them the opportunity to demonstrate what they know.[8] However, many of the criticisms of teacher-made tests can be overcome by properly designing criterion-referenced tests. CR tests can be adapted for diagnostic, mastery, and grading purposes.

CONSTRUCTING CRITERION-REFERENCED TESTS

The Domain Description

Central to developing a criterion-referenced test is the preparation of a "domain" description, that is, a clear specification of what the test will measure and a guide to writing the test items. The preparation of the domain description involves the following three steps.[9]

Step 1.   *Stimulus limits*—The term "stimulus limits" refers to the kinds of situations (content) students are to confront and for which instruction should prepare them. A stimulus limit may be narrowly defined (for example, as a fifth-grade word list or a pair of numbers—triple, double, or single digit) or broadly defined (for example, as editorial pages of newspapers). Stimulus can be thought of as a population that can vary from the specific (a particular word or problem) to the very general (all English novels). The degree of generality usually reflects the time span of instruction. Thus, a test covering one week of instruction will have more narrow stimulus limits than one assessing a semester of work.

Step 2.   *Directions and response option*—The next step for preparing the domain description is to state the kind of response that learners are expected to make when they confront the stimulus elements. The *Taxonomies of Educational Objectives* gives useful categories of response behaviors–know, comprehend, apply, analyze, synthesize, evaluate (cognitive behavior), attend, respond, value (affective behavior).[10] Other commonly stated responses are solve, interpret, identify, compare, classify, generate, demonstrate. The kind of response selected is related to the test direction–the charge that will be given to the person taking the test (for example, "Mark an X by the answer that is the best experiment for testing each of the hypotheses given").

To avoid ambiguity, the directions are stated as overt behaviors (for example, "*Select* (not *recognize*) from the alternative given the unstated assumption of the passage"). If the multiple-choice format is used, the teacher states the characteristics of the distractors or the incorrect answer choices. For example, the teacher might note that the distractors represent the most common errors, not the most simplistic choices.

Step 3. *Criterion of correctness*—The third step in describing the test domain is to state the "criterion of correctness," that is, what constitutes an acceptable response. The criterion of correctness is self-evident in many tests of basic skills (for example, spelling and math), although the teacher may elect to accept a given process generated by the student in answering a problem as a correct response, even if the answer to the problem is not the one validated by the rules of the discipline.

In judging responses to essay questions and to social studies and science situations, the teacher should indicate the attribute that signifies correctness–comprehensiveness, logical consistency, providing examples in support of main points. Similarly, in judging the responses in completing projects such as in art or mechanics, criteria for correctness should be explicit—presence of patterned and balance contrast, utility, practicality, uniqueness. In performance tasks found in athletics and vocational fields, the criteria may specify a time requirement and a particular accuracy of form. By informing students of the criterion of correctness in advance of instruction, teachers enable them to acquire the desired responses more quickly.

TEST FORMATS

Tests take several forms. The following are descriptions of the most popular formats and suggestions for writing the test items for each one.

Multiple Choice

Typical multiple-choice items consist of a problem (stem) and a list of suggested solutions (alternatives). The correct alternative is the "answer," and the other alternative (options) are "distractors."

For example, consider this item on an arithmetic exam:

Jane is putting cans of food in bags for the Red Cross. She has 18 cans. She puts 3 cans in each bag. How many bags can she fill?

a. $18 \div 3 =$

b. $3 \times 6 =$

c. $3 + 12 +$

d. $18 - 3 =$

Notice that the teacher does not use the option "none of the above" and that the reading level is kept low so that the test measures knowledge of math rather than of reading. Poorly designed tests keep students from revealing their knowledge because they do not understand what they are to do. In the preceding example, the answer and alternatives are brief. When the alternatives are comprised of words and phrases, they should be grammatically consistent with each other and the stem. It is, of course, important to avoid clues to the correct answer.

Matching

In the matching test format, the stems are listed in one column and the alternatives in another column. For example:

Directions: On the line to the left of each statement in Column A, write the name of the cloud in Column B that matches. Each cloud's name can be used more than once.

Column A

____ 1. thick, fleecy-looking clouds, medium height
____ 2. thin, feathery-looking clouds, high
____ 3. gray-colored clouds, low
____ 4. indicates the approach of a warm front
____ 5. indicates the approach of a cold front

Column B

a. cirrus
b. cumulus
c. status

The items in a matching test should be short and the responses shorter than the stems. The items should be stated positively to avoid assuming that because students know what is not, they know what is.

True-False

The items in the true-false format should be restricted to situations that are limited to two alternatives. For example:

Directions: For each of the following statements, put a T or F in the blank according to whether you believe it true (T) or false (F).

__The next term in the series 3,4,7,11,18 is 29.

In writing true-false statements, the teacher should avoid having one part of the item true while another part is false. Qualifying words such as "seldom," "frequently," or "always" should not be used. There should be approximately an equal number of true and false statements. A true-false test usually has more items than a matching or multiple-choice test to ensure reliability, since there is a 50 percent chance of guessing the correct response.

Essay

The essay test format allows students to express themselves in their own words using their own background and knowledge. It is a valuable activity in that it encourages students to clarify and organize their own ideas. Although the essay is relatively easy to prepare, it can be time consuming to score. Responses usually have to be judged according to attributes or qualities rather than predetermined specific correct answers. It is advisable to focus the topic of the essay so that students understand what is to be measured and the problem to be addressed. For example:

Directions: Write a two-page statement defending the importance of genetic research in agriculture. (Your answer will be evaluated in terms of its organization, comprehensiveness, and relevance of the arguments presented.)

In constructing an essay exam, the teacher should outline the ideal answer to the essay question before giving the test. Other suggestions include making the student aware of the time limits, starting the question with behavioral terms (for example, "compare," "contrast," "give the reason," "predict what would happen if," or "explain how"), and making sure each question matches the objective (content and behavior) and domain specifications.

Short-Answer Recall

The short-answer recall exam takes several forms. One form uses a direct question calling for a response (for example, "What elements combine to form water?"). Another is in the form of a completion test, which requires the student to write a word or phrase in one or more blanks to complete a sentence. Short-answer recall tests are often used because they are easy to construct and tend to be only a matter of identifying, naming, or associating facts. An example of improved short-answer tests is the "modified cloze" test, an excellent diagnostic tool for evaluating reading comprehension. In this test, specific categories of words are deleted in passages. For instance, if the teacher wants to learn whether students are using information together in a meaningful unit, the deleted word in a paragraph will be one that can only be supplied by attending to adjacent paragraphs. The following example of a modified cloze test item shows how the choice of an omitted word requires students to attend to subordinate and conjoined statements in the context of adjacent paragraphs.[11]

The New House

Mrs. Alexander was trying to fix dinner. First, though, she had to find where the boxes marked for the kitchen had _____. The boys had unloaded the station wagon
          (1)
in a hurry and _____ back to the old house to get the final load of boxes.
          (2)
     "What's the use?" she said aloud. "Put the food in the bedroom. Put the pots and pans in the bathroom. Put the underwear in the refrigerator." Her voice rose along with her _____.
          (3)
     "Mom, I don't have the _____." Little Mark looked around at the open boxes.
          (4)
"How come we have to put it in the 'frigerator? Why do we have to do everything different?" Mark started to cry while he talked and peeled _____ off boxes. "Can't we
          (5)
have drawers in our bedroom in this house? I don't like new houses. I like old apartments. I can't have my friends, can't ride elevators, can't have drawers for my stuff. And I'm hungry, too. No milk or apples in the 'frigerator in new houses."

ANSWER LIST

1.	a. passed	2. a. wrote	3. a. esteem	4. a. bucket	5. *a. tape
	b. burned	b. spread	b. prestige	*b. underwear	b. heat
	*c. gone	c. jumped	*c. frustration	c. newspaper	c. coffee
	d. left	d. paddled	d. appropriation	d. flashlight	d. thunder
	e. held	*e. rushed	e. technique	e. soap	e. bread
	(subordinate sentence)	(conjoined sentence)	(same paragraph)	(separate paragraph)	(local)

Curriculum-Embedded Tests

Curriculum-embedded tests are commercially available and accompany many textbooks and workbooks. They are useful internal tests that teachers are free to use or adapt. They are called "curriculum-embedded" because they are clearly related to the teacher's daily instruction. The tests themselves follow conventional forms—objective-based, multiple choice, and completion, as well as exercises.

A recent study reveals that teachers use curriculum-embedded tests mainly because they are readily available, save time in preparation, are useful in motivating students, and help them in the memorization of basic facts.[12] However, the results from these tests provide little information of value in decision making. The results are sometimes used to place students in a given instructional group but are seldom used to make decisions about what to teach (that is, to select content). Instead, teachers rely on informal assessments such as observation and teacher questioning to make instructional decisions. Also, the results from curriculum-embedded tests are seldom used to make decisions about marks or grades.

INFORMAL MEASURES IN THE CLASSROOM

Gullickson surveyed teachers in the elementary and secondary school levels, including science, social science, and language arts teachers, to determine which evaluation techniques they use. Dramatic differences were found among teachers of various grade levels, and some differences were found among the subject areas. The following techniques were rated highly across all grades and curriculum areas: objectives, teacher-made tests, discussion, and papers/notebooks. The study also found that laboratory activities, used in science as an evaluation tool, are increasingly used as grade level increases. At the elementary level, teachers rely on a diversity of techniques, especially nontest techniques such as class discussions, evaluation of student papers, and observations of student behavior. At the secondary level, the major evaluation tool is the test, particularly the teacher-made test.[13]

Basically, there are three informal ways of assessing student progress: self-reporting, observation, and work samples.

Self-Reporting

Self-reports are used to determine interests, attitudes, and processes. They can be either "direct" (that is, the student knows what information is being sought) or "indirect" (that is, the true focus of the inquiry is not revealed to the student). An example of a direct attitude measure is shown in Table 11.4.

"Indirect" self-reports require an inference or underlying theory of what the responses mean. For example, in a self-concept measure "Television Roles," primary children are asked to describe the role they would play in a television show. Some of the roles are aversive (for example, "a dirty-faced child"). The inventory is based on the theory that individuals who are willing to project themselves in a variety of roles have a more positive self-concept than those who won't. The following example illustrates the inventory:

"Will you play the part:"	a happy child	a pig
	a sad child	a tree that talks
	a worm	a bully

Table 11.4 Teacher-Made Self-Report: A Measure of Attitude Toward Math

Things We Do	Like	Just Okay	Don't Like
Math games			
Addition			
Subtraction			
Story problems			
Drawing shapes			
Measuring			
Telling time			
Making change			
Counting			

Indirect measures are used when the teacher believes students may be inclined to fake or give particular answers to please the teacher.

A useful variation in self-reporting is to ask students to describe aloud what they are thinking as they engage in learning tasks. For instance, students can list the steps they are following and tell where they are in the sequence of reading a book or solving a problem. They can state their purposes, indicate the information they need, and give their plan for getting the information. The teacher, of course, is interested not only in whether students answer correctly but also in noting how students behave when they have difficulties and when they do not know answers. Analysis of the student's own perspective of the learning task often suggests points of confusion and conflict with which the teacher must deal.

Observation

The key to observation is the teacher's awareness of what to attend to and his or her interpretation of what is seen and heard. Teachers identify those anticipated and unanticipated responses that occur as a result of instruction. The results often reveal the need for teaching new material, with instructional objectives following instruction. Only after the teacher has taught is it clear what students need to learn. Further, observation can occur under both natural (unplanned) and controlled conditions (the teacher arranges a situation designed to elicit student reaction). Often a checklist is employed in guiding and analyzing the observation (see Figure 11.1).

Changing beliefs about what is important are reflected in teacher observations. One study found that when oral pronunciation was a valued aspect of reading, as in the recent past, teachers recorded children's oral omissions, hesitations, substitutions, and mispronunciations. Today, when reading comprehension is more important, teachers have modified their observations. Accordingly, many of the so-called errors in reading are not errors at all.[14] Accordingly, the appropriate substitution of a familiar word for an unfamiliar one in the context of a passage, for example, demonstrates that the student is gaining meaning from reading, not merely word-calling. Consequently, reading teachers today observing the oral reading performance of students discriminate between miscues, which reveal comprehension, and errors in word recognition, which are caused by a semantic, syntactical, or sound-symbol deficiency. Also, to learn how learners are comprehending, it is recommended that teachers ask them to recall orally or to write a summary of what they have read. The recall protocol can then be interpreted in light of both text and what is recalled. If the material is expository, the teacher notes the main ideas that the learner recalls as well as whether details related to the main ideas are supplied. If the material is narrative, the teacher checks to see if the reader has identified key elements, such as characters, goals, and setting. Teachers tend to be original and creative in planning their observations.

Nonobtrusive measures and records provide indicators of student interest. Teachers sometimes place a variety of magazines and books on an open table, noting which materials are freely chosen on a regular basis. Smudge marks on particular pages, exhibits, and learning centers are evidence of student interest. Student attitudes toward themselves and their work can be judged by what they do with their classroom activity sheets—carefully carrying the work with them or throwing it in the wastebasket. In similar fashion, progress toward social goals can be observed by noting seat selection and free-grouping patterns during various school activities. Observation error can be minimized through triangulation—by making repeated observations and by comparing the results of one measure with the results of other measures.

Work Samples

An analysis of students' *work samples*—their writings, paintings, drawings, and other projects—can reveal pertinent things about the impact of teaching. Changes in learner products disclose progress (see Figure 11.2). For instance, the comparison of early in-course compositions with late in-course compositions may show differences in syntax deficiencies, vocabulary level, and spelling ability. The analysis might also include the extent to which imagination is employed.

---

1. Performs and acknowledges introduction according to accepted rules of etiquette in a specific situation.
2. Shows initiative by beginning the conversation with a topic of interest to all.
3. Develops the conversation topic of interest to others.
4. Considers the ideas of others.
5. Reveals knowledge of topics suitable for conversation in the specific situation.
6. Speaks with a pleasing voice that is easily understood and adapted to the situation.
7. Departs by withdrawing gracefully and giving proper farewell courtesies.

Figure 11.1 Observation Checklist: Conversation Rating Scale

Definition	A case for holding papers
	A purposefully selected collection
	Documentation of work
	Evidence of performance
Purpose	To measure effort, progress, or achievement
	A source of self-reflection
	An intersection of instruction and evaluation
	Student judged best work
Organizing Questions	What will the portfolio look like?
	What goes into the portfolio?
	What is the evaluation criteria?
	When will the portfolio be reviewed?
Sample Evidence	List of annotated readings
	Collection of notes, thoughts, quotes
	Reviews of research
	Diary of class reactions, thoughts
	Longitudinal ideas, drafts, questions
	Interviews
	Papers, products (drawings, tapes, models, designs)
	Emerging theories
	Analyses of problems
	Presentations
Student Input	Work samples, selected, best work organized and in order with distinct sections

Figure 11.2 Portfolio Assessment

Students should know the criteria or qualities that are being emphasized in judging a superior product. Sometimes the evaluation is in terms of overall (holistic) quality. Essays, for example, may be judged against a series of samples representing different degrees of quality or can be assessed by peers on the basis of whether the essay conveys a particular idea or feeling. Other times, products may be analyzed and graded by their separate features, such as consistency of the arguments, organization, and originality. Maryland uses a scale of 1–4 on its writing test. Evaluators take note of five criteria: content, organization, attention to audience, sentence formation, and convention (which includes punctuation, spelling, and capitalization). Students with egregious errors in spelling and punctuation may pass the test if they have done well in terms of the other criteria. Some teachers choose to collect samples of work completed when students had the opportunity to shape meaning for themselves. As one student said, "I like to write for someone other than the teacher—it's like taking the shackles off. I'm freer and can work within my own limits. My creativity is broken when I'm forced to do it somebody else's way. Usually, I figure I've got to do it their way or I'll get an F or I'm going to get it wrong because they're grading it the way they want it."

THE MISUSES OF TESTS

Serious problems are associated with using test results as a basis for teacher decision making. As noted earlier, external tests can negatively influence teaching, narrow the curriculum, and create personal pressures and anxieties about test taking. Although the impact of internal testing ultimately lies in the teacher's own philosophy and values (that is, in whether testing serves the individual or sorts individuals in the interest of others), knowledge of technical factors may also contribute to better use of tests in classrooms. The following discussion of the misuses of tests introduces common technical limitations and erroneous interpretations of tests and test scores.

Inaccurate Description

Standard tests often carry a title suggesting that important goals are assessed by the measure (for example, critical thinking, problem solving, reading comprehension, and other valued content). There are numerous tests in any content area, and each measures different aspects of knowledge, understanding, and skill. An extreme example is a test purporting to measure thinking but has items that measure memory rather than reasoning. For example, standardized tests from different corporations purport to measure achievement in the same area—math, science, language— but often one is easier or more difficult than another. The difference in difficulty may be due to (1) the population on which the test is normed (for example, urban area students versus those from the suburbs), (2) the particular range and kinds of items included, and (3) the test format used. Occasionally, newspapers express the public's shock at spectacular rises or declines in student performance in a subject area. Often these changes are due to the use of a different test but with a similar title and description. Examination of an old and new test of reading in New York, for instance, revealed differences in size of print, amount of silent reading, number and length of stories, vocabulary level, and sentence complexity; with the more difficult test, the students were also expected to get more items right.[15]

Cynics suggest that tests are often selected for the most useful results to the school or school district. The easy test that results in high scores is purchased when it is necessary to show improvement in achievement to the public; the difficult test that results in low scores is selected to qualify for federal funds earmarked for learning-disability and low-achieving students. Most importantly, however, teachers should evaluate the content of tests in terms of their own instructional goals and emphasis. The test publishers' technical manuals give information for judging the quality of a test. In addition, there are sources that review published standardized tests, such as *The Mental Measurement Yearbook,* and specialized measurement journals, which are available in most educational libraries.[16]

Ignoring the Standard Error of Measurement

It is unlikely that a student would get the same score two or more times on the same test. The "standard error of measurement" is an estimate of the amount of variation expected in the student's score. For example, if the error of measurement is 5, a student with a score of 97 has a "true" score of between 92 and 102. A teacher who is aware of the standard error of measurement does not make decisions on the basis of minor differences in test scores.

The amount of the standard error depends on the reliability of the test. Generally, longer tests have higher reliability and less error because they provide a better sampling of the behavior being tested. Similarly, criterion-referenced tests constructed to well-specified domains are more reliable.

Using Only a Single Score

A standardized norm-referenced test measures many different things. A reading test, for example, includes items that assess vocabulary, word identification, literal comprehension, inferential comprehension, and interpretive reading. A standardized test of arithmetic is likely to have items testing knowledge of number concepts, whole numbers, fractions, decimals, measurement, and the like. Before making decisions on the basis of the student's overall score on such a test, the teacher should know how the separate parts contribute to the score and note the number and kind of items measuring each factor.

The limitation of a single score points out the danger in making important decisions on the basis of a single test. Although colleges and universities may consider S.A.T. scores in deciding which students to admit, they make a more defensible decision when they take other information into account (for example, high school records, extracurricular activities, motivation, cultural background, and letters of recommendation).

Misunderstanding the Meaning of a Score

A test score may mean that a student answered 45 out of 50 easy items or that the student answered 45 out of 50 difficult items. A raw score converted to a percentile score also causes problems in interpretation. Gardner points out that on a norm-referenced test, one half of the students may fail because their scores are below the mean, even though their performance may be excellent.[17] For example, a percentile score of 20, by itself, does not represent good or bad performance. It merely indicates that among the group used as a frame of reference, the score is higher than that reached by 20 percent of its members. If the group was comprised of students of higher ability or with unusual skills, a percentile rank of 20 might indicate excellent performance.

Grade-equivalent scores are associated with other misinterpretations. A grade-equivalent score is one exceeded by 50 percent of the normative group and not attained by the other 50 percent at the time the test is given. It does not represent a standard to be attained nor does it represent the grade in which a student should be placed. For example, a grade-equivalent score of 7 attained by a fifth-grader on a math test does not mean that the student knows sixth- or seventh-grade math. Rather, it is more accurate to say that the student can do fifth-grade math as well as the average seventh-grader can do fifth-grade math.

Inferring Cause from a Score

A test score is a numerical description of a sample of performance at a given point in time. Why an individual obtains this score is not answerable from the score itself. When asked why S.A.T. scores have declined in the United States, test makers cited evidence about changes in the population of test takers (for example, an increase in students from lower socioeconomic classes) but could only speculate on other possible causes (for example, the influences of television, single-parent families, climatic changes, the quality of textbooks, and course offerings).

In classroom testing, teachers should look for patterns in students' responses to get clues as to what might account for incorrect answers. When general achievement tests indicate weakness in the learning of a basic skill, administration of diagnostic tests can help to pinpoint the difficulty. However, there are many possible causes, including untested factors such as social relations, health, personal development, and motivation.

Test Bias

Tests are supposed to discriminate—to reveal who knows or can do something specified and who cannot. A low score alone does not signify bias. If so, the spelling test would be biased against poor spellers. Most tests are designed to measure the competence of students in a specifically defined area, and the test scores indicate how adequately the questions defined by the domain are answered.

Bias occurs when the test score is influenced by factors that are not relevant to what the test purports to measure. A test designed to measure achievement in elementary science is biased, especially toward poor readers, if the items are presented in language and syntax above the students' level. Such a test should measure knowledge of science, including appropriate science vocabulary, but not general reading ability.

TESTING FOR PLACEMENT

Placing students in groups for instruction or providing them with particular learning opportunities (for example, textbooks written at a given difficulty level) rests on the principle that students should have success in their learning. The teacher does not seek to place students in situations where they already know what is to be taught, nor does the teacher want students in situations for which they lack the prerequisites for success.

A prerequisite test is a placement test. In preparing this test, the teacher first answers the question, "What must my students do to convince me that they have the skills, motivation, and background I have assumed they have?" After administering the prerequisite test to students soon after they enter the class and finding that only a few can perform according to the assumptions, the teacher has two choices: (1) send the student away for remedial instruction, or (2) teach what is missing, erasing the skill from the prerequisite list and adding it to the list of instructional objectives.

A danger in using placement tests for grouping students is the possibility of the "Pygmalion effect"—that the teacher may treat students in accordance with what is expected from them as indicated by testing. For example, the primary teacher who assigns children to one of three reading groups at the beginning of the school year on the basis of their responses to certain questions (for example, on letter recognition, rhyming words, and left-to-right orientation) might find that the children subsequently show differentiated progress, with the slow group advancing far behind the fast group—a self-fulfilling prophecy. In this case, it is better to teach the children readiness skills before making judgments about their ability to learn.

DIAGNOSING STUDENT PERFORMANCE

Diagnosis and remediation of learning difficulties involve determining the nature of the difficulties, the factors causing it, and applying remedial procedures. The new trend in diagnosis is to focus on the fundamental misconceptions that individuals harbor rather than on the number of errors that appear on their tests. The work of Brown and Burton well represents this new direction. These authors make it clear that it is much more difficult to diagnose what is wrong with a student's performance of a task than it is to perform the task itself.[18] Consider the following example of a student's work in mathematical addition and try to determine the error being made:

$$
\begin{array}{ccccc}
41 & 328 & 989 & 66 & 216 \\
+\ 9 & +\ 917 & +\ 52 & +\ 887 & +\ 13 \\
\hline
50 & 1345 & 1141 & 1053 & 229
\end{array}
$$

This student, after determining the carry, forgets to reset the "carry register" to zero so the amount is accumulated across the column. A study of 1,325 fourth-, fifth-, and sixth-grade students shows that most of the difficulties in arithmetic arise while borrowing, especially when zero is involved. The most common "bug" when borrowing from a column where the top digit is 0 is to change 0 to 9 but not continue borrowing from the next column to the left. This bug occurred 153 times in 1,325 student tests.[19] Analyzing a student's errors can be a way to discover how the student learns. The error may not be due to carelessness but instead involves a complex and logical thought process. Individuals often devise their own systems for resolving problems. Different types of problem examples must be given to be sure that the student understands. By looking carefully at a student's errors, it is sometimes possible to discover a pattern.

Standardized tests are sometimes used for diagnosing strengths and weaknesses in the past learning of individual or groups of students. In particular, test scores are used to generate instructional objectives in response to weaknesses in vocabulary, comprehension, word study, mathematics computation, mathematics application, and the like. More specific tests have been designed to provide more diagnostic information for limited areas. In reading, for example, a diagnostic test might assess literal reading comprehension, inferential reading comprehension, sound discrimination, blending, rate of reading, and vocabulary.

Although diagnostic tests provide more precise information than achievement tests do, they, too, have problems. Without an understanding of the processes that underlie, say, sound blending, it is difficult to come up with a prescription for teaching and learning that will help the student beyond simple practice, which may not be sufficient to remedy deficits in a skill such as sound blending. Diagnostic tests also provide a more reliable sample of student errors than general achievement tests because they have a larger number of items representing each particular aspect of the skill. However, a test is not enough. Other information should be collected by asking students to talk about their performance on the task.

Review and reteaching as remediation may be helpful in some instances. However, unless the teacher deals with students' existing conceptions by exposing their alternative framework and creating a conceptual conflict (that is, getting students to question what they are doing and why), the correction will not endure.

Testing for Mastery

The setting of a standard level for mastery or a passing score for a particular learning is complicated. What constitutes mastery? Perhaps it is the level of performance necessary for subsequent success in the next stage of learning. Perhaps it is the performance level attained by a recognized expert in the field at hand or the level of performance attained by top members of a normed-referenced group. If teachers could access data showing how different levels of test performance predict relative success in the future school and everyday situations, they could set more defensible standards. However, such data are seldom available. Instead, most standards are set arbitrarily, based perhaps on the teacher's knowledge of how well students in the past did on the tests, the perceived importance of the objectives the test purports to measure, and the instructional time and effort required to get students to a given level.

In classrooms, mastery outcomes are typically associated with the minimum essentials of a course, recognizing that many students are able to perform well beyond this level. In teaching mastery learning, the course is divided into a series of learning tasks. Objectives are specified for each task and test items that match each objective are prepared. The number of test items a student must answer correctly is the mastery standard for that objective. Usually, the standard is set at 80 or 85 percent for each test, but it may be adjusted to fit various learning tasks.[20] The performance of students who have previously taken the course can serve as a guide. Instructional materials and activities match each objective. After students complete instruction, they are given the appropriate test for mastery. Those who do not reach the criterion are given alternate remedial instruction and retested after correct study. It is expected that all students will master all objectives, although some students will need more time and help in achieving them. Grading is noncompetitive, in that any student who has mastered the curriculum is given an A. Although the theory of mastery learning assumes that all students can achieve mastery, a study conducted by Good and Dembo found that more than half of the teachers interviewed estimated that less than 50 percent of their students could master the material they had to teach.[21]

TESTING AS A BASIS FOR GRADING

The grades that teachers record become public messages. Grades may signify the progress of individual students in desired directions, a comparison of relative standing among peers, or a student's effort, cooperation, and social development. Grades tell the student many things—how well they are doing or have done in a course and what not to do. Grades may tell students they can get into college or that they should consider vocational careers.

Although school districts and individual schools have their grading policies, teachers are the sole arbiters of that policy. Most school districts issue a traditional report card and hold scheduled conferences for communicating with parents. The format of the report card calls for a letter grade and numerical marks to indicate social behavior. Some districts report standardized testing scores. At the primary level, the marks O (outstanding), S (satisfactory), N (needs improvement), and U (unsatisfactory) are common. Academic achievement may be reported by subareas. Social development (for example, listens, follows instruction, assumes responsibility, works with others, respects property) and effort are reported in two thirds of the schools in the United States.

In a 1985 study of the grading policies and practices of high school teachers, Agnew found that many factors influence the grade that teachers award, including the subject area, the department chairperson, school administration, and the status of the school. Further, most teachers are dissatisfied with grading policy, although on the surface they appear to control it. Teachers' perceptions of the consequences of failing students (for example, criticism from administrators, teachers, parents, students; having to deal with students repeating the course; and the effects of failing grades upon students) and their disapproval of the standards of others contribute to their dissatisfaction.[22]

There is much variability in grading among teachers. One survey of high school course grade standards reveals that higher grades are awarded by teachers in the visual and performing arts and in personal development courses than by teachers of math, English, and science. For example, the percentages of A's given by teachers in the arts and personal development courses is 2.5 times greater than the percentage of A's given in math courses—44 versus 17 percent. Further, good grades in the former courses require less homework effort than the latter courses.[23] Teachers also vary in their grading styles—some are more strict early in the course and more lenient at the end, whereas others are more lenient initially and more strict at the end.[24] Just being a hard or easy teacher accounts for about 6 percent of the grades given. About 16 percent of the grades can be explained in terms of the teacher's judging habits, interaction with students, and stereotyped knowledge of the student. According to Airaisian, teachers "size up" students as individuals, and their initial estimates remain stable. Students, in turn, are sensitive to the teacher's early assessment and learn their position in the "pecking order" of the class and respond accordingly. Nevertheless, about 84 percent of the grade can be attributed to the competence and performance of the student. Gender also accounts for variance in grades, with females being more likely to receive higher grades.[25] Further, elementary teachers tend to judge students in the absence of formal information such as standardized test scores. They give more emphasis to the social and background characteristics of students as well as to impressions formed through direct observation.[26] In making their judgments based on observations, teachers rely on two categories: social (for example, work habits, participation, and peer relations) and personal (for example, maturity, self-confidence, attention, health, and openness to ideas).

If letter grades are to serve as indicators of achievement, they should reflect the extent to which students have achieved the outcomes sought from the course. In making decisions about grades, teachers should consider the functions of the courses they are teaching. A grade in an exploratory course—one designed to help students explore an area new to them for the purpose of awakening them to possible future studies—should reflect the extent to which students have participated in classroom activities rather than a level of mastery. Grades for a remedial course designed for individual improvement should be based on the growth exhibited by the individual and be independent of the achievement of others. In courses established for the preparation of specialists (for example, competent secretaries, proficient mechanics, majors in advanced studies of math, science, and writing), grades should reflect a well-stated and justified criterion for competency. Grades in general education courses, in which the learners are to acquire the concepts and understandings necessary for civic purposes and shared communication in the larger society, should reflect participation as well as progress toward commonly held objectives.

Abuses in grading occur as a result of the teacher using grades to control students and to exercise power. To encourage learning by offering grades as incentives is contrary to the philosophy that says students should study because they are interested in the subject, not the grade. Also, the practice of rewarding grades in the absence of defensible criteria may adversely affect students' motivation, attributions, and ability to interpret how their behavior affects achievement. Critics of competitive grading systems contend that students learn more when the deleterious effects of competitive grading are reduced. Cooperative learning—a most effective form of learning—does not occur when only a few high grades are available to students.

EVALUATION IN THE CLASSROOM

The bottom line for all supervisory evaluations is the assessment of classroom teaching. It is at the classroom level that the supervisor will ultimately learn of the effectiveness of the school programs.

There are three major ideas that govern the evaluation of teachers in the classroom:

1. The teacher needs to see himself or herself as part of the curriculum, not apart from it.
2. The teacher needs to understand the intent of the planned program as well as its structure.
3. The teacher must clearly perceive evaluation and staff development as part of a program improvement effort.

Each of these ideas is treated more fully here.

Curriculum and Instruction

For years, the belief has been that teaching is an art. More recently, teacher effectiveness research has pursued the idea that the teaching act is comprised of a series of interrelated acts or skills that contribute to effectiveness. In truth, both of these positions are probably valid . . . to some degree. The judgment of teaching through formal classroom evaluations is totally dependent on a model of the aims of teaching. A teacher who is personable or entertaining may be an instructional delight without contributing significantly to learning. By contrast, a teacher who grinds through a curriculum without spirit or understanding may be equally ineffective as a teacher. Evaluation of classroom instruction must be based on some understanding of what is supposed to happen to students in the learning experience that is planned.

The beginning point for classroom evaluation is helping the teacher see himself or herself as an extension of the curriculum. Instruction is the implementation of the curriculum, and the teacher is the instrument by which the curriculum is delivered. At the lowest level, this would mean that the teacher is not a free agent who teaches what is familiar or interesting to him or her. At a higher level, this would mean that the teacher is always conscious of what is supposed to happen to the student and how teaching contributes to that end.

There are many lists of teacher behaviors that go into school-based teacher evaluation forms. Here is a list of eight categories that could be used to construct such an instrument. The critical question is, "Which of these performances actually contribute to the purpose of the curriculum?"

I. Dependability
   A. Punctual.
   B. Reliable.
   C. Fulfills duties.
II. Human Relations Skills
   A. *Helps development of positive self-images in learners.* Praises. Listens, making students feel important. Elaborates and builds on the contributions of students. Relates to students on an individual basis. Provides opportunities for successful experiences.

B. *Works effectively with different social/ethnic groups.* Relates well to students, parents, and staff from different ethnic and socioeconomic backgrounds.

C. *Demonstrates skills in various kinds of communications.* Enunciates clearly and correctly. Adjusts voice and tone to situation: large group, small group, and individuals. Listens accurately to pupils and staff. Recognizes nonverbal statements. Adjusts language and content to students' age level.

D. *Helps students become independent learners.* Helps students identify personal goals. Facilitates individual exploration. Provides opportunities for diversity. Offers alternative paths to skill acquisition.

E. *Facilitates students' social interactions and activities.* Helps in special activity: field trip, play, games, and PTA.

F. *Works effectively as a team member.* Gets along with staff. Assumes responsibility for tasks as a team member.

III. Managing the Classroom

A. *Maintains a safe environment.* Follows safety regulations.

B. *Maintains physical environment conducive to learning.* Arranges room with books, materials, and learning stations that produce a stimulating academic environment. Decorates room reflecting students' ages and interests. Maintains room lighting and temperature as comfortable as possible.

C. *Maintains socioemotional environment conducive to learning.* Uses students' mistakes as sources of new learning. Respects rights of individuals. Enthusiastic about class work. Sense of humor. Uses competition to allow for the success of many. Provides opportunities for students to share experiences and feelings. Provides opportunities for cooperation.

D. *Involves students in the management of the classroom.* Delegates responsibility of housekeeping tasks to students. Involves students in decision making concerning the identification, implementation, and enforcement of classroom regulations. Matches management duties with students' needs as an opportunity for personal enhancement.

E. *Manages disruptive behavior appropriately.* Implements rules and procedures consistently. Standards of behavior are publicly and professionally justifiable. Attends to disruptive behavior individually and privately. Maintains control.

F. *Designs procedures for handling routines in the class.* Gets class started within five minutes of signal and finishes on time. Establishes procedures for hall passes, lunch count, storage of materials. Keeps register accurately. Scores, reviews, and records grades properly.

IV. Planning Instruction

A. *Selects appropriate learning goals and objectives.* Develops units and daily lesson plans that include appropriate learning objectives.

B. *Demonstrates skills in organizing learners for instruction.* Organizes different-sized groups of students for various instructional purposes.

C. *Selects appropriate teaching strategies.* Lecture discussion, lecture demonstration, lecture, inductive, individualization, group investigation, open classroom, simulations, programmed instruction.

D. *Skillful in selecting and preparing resource materials.* Selects and prepares resource materials for lessons. Utilizes a variety of printed and electronic media.

E. *Involves students in design of the instructional plan.* Seeks students' suggestions in the designing of the instructional plan. Provides opportunity for student choices.

F. *Demonstrates skill in evaluating the instructional plan.* Provides a rationale for instructional plans. Establishes criteria for attainment objectives. Evaluates effects of the instructional plan.

V. Implementing Instruction

A. *Relates instruction to the world of the learner.* Relates learning objectives to students' perceptual world. Teaches at students' level in terms of language, examples, and activities. Deals with content in a problem-solving context. Provisions are made to learn by "doing" rather than by listening only. Points out implications of material learned for students' career development.

B. *Skillful in use of various teaching strategies.* Lecture discussion, lecture demonstration, lecture, inductive, individualization, group investigation, open classroom, simulations, programmed instruction.

C. *Applies group dynamics techniques.* Uses different group management and leadership styles when working with large, medium, and small groups of students.

D. *Skillful in the individualization of instruction.* Diagnoses individual levels of proficiency, prescribes appropriate activities, selects appropriate materials, manages learning procedures.

E. *Skillful in the use of A-V equipment and computers.* Operates overhead projector, opaque projector, recorder, movie projector, slide projector, ditto machine, mimeograph, CAI.

F. *Skillful in the use of multimedia resources.* Incorporates printed and electronic media into learning activities.

G. *Demonstrates skills in questioning and responding.* Asks questions at various levels of cognitive taxonomy. Phrases and times questions appropriately. Elicits student participation through questions. Uses rapid-fire questions to move students into work. Uses questions as a means of success for all learners. Builds new questions on students' answers. Challenges and probes through questions. Responds to answers by reinforcing or abstaining from judgment as the activity prescribes.

H. *Demonstrates skills in value-clarification techniques.* Raises questions in the minds of the students to prod them gently to examine personal actions, values, and goals.

I. *Evaluates and modifies his or her own performance.* Gathers self-evaluation data through VCR or audio tape playback, student oral and written feedback, supervisor feedback. Identifies areas of strength and weakness and formulates plan for improvement specifying criteria for accomplishment. Implements plan and evaluates report results.

VI. Knowledge of Subject Matter
  A. *Demonstrates adequate general academic preparation.* Makes accurate assessment of student knowledge in subject area and outside areas of specialization. Exhibits broad academic preparation.
  B. *Demonstrates knowledge of areas of specialization.* Well informed and skillful in field(s) of specialization.

VII. Assessing and Evaluating Students
  A. *Recognizes individual personality/learning styles.* Designs and implements curriculum plans that provide for alternative learning styles and different cognitive and affective make-up.
  B. *Demonstrates diagnostic skills.* Skillful in the analysis of learning tasks. Determines students' level of proficiency in content area(s).
  C. *Skillful in selecting and devising formal evaluation instruments.* Writes tests utilizing variety of types of items, appropriate to content area and students' level.
  D. *Skillful in devising and using informal evaluation procedures.* Uses informal evaluation techniques to assess progression in learning such as interviews, case studies, analyses of student performance data.
  E. *Skillful in providing feedback to students and parents.* Devises formative evaluation events: teacher evaluated, learner/parent evaluated.

VIII. Professionalism
  A. *Seeks to improve own professional competence.* Reads professional journals. Attends professional meetings. Visits other programs and teachers. Seeks and utilizes professional feedback.
  B. *Is accountable for professional actions.* Dependable. Fulfills responsibility of the professional teacher: planning, implementing, validating instruction, maintenance tasks, playground duties, and other tasks.
  C. *Demonstrates skill in professional decision making.* Possesses a rationale for professional action. Produces evidence to justify professional decisions. Evaluates the consequences of actions.
  D. *Demonstrates awareness of strength and weaknesses.* Identifies teaching roles and strategies most and least suited to own style. Identifies personal human interaction style and its effects in professional work. Identifies own value system and how it relates to teaching.
  E. *Behaves according to an accepted code of professional ethics.* Works to fulfill institutional goals. Bases public criticism of education on valid assumptions as established by careful evaluation of facts and hypotheses. Refrains from exploiting the institutional privileges of the teaching profession to promote partisan activities or political candidates. Directly uses information about students; refrains from unprofessional comments. Avoids exploiting the professional relationship with any student. Deals justly and considerately with each student.
  F. *Seeks to improve the profession.* Participates in professional organizations. Prepares plan for improvement of the profession to be implemented during first year of teaching.

SUMMARY

Evaluation is an essential tool for school supervisors. The use of evaluation as a means of communication with teachers will be an essential part of the new knowledge-based leadership role of supervisors in schools.

Schools routinely evaluate for a number of purposes, but most such evaluation is mechanical in nature. Supervisors can bring such evaluation to life by involving teachers. Not only will such a process make teacher evaluation a rational process, but using techniques such as action research will further the "collaboration movement" in education.

Supervisors need to be comprehensive in their school evaluation efforts aiming for a schoolwide plan. In addressing the many areas of need, we have made special note of the limitations of testing in schools. Focus on this area will help clarify practices in other related areas.

Finally, in the actual assessment of classroom teaching, supervisors should strive for objectivity. A performance-oriented and outcome-based instrument will help communicate to the teacher why supervision is occurring in their school.

IMPLICATIONS FOR SUPERVISION

1. How can the supervisor best determine relevant research to share with teachers? State the selection criteria.
2. Grading has always been a controversial part of the schooling process. How can teachers be better prepared to understand this complex area?
3. Using the eight areas of the teacher evaluation guide at the end of this chapter, list and defend the most important categories in order.

❧ CASE STUDY 1 ❧

Miss Morris is a well-known figure at Southland High. She should be, for this fall marks the thirtieth year she has been teaching in the home economics program. It is hard to believe that she represents the example "homemaker" of tomorrow. She is always sloppy, and her hair is never neatly groomed. Even boys notice her disheveled appearance when they see her in the halls. It seems that the faded lace on her slip shows beneath her dress quite frequently. But this doesn't seem to bother Miss Morris at all. She shuffles to her class at a snail's pace and relishes the last drag from her cigarette before the final bell rings.

Class is automatic for Miss Morris. She has read her notes so many times that they are now old and yellow. Sometimes, however, she doesn't instruct but talks to her pupils of when she was a young girl living in Cleveland, Ohio. Her stories are so worn that students write letters while she dreams of days gone by. When Miss Morris does instruct, she strictly follows her outline and lectures throughout the entire class period. She rarely uses available facilities and seems to ignore the questioning minds of her students.

Even though Miss Morris heads the home economics program, she never instigates committee meetings, nor is she receptive to the enthusiastic ideas of the newer teachers. She has held her position for the past ten years, and she feels she could really tell these young idealists about the problems of education. There has been neither appreciation of her hard work nor recognition—monetarily or otherwise. At this point, Miss Morris's only desire is to complete five more years of teaching so she can retire and go back to Cleveland to live out her remaining years.

A new principal has informed the superintendent that he intends to do something about Miss

Morris. He asks for help from the district office. The superintendent asks you, as Miss Morris's supervisor, to respond. He wants to support the new principal at Southland, yet suggests that fewer waves will be made if Miss Morris can improve her performance rather than be terminated.

Questions

1. Miss Morris is obviously a marginal teacher who has "gotten by" for years. What can you as a supervisor do, if anything, to improve the performance of Miss Morris?
2. What issues would you face if you recommend the termination of Miss Morris's employment?
3. Outline an incentive plan for teachers like Miss Morris to participate in staff improvement programs. How would you sell your plan to teachers? To the board?

⊱ CASE STUDY 2 ⊰

As part of the curriculum change to accommodate the middle school philosophy, guides were set up for the various disciplines. The science program was designed to give general subject area topics to each grade level. A general science background was to be provided in the sixth grade, biology was to be covered in the seventh grade, and the physical sciences, chemistry, physics, meteorology, and astronomy, were to be studied in the eighth grade. No one textbook was to be used as the basic book for any grade level; rather, there were several books that were suggested as having good material for various specific topics. As a first-year teacher in this system, Mark James was at a loss as to how to teach. The county office had provided him with a basic cognitive outline for the seventh-grade level. However, Mark realized after the first week of classes that the content was more than the majority of his students could handle. After consulting with his department head, Mark was disappointed to find little help. The basic backbone, biology, had already been given to him, he was told. The department head stated that this system was the best for personal freedom in teaching. Mark argued to no avail that some structure was needed. As a first-year teacher, he felt handicapped and frustrated with the system. At a county science meeting, Mark voiced his concern about this problem, and nearly all the other teachers present seemed to agree with him.

Questions

1. As district science supervisor, what steps would you take to resolve the concerns of teachers about the effectiveness of the new science program?
2. In what ways could you help first-year teachers like Mark become more effective teachers?
3. How would you assess the effectiveness of the new program other than listening to the complaints of teachers?

SUGGESTED LEARNING ACTIVITIES

1. Assume a teacher has asked you why you must come into her classroom to evaluate performance and why so many days are wasted on in-service activities. What is your response?
2. Explain why inconclusive primary research on teacher effectiveness has become so prescriptive in the 1990s.
3. What are some ways that a supervisor might get teachers more interested in research at the classroom level?
4. There is a special problem in testing the culturally different. Their performance is influenced by language differences, achievement motivation, and unfamiliarity with test-taking skills. For example, we know that many American Indians are at odds with the prevailing evaluation mode that works against them. In some tribes, speech is not organized around a single topic, and speakers do not make arguments substantiating their points of view nor draw conclusions from

unrelated remarks. Tribal leaders do not interpret information for the audience but give facts and defer decisions to the group. It is the listener's role to draw connections and conclusions. Notice how these communication patterns conflict with the criteria used to evaluate essay writing in our schools.

What sources of information could verify the accuracy or inaccuracy of the test results from low-achieving minorities? How can one best use test results in the interests of culturally different students?

5. State and defend what you believe is a satisfactory marking (grading) policy.

BOOKS TO REVIEW

Aiken, M., ed. *Encyclopedia of Educational Research,* 6th ed. New York: Macmillan, 1992.

Frisbie, D., and Ebel, R. *Essentials of Educational Measurement,* 4th ed. Englewood Cliffs, NJ: Prentice Hall, 1990.

Mullin, I. *Trends in Academic Progress.* Washington, DC: National Center for Educational Statistics, 1991.

National Association of Secondary School Principals. *Comprehensive Assessment of School Environments.* Reston, VA: 1990.

Northwest Regional Educational Laboratory. *Effective School Practices: A Research Synthesis.* Portland, OR: 1990.

CHAPTER 12 ≋

NEW DIRECTIONS FOR SUPERVISION

A new century always signals changes in American life, and public education is no exception to that rule.[1] The forces of change seemed to have gained momentum during the last two decades of the twentieth century.[2] Calls for reform have echoed from the classrooms to board rooms to the halls of our legislatures and Congress.[3] Those in leadership roles in education have two choices. They can stand by and watch business and political leaders shape the face of education or step forward and lead. Today's supervisors need all of the leadership skills discussed earlier in this text if they are to help shape the future of American education. They must understand human relations and be able to apply human relations skills. They must also be skilled in the area of curriculum, instruction, administration, staff development, and evaluation. They must be able to utilize technology and apply that technology to solving problems. They must be able to compete in the world of business and management and not be overwhelmed by instant solutions coming from those fields. Finally, today's supervisory leaders must understand the political arena. If politics is defined as "the art of working with people," then supervisors must be "people persons."

This chapter will examine four critical areas of concern facing modern supervisors. First will be an overview of how American education has changed, especially in the last decades of this century. Next, the role of business and schools will be examined. Policies and professionalism in schools will be covered. Finally, recommendations will be offered for better schools in the next century.

THE CHANGING FACE OF AMERICAN EDUCATION

Poverty in America

Data from the Census Bureau reveals that between 1966 and 1996 a growing number of Americans entered the category of "poor" (the poverty threshold for one person is about $7,200; for a family of four, about $14,500). Those reports also found that children were overrepresented among the poor. About 40 percent of those living in poverty are children under 18, although they represent only 26 percent of the population. In 1966, 30 percent of those over the age of 64 were in poverty, while 18 percent of those under 18 were classified as poor. By 1992, the figure for those over 64 and older had been reduced to 11 percent while the figure for those under 18 had risen to 22 percent.[4] Table 12.1 shows the government's projected percentages of poverty for nonwhite children under the age of 18 in the year 2010 for selected states and the United States. Figure 12.1 illustrates the 1994 poverty groups.

Who Are Our Children?

Many of our children are not only poor, but come from homes where there are single parents. Over half of marriages end in divorce today. Of those living with one parent, 50 percent of white children are with a mother who is divorced. Sixty percent of black children are with a never-married mother, and 35 percent of Hispanic mothers have not married. Poverty and single parenthood go hand-in-hand. The average income for married families in 1995 was about $37,000 whereas that for female households with children was about $14,000 (U.S. Census Department Figures, 1995).[5]

Today the nuclear "Leave It to Beaver" household of yesteryear (the 1960s television show depicting a near-perfect nuclear family in America) seems very atypical to say the least. Even in the days of the factory systems in America, the Great Depression or even World War II, the situation for children never seemed so bleak. Parenting has taken on a new meaning in the last quarter of the twentieth century. The majority of mothers of school-age children rose in the workforce, many are single parents, and many of our youth have succumbed to the scourges of drugs and street crime.

Yet, these children, by law, are served by our schools. We teach all children, regardless of circumstances, and that will continue. The stress on teachers, many

Table 12.1 Percent Nonwhite Youth—Ages 0-17 Years, Projections for 2010 for Selected States
Source: U.S. Department of Commerce, Bureau of the Census, 1995.

State	Percent Nonwhite	State	Percent Nonwhite
District of Columbia	93.2%	Louisiana	50.3%
Hawaii	79.5%	Mississippi	49.9%
Texas	56.9%	New Jersey	45.7%
California	56.9%	Maryland	42.7%
New York	52.8%	Illinois	41.7%
U.S.	38.2%		

Figure 12.1 1994 Poverty
Groups
Source: U.S. Department of Commerce, Bureau of the Census, 1995.

Number of People		Percent
36,880,000	=	14.5% of entire population
27,372,000	=	13.9% of people in urban areas
24,523,000	=	11.6% of whites (including Hispanic)
18,308,000	=	9.6% of whites (non-Hispanic)
18,281,000	=	11.7% of people 18 to 64 years old
14,763,000	=	16.9% of people in Southern states
14,763,000	=	40.0% of the poor live in the South
14,617,000	=	21.9% of people under 18 years old
10,613,000	=	33.3% of blacks
9,509,000	=	16.8% of people outside urban areas
8,955,000	=	16.9% of white children under 18
7,983,000	=	13.1% of people in Midwest states
7,983,000	=	21.6% of poor live in the Midwest
7,960,000	=	11.7% of all families
7,907,000	=	14.4% of people in Western states
7,907,000	=	21.4% of the poor live in the West
6,655,000	=	29.3% of Hispanics
6,227,000	=	12.3% of people in Northeast states
6,227,000	=	16.9% of the poor live in Northeast states
5,160,000	=	8.9% of white families (including Hispanic)
4,938,000	=	46.6% of black children under 18
4,171,000	=	34.9% of female-led households
3,983,000	=	12.9% of people older than 64
3,860,000	=	7.3% of white families (non-Hispanic)
3,318,000	=	6.2% of married-couple families
3,116,000	=	39.9% of black families
2,435,000	=	30.9% of black families
1,835,000	=	49.8% of black female-led households
1,395,000	=	26.2% of Hispanic families
912,000	=	12.5% of Asian/Pacific Islanders
486,000	=	13.0% of black married-couple families
199,000	=	12.0% of Asian/Pacific Islander families

with some of the same problems facing the general population, has continued to build so that the wellness of teachers has become a major issue in management–union regulations. Supervisors often find themselves in the role of counselor as they work with teachers who are fed up with student behavior that is antisocial. Teachers with middle-class work ethics and social values have also been slow to adjust to students who perform below grade level or below teacher expectations. Classroom disruptions by students and other classroom management problems often result from teacher frustrations and the inability to deal with students having different values.

It is interesting to note that differences in social classes have always existed in the United States. For instance, from 1900 to 1940, an overwhelming number of persons (75 percent) were classified as poor (see Figure 12.2).[6]

The 1990s saw a growing diversity in the family structure. U.S. Census charts (1995) show:

- Married couples filled about 50 percent of households compared to 70 percent of households in 1975. Married couples with children now make up less than 25 percent of U.S. households.
- For the first time in 50 years, childless couples outnumber couples with children.
- Of those couples who have children, half are stepfamilies.
- Single-parent households became the fastest growing family type, almost doubling to more than 10 percent of all households.
- Of children born out of wedlock, most are born to uneducated black women who are driven further in poverty.
- The proportion of the nation's single-parent households is highest in the central cities where a majority of children attend schools.
- In 1970, 11 percent of all births were to single mothers. By 1995, that figure had grown to 35 percent .
- Reflecting on the aging population, the number of people living alone rose from 20 percent of all households in 1970 to 30 percent by 1995.
- The estimated number of child abuse victims increased 50 percent from 1985 to 1995.
- The National Center for Health Statistics estimates 30 percent of girls age 15 are sexually active.
- Violence in our schools grew a whopping 371 percent from 1980–1995.
- In 1994, 65 percent of all married women with children were in the labor force compared to 45 percent in 1980 and 30 percent in 1970.
- In only 6 percent of American families does the mother stay at home and the father work outside the home.

Public elementary and secondary school enrollment, which decreased between 1971 and 1984 because of a decline in the school-age population, has been rising

Figure 12.2 The Changing Distribution of Wealth in America **Source:** U.S. Department of Commerce, 1995.

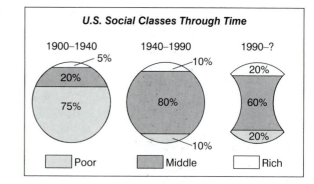

U.S. Social Classes Through Time

1900–1940   1940–1990   1990–?

Poor   Middle   Rich

Figure 12.3 Fastest Growing Racial Ethnic Groups in the United States in the 1990s
Source: U.S. Census Bureau, 1995.

Vietnamese	135%
Asian Indian	126%
Korean	125%
Chinese	104%
Filipino	82%
Hispanic	53%
Native American	38%
Japanese	21%
Black	13%
U.S. Average	10%
White	5%

ever since. Public school enrollment will hit an all-time record in 1997 of approximately 46.5 million students and will continue to increase in the early 2000s.

Although enrollment increased in elementary schools and declined in secondary schools in the late 1980s, enrollments rose at both levels in the 1990s and will continue in the next century.

Children from minority backgrounds continue to enter public and private schools in great numbers.[7] Between 1994 and 2000, the number of white children under five is expected to decline 10 percent while the number of black children will rise by 10 percent and Hispanic children by 15 percent. The number of children of elementary school age will increase between 1994 and 2000, with the number of white children increasing by 3 percent compared to an increase of 15 percent for black children and 28 percent for Hispanic children.[8] If present trends continue, Hispanic students will outnumber black students by 2020, and Asian students will outnumber black and Hispanic students by 2050 in the United States. There will be no more majority populations of students. America will indeed be a culturally pluralistic nation (see Figure 12.3).

Changing School Organizations

In 1930, there were 247,000 schools and 130,000 school districts in the United States. Today, there are only 85,000 schools and less than 15,000 school districts. The trend toward consolidation has brought a steady decline in the number of schools and school districts. However, the structure of public schools has also changed. Although the number of elementary schools dropped 11 percent between 1970 and 1985, that number has increased about 6 percent by 1995. Middle schools have risen in number from 25 in 1960 to 8,500 by 1995, replacing most of the junior high schools as the intermediate school.

The number of public school teachers is growing. There has been no downtrend in pupil–teacher ratios in the elementary schools because school enrollment has grown proportionately. Class size has remained about the same in public elementary schools (24 students) for the past twenty-five years. This has been attributed to the increased number of specialty teachers.

Spending per pupil has increased substantially over the past fifteen years, raising cries from conservatives that more money has not gotten us better results in achievement, graduation rate, and so on. A favorite habit of conservative writers is to point out that states with the highest S.A.T. scores were states that ranked lowest in per-pupil expenditures.

In 1994, for instance, the five states with the highest S.A.T. scores and their per-pupil expenditures were:

1. Iowa (27th)
2. North Dakota (44th)
3. South Dakota (42nd)
4. Utah (51st)
5. Minnesota (25th)

New Jersey spends the most per student while their S.A.T. scores rank 39th. Interestingly, proximity to Canada correlates more strongly with school excellence than does high spending on students. Between 1974 and 1994, expenditures for public education for grades kindergarten through 12 coincided with a 7 percent decline in school enrollment and 35 point decline in S.A.T. scores. Incidentally, the S.A.T. was renamed in 1994 from *Scholastic Aptitude Test* to *Scholastic Assessment Test.*

The United States ranks second only to Canada in the money it spends on education.[9] The 1995 Annual Report of the Organization for Economic Cooperation and Development points out that American teachers are outnumbered by school support staff such as counselors, coaches, bus drivers, and administrators. This phenomenon is unique to the United States. The United States spends more money on higher education per student than any other country except Australia.

Looking for problems or suggesting solutions to the problems facing American schools are not in short supply. Often apples are compared with oranges to make a point—"We spend too much on schools and get few results"; "Private schools will do a better job"; "We need vouchers"; "Home-school is the answer"—and so on.

The single factor on which most educators can agree is that the quality of schools correlates more positively with the quality of families from which children come to school than it does with educational appropriations or any other variable.[10]

Changing the School Day and/or School Year

In 1994, the National Commission on Time and Learning reported that high schools required students to spend barely 41 percent of classroom time on academic subjects. The Commission counted three hours a day for English, science, mathematics, civics, language, and history–half of what was spent on academic courses by students in Germany, France, and Japan.[11]

Calls for longer school days and longer school years for students have come from politicians and educators. In 1995 (after four decades of opposition), more than half of Americans polled responded in favor of extended classroom time for students.[12]

Year-round schools made a comeback in the 1990s, but most year-round schedules reflected extended use of facilities rather than increased student time. The 180-day standard for a student's school year is the same one used in year-round schools. Students simply spend the 180 days over a longer school year. There have been attempts to extend student time, especially for at-risk students. Those students often attend school between quarters of a year-round school, attend after-school programs, or special remedial summer programs. Gifted and talented students often experience extended-time opportunities through zero periods, after-school programs, or summer enrichment programs. The great majority of American students are still stuck in the time warp of a 180-day school schedule.

Reporting on the Status of Schools

The National Commission on Excellence in Education issued its report, *A Nation at Risk,* in 1983 and set off a decade of school bashing. Twelve years later, many observed that a majority of the schools were about the same as when the report was issued.[13] Although there was little reform of schools during those years, a flood of social problems plaguing children and young people emerged. Included were large increases in the number of teenage pregnancies, increases in drug abuse and juvenile crime, and a growing AIDS epidemic. The number of children in poverty in the United States grew to double that of other major industrialized nations. Meeting basic needs of students has become a great struggle within schools and is taking precedence over more traditional objectives. The school has become a great social system doing for children what families cannot do. A growing share of school budgets are being devoted to counseling and psychological services, and the curriculum is becoming increasingly therapeutic.

In 1990, the Secretary of Education enlisted three senior researchers at the Sandia National Laboratory to report on the status of elementary and secondary education. Released in 1993, the *Sandia Report* addressed the decline of S.A.T. scores and attributed that decline on a change in the test-taking pool. This meant that proportionately fewer test-takers were in the top 20 percent of their class than 15 years ago. Declining scores on the S.A.T. have also been addressed by other groups, but as pointed out earlier, conservative writers have given their own spin to the decline. The most common slant is to justify proposed reductions in federal spending for education. Federal spending for education was about 6.5 percent of the federal budget in 1995, down from a high of 8 percent in 1965.

The National Assessment of Educational Progress (NAEP) was established by Congress in 1969 to monitor trends in National Achievement. NAEP scores have been used since 1988 to make state-by-state comparisons although not all states participate in the testing program. Reviewing test scores over a twelve-year period, the Sandia researchers found that performance was steady or improving in nearly all subject areas tested and that the greatest gains were made in basic skills. A U.S. Department of Education Study in 1992 indicated that NAEP math scores increased in 18 of 37 states between 1990 and 1992.

Of course, as in previous years, any good news coming from NAEP received immediate criticism from such groups as the National Center for Education Statistics, the National Academy of Education, and the General Accounting Office (GAO) which faulted NAEP achievement levels (basic, proficient, and advanced) as unsuitable for reporting test results.

International comparisons of U.S. students have often drawn simplistic comparisons that match different groups of students. Harold Hodgkinson, the great demographer, noted in 1994 that American students in the lowest 40 percent would be on the streets in many other countries. We keep them in school until age 18.[14]

A 1993 report of the Organization for Economic Cooperation and Development found that the U.S. spends more on higher education than any other nation and graduates more postsecondary science and engineering degrees than any other country.

Reports comparing U.S. students within the country and with students in other countries are valuable tools if we use information gathered as information and not as a justification for or against a particular program.

Funding Public Schools

In 1994, the State of Michigan, where five previous sales-tax hikes for public education were defeated, rewrote the method of funding schools.[15] Shattering the traditional method of financing public education, the state voted to shift most of the burden from property taxes to sales taxes. It also tripled the cigarette tax to help pay the bills. A key goal of the plan was to smooth out the disparity among school districts. (The poorest spent $3,200 dollars per student each year while the richest spent $10,400.) By 1994, twenty-eight states were in the midst of lawsuits involving the distribution of school aid.

Full Inclusion of Children with Disabilities

An increasing number of children with severe disabilities are being taught in regular classrooms on the theory that they benefit more there than in segregated, special-education classes. It is also hoped their classmates without disabilities will gain a better understanding of them.[16]

Under the 1975 Individuals with Disabilities Education Act, children with disabilities were given the right to learn with peers without disabilities, "to the maximum extent appropriate." Through the 1980s, suits by parents of such children won three major court decisions to force districts to place their children who were mentally disabled in regular classes.

Inclusion has become a struggle both for parents and teachers in regular classrooms. In 1994, the American Federation of Teachers called for a halt to full inclusion. Other state-level teacher organizations have won concessions relating to full inclusion of these children in regular classrooms.

The controversy over how children with disabilities will be included in regular classes will continue. Teachers must have training and extra help if inclusion is to result in a better educational program for those students with disabilities and those without these challenges.

Programs for At-Risk Students

Disruptions and violence in schools received more attention than any other issues in the 1990s.[17] The breakdown of the family, poverty, and economic problems continue to fuel large numbers of disaffected youth. Schools have become centers of violence as problems of the streets and homes spill over to the hallways and playgrounds of our educational institutions. Strong anticrime laws passed by Congress in 1994 and by many states are attempting to address the needs of at-risk students. Guns have become everyday weapons for many school-age children. The Brady Bill, passed in 1994, attempted to limit certain types of guns, but the battle over ownership of guns continues. The constitutional right to bear arms was certainly one area of the Constitution mastered by Americans.

An ad by handgun control advocates in 1994 listed the following:

In 1994, handguns killed

> 22 people in Great Britain
> 13 in Sweden
> 91 in Switzerland
> 87 in Japan
> 10 in Australia
> 68 in Canada
> 10,500 in the United States

As the attacks on crime continues in the halls of Congress and in our legislatures, schools are seeking to present safe environments for students to learn and teachers to teach.[18] Metal detectors, radio communication between teachers and administrators, gun sweeps, and armed guards are commonplace in many schools. Large city school districts have become armed camps with schools looking more like prisons than places of learning.

New York City, which employs more educational bureaucrats than all of Western Europe, has a school security force bigger than most police forces of countries around the world. The city also has a million people on welfare, a total larger than the population of all but ten American cities. Crime, the AIDS epidemic, and drug abuse in New York City and other large cities have put a financial strain on cities, limiting funds for school programs.

Supervisory leadership in large urban school districts must deal with an increasing number of teachers under great stress. Supervisors will also have to struggle for resources for school programs that are educational and not just simply therapeutic or safety related.

The Religious Right

The 1990s saw renewed efforts on the part of many parents to gain more control over the curriculum of schools. Those efforts have included: all-out campaigns to gain support for schools of choice, the challenging of the teaching of values in public schools, and supporting the liberalization of laws regarding home schooling.[19]

Home schooling of students has increased with support from networking by parent groups and the use of television and computer programs especially designed for home teaching. Thirty-four states had specific statutes regulating home schooling in 1994. Some states require parents to be certified teachers or college graduates. However, parents who cite religious reasons are exempt. Also, thousands of home-schooling families register their residences as private schools to avoid running afoul of truancy laws. To avoid students being labeled as social outcasts, home-schooling families often link up with other home-schooling families for field trips and social activities.

An estimated 1.5 million children were home-schooled in 1995, about one percent of the school-age population. That figure is projected to grow about 15 percent a year according to the National Home School Research Institute. About 12 percent of the American school-age population attended private schools in 1995.

The fight over teaching values has been a continuous one during the 1990s. Which values to be taught is one issue. Another is that values should be taught at home or church (the Christian Fundamentalist view). The teaching of tolerance for certain groups (for example, the rainbow curriculum in New York City which emphasized understanding of homosexuals and bisexuals) came under furious attack from parents and other groups. "Moral education" or "character education" draws heated debate from groups either advocating or condemning those programs. Can honesty, democracy, the golden rule be addressed in our schools?

Again, supervisors must be able to work with groups on both sides of issues. They must be able to help groups find consensus on what should be taught. Those skills will be in great demand as our school population becomes more diverse in the next decades.

Privatization of Schools

Privatization of schools increased dramatically in the 1990s.[20] These privately run schools either started as a result of voucher plans or were existing schools that were simply contracted out to private firms. Private firms in districts such as Washington, DC; Baltimore; Atlanta; Albany, NY; Phoenix; and San Antonio were given control of school programs by state government.[21]

In 1994, the Minneapolis school board voted to transfer every public school to the Public Strategies Group, a private firm. The president of that firm was, in effect, the city's school superintendent.

In other cities, business leaders have decided to set up privately funded voucher programs to help struggling inner-city students and to demonstrate the benefits of competition. Pat Rooney, the chairman of Golden Rule Insurance Company, started the first program in Indianapolis in 1991. It provides more than eleven hundred students with scholarships in private schools paid by Golden Rule and other local companies.

In 1994, California turned down a referendum that would have allowed parents to use some of their taxes to send their children to private schools. Puerto Rico and Milwaukee did create taxpayer-funded voucher programs.

The debate over privatization of schools continues. Opponents argue that public schools will be left only with special students or low-achieving students. They also argue that formulas used to fund private schools with public tax dollars are often skewed to allow secondary funding (where specialized programs receive more funds) for an elementary school. Proponents say that public schools have failed and that competition and freedom (from unions and bureaucracy) will only result in better schools and increased student achievement.

Restructuring

Whether reforming or restructuring, proponents of school improvement believe school organizations and practices must change.[22]

While differing in terminology and specific strategies, new plans for education all share the idea that educational systems can't continue as they presently exist.

One plan focuses on student outcomes.[23] Proponents argue that simply earning credits does not mean success after graduation. They call on students to demonstrate their mastery of major outcomes. Rather than having students take courses in lock step, schools should reorganize their practices to support student attainment of significant outcomes. By 1994, at least thirty states had identified essential student outcomes according to the National Association of State Boards of Education. State outcomes usually are linked to state assessment programs and/or curriculum frameworks.

In contrast to the 1980s, when districts emphasized behavioral objectives, the purpose of outcome-based education is to involve critical thinking or the ability to solve complex problems.

The idea of restructuring school programs around new student outcomes drew immediate opposition, especially from the religious right. Opponents questioned affective outcomes and values that "strayed away too far from academics." Which outcomes are important and how to teach them continue to be addressed by both proponents and opponents of outcome-based education.

Restructuring of schools has also meant making schools more democratic. "Shared decision making," "school-based management," and "site management" are all terms frequently used.[24] Teachers have been empowered in the 1990s after experiencing a decade of top-down management processes. Often, legislatures have mandated that school or site-based management plans be implemented in school districts. It is ironic that a state legislature has to mandate that "you will be democratic."

For supervisory leaders, restructuring does mean forming new relationships with teachers and parents, borrowing less authority from administration, and using human relations skills to the maximum. Supervisors must help other educators move beyond the rhetoric of restructuring to a true participatory democracy in which problems and solutions are shared by all.

BUSINESS AND SCHOOLS IN THE TWENTY-FIRST CENTURY
The Corporate Role in Reforming Public Schools

In 1916, John Dewey said, "Democracy has to be born anew in each generation, and education is the midwife."[25]

Changes in the world of work have been profound in the 1990s.[26] "Lean and mean" has been a term used by business and industry to eliminate jobs, cut production costs, and become more competitive in the international arena. For the first time since the Great Depression, skilled workers and managers (white-collar workers) have been turned out on the streets. Union membership has declined, and many businesses have merged or closed their doors. Giant corporations like DuPont, IBM, Xerox, and others have eliminated 165,000 jobs between 1990 and 1994. As with other times of economic upheaval in the United States, attention has turned to public schools. Public schools are not producing the kind of workers America need in order to compete with the rest of the world, and schools and school districts are bloated with too many bureaucratics and too few new ideas. If business and industry can become "lean and mean," why can't our educational institutions? As in the period between 1900 and 1920, terms such as "efficiency" and "effectiveness" are being applied to education. The if-then syndrome of "if business can become more effective, then so can schools," has become a rallying cry in the marketplace. Business partnerships with schools have changed from the focus of what business can do to help the schools to how business can prod schools into greater reforms. In a school district in Florida, local business leaders actually hired an IBM official to help speed up reform in a school district—without first conferring with the superintendent or board of that district. Many corporate leaders are convinced that public schools have ruined the economy. From *A Nation at Risk* to plans for *America 2000,* increasingly harsher tones have emanated from corporate boardrooms about the future of public education. Top corporate officials are convinced that economic problems are linked to educational solutions and that educators either can't or won't make needed changes.

Citing declining scores on standardized tests by high school graduates, corporate leaders say that the solution is to equip students with the necessary knowledge, skills, and work habits to make America competitive again. Further, they say this can be done by setting clear goals, decentralizing operations so that managers and workers share responsibility for outcomes, and rewarding those who succeed and punishing those who fail since the public chooses the best product. Why not let private enterprise run schools and let parents choose companies that deliver the best products? That rhetoric has led to the call for national funding of corporate-run demonstration schools—the kind the Whittle Corporation and other private companies would love to run for profit.

Many believe that the corporate solution for running schools is a myth. They cite foreign industries whose workforces are less educated, yet their products outsell our own. Critics of the corporation solution also point out that there is little consensus that schools have caused the productivity crisis in the United States or that there is any connection between a decline in test scores and drops in worker productivity. Indeed, between 1990 and 1995, test scores have remained fairly stable while productivity increased and by mid-decade had grown so much that U.S. workers were outproducing those of other industrialized nations.

Focusing on Organizational Improvement

W. Edwards Deming, who died in 1994, left a legacy of promising practices for business and industry.[27] Since these practices were embraced by Japanese businesses, American,

soon saw them as holding potential for American businesses and also for public education.[28] Deming's principles of Total Quality Management (T.Q.M.) (discussed in Chapter 2) emphasized that if management can eliminate systemic problems in an organization—practices, rules, expectations, and traditions—over which individuals have little
control, then continued improvement can be made in the organization. Empowering
workers and eliminating competition between workers are important facets of T.Q.M.

T.Q.M. is a philosophy and a set of tools to enable an organization to pursue systematically a definition of quality and a means for attaining quality. Whether T.Q.M.
can change the culture of schools and have an impact on efficiency and effectiveness
is still unknown. It does hold promise for creating better ways of organizing schools
and creating more positive climates in classrooms.

Education and Work

Frederick Taylor (1856–1915) theorized that American factories needed "scientific
management." He was one of the first to say that managers and workers needed to
get along, but that message was lost on factory barons hearing a call for division of
labor. Managers had to be smart, and workers had to be dumb. Schools picked up on
that notion. Soon, managers were separated from workers by a merit system, and
students were separated from all-knowing teachers. Almost one hundred years of
that philosophy is hard to overcome in today's schools. Unions, in their desire to
protect worker rights, have built in that division of responsibility with negotiated
rules, regulations, and methods of evaluation. That philosophy is carried into classrooms where students move at a predictable rate—an assembly-line type of learning.

If the work place is to change, so must schools.[29] The factory-type, top-down
management of schools has to change. Principals need to share power with students,
parents, teachers, mental health workers, and other support staff. In the next century, schools must graduate students who are capable of production and creation,
not repetition.

Computers should be freeing students from lock-step, mundane learning, but it
is estimated that 85 percent to 90 percent of computer instruction has been devoted
to drill and practice, far from the participatory interaction with computer technology
that is found in most workplaces. There are, of course, exceptions to the use of computers for drill, but schools must make a concerted effort to use computers cre-
atively for both teachers and students.

For survival in a global economy, skills of systems thinking, experimental inquiry,
symbolic analysis, and collaboration must be mastered by our workers.

In the past decade, individuals who had those skills prospered while those lacking them fell even farther behind. In 1995, the richest 20 percent received over one
half of the nation's income; the top 5 percent, 26 percent. The poorest 5 percent
received only 3.5 percent, down from 5.5 percent in 1980. Between 1973 and 1993,
the income of high school graduates declined by 12 percent, while the number of
workers whose income fell below the poverty line rose by 43 percent.

The social divisions of society are paralleled by similar divisions in the quality of
schooling. Children from the top 20 percent do well. On the other hand, one fourth

of all American children under age three (47 percent of black children under age three) live in families below the poverty level.

Districts with large numbers of minority children tend to be those where there are also large numbers of disadvantaged children. Figure 12.4 illustrates the large U.S. cities where minorities have become the majority.

As a growing high-tech American economy emerges in the next century, we will still be faced with the quandary of what to do with a lost generation of inner-city minority youth and adults.

We know, too, that factory-era administration, supervisory leadership, and styles of learning are dysfunctional. Alternatives must be sought that allow for participative styles of management that, in turn, support local creativity and problem solving.

In 1991, the New American Schools Development Corporation (NASDC) was organized. This privately funded foundation, the creation of American business, was given

In 50 of the United States' largest cities (population at least 100,000), Blacks, Hispanics, Asians, and Native Americans collectively are more than half the population:

City	Minority	City	Minority
East Los Angeles, CA	97.2%	Baltimore, MD	61.4
Laredo, TX	94.4	Salinas, CA	61.3
Inglewood, CA	91.5	Elizabeth, NJ	60.3
Hialeah, FL	89.1	Houston, TX	59.6
Miami, FL	87.8	Richmond, VA	57.1
Gary, IN	85.9	New York, NY	56.8
El Monte, CA	84.8	Jackson, MS	56.6
Newark, NJ	83.5	Stockton, CA	56.4
Detroit, MI	79.3	Memphis, TN	56.4
Santa Ana, CA	76.9	Corpus Christi, TX	56.2
Paterson, NJ	75.6	San Bernardino, CA	54.5
Honolulu, HI	74.5	Bridgeport, CT	54.4
El Paso, TX	73.6	Vallejo, CA	53.8
Washington, DC	72.6	San Francisco, CA	53.4
Pomona, CA	71.8	Pasadena, CA	53.4
Oakland, CA	71.7	Macon, GA	53.2
Atlanta, GA	69.7	Ontario, CA	53.0
Hartford, CT	69.5	Dallas, TX	52.3
Oxnard, CA	67.7	Cleveland, OH	52.2
New Orleans, LA	66.9	Flint, MI	51.7
Birmingham, AL	64.2	New Haven, CT	51.0
San Antonio, TX	63.8	Fresno, CA	50.6
Jersey City, NJ	63.4	Long Beach, CA	50.5
Los Angeles, CA	62.7	San Jose, CA	50.4
Chicago, IL	62.1	Chula Vista, CA	50.2

Figure 12.4 Minorities in Majority
Source: U.S. Census Bureau data, 1994.

the mission of "breaking the mold" and encouraging the development of world-class schools. The NASDC solicited ideas from large and small companies, universities, and even individuals who bid for a chance to apply private enterprise solutions to public schools. Eleven projects from 686 submitted were selected. At the same time, then-President Bush proposed Congress fund 535 schools that would learn from and even replicate the NASDC-funded models. Congress rejected out-of-hand that proposal.

Those developments did not stop private firms such as Educational Alternatives, Inc. (EAI) and the Whittle Corporation (Edison Project) from proposing their own contracts with public school districts to run schools. Private, for-profit companies have joined the race, claiming they can combine business know-how with educational expertise—and make money.

In the 1970s, during the Nixon administration, there was another public–private venture called "performance contracting." That, too, was supported to save public education. Performance-contracting companies offered what looked like a no-lose proposition. They would undertake to improve student performance in a given subject or subjects and would be paid only if students met certain standards. The idea was so impressive that the federal governmental funded demonstration projects throughout the country. Soon, though, horror stories of teaching to tests, giving students answers, or giving the same tests over and over again began to emerge. Performance contracting ended in scandal because although companies had brilliant marketing ideas, they had no educational expertise and no curriculum. Will companies in the 1990s get contracts first, then figure out what to do next as many companies did with performance contracting? If a company does a poor job today and goes out of business, what will happen to students?

The nature of work in the twenty-first century will be affected by new workplace skills, increased technology, demographics of the workforce, and the global economy. School leaders face an immense challenge of getting our schools ready for the new world of work in the next century.

POLITICS AND PROFESSIONALISM IN SCHOOLS

The call for a national curriculum and national achievement test in the early 1990s emanated from a low level of public confidence in schools.[30] A national report card was also proposed to compare school achievement in reaching the goals set out in *America 2000.* Those goals, proposed by President Bush and endorsed by the fifty governors, included such lofty expectations as that America would be number one in mathematics and science by the year 2000.

Constitutional experts tell us the federal government cannot mandate a national curriculum or national test. As with the National Assessment of Educational Progress (NAEP), states and school districts would have to volunteer to be a part of such efforts. America has had a long tradition of state and local control of schools. The Constitution does not mention education, and what does not belong to the federal government becomes the province of the states.

There is a growing interest in the professionalism of teaching. Teachers are encouraged to become involved in defining the goals of schools. School-based management extends that notion. These conditions seem to conflict with proposals for a national curriculum in which aims and even educational practice are remote—controlled by the White House.

As mentioned earlier in this chapter, there is not a strong causal relationship between test scores and the state of the economy. To become "number one in the world in mathematics and science" does not necessarily mean our workforce will have a better production rate.

In 1993, six states passed charter school laws allowing groups to run schools outside the boundary of local school board authority. At least a dozen states authorized the seizing of failing schools or school districts in 1993. School boards are under attack by Christian fundamentalists and others seeking to promote their agendas through the school boards. In 1994, $258 billion was entrusted to about 13,500 school boards in the United States, yet only 46 percent of school taxes in 1994 were collected by local school boards.[31] All of those factors point to the waning influence of local school boards. States, where funding by local taxes is being challenged, may see even more local control of schools eroded as the majority of school funding comes from the state.

Teacher unions have come under intense attack in the 1990s. A recent cover story in *Forbes Magazine* referred to the National Education Association as the "National Extortion Association."[32] The article pointed out that one of eight delegates to the Democratic National Convention were National Education Association (NEA) members, the largest single bloc, as has been the case since 1976. *Forbes* (a conservative publication) warned that the rise of the NEA and its sister organization, the American Federation of Teachers (AFT), as powerful unions has coincided with rising costs and deteriorating quality of the nation's public schools.

Pro-market forces not only continue to argue that there is a relationship between productivity and quality of schools, but that as long as schools remain a government monopoly, forces such as teacher unions will continue to keep schools from the kind of reform needed to keep our country competitive.

Politics of the Right

Ten years ago, the religious right used secular humanism as a rallying point. Today multicultural programs that emphasize cultural diversity are under fire (an example was the Rainbow Curriculum in New York).[33] Outcomes education, character education, homosexual lifestyles, satanism, and even witchcraft are areas of concern for activists.

Tactics for the Far Right have changed. During the 1970s and 1980s, groups tended to challenge textbooks, supplemental materials, or counseling programs at public hearings or school board meetings. Today, national organizations provide training programs for parents to challenge local school boards. The same groups organize state groups to propose legislation or vouchers, schools of choice, and home schooling. The Hatch Amendment, federal legislation which protects students' rights by giving parents the right to reject certain types of psychological testing and which also gives parents the right, under certain conditions, to review classroom materials, has been stretched by certain groups to include the vetoing of total programs. The Hatch Amendment applies only to programs funded by the Department of Education and only to research or experimental programs that delve into one or more of seven areas such as potentially embarrassing psychological problems, sexual behavior, or self-incriminating behavior.

Textbook censorship remains a challenge for school districts. A certain amount of curriculum censorship has always existed, not as a matter of policy or law, but rather as a customary practice.

During the 1980s, covert censorship changed to overt censorship. Widespread textbook and school library battles erupted. Creationism versus evolution, family values, racial bias, sexism, obscene language, all became issues leading to calls for censorship. Caught in the middle were textbook publishers who were forced to compromise to an extent that certain texts contained nothing that was offensive, sometimes resulting in blandness. School boards were pressed to censor books, and teachers and librarians were afraid to take a stand on issues.

School leaders will need all the human relations skills they can muster as they work with groups holding extreme views. Finding areas of agreement and maintaining a professional atmosphere in the midst of heated debate will be critical skills for all supervisory leaders.

TOWARD BETTER SCHOOLS

What should we teach in schools? And who should decide? These questions and others have signaled a new challenge to educational leaders. The debate over what should be taught in schools extends from the cultural and epistemological origins of school subjects to the politics of control over the curriculum.

Following are ten major trends for the twenty-first century that can be identified:

Trend 1: *Shift from specialization to general knowledge*—The boundaries between fields of knowledge are disappearing in both work and general living. Citizens of the twenty-first century will need to use mathematical and scientific principles, historical and cultural knowledge, and stronger communication skills more than ever before.

Trend 2: *Rapidly changing knowledge base*—Knowledge is doubling every ten months. Much of what is current today will be obsolete tomorrow. The ability to learn and use new knowledge will be essential.

Trend 3: *New technology in all areas of life*—New technology will dramatically change the way we live, travel, communicate, work, and play.

Trend 4: *Instant worldwide communication*—New technology will make instant worldwide communication a part of everyday life in the home, business, and government.

Trend 5: *Increasing international interdependence*—Today's social, economical, political, and environmental events cross national boundaries. By the twenty-first century, it will be common for nations to pool resources and personnel to solve the problems they share.

Trend 6:   *Shift from manufacturing to service economy*—As we approach the next century, over 90 percent of the new jobs will involve the delivery of services to the public. Examples are services in the medical, legal, personal, and hospitality fields. Only 8 percent of new jobs will be in manufacturing.

Trend 7:   *Frequent changes in the workplace*—High-speed change will rule the workplace. Workers will need to adjust often to new methods, technology, products, and services. In addition, most workers will have to learn more than six different jobs during their working lives.

Trend 8:   *Increasing diversity in the U.S. population*—By the year 2000, over 50 percent of school-age children in large U.S. cities will be from minority groups. The percentage of elderly citizens across the U.S. will be larger than today.

Trend 9:   *Change in personal and family roles*—By the year 2000, over 40 percent of children in the U.S. will live in single-parent households. Disruptions in family life due to divorce or job changes will create stress in both parents and children. New roles for women will change the roles of other family members. Many children will receive less direct supervision from their parents.

Trend 10:   *Increasing emphasis on health and wellness*—The citizens of the next century will take greater responsibility for maintaining their own health. They will face more choices about nutrition, lifestyle, and preventive medicine than they do today.

In the past, parents and business leaders trusted educators to make their decisions, but those same groups now believe others, outside the educational establishment, have better solutions than those within the system.

Can we develop educational leaders who can regain the confidence of those outside of educational systems? What can those in leadership positions do to be recognized as leaders who can improve public schools? Reclaiming a voice can occur if those in leadership positions can master the skills discussed earlier in the text. Scholarship and vision must undergird all activities of supervisory leaders. After all, it is their field, and they do have the expertise to improve schools. In no other profession— medical, law, business—do outsiders actually believe they can run that profession better than those in it.

Those in other professions often call for "greater accountability" in the education profession, but do they offer to eliminate fees for a client if they lost a court decision or botch an operation? Do we offer to put businesses out for bid when they fail to make a profit one year? Educators do have the knowledge and skills needed to develop an educational system that will continue America's economic leadership into the next century, but they must have the respect outside the education establishment to make it happen. That respect will be attained by educational leaders who stand up for what is right in education and have the courage to challenge what is wrong. Simply bowing to teacher unions or to outside pressure groups in the union will not result in the respect needed.

Vision is needed by our supervisory leaders to project ahead. John Dewey and other educators were "progressive" because they were ahead of their times. While others were singing the praises of the factory system, with its bureaucracy, top-down management, and undemocratic structure, Dewey was challenging those premises. Rather than "snoopervisors," Dewey said educational leaders should be helping persons, treating teachers as human beings. Learning for students in the classroom should be democratic, rather than spoon-fed in a dictatorial atmosphere. The *Eight Year Study* and other studies confirmed Dewey's philosophy.[34] The important point is that Dewey, Counts, Kilpatrick, Rugg, and other great leaders were *educators*—not business or industry leaders proposing answers for educational leaders.

SUMMARY

Earlier in this book, the authors discussed skills needed for supervisory leaders. Knowledge is a prerequisite for all good decisions, and tomorrow's supervisors must know more than others around them. They must be the scholars who can refute wild claims by others with good, solid research. Preparation programs for future supervisory leaders must be rigorous. Weekend graduate preparation programs will not be enough. Being able to link curriculum, instruction, administration, human relations, human development research, and management skills to prevent a holistic approach to educational change will demand that supervisors read, write, and conduct quality research as well as having the practical knowledge to relate to teachers in the field.

The global economic relationships of the United States in the new century will also demand a greater participation in global education. The electronic linking of schools around the world will open up new vistas to our students and teachers. Travel between countries on supersonic transports will allow us to visit easily and gain a better understanding of the cultural differences and bonds of people around the globe.

The information revolution will create better opportunities to learn for students and better ways to teach for teachers.[35] We have just scratched the surface in the 1990s with the use of computers, CD-ROMs, and interactive networks. An electronic network in this country will allow learning to move beyond the walls of our school buildings. Not since the invention of the printing press and instruction

of books has the potential for learning been so dramatically affected. The excitement of this new learning will bring new challenges to educational leaders. We can no longer afford to shape technology into a curriculum design for nineteenth century classrooms. We must couple technology with new visions about the work of teachers and students.

If education is aimed at preparing our students to live happily and productively in a new century whose demands we can only imagine, we have an enormous task ahead in education.

In talking of school reform, technology in and of itself is not *the* solution to our educational problems, but it is an essential part. Armed with the tools of technology, along with new ideas, we can meet the challenge of the new century head on and build a better life for all our citizens.

Finally, if we are to have better schools, we must do more than just set goals. *America 2000's* goals of having American students be first in the world in mathematics achievement and attain a graduation rate of 90 percent by the year 2000 will not happen unless this country discovers again the importance of family.

In 1964, the sociologist James Coleman and colleagues published data from a huge survey of public schools and students. Postwar education had been focused on where the education lobby wanted it, on financial inputs such as per-pupil spending, teachers' salaries and per-pupil ratios. Coleman's report concluded that schools were remarkably similar in the effect they had on the achievement of their pupils when the socioeconomic background of the students was taken into account. The best predictor of a school's performance is the quality of the homes from which students come.

Differences in academic achievement have been explained by factors such as number of days absent from school, number of hours spent watching television, number of pages of homework read, quantity and quality of reading materials in the home, and *two parents in the home*. Unless the government is willing to mandate two caring parents at home providing quality reading materials, regulating television viewing, and helping with homework, it makes it hard to imagine that attaining the goals set in the Goals 2000 Plan will be achieved.

Between 1910 and 1990, the graduate rate rose from 8.8 percent to 77.1 percent. By 1980, it had receded to 71.6 percent. In 1994, the rate was 73.8 percent. It has never been higher than 77.1 per-cent.[36] Whether the graduation rate will be 90 percent by the year 2000 is doubtful. Yet, it does not mean it is impossible. Nor is the goal of being first in mathematics and science.

The United States has always been challenged by the influx of immigrants into our school system and by strains on the American family. We have a strong national will as a country, and when we set out to do something we do it. Winning World War Two in the face of two superpowers, winning the Cold War, walking on the moon all were "impossible" tasks that Americans made possible.

Americans are fighting back against drugs and crime, and the American family is receiving more attention and getting better. With strong national will and strong leadership from our school leaders, we can use our schools as the force they should be to build a better tomorrow for our young people.

IMPLICATIONS FOR SUPERVISION

1. The statistics presented in this chapter have many implications for local school districts. List ten such implications for the 1990s.
2. Schools in the twenty-first century in America will be educating a diverse population of students. What changes must occur in the curriculum and its instructional delivery?
3. Business in the 1990s is continually pressing schools for reform. What changes does the business community want? How many are compatible with traditional school values?

⨳ CASE STUDY 1 ⨳

Your school has been a subscriber to the Whittle Corporation television service "Channel One" for two years. This twelve-minute daily broadcast contains two minutes of advertisement and ten minutes of news programming. Teachers in the classrooms have begun to turn off the sound when the program begins each day.

Questions

1. By what criteria should this private corporation be allowed, or not allowed, to broadcast into public school classrooms? Write a policy statement defining this issue.
2. What safeguards would you insist on for ensuring the objectivity of such privately developed "news"?

❧ CASE STUDY 2 ❧

Charter schools will enable parents and other concerned groups to sponsor schools free from regulations at public expense. This movement was supported by law in six states by 1995 and had legislation pending in other states as this book was written.

Questions

1. As a supervisor assigned to oversee the development of charter schools in your district, what concerns would you have? Please list and then prioritize these concerns.
2. What advantages might charter schools bring for students in your attendance area? Using the secondary school as a model, try to envision positive changes that might occur as the charter school movement progresses.

SUGGESTED LEARNING ACTIVITIES

1. Develop a list of controversial issues that a supervisor might face in today's schools.
2. Outline a plan of action for parent involvement in a school district.
3. Write a plan to increase technology in classrooms in your school district.
4. Prepare a list of reading resources on school restructuring.
5. Write a position paper on global education in the twenty-first century.

ADDITIONAL READING

America 2000: An Education Strategy, rev. ed. Washington, DC: U.S. Department of Education, 1991.

Joseph, Pamela, and Bumaford, Gail, eds. *Images of School Reading in 20th Century America.* New York: St. Martin's Press, 1994.

National Commission on Excellence in Education. *A Nation at Risk.* Washington, DC: National Commission on Excellence, 1983.

National Governor's Association. *A Time for Results.* Washington, DC: National Governor's Association, 1984.

Newmann, Fred. *Student Engagement and Achievement in American Secondary Schools.* New York: Teachers College Press, 1992.

Schultz, Fred, ed. *Annual Editions,* 94, 95, 21st eds. Guilford, CT: Dushkin Publishing Group, 1994.

Wiles, J., and Bondi, J. *Curriculum Development: A Guide to Practice,* 4th ed. Englewood Cliffs, NJ: Merrill/Prentice Hall, 1993.

BOOKS TO REVIEW

Cawelti, Gordon, ed. *Challenges and Achievements of American Education,* 1993 ASCD Yearbook. Alexandria, VA: Association for Supervision and Curriculum, 1993.

Elmore, Richard, and Fuhrman, Susan, eds. *The Governance of Curriculum,* 1994 ASCD Yearbook. Alexandria, VA: Association for Supervision and Curriculum Development, 1994.

Glickman, Carl, ed. *Supervision in Transition,* 1992 ASCD Yearbook. Alexandria, VA: Association for Supervision and Curriculum Development, 1992.

Joyce, Bruce; Wolf, James; and Calhoun, Emily. *The Self-Renewing School.* Alexandria, VA: ASCD, 1993.

Kowalski, Theodore, and Reitzug, Ulrich. *Contemporary School Administration.* New York: Longman, 1993.

Noll, James, ed. *Taking Sides: Clashing Views on Controversial Educational Issues,* 7th ed. Guilford, CT: Dushkin Publishing Group, 1993.

Ornstein, Allan, and Hunkins, Francis. *Curriculum Foundations, Principles and Theory,* 2nd ed. Boston: Allyn and Bacon, 1993.

Patterson, Jerry. *Leadership for Tomorrow's School.* Alexandria, VA: Association for Supervision and Curriculum Development, 1993.

Spring, Joel. *Conflict of Interests: The Politics of American Education.* 2nd ed. New York: Longman, 1993.

APPENDIX

RESOURCES FOR SUPERVISORS

Because supervision in an educational setting is not always clearly defined, procedures and techniques are often improvised. Supervisors often must find their own means of solving problems. For this reason, supervisors should be aware of the wealth of resources available to them through agencies and professional organizations. Some of these general resources follow.

NEWSLETTERS

ASCD News Exchange
Association for Supervision and Curriculum
 Development
1250 N. Pitt Street
Alexandria, VA 22314

Department of Classroom Teachers
News Bulletin
National Education Association
1201 16th Street, NW
Washington, DC 20036

Education U.S.A.
National School Public Relations Association
1201 16th Street, NW
Washington, DC 20036

Educational Product Report
Educational Products Information Exchange
 Institute (EPIE)
386 Park Avenue South
New York, NY 10016

Educational Recaps
Educational Testing Service
Princeton, NJ 08540

Educational Researcher
American Educational Research Association (AERA)
1126 16th Street, NW
Washington, DC 20036

NASSP Newsletter
National Association of Secondary School Principals
1201 16th Street, NW
Washington, DC 20036

National Elementary Principals
National Elementary Principals
Department of Classroom Teachers
1201 16th Street, NW
Washington, DC 20036

SLANTS
School Information and Research Service (SIRS)
100 Crochett Street
Seattle, WA 98109

DIRECTORIES

Current Index to Journals in Education (CIJE)
CCM Information Corporation
909 Third Avenue, New York, NY 10022

Directory of Educational Information Services
Division of Information Technology and
Dissemination
Bureau of Research
U.S. Office of Education
Washington, DC 20036

The Directory of Publishing Opportunities
Academic Media
Cordura Corporation
32 Lincoln Avenue
Orange, NJ 07050

Directory of Special Libraries and Information Centers
Gale Research Company
The Book Tower
Detroit, MI 48226

The Education Index (authors and titles in education)
The H.W. Wilson Company
950 University Avenue
New York, NY 10452

Encyclopedia of Associations
Gale Research Company
The Book Tower
Detroit, MI 48226

REFERENCE BOOKS

Dictionary of Education
Edited by Carter V. Good. New York: McGraw-Hill, 1959. Definitions of educational terminology.

Digest of Education Statistics
Available from U.S. Government Printing Office, Washington, DC 20402. A statistical abstract of American education activity.

Encyclopedia of Educational Research
Sixth ed., edited by M. Aikens. New York: Macmillan, 1992. Describes research findings on broad range of topics in education.

Handbook of Research in Teaching
Third ed., edited by Merlin C. Wittrock. New York: Macmillan, 1986.

Handbook of Research on Teacher Education
Edited by W. Robert Houston. New York: Macmillan, 1990.

The International Encyclopedia of Teaching and Teacher Education
Edited by Michael J. Dunkin. New York: Pergamon Press, 1987.

National Society for the Study of Education Yearbook (NSSE)
Published by the University of Chicago Press. An in-depth treatment of an educational concern each year. More information from NSSE, 5835 Kimbark Avenue, Chicago, IL 60639.

The World Yearbook of Education
Available from Harcourt, Brace, and Jovanovich, New York. Provides articles on various topic areas in education by year.

INFORMATION SERVICES

ERIC (Educational Resources Information Center)

ERIC is a network of information centers by topic areas established by the United States Office of Education. ERIC disseminates research findings and other resource materials found effective in developing school programs.

ERIC publishes a monthly catalog, *Resources in Education* (RIE). Reports in RIE are indicated by an "ED" number. Journal articles that are indexed in ERIC's companion catalog, *Current Index to Journals in Education,* are indicated by an "EJ" number.

Most items with ED numbers are available from ERIC Document Reproduction Services (EDRS), P.O. Box 190, Arlington, VA 22210. To order from EDRS, call 1-800-227-3742 for price information.

ORGANIZATIONS AND ASSOCIATIONS

Citizens' Organizations

Council for Basic Education
725 15th Street, NW
Washington, DC 20005

National Center for Middle School Materials
P.O. Box 16545
Tampa, FL 33687

National Coalition for Children
6542 Hitt Street
McLean, VA 22101

National Congress of Parents and Teachers
1715 25th Street
Rock Island, IL 61201

SRIS (School Research Information Service)
Phi Delta Kappa Research Service Center
Eighth and Union Streets
Bloomington, IN 47401

Educationally Related Organizations and Associations

American Association for Higher Education
One Dupont Circle, NW
Washington, DC 20036

American Association of School Administrators
1800 North Moore Street
Arlington, VA 22209

American Council on Education
One DuPont Circle, NW
Washington, DC 20036

American Educational Research Association
1126 16th Street, NW
Washington, DC 20036

American Vocational Association, Inc.
1510 H Street, NW
Washington, DC 20005

Association for Supervision and Curriculum
   Development
(ASCD)
1250 N. Pitt Street
Alexandria, VA 22314-1403

Children's Television Workshop
One Lincoln Plaza
New York, NY 10023

College Entrance Examination Board
888 7th Avenue
New York, NY 10019

Council for American Private Education
1625 I Street, NW
Washington, DC 20006

Council of Chief State School Officers
1201 16th Street, NW
Washington, DC 20036

International Reading Association
800 Barksdale Road
Newark, DE 19711

Joint Council on Economic Education
1212 Avenue of the Americas
New York, NY 10036

National Art Education Association
1916 Association Drive
Reston, VA 22091

National Association for Education of Young Children
1834 Connecticut Avenue
Washington, DC 20009

National Association of Elementary School
   Principals
1801 North Moore Street
Arlington, VA 22209

National Association for Public Continuing Adult
   Education
1201 16th Street, NW
Washington, DC 20036

National Association of Secondary School Principals
1904 Association Drive
Reston, VA 22091

National Council of Teachers of English
1111 Kenyon Road
Urbana, IL 61801

National Council of Teachers of Mathematics
1906 Association Drive
Reston, VA 22091

National Education Association
1201 16th Street, NW
Washington, DC 20036

National Middle School Association
P.O. Box 968
Fairborn, OH 45324

National School Boards Association
800 State National Bank Plaza
P.O. Box 1496
Evanston, IL 60204

National Science Teachers Association
1742 Connecticut Avenue, NW
Washington, DC 20009

Ethnic and Minority Organizations

Bilingual Education Service Center
500 South Dwyer
Arlington Heights, IL 60005

National Council of Negro Women, Inc.
1346 Connecticut Avenue, NW
Washington, DC 20036

National Indian Education Association
3036 University Avenue, SE
Minneapolis, MN 55419

National Organization for Women (NOW)
1424 16th Street, NW
Washington, DC 20036

Federal Agencies

National Institute of Education
1200 19th Street, NW
Washington, DC 20208

National Science Foundation
5225 Wisconsin Avenue, NW
Washington, DC 20015

Office of Education
Office of the Assistant Secretary
Room 3153
400 Maryland Avenue, SW
Washington, DC 20202

Organizations for Children with Special Needs

ACLU Juvenile Rights Project
22 East 40th Street
New York, NY 10016

American Academy for Cerebral Palsy
University Hospital School
Iowa City, IA 52240

American Association for the Education of Severely
and Profoundly Handicapped
1600 West Armory Way
Garden View Suite
Seattle, WA 98119

American Association for Gifted Children
15 Gramercy Park
New York, NY 10003

American Epilepsy Society
Department of Neurology
University of Minnesota
Box 341, Mayo Building
Minneapolis, MN 55455

American Foundation for the Blind
15 West 16th Street
New York, NY 10011

American Medical Association
535 North Dearborn Street
Chicago, IL 60610

American Psychological Association
1200 17th Street, NW
Washington, DC 20036

Association for the Aid of Crippled Children
345 East 46th Street
New York, NY 10017

Association for Children with Learning Disabilities
2200 Brownsville Road
Pittsburgh, PA 16210

Association for Education of the Visually
Handicapped
919 Walnut Street
Philadelphia, PA 19107

Bureau for Education of the Handicapped
400 6th Street
Donohoe Building
Washington, DC 20202

Council for Exceptional Children
1920 Association Drive
Reston, VA 22091

Institute for the Study of Mental Retardation and
Related Disabilities
130 South First
University of Michigan
Ann Arbor, MI 48108

Muscular Dystrophy Association of America
810 7th Avenue
New York, NY 10019

National Association for Retarded Citizens
2709 Avenue E, East
P.O. Box 6109
Arlington, TX 76011

National Association of Social Workers
2 Park Avenue
New York, NY 10016

National Committee for Multi-Handicapped Children
239 14th Street
Niagara Falls, NY 14303

President's Committee on Employment of the
    Handicapped
U.S. Department of Labor
Washington, DC 20210

PROFESSIONAL ORGANIZATIONS AND JOURNALS

American Educational Research Association (AERA)

Association for Supervision and Curriculum Development (ASCD)

National Association of Secondary School Principals (NASSP)

National Education Association (NEA)

National Elementary Principals Association (NAESP)

National Middle School Association

Phi Delta Kappa (PDK)

Among other functions, these professional organizations produce excellent journals that allow educators to communicate with one another over a broad range of concerns. The following journals are thought to be valuable resources for those persons engaged in supervision work:

Academy of Management Journal

American School Board Journal

Educational Administration Quarterly

Educational Forum

Educational Leadership

Educational Technology

Elementary School Journal

Harvard Educational Review

Journal of Research and Development in Education

Journal of Secondary Education

Learning Magazine

Management Review

Middle School Journal

NASSP Bulletin

National Elementary Principal

Phi Delta Kappan

ENDNOTES

Chapter 1

1. V. Collier, "How Long? A Synthesis of Research on Academic Achievement in a Second Language," *TESOL Quarterly* 23 (September 1988), pp. 509–530.

2. A. Trow, "The Second Transformation of the American Secondary Education," in *Power and Ideology in Education,*" eds. J. Karabel and A. Halsey (New York: Oxford University Press, 1977), p. 41.

3. J. Nolan and P. Francis, "Changing Perspectives in Curriculum and Instruction," in *Supervision in Transition, Association for Supervision and Curriculum Development Yearbook,* 1989.

4. R. Callahan, *Education and the Cult of Efficiency* (Chicago: University of Chicago Press, 1962), p. 6.

5. See Ellwood Cubberley, *The History of Education* (Boston: Houghton-Mifflin, 1930), Chapters 27 and 28.

6. The best-known example being the "Hawthorne Effect" revealed by Western Electric studies.

7. Morris Cogan, *Clinical Supervision* (Boston: Houghton-Mifflin, 1973).

8. From 1965 to 1980, the number of teachers who were union members rose from 25 percent to 80 percent.

9. See Carnegie Foundation for the Advancement of Schooling, *An Imperiled Generation* (Princeton, NJ: The Carnegie Foundation, 1988).

10. J. Loveil and K. Wiles, *Supervision for Better Schools,* 5th ed. (Englewood Cliffs, NJ: Prentice Hall, 1983).

11. A. Glatthorn, "Teacher Planning: A Foundation for Effective Instruction," *NASSP Bulletin* 77, no. 551 (March 1993): 1–7.

12. B. Harris and W. Bessent, *In-service Education: A Guide to Better Practice* (Englewood Cliffs, NJ: Prentice Hall, 1969), p. 11.

13. M. Cogan, *Clinical Supervision* (Boston: Houghton-Mifflin, 1973), p. 9.

14. James Curtin, *Supervision in Today's Elementary Schools* (New York: Macmillan, 1964), p. 162.

15. Association for Supervision and Curriculum Development, *Role of the Supervisor and Curriculum Director in a Climate of Change,* 1965 Yearbook (Washington, DC: Association for Supervision and Curriculum Development, 1965), pp. 2–3.

16. James R. Marks, Emery Stoops, and Joyce King-Stoops, *Handbook of Educational Supervision: A Guide for the Practitioner,* 2nd ed. (Boston: Allyn and Bacon, 1978), p. 15.

17. Kimball Wiles, *Supervision for Better Schools,* 3rd ed. (Englewood Cliffs, NJ: Prentice Hall, 1967), p. 10.

18. Thomas Sergiovanni and Robert Starratt, *Emerging Patterns of Supervision: Human Perspectives* (New York: McGraw-Hill, 1971), p. 3.

19. Draft statement, Association for Supervision and Curriculum Development 1982 Yearbook Committee, *Supervision* (working title).

20. Robert Alfonso, Gerald Firth, and Richard Neville, *Instructional Supervision: A Behavior System* (Boston: Allyn and Bacon, 1975), p. 3.

21. Ralph Mosher and David Purpel, *Supervision: The Reluctant Profession* (Boston: Houghton-Mifflin, 1972), p. 4.

22. Allen Sturges (ed.), *Certifying the Curriculum Leader and Instructional Supervisor* (Washington, DC: Association for Supervision and Curriculum Development, 1978), p. 28.

23. Ralph Mosher and David Purpel, *Supervision: The Reluctant Profession* (Boston: Houghton-Mifflin, 1972), p. 4.

24. Ibid., p. 29.

25. Ben Harris, *Supervisory Behavior in Education* (Englewood Cliffs, NJ: Prentice Hall, 1963), p. 28.

26. Edward Pajak (ed.), *Identification of Supervisory Proficiencies Project* (Washington, DC: Association for Supervision and Curriculum Development, 1989). Used with permission of ASCD.

Chapter 2

1. Frederick W. Taylor, *Principles of Scientific Management,* 2nd ed. (New York: Harper and Row Publishers, 1947).

2. Frank Gilbreth, *Field Systems* (New York: Myron C. Clark Publishing Company, 1908).

3. Henry L. Gantt, *Organizing for Work* (New York: Harcourt, Brace and Howe, 1919).

4. Henri Fayol, *General and Industrial Management* (Geneva: International Management Institute, 1929).

5. The reader is encouraged to review a later attempt to codify these principles in Lyndall Urwick, *Elements of Administration* (London: Pitman, 1947).

6. Max Weber, *The Theory of Social and Economic Organizations,* trans. A.M. Henderson and T. Parson, ed. T. Parsons (New York: Free Press, 1947).

7. Daniel E. Griffith, "Toward a Theory of Administrative Behavior," in *Administrative Behavior of Education,* ed. Roald Campbell and Russell T. Gregg (New York: Harper and Row, 1957), p. 368.

8. Robert Katz, "Skills of an Effective Administrator," *Harvard Business Review,* January/February 1955, pp. 35–36.

9. For a complete coverage of systems application in education, see Kathryn Feyereisen et al., *Supervision and Curriculum Renewal: A Systems Approach* (New York: Appleton-Century-Crofts, 1970).

10. See Richard Schmuck and Matthew Miles, *Organizational Development in Schools* (Palo Alto, CA: National Press, 1971).

11. Elton Mayo, *The Human Problems of an Industrial Civilization* (New York: Macmillan, 1933).

12. Kurt Lewin, *Field Theory in Social Science* (New York: Harper Torch Books, 1951).

13. Abraham Maslow, *Motivation and Personality* (New York: Harper Row, 1954).

14. Frederick Herzberg, *Work and the Nature of Man* (Cleveland: World Publishing Company, 1966). Used by permission.

15. Chris Argyris, "The Individual and the Organization: Some Problems of Mutual Adjustment," *Administration Science Quarterly* 2(1957): 327–38.

16. Rensis Likert, *New Patterns of Management* (New York: McGraw Hill, 1961).

17. Peter M. Blau and W. Richard Scott, *Formal Organizations* (San Francisco: Chandler, 1962), p. 90.

18. Douglas McGregor, *The Human Side of Enterprise* (New York: McGraw-Hill, 1960).

19. Egon Guba, *The Role of Educational Research in Educational Change* (Bloomington, IN: National Institute for the Study of Educational Change, 1967).

20. Warren G. Bennis, *Changing Organizations* (New York: McGraw-Hill, 1966).

21. H. Lionberger, *Adoption of New Ideas and Practices* (Ames: Iowa State University Press, 1961).

22. R. Lippit, J. Watson, and B. Westley, *The Dynamics of Planned Change* (New York: Harcourt, Brace, and World, 1958), p. 264.

23. W. Bennis, K. Benne, and R. Chin, *The Planning of Change* (New York: Holt, Rinehart and Winston, 1969), pp. 34–35.

24. Ibid., pp. 67–68.

25. D. Klein, "Some Notes on the Dynamics of Resistance to Change," in *Concepts for Social Change,* ed. G. Watson (Washington, DC: Cooperative Project for Educational Development, National Training Laboratories, 1967), p. 13.

26. R. M. Stogdill, "Personal Factors Associated with Leadership," *Journal of Psychology* 25 (1948): 64.

27. See M. Sherif and C. W. Sherif, *Reference Groups* (New York: Harper and Row, 1964).

28. See Bryce Ryan, "A Study of Technological Diffusion," *Rural Sociology,* September 1948, pp. 273–85.

29. See Arthur Combs and Donald Snygg, *Individual Behavior: A Perceptual Approach to Behavior* (New York: Harper and Row, 1949).

30. Jon Wiles and Joseph Bondi, *Curriculum Development: A Guide to Practice* (Englewood Cliffs, NJ: Merrill/Prentice Hall, 1989), pp. 213–51.

31. Robert Agger, Daniel Goldrich, and Bert Swanson, *The Rules and the Ruled* (New York: John Wiley, 1964), p. 78.

32. Roald Campbell et al., *The Organization and Control of American Schools* (Englewood Cliffs, NJ: Merrill/Prentice Hall, 1980), p. 340.

33. Herbert Goldhammer and Edward A. Shils, "Types of Power and Status," *American Journal of Sociology* 95 (September 1939): 171.

34. Michael Nunnery and Ralph Kimbrough, *Politics, Power, Polls, and School Reform* (Berkeley, CA: McCutchan Publishing, 1971), p. 8.

35. Floyd Hunter, *Community Power Structure* (Chapel Hill, NC: University of North Carolina Press, 1953), p. 9.

36. Ralph Kimbrough, *Political Power and Educational Decision Making* (Chicago: Rand McNally, 1964), p. 144.

37. Nunnery and Kimbrough, *Politics, Power, Polls and School Reform,* p. 7.

38. McGregor, *The Human Side of Enterprise,* p. 64.

39. Ronald Havelock, Institute for Social Research, University of Michigan, 1969. Unpublished manuscript.

40. J. M. Burns, *Leadership* (New York: Harper and Row, 1978), p. 66.

41. Ralph M. Stogdill, *Handbook of Leadership* (New York: Free Press, 1974), p. 116.

42. Kimball Wiles and John Lovell, *Supervision for Better Schools,* 5th ed. (Englewood Cliffs, NJ: Prentice Hall, 1983).

43. For an analysis of Deming's contribution, see Peter M. Senge, "The Leader's New Work: Building a Learning Organization," *Sloan Management Review* 221 (1990): 7.

44. See John McNeil and Jon Wiles, *The Essentials of Teaching* (New York: Macmillan, 1990) for a more detailed discussion of their topic.

Chapter 3

1. Wilford Aiken, *The Story of the Eight Year Study* (New York: Harper and Brothers, 1942).

2. Barak Rosenshine and Norma Furst, "Research on Teacher Performance Criteria," in *Research in Teacher Education,* ed. B. O. Smith (Englewood Cliffs, NJ: Prentice Hall, 1969), pp. 43–51.

3. Robert Stake and Terry Denny, "Needed Concepts and Techniques for Utilizing More Fully the Potential of Evaluation," in *Educational Evaluation—New Roles, New Means* (Chicago: National Society for the Study of Education, 1969), p. 32.

4. Jere Brophy and Carolyn Evertson, "Teacher Behavior and Student Learning in the Second and Third Grades," in *Appraisal of Teaching,* ed. Gary Borich (Reading, MA: Addison-Wesley Publishing, 1977), pp. 79–89.

5. Robert Soar, *Follow Through Classroom Process Measurement* (Gainesville, FL: Research and Development Council, 1970), p. 10.

6. Frederick MacDonald, "Report on Phase II of the Beginning Teacher Evaluation Study," *Journal of Teacher Education,* 27 (Spring 1976): 39.

7. Frederick MacDonald and Patricia Elias, *The Effects of Teacher Performance on Pupil*

Learning, BTES Phase II (Princeton, NJ: Educational Testing Service, 1975), pp. 368–369.

8. Barak Rosenshine and Robert Stephens, "Teaching Functions," in *Handbook of Research on Teaching,* 3rd ed., ed. Merlin Wittrock (New York: Macmillan, 1986), pp. 376–391.

9. K. Jenks and B. Mayer, as cited in "Social Influences," *The Encyclopedia of Educational Research,* 6th ed., ed. M. Aiken (New York: Macmillan, 1992), pp. 562–567.

10. P. Crone and M. Tashakkori, "Variance in Student Achievement in Effective and Ineffective Schools: Inconsistencies Across SES Categories" (Paper, American Educational Research Association, 1992).

11. Robert Havighurst, *Growing Up in River City* (New York: John Wiley and Sons, 1962).

12. A. Friedkin and P. Necochen, as cited in "Social Influences," *The Encyclopedia of Educational Research,* 6th ed., ed. M. Aiken (New York: Macmillan, 1992), pp. 562–567.

13. K. Howze and W. Howze, "Children of Cocaine: Treatment and Child Care" (Paper, National Association for the Education of Young Children, Annual Conference, 1989).

14. M. Poulson and P. Cole, "Children at Risk Due to Prenatal Substance Exposure" (Paper, Los Angeles Unified School District, December 1989).

15. J. Daniels, "Empowering Homeless Children Through School Counseling," *Elementary School Guidance and Counseling,* 27 (December 1992): 105–111.

16. A. Shoho, "A Historical Comparison of Parental Involvement of Three Generations of Japanese Americans in the Education of Their Children" (AERA Paper, 1992).

17. D. D'Andrea, R. Daniels, and H. Morioka, *Building Strategies to Meet the Developmental Needs of Homeless Children* (Ann Arbor: University of Michigan Press, ERIC/CAPS, 1990).

18. N. Jordon, "Differential Calculations Abilities in Young Children from Middle and Low Income Families," *Developmental Psychology,* 26, 4 (1992): 644–653.

19. F. H. Palmer, "The Effects of Minimal Early Intervention on Subsequent I.Q. Score and Reading Achievement" (Final Report, Educa-tion Commission of the States, Denver, 1976).

20. A. Smith, "The Impact of Head Start on Children, Families, and Communities," Final Report, U.S. Department of Health and Human Services, 1985).

21. R. Hubbell, *A Review of Head Start Research Since 1970* (Washington, DC: U.S. Department of Health and Human Services, 1985), pp. 14–18.

22. T. Toch, "Giving Kids a Leg Up: How to Best Help Kids Succeed in School," *U.S. News and World Report,* October 22, 1990, p. 63.

23. T. Fagan and C. Held, "Chapter One Program Improvement," *Phi Delta Kappan* 72 (1991): 562–564.

24. V. Collier, "How Long?: A Synthesis of Research on Academic Achievement in Second Language," *TESOL Quarterly* 23 (September 1988): 509–530.

25. K. Baker and A. deKanter, "1990 U.S. DOE Study," in *Bilingual Education: History, Politics, Theory,* ed. J. Crawford (Newark, NJ: Crane Publishing Co., 1991).

26. J. Crawford, *Bilingual Education: History, Politics, Theory, Practice* (Newark, NJ: Crane Publishing Company, 1991), pp. 210–219.

27. D. Larsen-Freeman, "Second Language Acquisition Research: Staking Out the Territory," *TESOL Quarterly* 25, 2 (1991): 215–260.

28. *Learning 94* (Springfield Corporation, 111 Bethlehem Pike, Springhouse, PA 19477).

29. G. Greenwood, "Research and Practice in Parent Involvement: Implications for Teacher Involvement," *The Elementary School Journal* 91, 3 (January 1993): 279–286.

30. J. Epstein, "Longitudinal Effects of Family-School Interaction on Student Outcomes," in *Research in the Sociology of Education,* ed. A. Kerchhoff. Greenwich, CT: Kingsman, 1989, pp. 171–189.

31. Baker and deKanter, "1990 U.S. DOE Study."

32. J. Epstein, "Longitudinal Effects of Family-School Interaction on Student Outcomes," *The Principal* 66 (1987): 6–9.

33. S. Scalover, "The Relationship Between Parent Involvement and Academic Achievement in High School Students (Ph.D. diss., Penn State University, 1988).

34. A. Milne et al., "Single Parents, Working Mothers, and the Educational Achievement of School Children," *Sociology of Education* 59, 3 (1986): 14–139.

35. H. Loucks, "Increasing Parent/Family Involvement," *NAESP Bulletin,* April 1992, pp. 39–42.

36. W. Shreeve, *Single Parents and Student Achievement: A National Tragedy* (Baltimore: HDA Research Report, 1985).

37. C. Roy and D. Fuqua, "Social Support Systems and Academic Performance of Single-Parent Students," *School Counselor* 30, 3 (1983): 183–192.

38. M. Shinn, "Father Absence and Children's Cognitive Development," *Psychological Bulletin* (APA), 1978, pp. 295–324.

39. E. Hetherington, *Cognitive Performance, School Behavior and Achievement of Children from One-Parent Households* (Washington, DC: National Institute of Education, 1981).

40. J. Gelbrich and E. Hare, "The Effects of Single-Parenthood on School Achievement in a Gifted Population," *Gifted Child Quarterly,* 33, 3 (1989): 115–117.

41. J. Somer and K. Ross, "1958 Study of Hospital Cafeterias," in *The Hidden Dimension,* ed. E. Hall (Garden City, NY: Doubleday, 1966), p. 36.

42. E. Hall, *The Hidden Dimension* (Garden City, NY: Doubleday, 1966).

43. M. Dunkin and B. Biddle, *The Study of Teaching* (New York: Holt, Rinehart & Winston, 1974).

44. S. R. Neill, *Classroom Nonverbal Behavior* (New York: Routledge, 1991).

45. W. Hathaway, *A Study into the Effects of Light on Children of Elementary School Age—A Case of Daylight Robbery* (Edmonton: Alberta Department of Education, 1992, ERIC 343686), pp. 3–37.

46. F. Knirk, "Facility Requirements," *Educational Technology,* September 1992, pp. 26–32.

47. W. Hathaway, "A Study into the Effects of Light on Children of Elementary School Age," pp. 3–37.

48. Ibid.

49. M. Sanders and E. McCormick, *Human Factors in Engineering and Design* (New York: McGraw-Hill, 1987), p. 14.

50. K. Glass, "Sonic Environment," *CEFP Journal,* July–August 1985, pp. 6–11.

51. N. Kwallek and C. Lewis, "Effects of Environmental Color on Males and Females," *Applied Ergonomics,* 1990, 257–278.

52. E. Babey, "The Classrooms: Physical Environments That Enhance Teaching and Learning" (Paper presented at the American Association of Higher Education, Washington, DC, 1991).

53. F. Knirk, "Facility Requirements," pp. 26–32.

54. K. Cotton, "Schoolwide and Classroom Discipline," *School Improvement Research Series,* V (1990): 1–12.

55. W. Goldstein, "Group Process and School Management," in *Handbook of Research on Teaching,* ed. M. Wittrock (New York: Macmillan, 1986), pp. 430–435.

56. E. Emmer and A. Ausikker, "School and Classroom Discipline Programs: How Well Do They Work?" in *Student Discipline Strategies: Research and Practice,* ed. D. Moles (Albany: State University Press, 1990), pp. 89–104.

57. N. Sprinthall and K. Sprinthall, *Educational Psychology: A Developmental Approach* (New York: McGraw-Hill, 1990).

58. Shepard and Smith, "Synthesis of Research on Grade Retention," pp. 113–118.

59. I. Balow, *Retention in Grade: A Failed Procedure* (Riverside: California Education Research Cooperative, 1990).

60. Shepard and Smith, "Synthesis of Research on Grade Retention," pp. 113–118.

61. N. Karweit, "Repeating a Grade: Time to Grow or Denial of Opportunity" (Pamphlet, Johns Hopkins University Press, May 1991).

62. A. Thomas, "Alternative to Retention: If Flunking Hasn't Worked, What Does?" *Oregon School Study Council,* 35, 6 (February 1992): 23–27.

63. Projecting ahead, dropping out leads to social problems. In Florida, for instance, 90

percent of all persons incarcerated are dropouts from school.

64. N. Baenan, *Perspective After Five Years— Has Grade Retention Passed or Failed?"* (Austin: Austin Independent School District, 1988), pp. 1–51.

65. Massachusetts Board of Education, 1989.

66. G. Yamomoto, "Survey of Preadolescent Fears," Arizona State University Study, 1980.

67. Shepard and Smith, "Synthesis of Research on Grade Retention," pp. 113–118.

68. Balow, *Retention in Grade: A Failed Procedure.*

69. P. Peterson, "Direct Instruction Reconsidered," in *Research on Teaching: Concepts, Findings, Implications,* ed. P. L. Peterson (Berkeley, CA: McCutchan, 1987), pp. 11–27.

70. President George Bush, State of the Union Address, 1991.

71. R. Jaeger, "Weak Measurement Serving Presumptive Policy," *Phi Delta Kappan,* October 1992, pp. 116–126.

72. O. Bacoats, "The Relationship of the Florida State Student Assessment Test and the Grade Performance of Students in a Medium Sized School District in Florida" (Ph.D. diss., University of South Florida, 1992).

73. M. Fleming and R. Chambers, "Teacher-Made Tests: Windows on the Classroom," in *New Directions for Testing and Measurement,* ed. W. Hathaway (San Francisco: Jossey-Bass, 1983), pp. 29–38.

74. D. Kirby, *Testing for Critical Thinking* (Mobile, AL: Mid-South Education Research Association, 1987), pp. 16–18.

75. C. Wolfe, "Getting Our Students to Think Through Simulation," *Contemporary Education* 63 (1992): 219–220.

76. L. Hales and E. Tokar, "The Effects of Quality of Preceding Responses on the Grades Assigned to Subsequent Responses to an Essay Examination," *Journal of Educational Measurement* 12 (1975): 115–117.

77. P. Airaisian, "Classroom Assessment and Educational Improvement" (Paper, Conference on Classroom Assessment, Portland, OR, NWREL, 1984).

78. J. Hughes, "What's in a Grade?" (Paper presented at Speech Communication Association, Washington, DC, November 1983), p. 1–19.

79. David Elkind, "Developmentally Appropriate Practice: Philosophical and Practical Implications," *Phi Delta Kappan,* October 1989, pp. 113–116.

80. J. Kulik and C. Kulik, "Meta-Analysis: Findings on Grouping Programs," *Gifted Child Quarterly,* 36, 2 (Spring 1992): 73–76.

81. J. Nevi, V. Dar, D. Flemings, and A. Chankeer, as cited in *School Practices Series,* "Ability Grouping and Achievement Mathematics in the Middle School" (Tampa: Wiles, Bondi and Associates, 1990), pp. 3–4. Also, R. Jaeger, "Weak Measurement Serving Presumptive Policy," *Phi Delta Kappan,* October 1992, pp. 118–128.

82. C. Wolff, "Getting Our Students to Think Through Simulation," *Contemporary Education* 63 (1992): 219–220.

83. C. Hill, "Cooperative Learning and Ability Grouping: An Issue of Choice," *Gifted Child Quarterly* 36, 1 (1992): 11–16.

84. A. Kerckhoff, "Effects of Ability Grouping in British Secondary Schools, *American Sociological Review* 51 (December 1986): 642–658.

85. M. Hallihan, "The Effects of Ability Grouping in Secondary Schools, *Review of Educational Research* 60 (1990): 501–504.

86. R. Slavin, "Achievement Effects of Ability Grouping in Secondary Schools: A Best-Evidence Synthesis," *Review of Educational Research* 60 (1990): 471–499.

87. J. Oakes, "Detracking Schools—Early Lessons from Field," *Phi Delta Kappan* 72, 6 (February 1992):448–454.

88. R. Valdiviesco, "Hispanics and Schools: A New Perspective," *Educational Horizons* 11 (1986): 190–196.

89. J. Oakes, *Keeping Track: How Schools Structure Inequality* (New Haven: Yale University Press, 1985), pp. 32–35.

90. Slavin, "Achievement Effects of Ability Grouping in Secondary Schools."

91. M. Hallinan, "The Effects of Ability Grouping in Secondary Schools."

92. H. Marsh, "Failure of High Ability High Schools to Deliver Academic Benefits Commensurate with Their Students' Ability Levels," *American Educational Research Journal* 28 (Summer 1991): 445–480.

93. R. Rosenthal and L. Jacobson, *Pygmalion in the Classroom* (New York: Holt, Rinehart, Winston, 1968).

94. Ibid., p. 84.

95. G. Farkas et al., "Cultural Resources and School Success: Gender, Ethnicity, and Poverty Groups within an Urban School District," *American Sociological Review* 55 (1990): 127–142.

96. C. Whelen and C. Teddlie, "Self-Fulfilling Prophecy and Attribution for Responsibility: Is There a Causal Link to Achievement?" March 1989 ERIC Ed 323211.

97. T. Good, "Two Decades of Research on Teacher Expectation: Findings and Further Directions," *Journal of Teacher Education* 38 (1987): 32–48.

98. R. Sternberg, "Thinking Styles: Keys to Understanding Student Performance," *Phi Delta Kappan* 71 (1990): 366–371.

99. S. Pflaum, *The Development of Language on Literacy of Young Children* (Columbus, OH: Merrill, 1986), p. 19.

100. S. Rodenbush, "Magnitude of Teacher Expectancy on Pupil I.Q. as a Foundation of the Credibility of Teacher Induction," *Journal of Educational Psychology* 76 (1984): 85–97.

101. R. Tauber, "Criticisms and Deception: The Pitfalls of Praise," *NASSP Bulletin* 74, 528 (October 1990): 95–99.

102. N. Flanders, "Teacher Influence—Pupil Attitudes and Achievement (Washington, DC: H.E.W Monograph 12, 1965).

103. M. Dunkin and B. Biddle, *The Study of Teaching* (New York: Holt, Rinehart & Winston, 1974).

104. J. Brophy, "Teacher Praise: A Functional Analysis," *Review of Educational Research* 51, 2 (1981): 5–32.

105. S. Henerey, "Sex and Locus of Control as Determinants of Children's Response to Peer Versus Adult Praise," *Journal of Educational Psychology* 67 (1979): 604–612.

106. T. Gordon, *Teacher Effectiveness Training* (New York: Wyden Press, 1974).

107. M. Rowe, "Wait Time and Reward as Instructional Variables," *Journal of Research on Science Teaching* 2 (1974): 81–97.

108. J. Brophy, "Teacher Praise: A Functional Analysis," pp. 5–32.

109. G. Morine-Dershimer, "Pupil Perception of Teacher Praise," *Elementary School Journal* 82, 5 (1982): 421–434.

110. P. Meyer et al., "The Informational Value of Evaluative Behavior: Influences of Praise and Blame on Perception of Ability," *Journal of Educational Psychology* 71 (1979): 259–268.

111. C. Shiang, *The Effectiveness of Questioning on the Thinking Process* (San Francisco: American Educational Research Association, 1989, ERIC ED 013704), pp. 13–14.

112. M. Gall, "The Use of Questions in Teaching," *Review of Educational Research* 40 (1970): 707–720.

113. M. Mystrand and A. Gamoran, "Student Engagement: When Recitation Becomes Conversation" (Report, National Center on the Effectiveness of Secondary Schools, Madison, WI, February 1990), pp. 707–720.

114. J. J. Gallagher and M. J. Aschner, "A Preliminary Report: Analyses and Classroom Interaction," *Merrill Palmer Quarterly* 9 (1963): 183–194.

115. B. Winne, as cited in W. Carlson, "Questions in the Classroom: A Sociolinguistic Perspective," *Review of Educational Research* 61 (1991): 165.

116. J. Redfield and P. Rousseau, as cited in W. Carlson, "Questions in the Classroom: A Sociolinguistic Perspective," *Review of Educational Research* 61 (1991): 165.

117. H. Walberg, as cited in W. Carlson, "Questions in the Classroom: A Sociolinguistic Perspective," *Review of Educational Research* 61 (1991): 165.

118. D. Daines, *Teacher Oral Questions and Subsequent Verbal Behaviors of Teachers and Students,* (Provo, UT: Brigham Young University, 1982).

119. Sylvester and Cho, as cited in M. Imal, "Properties of Attention During Reading Lessons," *Journal of Developmental Psychology* 84, 2 (June 1992): 160–172.

120. C. W. Fisher, "Teaching and Learning in the Elementary School: A Summary of the Beginning Teacher Evaluation Study" (Report VII-1, BTES Technical Report, 1978).

121. P. Peterson et al., "Student Attitudes and Their Reports of Cognitive Processes During Direct Instruction," *Journal of Educational Psychology* 74 (1982): 535–546.

122. H. Laharderne, "Attitudinal and Intellectual Correlates of Attention," *Journal of Educational Psychology* 59, 5 (1968): 321–323.

123. M. Imai, "Properties of Attention During Reading Lessons," *Journal of Educational Psychology* 84 (June 1992): 160–172.

124. A. Bardos, "Gender Differences on Planning, Attention, Simultaneous and Successive Cognitive Planning Tasks," *Journal of School Psychology* 3 (1992): 297–299.

125. R. Sylvester, "What Brain Research Says About Paying Attention, *Educational Leadership* 50, 4 (December 1992): 71–75.

126. T. Newby, "Strategies of First Year Teachers," *Journal of Educational Psychology* 83 (1991): 195–200.

127. B. Weiner, *An Attributional Theory of Motivation and Emotion* (New York: Springer-Verlag, 1986), p. 8.

128. J. Lahti, in *Handbook of Research on Teaching,* 3rd ed., ed. M. Wittrock (New York: Macmillan, 1986), p. 704.

129. C. Dweck, "The Role of Expectations and Attributions in the Alleviation of Learned Helplessness," *Journal of Personality and Social Psychology* 31 (1975): 674–685.

130. C. Dweck, "Motivational Processes Affecting Learning," *American Psychologist* 41 (1986): 1040–1048.

131. S. Graham and V. Folkes, *Attribution Theory: Applications to Achievement, Mental Health, and Interpersonal Conflict* (Hillsdale, NJ: Lawrence Erlbaum and Associates, 1990).

132. D. Meichenbaum and J. Asarnow, "Cognitive Behavior Modification and Metacognition," in *Cognitive Behavior Interventions,* ed. P. Kendall (New York: Academic Press, 1979), pp. 137–211.

133. K. Baker and A. deKanter, "1990 U.S. DOE Study."

134. R. Garner, *Metacognition and Reading Comprehension* (Norwood: NJ: Ablex Publishing, 1987).

135. B. Moely et al., "How Do Teachers Teach Memory Skills?" *Educational Psychologist* 21 (1986): 55–71.

136. B. Rosenshine and J. Guenther, "Using Scaffolding for Teaching Higher Level Cognitive Strategies," in *Teaching for Thinking,* ed. H. Walberg (Reston, VA: NAASP, 1992), pp. 35–48.

137. L. Vygotsky, *Mind in Society: The Development of Higher Psychological Processes* (Cambridge, MA: Harvard University Press, 1978), p. 8.

138. R. C. Anderson, "The Notion of Schemata and the Educational Enterprise," in *Schooling and the Acquisition of Knowledge* (Hillsdale, NJ: Lawrence Erlbaum and Associates, 1977).

139. K. Kelly and L. Jordon, "The Effects of Academic Achievement on Self-Concept: A Reproduction Study," *Journal of Educational Psychology* 84 (1992): 345–355.

140. M. Marsh, "Content Specificity of Relations Between Academic Achievement and Academic Self-Concept," *Journal of Educational Psychology* 84, 4 (1992): 3–51.

141. T. Yawkey, *The Self-Concept and the Young Child* (Provo, UT: Brigham Young University Press, 1990), pp. 151–155.

142. M. Marsh, "Age and Sex Effects in Multiple Dimensions of Self Concept: Preadolescence to Early Adulthood," *Journal of Education* 81 (1989): 417–430.

143. M. Rosenberg, *Conceiving of Self* (New York: Basic Books, 1979).

144. S. Gehshan, "College Admission Tests: Opportunity or Roadblocks," *AAUW,* June 1988, pp. 1–6.

145. A. Williams, "Class, Race, and Gender in American Education," *AAUW,* November 1989, p. 5.

146. J. Parsons et al., "Sex Differences in Attribution and Learned Helplessness," *Sex Roles* 8, 4 (1982): 421–432.

147. D. Stipek, "Sex Differences in Children's Attributions for Success and Failure on Math and Spelling Tests," *Sex Roles* 11, 11 & 12 (1984): 969–980.

148. B. Rosenshine, "Synthesis of Research on Explicit Teach," *Educational Leadership* 43 (April 1986): 65.

149. G. Greenwood, "Research and Practice in Parent Involvement: Implications for Teachers," *The Elementary School Journal* 91, 3 (January 1993): 279–286.

150. K. Berendt, "A Study of Friendship and Attitude Formation in Relation to Achievement Motivation," *Journal of Educational Psychology* 82, 4 (1990).

151. F. Newman and J. Thompson, *Effects of Cooperative Learning on Achievement in Secondary Schools: A Summary of Research* (Madison: University of Wisconsin–Madison, 1987), pp. 12–15.

152. R. Slavin, "Achievement Effects of Ability Grouping in Secondary Schools: A Best Evidence Synthesis," *Review of Educational Research* 60 (1990): 471–499.

153. D. Johnson and R. Johnson, *Cooperation in the Classroom* (Edina, MN: Interaction Book Co., 1990).

154. E. Aronson et al., *The Jigsaw Classroom* (Beverly Hills: Sage, 1978).

155. R. Larazowitz, "Academic Achievement and On-Task Behavior of High School Biology Students Instructed in Cooperative Small Investigation Groups," *Science Education* 72, 4 (1988): 475–487.

156. A. Kohn, "It's Hard to Get Left Out of a Pair," *Psychology Today,* October 1987, pp. 53–57.

157. R. Slavin, "Synthesis of Research on Cooperative Learning," *Educational Leadership,* May 1981, pp. 655–660.

158. R. Slavin, "Synthesis of Research on Cooperative Learning," *Educational Leadership,* 48 (1992): 71–82.

159. J. Stallings, "Research on Early Childhood and Elementary Teaching Programs," *Handbook of Research on Teaching* (New York: Macmillan, 1986), pp. 746–750.

160. A. Kohn, "Group Grade Grubbing Versus Cooperative Learning," *Educational Leadership,* 48 (1992): 83–88.

161. P. Okebukola, "The Influence of Preferred Learning Styles on Cooperative Learning in Science," *Science Education* 70 (1986): 509–576.

162. A. Chambers and B. Abrami, "The Relationship Between Student Team Learning Outcomes and Achievement: Causal, Attributes, and Affect," *Journal of Educational Psychology* 83 (1991): 145.

163. C. Mulryan, "Student Passivity During Cooperative Small Groups in Mathematics," *Journal of Educational Psychology* 85 (1992): 261–273.

164. T. Good, "Using Work Groups in Mathematics Instruction," *Educational Leadership* 47, 4 (1990): 4.

165. G. Hooper, "The Effects of Interaction During Computer-Based Mathematics Instruction," *Journal of Educational Research* 85, 3 (1992): 180.

166. A. Gregorc, "Learning/Teaching Styles: Their Nature and Effects," *Student Learning Styles* (Reston, VA: NASSP,), pp. 19–26.

167. B. McCarthy, "Using the 4MAT System to Bring Learning Styles to Schools," *Educational Leadership* 48, 2 (1990): 31–37.

168. J. Hansen and H. Silver, *The Learning Style Preference Inventory* (Moorestown, NJ: Hansen, Silver & Associates, 1978).

169. T. Gusky and S. Gates, "Synthesis of Research on Mastery Learning," *Educational Leadership* 43 (1986): 3–8.

170. T. Titus, "Adolescent Learning Styles," *Journal of Research and Development in Education* 23, 3 (Spring 1990): 165–170.

Chapter 4

1. Excellent resources for supervision in understanding physical development are the writings of David Elkind. See especially, *A Sympathetic Understanding of the Child: Birth to Sixteen* (Boston: Allyn and Bacon, 1971).

2. Adapted by Jon Wiles and Joseph Bondi in *The Essential Middle School*, 2nd edition (Columbus, OH: Merrill, 1984).

3. A. Maslow, *Motivation and Personality* (New York: Harper and Row, 1954).

4. For an in-depth discussion, see L. Kohlberg and E. Turrel, "Moral Development and Moral Education," in *Physical and Educational Practice,* ed. G. Lesser (Chicago: Scott Foresman, 1971), pp. 410–415.

5. R. Gorman, *Discovering Piaget: A Guide for Teachers* (Columbus, OH: Merrill, 1972), pp. 60–84.

6. Statistics cited are from the Center for Health Statistics, National Institute of Mental Health Annual Reports, 1994; National Center for Education Statistics, Center for Disease Control and Prevention, 1994; and other reports from Congressional Committees, 1994–95.

7. *America 2000 Goals*, 1991.

8. Barbara Jackson, "New Directions for Federal Education Policy Spell Hope," Association for Supervision and Curriculum Development *Update*, February 1994, p. 2.

9. *Starting Points: Meeting the Needs of Our Youngest Children*. Carnegie Corporation of New York, 1994.

10. Lillian Katz, *ERIC Clearinghouse on Elementary and Early Childhood* (Urbana-Champaign: University of Illinois, 1994).

11. "Inclusive Education Gains Adherents," ACSCD *UPDATE,* November 1993, pp. 4–5.

12. Martha Riche, "We're All Minorities Now," *American Demographics,* October 1991, p. 26.

13. Thomas Armstrong, *Multiple Intelligences in the Classroom* (Alexandria, VA: Association for Supervision and Curriculum Development, 1994).

14. Carl Glickman, "Pretending Not to Know What We Know," Association for Supervision and Curriculum Development, *Educational Leadership,* May 1991, p. 5. See also Gerald Bracey, "Against Ability Grouping—Again, *Phi Delta Kappan,* March 1993, pp. 573–576.

15. R. Slavin, "Class Size and Student Achievement: Small Effects of Small Classes, *Educational Psychologist,* 29 (1989): 99–110.

16. "Outcomes-Based Education Comes Under Attack," Association for Supervision and Curriculum Development, *UPDATE*, March 1994. See also John O'Neil, "Aiming for New Outcomes: The Promise and the Reality," Association for Supervision and Curriculum Development, *Educational Leadership*, May 1994, pp. 6–10.

17. "Corporal Punishment" (Monograph, National Center for Corporal Punishment, 1992.)

18. See "Grade Level Retention," a position paper of the Florida Department of Education, 1990, and "Retention in Grade: A Failed Procedure," by I. Balow and A. Schlinger, California Research Corporation, University of California, 1990. See also M. Dawson and M. Raforth, "Why Student Retention Doesn't Work," National Association of Elementary School Principals, *Streamlined* Seminar, January, 1991.

19. K. Rogers and R. Kimpston, "Acceleration: What We Do Vs. What We Know," Association for Supervision and Curriculum Development, *Educational Leadership,* October 1992, pp. 58–61.

20. Erik Erikson, *Childhood and Society,* 2nd ed. (New York: Norton, 1963).

21. Gail Sheehy, *Passages: Predictable Crises of Adult Life* (New York: E.P. Dutton, 1976), p. 42.

22. Ibid.

Chapter 5

1. Ralph W. Tyler, *Principles of Curriculum and Instruction* (Chicago: University of Chicago Press, 1947).

2. H. Taba, "General Techniques for Curriculum Planning," in *American Education in the Postwar Period,* 44th Yearbook, Part I, National Society for the Study of Education (Chicago: University of Chicago Press, 1945), p. 85.

3. J. McNeil, *Designing Curriculum: Self-Instructional Modules* (Boston: Little, Brown, 1976), pp. 91–92.

4. LeRoy V. Goodman (Ed.), *Standards for Quality Elementary Schools: Kindergarten Through Eighth Grade* (Reston, VA: National Association of Elementary School Principals, 1984), p. 12.

5. Anita Harrow, *A Taxonomy of the Psychomotor Domain* (New York: Longman, 1972).

Chapter 6

1. John Dewey, "The Relation of Theory to Practice in Education," in *NSSE Yearbook* (Bloomington, IL: Public School Publishing Company, 1904), pp. 80–83.

2. W. Pink, "Effective Development for Urban School Improvement" (Presentation at American Educational Research Association,

San Francisco, 1989). Also see Association for Supervision and Curriculum Development, *Changing the School Culture Through Staff Development* (Washington, DC: 1990).

3. Manuscript, Jon Wiles and David Wiles, working title, *The Principal as Coach* (Scholastic Publishing Company).

4. Ronald Edmonds, "Programs of School Improvements: An Overview," *Educational Leadership* 40 (December 1982): 4–11.

5. T. M. Stinnert, *The Teacher Dropout* (New York: Doubleday, 1970).

6. Francis Fuller, "Concerns of Teachers: A Developmental Characterization," *American Educational Research Journal* 6, 2 (March 1969): 207–226.

7. Erik Erikson, *Childhood and Society,* 2nd ed. (New York: Norton, 1963), pp. 30–36.

8. Fred Pigge, "Teacher Competency: Need Proficiency and Where Developed," *Journal of Teacher Education* 29, 4 (July 1978): 70–76.

9. John McNeil and Jon Wiles, *The Essentials of Teaching* (New York: Macmillan, 1990), Chaps. 2 and 4.

10. P. Jackson, *Criteria for Theories of Instruction* (Alexandria, VA: Association for Supervision and Curriculum Development, 1968), pp. 29–35.

11. W. B. Weiner and D. Palmer, eds., *Cognition and the Symbolic Process* (Hillsdale, NJ: Lawrence Erlbaum and Associates, 1974), pp. 370–393.

Chapter 7

1. Cited in Robert Snider, "The Machine in the Classroom," *Phi Delta Kappan,* 74, 4 (December 1992): 316–323.

2. Ernest Boyer, *High School* (New York: Harper and Row, 1983), p. 189.

3. A study by Hillsborough County Schools (Tampa), Florida, found that using such systems.

4. See Charles Silberman, *The Crisis in the Classroom* (New York: Random House, 1970).

5. Earth Lab project at Ralph Bunche Elementary School, New York Public Schools, cited in Dennis Newman, "Technology as Support

for School Structure and Restructuring," *Phi Delta Kappan,* December 1992, pp. 308–315.

6. *Redbook Magazine* annually identifies exemplary schools in its spring issue (March 1994).

7. This phrase attributed to Kathryn Feireisen, *Supervision and Curriculum Renewal: A System Approach* (New York: Appleton-Century-Croft, 1970) p. 204.

8. Gilbert Valdez, "Realizing the Potential of Educational Technology," *Educational Leadership,* 43 (March 1986): 5–7.

9. Steven Wozinak, "Getting Personal," *Apple Magazine,* 2 (1981): 16.

10. Education Management Group, Tucson, AZ.

11. Robert Gagne, *Instructional Technologies Foundations* (Hillsdale, NJ: LEA Publishers, 1987), p. 316.

12. Marshall McLuhan and Quentin Fiore, *The Medium Is the Message* (New York: Bantam Books, 1967), p. 3.

13. Ronald Anderson, *Selecting and Developing Media for Instruction* (New York: Norstrand-Reinhold, 1983), p. 18.

14. David Easton, *A Systems Analysis of Political Life* (New York: Wiley and Sons, 1965), p. 40.

Chapter 8

1. George H. Litwin and Robert A. Stringer, *Motivation and Organizational Climate* (Boston: Division of Research, School of Business, Harvard University, 1968), p. 100.

2. Ibid.

3. Elton Mayo, *The Human Problems of an Industrial Civilization* (New York: Macmillan, 1933).

4. Chester Barnard, *The Function of the Executive* (Cambridge, MA: Harvard University Press, 1938).

5. William Ouchi, *Theory Z: How American Business Can Meet the Japanese Challenge* (Reading, MA: Addison-Wesley, 1981).

6. Wayne Hoy and Cecil Miskel, *Educational Administration Theory, Research and Practice,* 4th ed. (New York: McGraw-Hill, 1991), pp. 220–222.

7. Rensis Likert, *The Human Organization* (New York: McGraw-Hill, 1967), p. 81.

8. J. Burns, *Leadership* (New York: Harper & Row, 1978), pp. 14–31.

9. Robert Owens, *Organizational Behavior in Education,* 4th ed., (Boston: Allyn and Bacon, 1991), p. 135.

10. H. Fayd, *General and Industrial Management* (Geneva: International Management Institute, 1929).

11. Thomas Peters and Robert Waterman, *In Search of Excellence: Lessons Learned from America's Best-Run Companies* (New York: Harper and Row, 1982).

12. M. Weber, *The Theory of Social and Economic Organizations,* eds. A. M. Henderson and T. Parsons (New York: Free Press, 1947).

13. Kimball Wiles, *Supervision for Better Schools* (Englewood Cliffs, NJ: Prentice Hall, 1975), p. 53.

14. J. R. Gibb, "Defense Level and Influence Potential in Small Groups," in *Leadership and Interpersonal Behavior,* ed. L. Petrollo (New York: Holt, Rinehart 1991), pp. 120–135.

15. D. Berlo, *Avoiding Communication Breakdown,* BNA Effective Communication Film Series, 1995.

16. "Enriching Schools through Multicultural Education," *ASCD Program News,* May 1994, p. 4.

17. "Critical Report Urges St. Paul to Address Increasing Diversity in Schools," *Education Week,* May 25, 1994, p. 3.

18. Martha McCarthy, "Challenges to the Public School Curriculum: New Targets and Strategies," *Phi Delta Kappan,* September 1993, pp. 55–60.

19. Robert Marzano, "When Two Worldview Collide, *Educational Leadership,* January 1994, pp. 6–9.

20. Ralph G. Nicholas, "Listening is a Ten-Part Skill," in "Managing Yourself," *Nations Business,* May 1995, p. 44.

Chapter 9

1. Judith Little et al., *Staff Development in California: Effective Summary* (San Francisco: Far West Laboratory for Educational Research and Development, 1989).

2. See Hilda Taba, *Curriculum Development: Theory and Practice* (New York: Harcourt, Brace & World, 1962).

3. K. Darling and Linda Hammond, "Teacher Supply, Demand and Quality: A Mandate for the National Board" (Paper prepared for the National Board for Professional Teaching Standards, 1990).

4. William Nallia, ed., State of Georgia Study of Teacher Training, 1984.

5. Carl Glickman, "Pretending Not to Know What We Know," Association for Supervision and Curriculum Development, *Educational Leadership,* May 1991, pp. 4–9.

6. J. H. Duval, "Dedication/Commitment: A Study of Their Relationship to Teaching Excellence" (Ph.D diss., University of Vermont, 1990), p. 8.

7. The Carnegie Foundation for the Advancement of Teaching, "The Conditions of Teaching: A State by State Analysis" (Princeton, NJ: 1990), p. 20.

8. Fred Wood and Steven Thompson, "Assumptions About Staff Development Based on Research and Best Practice," *Journal of Staff Development,* 14, 4 (Fall 1993): 52–57.

9. Morris Cogan, *Clinical Supervision* (Boston: Houghton Mifflin, 1992).

10. Gordon Lawrence, "Problems of Effective Inservice Education" (Monograph, Florida Department of Education, 1983.

11. Thom Guskey and Dennis Sparks, "What to Consider When Evaluating Staff Development," *Educational Leadership,* 49, 3 (November 1991): 303–309.

12. M. G. Fuller, "Staff Development, Innovation and Instructional Development," *In Changing School Culture Through Staff Development,* 1990 Yearbook of the Association for Supervision and Curriculum Development, ed. B. Joyce (Alexandria, VA: Association for Supervision and Curriculum Development, 1990) pp. 37–51.

13. H. Olaf, P. Grimmet, J. Rosind, and B. Ford, "The Transformation of Supervision," *Supervision in Transition,* 1992 Association for Supervision and Curriculum Development Yearbook (Alexandria, VA: Association for Supervision and Curriculum Development, 1992), pp. 86–102.

14. Neil Davidson, Jim Henkelman, and Helen Stasinowsky, "Findings from a NSDC Status

Survey of Staff Development and Staff Developers," *Journal of Staff Development,* 14, 4 (Fall 1993): 58–64.

15. P. Holland, R. Cliff, M. Veal, M. Johnson, and J. McCarthy, "Linking Preservice and Inservice Supervision Through Professional Inquiry," *Supervision in Transition,* 1992 ASCD Yearbook (Alexandria, VA: Association for Supervision and Curriculum Development, 1992), pp. 67–79.

16. H. Olaf, P. Grimmet, J. Rosind, and B. Ford, "The Transformation of Supervision," *Supervision in Transition,* 1992 Association for Supervision and Curriculum Development Yearbook (Alexandria, VA: Association for Supervision and Curriculum Development, 1992), pp. 86–102.

Chapter 10

1. Robert Katz, "Skills of an Effective Administrator," *Harvard Business Review,* January-February 1955, pp. 35–36.

2. Peter Drucker, *The Effective Executive* (New York: Harper & Row, 1967), p. 83.

3. For more information on this planning function, see Jon Wiles, *Planning Guides for Middle School Education* (Dubuque, IA: Kendall-Hunt, 1975); Wiles and Bondi, *Making Middle Schools Work* (Alexandria, VA: ASCD, 1986); or Jon Wiles, *Promoting Planned Change in Schools* (New York: Scholastic, 1993).

5. Aaron Wildavsky, *The Politics of the Budgetary Process,* 2nd ed. (Boston: Little, Brown, 1974), p. 4.

Chapter 11

1. Daniel Stufflebeam, "Toward A Science of Educational Evaluation," *Educational Technology,* June 1968, p. 33.

2. L. Dembart, "Researchers: Evidence Implies Biology, Math Linked," *Los Angeles Times,* January 15, 1984, p. 11-A.

3. *The Gallup Poll: Public Opinion 1988* (Wilmington, DE: Scholarly Resources, 1989), p. 162. Cited in *Phi Delta Kappan,* November 1993.

4. George F. Madaus, "The Influence of Testing on the Curriculum" in *Cultural Issues in Curriculum,* ed. Laurel M. Tanner (Chicago: University of Chicago Press, 1988), pp. 82-122.

5. Anne Bridgman, "Standardized Tests Deficient, English Teachers Assert," *Education Week,* December 4, 1985, p. 4.

6. John L. Herman and Donald W. Door-Bremme, *Testing and Assessment in American Public Schools* (Los Angeles: University of California at Los Angeles, Center for the Study of Evaluation, UCLA Graduate School of Education, 1984), p. 130.

7. M. Fleming and B. Chambers, "Teacher-Made Tests: Windows on the Classroom," *New Directions for Testing and Measurement: Testing in the Schools,* W. Hathaway, ed. (San Francisco: Jossey-Bass, 1983), pp. 29–38.

8. F. Stetz and F. Beck, "Comments from the Classroom: Teacher and Student Opinion of Achievement Tests" (Paper presented at the Annual Meeting of the American Educational Research Association, San Francisco, 1977).

9. These procedures are adapted from those suggested by W. James Popham, *Educational Evaluating,* 2nd ed. (Englewood Cliffs, NJ: Institutional Exchange, 1988), pp. 129–150.

10. Benjamin S. Bloom, ed., *Taxonomy of Educational Objectives: Handbook 1: Cognitive Domain* (New York: The David McKay Company, 1956); David R. Krathwohl et al., *Taxonomy of Educational Objectives: Handbook II: Affective Domain* (New York: The David McKay Company, 1956); Anita Harrow, *A Taxonomy of the Psychomotor Domain: A Guide for Developing Behavioral Objectives* (New York: The David McKay Company, 1972).

11. Thomas Dieterick, Cecilia Freeman, and Peg Griffin, "Assessing Comprehension in a School Setting," *Linguistics and Reading Series: 3,* Peg Griffin, ed., (Arlington, VA: Center for Applied Linguistics, 1977), pp. 99–100.

12. Therese Kuhs et al., "Differences Among Teachers in Their Use of Curriculum Embedded Tests," *The Elementary School Journal,* November 1985, pp. 141–153.

13. Arlen R. Gullickson, "Teacher Perspectives and Their Instructional Use of Tests," *Jour-*

nal of Educational Testing, 5 (1984): 222–246.

14. Kenneth Goodman and Yetta Goodman, "Miscue Analysis: Theory and Reality," *New Horizons in Reading,* John Merrit, ed. (Newark, DE: International Reading Association, 1976), pp. 171–173.

15. Ann Cook, "New York's Great Reading Score Scandal," *The National Elementary Principal,* 59 (January 1980): 77–80.

16. Oscar Buros, *The Eighth Mental Measurement Yearbook* (Highland Park, NJ: Grylon Press, 1978). (Future editions of the *Yearbook* will be published by the University of Nebraska Press.)

17. Eric F. Gardner, "How Can Tests Be Misused?" (Paper presented at the Meeting of the National Council on Measurement in Education, Chicago, Illinois, April 1985).

18. John Seely Brown and Richard R. Burton, "Diagnostic Models for Procedural Bugs in Basic Mathematical Skills," *Testing, Teaching, and Learning* (Washington, DC: National Institute of Education, October 1979), pp. 273–307.

19. Ibid.

20. James Block, ed., *Mastery Learning: Theory and Practice* (New York: Holt, Rinehart & Winston, 1971), p. 13.

21. Thomas Good and M. Dembo, "Teacher Expectations: Self-Report Data," *School Review,* 81 (1983): 247–253.

22. John E. Agnew, "The Grading Policies and Practices of High School Teachers" (Paper presented at the Annual Meeting of the American Educational Research Association, Chicago, March 31–April 1, 1985).

23. *High School Course Grade Standards,* National Center for Education Statistics Bulletin (Washington, DC: National Center for Education Statistics, November 1984), pp. 82–83.

24. Jim Hughes and Bena Harper, "What's in a Grade?" (Paper presented at the Annual Meeting of the Speech Communication Association, Washington, DC, November 10–13, 1983).

25. Peter Airaisian, "Classroom Assessment and Educational Improvement" (Paper presented

at the Conference of Classroom Assessment, Portland, OR, Northwest Regional Educational Laboratory, 1984).

26. L. Salmon-Cox, "Teachers and Standardized Tests: What's Really Happening?" *Phi Delta Kappan,* 62, 9 (1982): 631–634.

Chapter 12

1. "Calling Up the Future," *The Executive Educator,* March 1992, p. 5.

2. Harold Hodgkinson, "Reform versus Reality," *Phi Delta Kappan,* September 1991, pp. 9–16.

3. Alex Molnar, "City Schools Under Attack," Association for Supervision and Curriculum Development (ASCD), *Educational Leadership*, May 1994, pp. 58–59.

4. Thomas Snyder, "Trends in Education," *Principal,* September 1993, pp. 9–10.

5. Elliot Eisner, "Educational Reform and the Ecology of Schooling," *Teacher College Record,* 93, 4 (Summer 1992): 152–160.

6. Thomas Toch et al., "The Perfect School," *U.S. News and World Report,* January 11, 1993, pp. 56–57.

7. May McClellan, "Why Blame Schools?" *Research Bulletin,* Phi Delta Kappa, Center for Education, Development and Research, March 1994, pp. 1–6.

8. "Enriching Schools Through Multicultural Education," Association for Supervision and Curriculum Development, *Program News,* May 1994, pp. 1–2.

9. The Organization for Economic Cooperation and Development, 1995 3rd Annual Report.

10. George Will, "Politicians Promise the Impossible," *Washington Post,* February 17, 1994, p. 13.

11. "The Rocky Road to Empowerment," Association for Supervision and Curriculum Development, *Update,* February 1994, pp. 1–3.

12. Linda Darling-Hammond, "Reforming the School Reform Agenda," *Phi Delta Kappan,* June 1993, pp. 753–761.

13. Elliot Eisner, "What Really Counts in Schools," Association for Supervision and Curriculum Development, *Educational Leadership,* February 1991, pp. 10–17. See also Eisner, "The Federal Reform of Schools:

Looking for the Silver Bullet, *Kappan,* May 1992, pp. 722–723.

14. Harold L. Hodgkinson, "A Demographic Look at Tomorrow," Institute for Educational Leadership, Washington, DC, 1994.

15. John Engle (Governor of Michigan), "Let's Revolutionize Public Education," *Wall Street Journal,* March 11, 1994, p. A–10.

16. Sarah Lubman, "More Schools Embrace Full Inclusion of the Disabled," *Wall Street Journal,* April 13, 1994, p. B–1.

17. "Schools Test New Ways to Resolve Conflict," Association for Supervision and Curriculum Development, *Update,* December 1993, pp. 1–8.

18. Richard Neumann, "A Report From the 23rd International Conference on Alternative Education," *Phi Delta Kappan,* March 1994, pp. 547–549.

19. Janet Jones, "Targets of the Right," *American School Board Journal,* April 1993, pp. 22–29.

20. Martha Brown, "School Choice Foes Defend the Indefensible," *Wall Street Journal,* June 25, 1992, p. A–16.

21. Jonathan Weisman, "Skills in the Schools: Now It Is Business' Turn," *Phi Delta Kappan,* January 1993, pp. 297–309.

22. Larry Cuban, "The Corporate Myth of Performing Public Schools," *Phi Delta Kappan,* October 1992, pp. 157–159.

23. John O'Neil, "The Challenges of Outcome-Based Education—Aiming for New Outcomes: The Promise and the Reality," Association for Supervision and Curriculum Development, *Educational Leadership,* March 1994, pp. 6–10. (See also "Outcome-Based Education Comes Under Attack," Association for Supervision and Curriculum Development *Update,* March 1994, pp. 4–5.

24. Ron Brandt, "On Restructuring Roles and Relationships: A Conversation with Phil Schlechty," Association for Supervision and Curriculum Development, *Educational Leadership,* October 1993, pp. 8–11.

25. J. Dewey, *Experience and Education* (New York: Macmillan, 1938), p. 37.

26. Arthur Wirth, "Education and Work: The Choices We Face," *Kappan,* January 1993, pp. 361–366.

27. Daniel Seymour, "Total Quality Management (TQM): Focus on Performance, Not Results," *Educational Record,* Spring 1993, pp. 6–14.

28. "Creating Total Quality Schools," Association for Supervision and Curriculum Development, *Update,* February 1993, pp. 1, 4.

29. Phillip Schlechty and Bob Cole, "Creating a System That Supports Change," *Educational Horizons,* Winter 1991, pp. 78–82.

30. Elliot Eisner, "Should America Have a National Curriculum?" Association for Supervision and Curriculum Development, *Educational Leadership,* October 1991, pp. 76–81.

31. *Education in States and Nations,* National Center for Educational Statistics, Report 94, 1994.

32. Peter Brimelow and Leslie Spencer, "How the National Education Association Corrupts Our Public Schools," *Forbes Magazine*, June 7, 1993, pp. 72–84.

33. Associated Press, "School Census Growing Stronger," *The New York Times,* May 19, 1994, p. 5. See also "Battle over Patriotism Curriculum," *The New York Times,* May 15, 1994, p. 12.

34. Wilford Aiken, *The Story of the Eight-Year Study* (New York: Harper & Row, 1942).

35. Isabelle Bruder et al., "School Reform: Why You Need Technology to Get There," *Electronic Learning,* May/June, 1992, pp. 41–42. See also David Dover, "Apple Classrooms of Tomorrow: What We've Learned," Association for Supervision and Curriculum Development, *Educational Leadership,* April 1994, pp. 4–10.

36. *American Demographics,* U.S. Bureau of the Census, 1994.

NAME INDEX

SUBJECT INDEX

THE AUTHORS

Jon Wiles (left) and Joseph Bondi (right) are professors of education at the University of South Florida. As a writing team, they have co-authored fifteen major texts in the areas of supervision, curriculum, administration, and middle schools. In addition to *Supervision: A Guide to Practice,* texts for Merrill (an imprint of Prentice Hall) include *The Essential Middle School* and *Curriculum Development: A Guide to Practice.*

Dr. Wiles and Dr. Bondi have served in a variety of educational roles—as teachers, school and college supervisors and administrators, and researchers. As consultants with their firm of Wiles, Bondi and Associates, they have worked in forty-five states and ten foreign countries.

Both authors received their doctoral degrees from the University of Florida.

ISBN 0-02-427641-3

90000

9 780024 276414